# BEYOND
# 2012
## Catastrophe or Ecstasy
### A Complete Guide to End-of-Time Predictions

# Geoff Stray

**Dedicated to the memory of Terence McKenna and John G. Stray**

First published in 2005 by Vital Signs Publishing
3 Old House Courtyard, Southover High Street, Lewes, East Sussex, BN7 1HT, UK
Website: *www.vitalsignspublishing.co.uk*
E-mail: *info@vitalsignspublishing.co.uk*

*Revised 2006, reprinted 2007, 2008, revised cover 2009*

Edited by Andy Thomas

Cover design by Andy Thomas and Geoff Stray
Book illustrations by Geoff Stray, unless otherwise noted

ISBN: 978-0-9550608-0-9

**Other Books by Geoff Stray:**
*The Mayan and Other Ancient Calendars* (Wooden Books, 2007)
*The Mystery of 2012* [ed. Gregg Braden, chapter by Geoff Stray] (Sounds True Inc., 2007)
*2012 in Your Pocket* (Straydog Books, 2008)

**Also available from Vital Signs Publishing:**
*The Truth Agenda: Making Sense of Unexplained Mysteries, Global Cover-Ups
and 2012 Prophecies* - by Andy Thomas (Vital Signs Publishing, 2009)

***www.vitalsignspublishing.co.uk***

Printed by InPrint AS (Dardedze Holography), Latvia - *www.dardedze.lv*

# Contents

## Part 4: Diagnosis

## Appendices & References

# Acknowledgements

Thanks goes to *Terence McKenna* for the initial inspiration and for the many spoken word and musical recordings that sustained that inspiration throughout this project. For their enthusiasm over the first wads of feint A4 summaries, and for lending me their house when I was heartbroken and homeless, a big thank you to *Jason Porthouse* and *Di Brown*. For interest, encouragement and reading more of my early writings than anyone, thanks goes to *Jon Adie* and secondly to *Colin Johnson*. Thanks also to *Youri*, a.k.a. *Carl Sullivan*, for his interest and help when reading the first illustrated summary that developed into the original *Beyond 2012* stapled booklet. Massive appreciation to *Andy Thomas*, for applying his proof-reading, editing and publishing skills, and whose encouragement, suggestions and friendship have been a guiding light over the last seven years. Much appreciation also goes to all the people at *Southern Circular Research* for listening to my rantings, especially *Joy Byner* who risked a high dosage of them, and *Barry Reynolds*, *Martin Noakes* and *Marcus Allen* for their help. To *Michael Glickman*, for his friendship and appreciation, and to *Karen Douglas* and *Sheila Martin* who, along with Andy Thomas, provided me with the opportunity to spout forth repeatedly at the Glastonbury Symposium, and to *Steve Alexander* for allowing use of his crop circle images on the *Diagnosis 2012* website. Thank you, my friends.

Special thanks go to *John Major Jenkins* for his honesty, integrity and persistence in uncovering and disseminating the truth, for friendship and support, for the use of his images and for writing a great introduction to this book. Many thanks also to *Vincent Bridges* and *Darlene* for their help and support and for the use of Darlene's excellent drawings and photographs. I would also like to give credit to *Andrew C. Stewart* of *www.cosmic-art.co.uk* for supplying the background image (*Super Nova*) for the front cover of the book, and to NASA for the Earth image.

Thanks to my ex-lodger *Jan Maloney* for unwavering friendship, teaching me to use a computer, and for her Scrabble and creative writing skills used in proof-reading the text, and also to her lodger *Ian Sheard* for proof-reading, and *Lee* for support. Further thanks to *Nikki Macbeth*. Gratitude to *Helen Sewell* and *Paul Wright* for astrological checking and support. Thanks to *Ian Crane* for believing in me, and to both he and *Lori* for their much-needed help during my nomadic period, and to *Debbie Parkes* for emotional rescue. For help with the Mac (no, not the plastic one) and fine-tuning of the cover design, huge thanks goes to *Jason Porthouse* (again) and *Allan Brown*. Further thanks also to *Emma Holmwood* and *Andrew Prince* for computer assistance.

To *Joel Keene, Zyzygyz, Hugh Newman* (the New Human), *Ian Baillie, Jay Weidner, Caroline Taylor, Val Mister, John Martineau, Elliot Cooper, Richard Coppens, Laurence* and *Suzie, Melanie Gambrill* and *Tibor, Tony Gambrill, Louis, Bryn, Clare, Mark* and *Daphne, Rachel* and *Sandie*: thank you all for your support. To *Carleen, Di* and *Martine*, thanks for being my smallest audience (so far). To my family: *John, Eileen, Phyllis, Ange, Keith, Ruth, Nick, Daniel, James, Marina, Alec, Simon*, and those talented rock-stars *Emily* and *Chris*: thanks for your love and not openly saying I've lost my marbles. Thanks too, to all those who have contributed to this project via conversation, e-mails or their own research and writings, or who have allowed me to use their images, or invited me to speak at their meetings and conferences. I thank *Tania Woodward* for her love and support throughout our five-year journey together, for believing in this project and for tolerating my affair with the computer almost to the project's completion...

Finally, I thank *Sue McCormick* for her love, encouragement and moral support.

# Foreword
## by John Major Jenkins
author of *Maya Cosmogenesis 2012*, *Tzolkin* and *Galactic Alignment*

### *Into the Beyond (Laying the End to Rest)*

Writings on 2012 have multiplied exponentially over the last five years. As we draw closer to 2012, interest focusing on that enigmatic, co-opted, perplexing date will be growing. It is a true and multi-faceted vector for all kinds of ideas. The plethora of writings on it is a phenomenon in itself, and while the discussion of Year 2000 centred largely around Y2K ('The Millennium Bug'), which proved to be as much a phantasm as many of the much more wacky millennial ideas, there is as yet no discernable loci of the 2012 discussion.

It is for this reason that the *Diagnosis 2012* website has been valuable to the ongoing discussion. Since 1998, Geoff Stray has collected and organized a wide spectrum of writings, reports, dreams, sci-fi and non-fiction studies on the 2012 theme. Although the centre of the discussion has yet to be discerned, at least the voices are now assembled under one roof. Stray has been unbiased in what he has allowed into the pavilion of purview. He is a true pioneer, the first 2012ologist who has sought to collect, survey, contextualize and comment on the wide spectrum of manifestations related to 2012. Because of his familiarity with all things 2012, he is our best guide into the labyrinths of kaleidoscopic creation and consternation that typify the inner landscape of 2012-land.

While his pavilion has been open to all, Stray has used common sense and discerning analysis to critique the contributions, such that basic errors in theories have been identified, always involving internal inconsistencies in the theory itself, rather than by reference to a set of preconceived doctrines of what 2012 'really' means. I appreciate this quality in Stray's book on 2012, because it allows us to categorize the wide spectrum of writings into fiction and non-fiction, trace the inter-relationships and discern, sometimes, the shared sourcings between different contributions. A bit of order has thus been given to the chaos of creativity that 2012 has spawned.

Geoff Stray clearly leans in a certain direction when it comes to his own views - views that have been distilled, it should be said, from his immersion in the field of ideas - but it is possible to give allegiance to one's own preferential viewpoint while retaining objectivity in assessing all others, and Stray has done this. Another admirable quality evinced by Stray is essential for continuing the conversation on 2012: open-mindedness. We can all strive to practice this virtue, as it is clear even in this incipient phase of the birth of 2012ology that many views are going to be mutually contradictory, irreconcilable with each other, and thus 'unity in multiplicity' may be the ultimate teaching to emerge from our passage through 2012. Open mindedness, rather than meaning the uncritical endorsement of everything, thus takes on the connotation of an inclusive mentality that can embrace contradictory views (even while retaining ones own perspective).

The creation and nurturing of that state of consciousness, that transcendent viewpoint, may initially seem to simply be a prerequisite of furthering serious discussion on 2012. However, such a meta-view may indeed coalesce as a supremely important emergent property from our collective dance with 2012. The 'lesson' distilled is simple: *higher perspectives are needed to resolve problems and conflicts.* And in that speculation we glimpse that something might lie beyond 2012 - beyond it in time and space, and beyond it in our own minds. In other words, there can be a 'beyond 2012' if we mentally create the space that can embrace that possibility, in effect transcending the apocalyptic nihilism that defines modern civilization and pollutes modern consciousness. Transcendence does not escape or deny that which is transcended, but includes it in a higher vision. We may all come to agree that 2012 is not a final end, which is a notion that seems to be one of the largest and potentially most counter-productive assumptions about it.

This book is called *Beyond 2012*. How are we to go beyond 2012? *Is* there anything beyond 2012? What is the intended meaning of this phrase? Geoff Stray tells me *"the title intends to impart optimism to the subject, decreasing anxiety that the end of the world is approaching, since it turns out that many of the catastrophe theories are inherently faulted."* And so *Beyond 2012* takes the courageous position of clarifying and simplifying the 2012 discussion by winnowing out theories of dubious merit. The 2012 discussion shows that people tend to gravitate towards one of two positions - that 2012 represents a catastrophic end or it represents a new beginning (in some sense). These are difficult questions to resolve, as they touch upon profound meditations on death and immortality, vast cycles of time and ancient insights into human consciousness that are just recently coming to light. Could it be that our own educational institutions and our own civilization's preconceptions have left us ill-prepared to deal with such profound questions? We, the denizens of the *Kali Yuga*, the age of spiritual darkness, are struggling to embrace profound higher wisdom, and thus our own transformation does indeed seem to be the prerequisite for any clear understanding of what 'the end of time' means. Getting beyond 2012 is about transcending preconceived biases and limitations born from Western civilization's limited worldview.

The 2012 date itself is specifically an artefact of the Mayan calendar. It is not a New Age creation of any particular author; it is a reconstructed artefact of the Mayan Long Count calendar tradition. Why the ancient calendar makers ended their 13-baktun cycle on the date we call December 21st, 2012 has been an open question. I believe that date was intended (by its creators) to target a rare alignment between the Earth, our Sun, and the centre of our Milky Way galaxy - a factual astronomical alignment that takes place only once every 26,000 years. My research follows academic principles of argument and documentation to arrive at this surprising synthesis and reconstruction. After subsequent research, this knowledge of a rare 'galactic alignment' also appears to be the centrepiece of other wisdom traditions from around the globe. As such, while the emergence of the 2012 date into contemporary thought is traceable to Mayan calendric tradition, the inner wisdom of 2012 is universal. We might even say that 2012 is emerging as an archetype of the end times, and thus resonates with the universal human questions about death and immortality. This avenue of association rightfully opens up 2012 to entire categories of approach that have little to do with my cosmological reconstruction, or even with Mayan culture *per se*. Having said this, we must also honour Mayan genius in what is, above all, a profound and advanced cosmological model of human development that uses the Galactic Centre as its evolutionary centrepiece.

Human beings, by their different natures and preferences, will gravitate to different categories in this discussion, revealing the relative merit they see in each approach. For some, my archaeo-philosophical resurrection of a lost Galactic Cosmology may seem hopelessly inaccessible, while dream visions catalysed by ingesting the sacred plant *Salvia divinorum* reveal more interesting data on what 2012 is 'really' about. Truth can appear relative - related to ones own position - and that egalitarian principle must be held high, to uphold freedom of expression and belief. But it must also be noted that some of the theories surveyed in *Beyond 2012* - especially in their more recent iterations - gratuitously toss in 2012 to lend superficial support to a theory that otherwise has nothing to do with Mayan calendrics or recognizable Mayan beliefs. These cut-and-paste cosmologies, such as the new connection between 'Planet X' and 2012, indirectly attribute to the Maya ad-hoc theories that are poorly supported and that, in fact, espouse beliefs counter to Mayan tradition. This is a marketing ploy, plain and simple, to co-opt the awe and apocalyptic punch that 2012 has gained within popular consciousness. It's like name-dropping, and name-dropping doesn't mean you know anything at all about the person named.

Thus some of the theories presented here unfairly latch onto 2012, basically as a marketing ploy, while others are dealing head-on with the real issues of the Mayan intention behind 2012. Adhering to the latter approach, I base my reconstruction of the true intention behind the 2012 date on examining the early Maya site that formulated the 2012 calendar. This early Mayan site, which experienced its heyday some 2,100 years ago, is called Izapa.  In this I am alone among academics and popular writers alike, and my work has therefore generated unique conclusions that are nevertheless backed up by archaeological, iconographical, calendrical, mythological, and astronomical evidence. So we have two extremes of the spectrum: on the one hand the carefully argued reconstruction of authentic (although up until now, forgotten) Mayan traditions, and on the other hand the spurious concoctions of ad-hoc ideas that threaten to inject modern distortions into ancient wisdom. Many of the ideas presented in *Beyond 2012* fall somewhere in-between, into an intriguing domain of deeper mysteries and higher faculties, of shamanic visions, alternative science, resurfacing traditions and recovered histories. This domain is worth exploring.

Shall the 2012 discussion be open *only* to scholars and academics? I don't think so. More to the point, what can we expect from academic social commentators as the 2012 discussion becomes louder and better known? For this we can look to a recent end-point date that was essentially similar to the 2012 date.

Boston University's Centre for Millennial Studies was a focus for Year 2000 dialogues.

Founded in 1995, it quickly began soliciting for papers on the millennial theme in cultural beliefs, with a special interest in Native American lore. In 1999, they rejected my submission outlining the galactic alignment thesis, even though the minimal alignment zone of 36 years (1980-2016) embraces Year 2000 (see chapter 23 in my book, *Galactic Alignment*). My book *Maya Cosmogenesis 2012* came out in 1998, which clearly laid out the thesis in rigorous detail, but although Year 2012 and Year 2000 both fall within the galactic alignment zone, my offer to send this book for review was refused.

The oversight was compounded by the Institute's director, Richard Landes, categorizing 2012 as a 'New Age' topic during an interview with National Public Radio's Terry Gross (*Fresh Air*, 16th December 1997). He propagated mistaken notions about the 2012 date when he said, "*there's a Mayan calendar that gives us information up to 2012, and then after 2012 it stops.*" He goes on to say that a sector of New Age thinkers have thus adopted 2012 as their favourite doomsday point, which is true, but Landes fails to emphasize that 2012 is a real artefact of Mayan calendar tradition, and the associated World Age doctrine never predicts a final end, but always a transformation. This particular interpretation is not my own, but is available in basic books on the Maya. Landes also mentioned the Harmonic Convergence of 1987 in relation to the 2012 end-date, which reveals that he was relying heavily on ideas in José Arguelles' *The Mayan Factor* and related manifestations. Since the Centre for Millennial Studies is still, as of 2004, a funded research think-tank, one can only hope that more serious research on 2012 will be assessed with an open mind.

The 2012 discussion is already formulating itself as a widespread, grass-roots, popular movement - much more so than Y2K/Year 2000. Such widespread interest may itself be the antidote to official myopia. If a university thinktank emerges to conference on 2012, scholars should refer to *Beyond 2012* as a guide to the multiple theories on 2012. Since the material runs the gamut from inner-dream visions to serious PhD-level studies, academics and social commentators will not be able to toss everything here into an easily dismissed bin of New Age fantasy. I support and encourage serious discussion of 2012, and the current level of the discussion - in quality and cogency - must be raised. *Beyond 2012* does this with admirable comprehension and comprehensiveness, inviting us all to engage with this topic in deeper ways.  Again, the keys, exampled by Geoff Stray, are open-mindedness and discernment.

So let us go to the next level in the evolving discussion. Let us have conferences, symposia, thinktanks, Yahoo e-mail groups and café salons. Let us write treatises and poetry, songs and equations.  Let us visit Chichen Itza, Izapa, Egypt, and inner planes of higher wisdom, and let us reconvene in 2013, when we are beyond 2012, and talk about what accompanies us unscathed through the eye of the needle, the Sun Door at World's End, the *ginnungagap* between the Ages, the eschatological *symplegades*, the still-point threshold crossing - the nexus between death and rebirth.

*Vincit omnia veritas*: Truth Conquers All.

**John Major Jenkins**, *1 Chicchan, 12.19.11.3.5*

# Introduction

The Maya civilization flourished between 200 AD and 900 AD in Mesoamerica - an area that corresponds to modern Southern Mexico, Guatemala, Belize, Honduras and part of El Salvador. They had a complex system of calendars, including one called the *Long Count*, that measured vast stretches of time with uncanny accuracy. It now seems certain [1] that the Long Count originated in Izapa, which was first inhabited around 1500 BC, but it may have been as late as 355 BC before the Long Count was conceived.

The Long Count includes a cycle that lasts 1,872,000 days, or approximately 5,125 years, and that is known as the *13-baktun cycle* (some refer to it as the *Great Cycle*, but this term has also been used to describe other cycles, so to avoid confusion I shall call it the 13-baktun cycle throughout this book). For the last hundred years or so, archaeologists have argued over the correlation of Long Count dates to the Gregorian calendar that we use today, and have now mostly agreed on one of two correlations. The two correlations are only two days apart, and they correlate the beginning (or zero-date) of the current 13-baktun cycle to a Gregorian historical date of either 11th August 3114 BC or 13th August 3114 BC. This means that the cycle ends 1,872,000 days later, on December 21st 2012 AD or December 23rd 2012 AD respectively. What the archaeologists or Mayanists have yet to agree on is why the Maya chose December 2012 as the end-point of the 13-baktun cycle.

In 1987, José Arguelles published a book called *The Mayan Factor*, [2] in which he brought the 2012 end-point of the 13-baktun cycle to the attention of the world at large. I was among the readers of that book, and was particularly fascinated because, for the previous five years, *I had already been studying a calendrical system from another part of the world, with a 2012 termination point!*

Terence and Dennis McKenna had published a book in 1975, *The Invisible Landscape*, [3] in which they showed that the Chinese oracle, the *I Ching*, had originally been used as a lunar calendar in which the 64 six-line hexagrams - 384 lines in all - had represented the 384 days in a thirteen-month lunar year. Following their 1971 journey down to the Amazon jungle, in which the brothers had a shared hallucinogenic experience, they developed their insights, and devised a method by which to convert the Chinese Book of Changes - the I Ching - into a complex wave that mapped the timing of all the changes in the universe, or *"the ingression of novelty into space-time"*. The complex wave was composed of a hierarchy of waves - each one of a magnitude 64 times greater than the one below it - that mapped all change, from sub-atomic event durations up to the duration of the three-dimensional physical universe. The explosions of the atomic bombs at the end of the Second World War were taken to be sufficiently novel events that they should correlate to a major peak on the Timewave, and when lined up with these events in the Gregorian calendar, it was found that late in 2012 AD, all the waves and sub-waves would peak together, signifying *"concrescence"* - an evolutionary pinnacle and dimensional transition.

Incredibly, knowing nothing of the McKennas or the Timewave, Arguelles had already published a book - *Earth Ascending* 4 - in 1984, in which he revealed a relationship between the I Ching and the Maya *tzolkin* (260-day) calendar. In 1987, in *The Mayan Factor*, Arguelles went on to show that the tzolkin was a microcosm of the 13-baktun cycle (260 katuns of 7,200 days each). Likewise, when the McKennas wrote the 1975 edition of *The Invisible Landscape*, they knew nothing of Arguelles or the end of the 13-baktun cycle of the Maya.

There are too many 'coincidences' here to use the word coincidence! The word developed by psychologist Carl Jung to describe a meaningful coincidence, *synchronicity*, is doubly apt; *syn* means *same*; *khronos* means *time*.

I started a research project to try to find out what might be scheduled for 2012 and eventually condensed my findings into summary paragraphs in an A4 booklet called *Beyond 2012*. The booklet developed into a website, *www.diagnosis2012.co.uk*, 5 attracting the input of people from all over the world, and now this book version will attempt to bring all the research together, to find any pattern that underlies the information, misinformation and disinformation that has been circulating regarding 2012.

Part One, *Ancient Calendars and Prophecies*, looks at the ancient sources of information that are coming to light, suggesting that ancient cultures knew something about an event far in their future, and tried to preserve knowledge about it, sending us a message across time. We look at the calendars of the Maya and the tribal prophecies of Mesoamerica, North America and South America, and others as far as Africa and New Zealand. We also take a look at Oriental and Asian calendars, so-called 'Western' or Abrahamic religions and the I Ching.

In Part Two, *2012 Theories*, we look at the many ideas that have been prompted by the recent publicity surrounding the calendars and prophecies. Several speculations attempt to prove that our ancestors were trying to warn us about a forthcoming cataclysm, but how convincing are they? Are these just another attempt to get some kind of meaning out of the *Book of Revelation*? The theories concern solar cycles, asteroids and comets, rogue planets, plasma bands, the exploding galactic core and other ideas, and the results are predicted to be anything from burnt-out power stations to total wipe-out. One thing is for sure - they can't all be right!

In Part Three, *Beyond the Veil*, we look at contemporary sources of information on 2012, from Nostradamus to modern visionaries and prophets, and from altered states of consciousness, channellers, UFO contactees, near-death experiencers, psychedelic voyagers, remote viewers and out-of-body travellers. Even crop circles, those mysterious shapes that appear in our cereal crop fields every year, have been connected to 2012.

In Part Four, *Diagnosis*, we take some of the most interesting and convincing items that have emerged during the investigation, apply prehistoric wisdom, and come to a surprising conclusion.

Following Part Four are three appendices that extend the conclusion of this study. Appendix 1 consists of two quotations with comments. Appendix 2 was posted on the

*Diagnosis 2012* website in 2001, and Appendix 3 is a slightly modified version of a short article posted on the *Swirled News* crop circle website (*www.swirlednews.com*) in 2002.

There is a comprehensive *Notes and References* section, in which I have tried to keep the extra-detailed information for those more familiar with this subject, and this includes book and website references (a book-mark positioned at the Notes pages would be advisable). There is also a separate bibliography section, to avoid the annoying 'op. cit' system, which involves searching back in the notes for the first mention of the source in question.

The conclusions reached in this book should not be seen as 'the answer', since we should always be ready to look at new information and re-examine our position. It is hoped that by looking closely at all the current theories regarding 2012, this book will save people a lot of time in trying to reconcile differing, contradictory and often confusing collections of information, and thus improve communication, reduce anxiety and allow research to progress faster.

During the course of the study, we shall discuss the experiences of various people gained while using hallucinogenic plants and compounds. This does not mean I am recommending that any readers do the same, any more than I recommend that anyone try to have a near-death experience. The information that these psychonauts have brought back from inner space is crucial to the discussion and I am very grateful to all those who provided it. I am also very grateful to all the theorists who have already grappled with the 2012 enigma, regardless of whether or not I ended up agreeing with some or none of their ideas. The possibility that we may be approaching a very rare event in the history of the planet means this is an essential topic deserving our attention.

If you have any ideas or information to contribute to the ongoing *Dire Gnosis* project, * please contact me through the e-mail address given on the index page of the *Diagnosis 2012* website at *www.diagnosis2012.co.uk*.

**Geoff Stray**

* *Dire means 'serious' or 'urgent', as well as 'dreadful', and thus sums up the ambiguous nature of the 2012 phenomenon. Dire Gnosis therefore means, primarily, "important knowledge," as well as inferring a diagnostic approach.*

NOTE ON 'MAYA' TERMINOLOGY:
*The reader may note a varied use of 'Maya' and 'Mayan' throughout the book. I have attempted for the most part to follow the protocol of Mayanists such as Linda Schele, in which the word 'Mayan' is used only in reference to the language spoken by the Maya, and the word 'Maya' is used to describe things pertaining to the Maya, such as 'Maya calendars'.*

# PART 1:
## Ancient Calendars and Tribal Prophecies

Probably the wisest view is to say: the truth - like the Self - is splintered up over thousands of miles and years; bits are found here and there, then and now, and must be re-collected; bits appear in the Greek naturalists, in Pythagoras, in Plato, Parmenides, in Heraclitus, Neo-Platonism, Zoroastrianism, Taoism, Mani, Gnosticism, orthodox Christianity, Judaism, Brahmanism, Buddhism, Orphism, the other mystery religions. Each religion or philosophy or philosopher contains one or more bits, but the total system interweaves it into falsity, so each as a total system must be rejected, and none is to be accepted at the expense of all the others (e.g. "I am a Christian" or "I follow Mani"). This alone, in itself, is a fascinating thought: here in our spatiotemporal world we have the truth but it is splintered - exploded like the EIDE - over thousands of years and thousands of miles and (as I say) must be re-collected, as the Self or Soul or EIDOS must be. This is my task.

**Philip K. Dick, in his Exegesis, 3/10/80** [1]

# Chapter 1:
# The Maya Calendars

## Tzolkin, Haab and Long Count

The *tzolkin*, or sacred calendar, of the Maya is a 260-day system based around the period of human gestation, according to the still-surviving descendants of the Maya, who live in the highlands of Guatemala and have used the same unbroken count of days for more than a thousand years. It is composed of twenty day-signs, each of which has thirteen variations, and was (and still is) used to determine character traits and time harmonics. It is a little reminiscent of Western astrology, except that the tzolkin does not directly involve the movement of planets relative to stars. Each of the 260 different combinations of day-sign and number indicates a unique quality for that day, and the tzolkin day that a person is born on is repeated at 260-day intervals as a *tzolkin birthday*, when the quality of the day that determined his/her character traits is repeated. According to John Major Jenkins' book, *Tzolkin*, [1] astronomical cycles that may connect with the tzolkin include such things as the zenith passage interval of the Sun at the latitude of Izapa, Mexico, and the synodic cycle of Mars (one solar orbit by Mars in relation to the Earth), which is exactly three tzolkins, at 780 days. It is also an intriguing fact that two of Jupiter's moons have a 260-day cycle. Another consideration is that the morning and evening star phases of Venus last 263 days on average, according to Anthony Aveni, [2] but Jenkins says the period between Venus rising as an evening star and its emergence as a morning star is 258 days, as recorded in an eleventh-century Maya picture book called the *Dresden Codex*. In addition, three eclipse half-years are equal to two tzolkins. [3] 260 days is also the length of time between planting and harvesting maize - the staple diet of the Maya. However, most significant of all is the fact that the Maya daykeepers who live in the Guatemala highlands and still use the tzolkin, say that it is based around the period of human gestation. [4]

Bruce Scofield did ten years of research through the 1980s, piecing together the odd scraps of information that remain about the meanings of each of the days in the 260-day calendar. He used "*historical documents, reports from oral tradition, psychic-archaeological techniques, and common sense*". [5] He looked at myths connected with the gods associated with each day-sign and, being an astrologer, used a database of about 400 celebrities and friends with known birthdays and personality traits to look for patterns to "*crack the code*". A summary of the process and the results can be found in his book *Day-Signs*. [6] It was while reading this book and the definitions of the twenty day-signs that I clearly recognised my father's character. Before checking to see if the day of his birth did actually occur on the day-sign with the characteristics I recognised, I looked through the thirteen variations of it that occur over 260 days. There were two variations that seemed to describe him the best, and when I checked, I was amazed to find that he *was* born on one of these two signs, at odds of 130-to-one against.

The Maya also used a 365-day calendar called the *haab*, consisting of eighteen 'months' of twenty days each (360 days), plus five extra days called *uayeb*. Each of the months had a different name, and the days progressed numerically, like ours where January 1st is followed by January 2nd. An example from the haab would be *1 Pop* followed by *2 Pop*, whereas in the tzolkin, the number and day-sign both change from one day to the next. For example, *One Imix* would be followed by *Two Ik*. Each day therefore had a tzolkin name and a haab name, and the combination would only happen once every 52 'years' (haabs of 365 days each), or 73 tzolkins. This period is called a *Calendar Round*, which we shall return to shortly.

The Maya measured long time periods by means of a *Long Count*, in which one 360-day year (a *tun*), consists of eighteen twenty-day 'months' (*uinals*). Twenty of these tuns add up to a *katun*; twenty katuns make a *baktun* (nearly 400 years), and thirteen baktuns add up to a *13-baktun cycle* of 1,872,000 days (5,200 tuns, or about 5,125 years). The first day, or zero-day, is written in Arabic numerals (the numbering system we use today) as 0.0.0.0.0.

Scholars specialising in the Maya have been attempting to correlate the Long Count to our Gregorian calendar since the beginning of the 20th century. There has been massive variation in the suggested correlations, but as early as 1897, Joseph Goodman suggested that the Maya Creation date was in 3114 BC. In 1905, he refined the correlation to *#584283* (the number refers

*Fig.1.1: The twenty Maya day-signs. From L-R, top to bottom, with Aztec variations: Crocodile, Wind, Night (House), Lizard, Serpent, Death, Deer, Rabbit, Water, Dog, Monkey, Road (Grass or Tooth), Corn (Reed), Jaguar, Eagle, Vulture, Incense (Earthquake, Movement), Flint (Knife, Mirror), Storm (Rain), Ancestors (Flower, Lord).*

to the Julian day number to which the zero-day is correlated). This was unpopular until 1926, when Juan Martinez Hernandez confirmed it.  In 1927, Eric Thompson applied lunar and Venus data to arrive at a two-day adjustment - the *#584285 correlation*, later confirmed by Floyd Lounsbury, who found evidence to support it by cross-referencing astronomical phenomena with those recorded in the Dresden Codex.  In this calculation, the zero-day correlates to 13th August 3114 BC, and the end-date to 23rd December 2012 AD.  In 1950, Thompson did a final re-examination of Goodman's work, combining it with the latest findings, and settled on the original *#584283 correlation* (Goodman-Martinez-Thompson-2, or GMT-2).  This puts the start of the 13-baktun cycle (day 0.0.0.0.0) on 11th August 3114 BC, and the end-date (known as 13.0.0.0.0) on 21st December 2012 AD. This correlation coincides with the unbroken count of days that has been followed by the Maya people still living in the Guatemala highlands (now known as the *True Count*).

*Fig.1.2: If a stela were found bearing the date of the next Creation, 13.0.0.0.0, 4 Ahau, 3 Kankin, corresponding to December 21st 2012 AD, it would look like this. Under the large introductory glyph, the first line reads (L-R): 13 baktuns, zero katuns. The second line reads: zero tuns, zero uinals. The third line reads: zero kin, plus the tzolkin date 4 Ahau. The bottom line shows the haab date 3 Kankin and the ruling Night-lord, Night-lord 9.*

There is a point to notice here, if you ever want to check any dates, or understand the various 2012 theories. To calculate periods of time that traverse the start of our calendar at the theoretical birth of Christ, you have to add an extra year to the calculation due to the fact that we have no 'year zero' in the Gregorian historical year. Since the eighteenth century, astronomers calculating past the BC-AD divide have used their own convention so that they don't have to add the extra year to calculations. Originally, they differentiated their system by calling it the "*Gregorian astronomical*", as opposed to the "*Gregorian historical*" system. Later, they abbreviated it to just using a minus sign. Thus, the 13-baktun cycle started in *3113 BC astronomical*, or year *-3113*, both of which are equivalent to *3114 BC historical*. The first two examples do not need to have an extra year added to calculations going into AD years; the last one does need the extra year added. The only problem is that some Mayanists (I am still researching who and when) forgot to include the "*astronomical*" tag on their 3113 BC start date, or the "*historical*" tag on their 3114 BC start-date. Others presumed that 3114 BC was an astronomical date, did not add a year and miscalculated an end-date of 2011. Some researchers made the alternative mistake of taking the 3113 BC date as a historical date, added an extra year and miscalculated an end-date of 2013.

*Fig.1.3: The sacred calendar of 260 days; the tzolkin or Chol Qij. Reading down all the columns, starting at top left, notice that after number 13, the numbers go back to 1 again. It takes 260 days for all the combinations of thirteen numbers and twenty day-signs to occur. The darker squares were conceived by Tony Shearer (see Shearer 1975, p.82), since the sum of the numbers of the four corners is 28, and the pattern then continues inwards, mirrored around a central axis. However, each of the squares on the tzolkin (excepting the central axis) can actually be summed to 28 with their three counterparts.*

| BAKTUN STARTS: | 11th August 3114 B.C. | 2720 B.C. | 2325 B.C. | 1931 B.C. | 1537 B.C. | 1143 B.C. | 748 B.C. | 354 B.C. | 41 A.D. | 435 A.D. | 830 A.D. | 1224 A.D. | 1618 A.D. |
|---|---|---|---|---|---|---|---|---|---|---|---|---|---|
| Baktun #: | 0 | 1 | 2 | 3 | 4 | 5 | 6 | 7 | 8 | 9 | 10 | 11 | 12 |
| Date: | 0.0.0.0.0 | 1.0.0.0.0 | 2.0.0.0.0 | 3.0.0.0.0 | 4.0.0.0.0 | 5.0.0.0.0 | 6.0.0.0.0 | 7.0.0.0.0 | 8.0.0.0.0 | 9.0.0.0.0 | 10.0.0.0.0 | 11.0.0.0.0 | 12.0.0.0.0 |

KATUN START DATES IN THE CURRENT BAKTUN:

| | |
|---|---|
| 1618 A.D. | 12.0.0.0.0 |
| 1638 A.D. | 12.1.0.0.0 |
| 1658 A.D. | 12.2.0.0.0 |
| 1677 A.D. | 12.3.0.0.0 |
| 1697 A.D. | 12.4.0.0.0 |
| 1717 A.D. | 12.5.0.0.0 |
| 1736 A.D. | 12.6.0.0.0 |
| 1756 A.D. | 12.7.0.0.0 |
| 1776 A.D. | 12.8.0.0.0 |
| 1796 A.D. | 12.9.0.0.0 |
| 1815 A.D. | 12.10.0.0.0 |
| 1835 A.D. | 12.11.0.0.0 |
| 1855 A.D. | 12.12.0.0.0 |
| 1874 A.D. | 12.13.0.0.0 |
| 1894 A.D. | 12.14.0.0.0 |
| 1914 A.D. | 12.15.0.0.0 |
| 1934 A.D. | 12.16.0.0.0 |
| 1953 A.D. | 12.17.0.0.0 |
| 1973 A.D. | 12.18.0.0.0 |
| 1993 A.D. | 12.19.0.0.0 |
| 2012 A.D. | 13.0.0.0.0 |

END OF 13-BAKTUN CYCLE:
21st DECEMBER 2012A.D.

*The 260-unit tzolkin can be used as a map of the 13-baktun cycle, which consists of 260 katuns of around twenty years each. Each column represents one baktun, the start-dates of which are listed along the top in Long Count notation with the equivalent Gregorian historical year. Katun start-dates in the current baktun are shown in the right hand margin.*

José Arguelles was probably the first to point out (in *The Mayan Factor*) [7] that since the tzolkin is composed of 260 *kin*, or days, and the 13-baktun cycle is composed of 260 katuns, the 13-baktun cycle is thus a harmonic of the tzolkin, being exactly 7,200 times larger. This means that the 13 x 20 tzolkin layout can be used to map history, as if it is measuring not *individual* gestation, but *species* gestation, and five of the 13-baktun cycles add to exactly 26,000 tuns; the "*Grand Year*," or precession of the equinoxes (see Fig 1.4), [8] a yet higher harmonic of 260.

## Galactic Alignment

John Major Jenkins has studied the mythology, architecture, king-accession rites and mysterious ball games of the Maya (the ball game was played in ball courts all over Mesoamerica and was developed into a symbolic mystery play), and he found encoded there the meaning behind the Maya 13-baktun cycle. Jenkins' work is so thorough and his approach so scholarly that he has even convinced some of the archaeological community (usually very entrenched in their views) that he has cracked the meaning of the Long Count and its 13-baktun cycle. In his book *Maya Cosmogenesis 2012*, [9] he shows that the 13-baktun cycle is a fifth and final cycle in the 26,000-year precession of the equinoxes, except that the Maya measured it from the Winter Solstice instead of the Spring Equinox. On December 21st 2012, the solstice Sun will align with the Dark Rift in the Milky Way, which the Maya called the *Mouth of the Crocodile* (or jaguar-toad), the *Crocodile Tree* being the Milky Way itself.

The Dark Rift is in the widest part of the Milky Way, and corresponds to the direction of the centre of the galaxy. As the alignment occurs, the *Solstice Meridian* will align with the plane of the galaxy, or *Galactic Equator*, and pass onto the other side, which Jenkins says will signal a "*field-effect energy reversal*", [10] allowing us to resonate with the source of the field. The source of the "*energy*" field (which includes the electromagnetic spectrum and beyond) is the

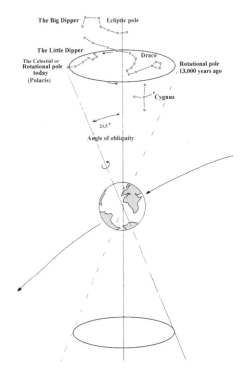

*Fig.1.4: This diagram shows how the rotational pole moves in a circle around the ecliptic pole over approximately 26,000 years. This can be measured by noting the slow movement of the zodiac constellations behind the rising point of the Sun on solstices or equinoxes. The rising point moves back through the zodiac in the opposite direction to their daily and annual movement - hence the 'precession of the equinoxes'.*

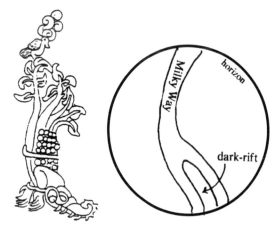

Fig.1.5: *The* Crocodile Tree *as the Milky Way, and the mouth of the crocodile as the Dark Rift. Compare to Fig.3.2. From Jenkins [1998].*

Galactic Centre, and just as water spirals down a plughole in opposing directions in each of Earth's hemispheres, which are divided by the Earth's equator, so our changing orientation to the Galactic Equator will affect us in a similar way. This will be the completion of the "*human spiritual embryogenesis*" [11] that is measured by the Maya Long Count calendar, culminating in "*a pole shift in our collective psyche*" [12] and the birth of our Higher Selves. This very last day of the 13-baktun cycle, the Maya called *Creation Day*.

Astronomically speaking, the actual crossing of the Winter Solstice Sun (or Winter Solstice meridian) and the Galactic Equator occurred in 1998, but since the Sun is half a degree wide, this is the halfway point in a process that takes 36 years to complete. In other words, it seems likely that any field effects connected with the crossing have already started, and the process will complete around 2016, when the Sun clears the equator. Astronomers have only recently been able to give an accurate estimation of the length of the precession cycle at around 25,800 years, [13] and even with today's technology they would be hard pressed to give a solstice prediction over 2,000 years in the future, to an accuracy of plus/minus fourteen years like the Maya did. However, some people think that there is no inaccuracy, and that the Maya were using this galactic alignment process to highlight some other event that coincides with it.

## The Aztec Sunstone

In 1790, while installing water pipes in Mexico City's Central Plaza, labourers unearthed a huge carved stone disc (see colour pages I and II). Archaeologists tell us it was carved in AD 1479, in the reign of Axayacatl, just 40 years before the Spanish arrived. It is twelve feet in diameter, weighs 24 metric tons, and is on display in the National Museum of Anthropology in Mexico City. The disc is known as the *Aztec Sunstone*, or *Calendar Stone*, since the central motif is said to show the five gods that represent the five ages of the world, called *Suns*. The four rectangular panels show the four previous Suns, while the central circle shows the face of Tonatiuh (or Huitzilpochtli), the Sun god who rules the present era - the fifth and final Sun.

The current, or Fifth Sun, is called the *Sun of Movement*, since it is at the centre of the day-sign *Ollin*, which means movement or earthquake. The four previous Suns are shown as

Fig.1.6: Stela 25 from Izapa, showing a scene from the Maya creation myth, the Popol vuh. Hunahpu shakes Seven Macaw from his perch. Seven Macaw represents the seven stars of the Big Dipper, and precession moved it from its perch (the rotational pole) between 1500BC and 1000BC. From Jenkins [1998].

Fig.1.7: Stela 11 from Izapa, showing the rebirth of First Father, One Hunahpu (father of Hunahpu), in the mouth of the jaguar-toad, representing the rising of the Winter Solstice Sun in the Dark Rift - Galactic Alignment. From Jenkins [1998].

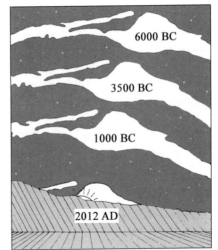

Fig.1.8: The convergence of December Solstice Sunrise and Galactic Equator over 8,000 years, as seen on the horizon from Izapa, Mexico. From Jenkins [2002].

Fig. 1.9: The slow approach of the Winter Solstice Sun to the Crocodile's Mouth, or Dark Rift, which the Maya also knew as xibalba be, the black road, or road to the underworld. A: 5,000 years ago. B: 2,000 years ago. C: 2012. From Jenkins [1998].

the gods or day-signs of Jaguar, Wind, Rain (or rain of fire) and Water, representing the four types of disaster that ended the four previous Suns. The *Cuauhtitlan Annals*, a Nahuatl manuscript, suggests that Jaguar Sun ended with an eclipse accompanied by the descent of *tzitzimime*, celestial demons that devoured mankind. John Major Jenkins says the tzitzimime are also predicted by the Aztecs for the end of the Fifth Sun, and sees them as either our own subconscious fears or as "*autonomous transdimensional entities.*" [14] The picture of one of these tzitzimime that Jenkins shows in *Maya Cosmogenesis 2012* [15] (from *Codex Magliabecchiano*) appears to be very similar to the god at the centre of the Aztec Sunstone, with claw hands and a flint-knife tongue (see picture).  Professor Gordon Brotherston has shown evidence that the Aztec Sunstone encodes the length of one Sun as 5,200 years, and that the five eras on the stone are thus equal to a 26,000-year cycle of the precession of the equinoxes. [16] Brotherston also shows that the 16th century Quiché Maya epic, the *Popol vuh*, encodes the same four past eras that are shown on the Sunstone, in the same order as those listed in the *Cuautitlan Annals*, which originated close to the Aztec capital city, Tenochtitlan. The first of the four previous eras ended in a flood (the sign of Water), the second with an eclipse (the descent of flesh-eating tzitzimime, symbolized in the sign of the Jaguar), the third in a rain of volcanic ash (the sign of Rain) and the fourth ended in fierce winds (the sign of Wind). Some Aztec accounts reverse the order of these apocalyptic calamities.

I have taken this a step further with a controversial computer animation I spent several months working on. An examination of the Sunstone showed that it could have been based on an original with layered, moving parts, which makes it actually possible to track the tzolkin. It would also have been possible to track the haab, using a partially concealed part of the theoretical original model that I call the *Secret Dial*, but it could not track the tzolkin and the haab at the same time. However, the tzolkin could be tracked at the same time as the 13-baktun cycle of the Maya, using the Secret Dial. This is the most controversial part, since the Aztecs are not normally thought to have had any knowledge of the Long Count calendar (however, they might have based the design on an original with moving parts, belonging to another, earlier civilization). The result is a mechanism that can give every day its own unique day/date position over a period of two 13-baktun cycles. This is around 10,250 years! See Chapter 16, *The Aztec Pizza*, for more details, and check *www.diagnosis2012.co.uk* for availability of the animation.

*Fig.1.10: An Aztec Tzitzimitl sky demon, from the Codex Magliabechiano.  From Jenkins [1998].*

## The Calendar Round

The civilisations of Mesoamerica all used a 365-day calendar (the haab) alongside their 260-day sacred calendar (the tzolkin), and also, in the case of the Maya, their 360-day tun (part of the Long Count calendar). Each day had a tzolkin name and a haab name, and it took exactly 52 haabs, or 18,980 days, for the combined day name to be repeated. Every 52 (365 day) years - one Calendar Round - there would be an Aztec *New Fire Ceremony*, in which sacrifices were made to stop the world from ending (see colour page I). The movement of Venus was connected to the Calendar Round, since two Calendar Rounds, or 104 haabs, and 146 tzolkins was equal to 65 Venus cycles of 584 days each.

*Fig.1.11: Seashell from Teotihuacan, decorated with two hieroglyphs meaning time cycle, and the numbers twelve and nine. After Séjourné [1957, 1978].*

The period of two calendar rounds is known as a *Venus Round* for this reason. In an anonymous manuscript dated 1558, called *Leyenda de los Soles* (*The Legend of the Suns*) [17], it is recorded that the First Sun lasted 676 years (52 x 13); the Second Sun lasted 364 years (52 x 7); the Third Sun lasted 312 years (52 x 6); and the Fourth Sun lasted 676 years (52 x 13).

It seems that the latter civilizations, such as the Aztecs, had either not inherited, or had forgotten or discarded, the Long Count calendar, so the concept of five eras or world ages was explained in terms of Calendar Rounds. Evidence that the Aztecs had lost some calendrical knowledge lies in the fact that the earlier Toltecs, from whom they inherited their knowledge of the Calendar Round and New Fire Ceremony, were using the Calendar Round to track precession by the movement of the Pleiades constellation, and when they moved south to the Yucatan, encoded this knowledge into the Pyramid of Kukulcan (more on this later). A pair of glyphs engraved on a seashell from Teotihuacan, [18] the ancient city taken over by the Toltecs, show date glyphs that include 'bar and dot' number symbols, as used by the Maya. The Aztecs reverted to a much cruder 'dots only' number system.

Tony Shearer, in his 1971 book *Lord of the Dawn*, [19] says that when Quetzalcoatl (the feathered serpent god of the Aztecs) departed, he left a prophecy of *"thirteen Heavens and nine Hells"*. Each Heaven and Hell cycle was 52 years ('years' being 365-day haabs) in length, and he would return at the end of the thirteen Heavens, then the nine Hells would start. This thirteen-Heaven cycle seems to correspond to the periods given in the *Leyenda de los Soles*, implying that the Fifth Sun lasts 468 (52 x 9) years (haabs). However, some sources say that the fifth era consists of the thirteen Heavens plus the nine Hells; 676 + 468 = 1,144 years. [20]

Since Quetzalcoatl was white-skinned and bearded and was expected to return in the year One Reed, and the Spanish tyrant Cortés landed in Mexico in the year One Reed, bearing the sign of Quetzalcoatl (the cross of four directions) on the sails of his fleet, the Aztecs welcomed Cortés as the returning Quetzalcoatl. The Spanish then slaughtered them all, burned their books and destroyed their cities, in the name of their own god.

If nine Calendar Rounds are added to the time of the arrival of Cortés, we arrive at 1987, and this is the thinking behind the *Harmonic Convergence* (conceived and promoted by José Arguelles), which took place on August 16th and 17th 1987. [21] To try and unify this Aztec end-point with the 13-baktun cycle of the Maya and other calendars and philosophies, Arguelles postulated a 25-26 year period between 1986/1987 and 2012 as a "*synchronization phase*". In the *Tribal Prophecies* chapter, which follows below, several elders mention a "*Period of Purification*" that seems to correlate to the synchronization phase of Arguelles. Were any of these revelations of ancient prophecy influenced by more recent sources of speculation? Perish the thought!

Since the 13-baktun cycle is not divisible by the Calendar Round (or even the haab), they could not both begin and end at the same point. However, there is a *Tikal* Calendar Round that will end on April 2nd 2012, and there is a *Teotitlan* Calendar Round that ended in 1987 [22] (1st March 1987).

# Chapter 2:
# Tribal Prophecies

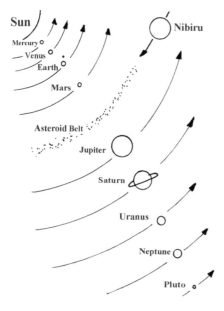

Fig.2.1: *The trajectory of Nibiru as it enters the solar system. After Sitchin [1976, 1978].*

## Maya Daykeeper: Hunbatz Men

In his book *Secrets of Maya Science/Religion*, [1] Hunbatz Men, a modern Maya Daykeeper, says that we should visit sacred sites to correct the outcome of a flaw in human DNA. This will "*strengthen our energy bodies*" for the coming transition at the end of the 13-baktun cycle.

More recently, Hunbatz Men held an eight-day course in March 2002, called *Initiation in the Cosmic Mayan Healing for Humankind*. During the course, he announced that the Maya knew about a massive planet on an elliptical orbit, which was known to the Sumerians as *Nibiru* (for more information on this, see Part 2, 2012 Theories). The Maya called it *Tzoltze ek'*. There may have been a connection with "*the 26,000-year Cosmic Mayan Calendar*", which has a "*relationship with the Pleiades and the Mother Earth*" and "*the major changes taking place on our Sacred Planet*". [2]

He says that the seventh moon of Nibiru will

activate *Kundalini* - the serpentine energy that in turn activates the seven *chakras* or power-zones along the spine (Men's book *Secrets of Mayan Science/Religion* provides evidence that this was *not* an exclusively Indian and Tibetan teaching). Tzoltze ek' will also activate our genetic memories and all the pyramids on Earth *and* underwater, so we are advised to visit them when it appears in the skies. The planet has a period of 6,500 years, not 3,600, he says, and visits us four times every 26,000 year cycle (*"The Great Calendar of the Pleiades"* that ends on 21st December 2012). The planet is inhabited by beings that operate on a higher *"mental frequency"*.

Fig.2.2: The positions of the seven chakras or power-zones.

## Maya-Aztec Shaman: Quetza-Sha

The Maya-Aztec shaman Quetza-Sha explained in an interview [3] that on 11th July 1991, during the total eclipse over Mexico, a *"sacred dimensional doorway of the equilibrium opened"*, and this was the *"Return of Quetzalcoatl"*. This was the start of an information-download process, which Quetza-Sha describes using Philip K. Dick's enigmatic terminology [4] - *"It will leave us plasmated with the millenary knowledge of the new time"*, and this information is to prepare *"for the dimensional birth of a new race that comes from the Pleiades."*

   The creation of the new race is due to occur in 2012. *"The year 2012 is not the destruction of the planet, but is the transformation of the spirit, sexual energy, the energy of your heart and your mind in all the dimensions of our existence in the solar system"*. The process continues through 2024, with a fifth dimensional transformation, to 2029 when humans themselves transform to fifth dimensional beings.

## Maya Elder: Don Alejandro

At the Latinola website, [5] there is an announcement by Maya elder, Don Alejandro Cirilo Pérez Oxlaj (Head of the National Council of Elders of Guatemala), which says:

*"...On Dec. 20, 2012, Mother Earth will pass inside the centre of a magnetic axis and that it may be darkened with a great cloud for 60 to 70 hours and that because of environmental degradation, she may not be strong enough to survive the effects. It will enter another age, but when it does, there will be great and serious events. Earthquakes, maremotos (tsunamis), floods, volcanic eruptions and great illness on the planet Earth. Few survivors will be left."*

Don Alejandro has been sent as a messenger from a council of elders to warn the world that we must change the way we live and take care of Earth. We shall return to Don Alejandro later in the book.

## Guatemalan Ajq'ij: Carlos Barrios

Steven McFadden has written an article - *Steep Uphill Climb to 2012* [6] - on the talk by Guatemalan *Ajq'ij*, priest-anthropologist Carlos Barrios in Santa Fe in Autumn 2002. Barrios says that the 25-year period between 1987 and 2012 is the period between the Fourth and Fifth Worlds. [7] He also says 2012 will not be the end of the world, but it will be transformed. He says the "*alignment with the heart of the galaxy in 2012 will open a channel for cosmic energy to flow through the Earth, cleansing it and all that dwells upon it, raising all to a higher level of vibration.*" However, in another article, [8] Carlos' brother, Gerardo Barrios says the Thirteen Heavens cycle began in 1991, but will "*gestate*" for nine years until 2001, when it will be "*born*".

Fig.2.3: *Comparative sizes of (L-R) Earth, Jupiter and Nibiru.*

## Inca Prophecy: Willaru Huayta

Willaru Huayta, a Peruvian "*spiritual messenger*" and descendant of the Quechua nation, says that 2013 will mark the end of the Inca calendar, and in that year a "*huge magnetic asteroid*" three times larger than Jupiter will pass close to Earth, "*activating the purification of the land*", causing cataclysms that will kill off most of humankind. A core of people will survive to become the "*seed-people*" of the "*Sixth Generation*". To become a part of that core, we must heal our spiritual sickness by conquering our egos. [9]

## Inca Prophecy: Q'ero Priesthood

In her 1999 book *Keepers of the Ancient Knowledge*, [10] Joan Parisi Wilcox, who has been trained in Peru to the highest current level of Q'ero priesthood (the fourth level), reveals the Q'ero prophecy of spiritual evolution and a Golden Age. The prophecy is incorporated into a 16th century Catholic philosophy of three ages. These are; the Age of the Father, the Age of the Son, and the Age of the Holy Spirit (see colour page III). The latter, which the Q'ero call *Taripay Pacha*, began in the period between August 1st 1990 and August 1st 1993, when the world underwent a cosmic transmutation called a *pachakuti*. Wilcox quotes William Sullivan's translation of the word pachakuti from his 1996 book *The Secret of the Incas*, in which he translates it as "*an overturning of space-time*". Taripay Pacha is the period extending approximately from 1993 to 2012, during which mankind will spiritually evolve - it is the "*Age of Meeting Ourselves Again*", when time will end. It is divided into two phases, a seven-year phase to the year 2000, then a twelve-year phase until 2012, when something happens to time, or our perception of it, and the Taripay Pacha becomes the Golden Age. The three worlds of the Andean cosmos will unite - the *hanaq pacha*, or upper world, the *ukhu pacha*, or lower world, and the *kay pacha*, or mundane physical world, will merge into one. We shall return to this subject in Chapter 21. The process is assisted by a technique of Andean shamanism, called the *"engaging of the energy body"*.

## Hopi Elders

The Hopi Native Americans of Arizona believe that we are living in the fourth of seven eras, the Fourth World, and that there will be a *"Great Purification"* just before the start of the Fifth World (and, like the Aztec version, they say that the previous era ended in a flood). Frank Waters' *Book of the Hopi* [11] provides the details, which I summarise below.

The First World ended by fire; the Second World ended when the Earth *"teetered off balance"* and rolled over twice, causing floods and an ice age; the Third World ended in a flood. The transition from one era to the next is called an *Emergence* by the Hopi, and is symbolised by a labyrinth symbol that is identical to ones shown on early Cretan coins. It is also known as the Mother Earth symbol, or Mother and Child. The whole process is seen as a birth process and is re-enacted during an annual ceremony called *Wúwuchim*, in which *"initiates undergo spiritual rebirth"*. [12] This ceremony is held in November and includes a *"New Fire Ceremony,"* similar to that which the Aztecs held in November, once every 52 years. The Emergence is symbolized in an underground ceremonial chamber (a *kiva*) with a hole in the floor and a hole in the roof.

*Fig.2.4: The Hopi symbol of Emergence, which is exactly the same as the Cretan labyrinth.*

The hole in the floor is the emergence-point (*sipápu* or *sipápuni*) into the Third World, and the ladder to the hole in the roof is the emergence-point into the Fourth World. [13]

Exactly as John Major Jenkins has found with the Aztec New Fire Ceremony, the Hopi New Fire Ceremony culminates at midnight, when the Pleiades are overhead. This shows a direct connection to the way in which the Toltecs tracked precession and

*Fig.2.5: A plan of Mesa Verde, a ruined town of the Anasazi - an extinct tribe of Pueblo Native Americans that lived over 1,000 years ago in Arizona. Note the many kivas or underground ceremonial rooms.*

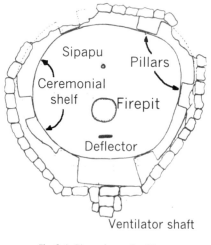

*Fig.2.6: Plan view of a kiva.*

encoded the results into the Pyramid of Kukulcan (see Chapter 8). At this point in the ceremony, "*a lone white-robed figure wearing a large white star enters the kiva and announces, 'I am the Beginning and the End'*". Shortly after this, the fire is extinguished, while priests, godfathers and initiates throw off their clothes and the stars they have been wearing on their foreheads. Chaos ensues as everyone tries to get up the ladder and out before the World ends.

The Hopi believe that the human body has a series of psychophysical centres, and this system is uncannily similar to that of the Hindu and Buddhist *chakras*, except that they only list the upper five centres, whereas the Hindu system lists two additional lower ones. The first Hopi centre is at the top of the head and is like a door that is open at birth and death. Originally, mankind communicated with the Creator through it, but during the First World it closed up (this is comparable to the Fall of Man); the second centre is the brain; the third is at the throat; the fourth is at the heart; the fifth is the naval/solar plexus centre. The living body of the Earth is based on the same design, with vibratory centres along an axis. [14] In each era, or World, mankind became governed by the next centre down, each more material and less spiritual than the one above. The Fourth World, in which we are currently living, is the most material, and at the next transition, development reverses and goes upwards, being governed by each higher centre in turn. [15] Waters does not state whether each higher centre will predominate for a whole era, or whether it will be possible to rise through the centres in one era, but the culmination will be a re-opening of the "*door*" at the crown.

## Blue Star Kachina

*Kachinas* are spirits, of which there are over 300 different ones, and they are represented in Hopi ceremonials by dancers wearing costumes and masks, who are then 'taken over' by the kachinas. In 1914 a song was first sung at the Wúwuchim ceremony predicting that the "*Emergence into the Fifth World*" would come when the Saquasohuh danced in the plaza. The *Saquasohuh* is Blue Star Kachina, and according to the *Book of the Hopi*, "*represents a blue star, far off and invisible, which will make its appearance soon.*" [16] The other main source on this Blue Star prophecy is said to originate from a Native American elder called White Feather, of the Bear Clan, who hitched a lift in 1958 with a Methodist minister and told him of nine prophecies, starting with the coming of white men with guns (which occurred in the sixteenth century). After that, the ancient prophecies were said to have predicted covered wagons, longhorn cattle, railroad tracks, power and telephone lines, concrete roads and oil spills. The eighth prophecy is the hippie era, which was manifested in the 1960s. The only remaining prophecy to be fulfilled is the ninth and last one:

"*You will hear of a dwelling-place in the heavens, above the Earth, that shall fall with a great crash. It will appear as a blue star. Very soon after this, the ceremonies of my people will cease.*" [17]

Some have suggested that this referred to the Russian *Mir* space station that crashed back to Earth in March 2001. Others say that the Blue Star was the comet Hale-Bopp of 1997. Moira Timms suggested that it was a supernova that appeared on February 23rd 1987, and was known as SN1987A. It was the brightest supernova in four centuries, and showered the Earth with sub-atomic particles and a whole spectrum of radiations. [18] In 1963, Frank Waters wrote that "*the Emergence to the future Fifth World has begun,*" [19] and since then other Hopi elders have added that the final stage of this transition period is known as *The Great Day of Purification*, [20] but all the subsequent Blue Star prophecies seem to be based on the two above, from the *Book of Hopi* and from White Feather (see colour page III).

In Steven McFadden's book *Profiles in Wisdom*, [21] the Hopi elder Oh Shinnah Fastwolf says the Great Purification will be over by 2011, and also says "*it will be marked by the appearance of a new star.*" However, it seems that Oh Shinnah variously claims to be an "*Apache healer*" or "*Cherokee Grandmother*", as well as a Hopi elder, and has been accused by the Fastwolf family of being an Irish Folk Singer from Chicago. [22] Frank Waters first published the *Book of the Hopi* in 1963, and to research it he had lived on the Hopi reservation for three years (probably 1959-1961) and was subsequently seen as an authority on Hopi matters. In the book, Waters says that the Hopi believe that the Maya, Toltecs and Aztecs were "*aberrant Hopi clans*" [23] who remained in Mesoamerica while the Hopi migrated north. In 1975 he brought out his book *Mexico Mystique*, [24] in which he showed common points in the cosmology, mythology and ceremony of the Hopi to those of the Aztecs and Maya. He equates the catastrophic end of the Fifth Sun of the Aztecs with the end of the Fourth World of the Hopi. [25] Also in *Mexico Mystique*, Waters says that the 13-baktun cycle began on 12th August 3113 BC and ends on December 24th 2011 AD. He got this end-date of 2011 from *The Maya* by Michael Coe (first published in 1966, but Coe's later works give a revised end-date of 23rd December 2012 [26]). This is obviously why some people have got the impression that the Hopi prophecies end in 2011.

Murry Hope says the Hopi "*share with the ancient Egyptians a knowledge of Sirius, which they know as 'Blue Star Kachina'*". [27] However, according to the glossary in the back of the *Book of the Hopi*, the word for Sirius, the Dog Star, is *Ponóchona*, while the word for Blue Star Kachina is *Saquasohuh*. The "*futurist*" Gordon Michael Scallion (who claims he had visions and dreams of the Blue Star before he knew about the Hopi prophecy), provides a possible (or impossible) explanation linking Sirius and the Blue Star:

*"This solar system shall become a binary sun system, when the Blue Star returns... During the day it will appear as a silvery light, one hundred times brighter than the morning star... During the evening, it will appear as a moon... The Blue Star is a companion to Sirius B... The vibrations given off by the Blue Star will enable the soul to have an easier time in communication with its host... A new light body is being created."* [28]

We will have more to say about Mr Scallion later in the book.

## Dogon Connection

Readers of Robert Temple's *The Sirius Mystery* [29] may recall that the Dogon tribe of Mali, West Africa, have known for centuries that Sirius (the Dog Star) is a binary star system, and that Sirius B is a white dwarf - facts they say were given to their ancestors by visitors *from* Sirius. They based their *Sigui* calendar on the orbit-time of Sirius B around Sirius A - originally a period of 49 to 50 years, as in the case of the orbit, but the Sigui was later reformed to a 60-year period. [30] In the first edition (1976), Temple told us that the Dogon knew of a third star, and that he thought it would be a red dwarf if and when it was discovered. What you may not have heard, if you haven't read the 1998 edition of *The Sirius Mystery*, is that astronomers have recently discovered Sirius C! In 1995, twenty years after the publication of the first edition, French Astronomers Daniel Benest and J. L. Duvent announced in *The Journal of Astronomy and Astrophysics* their discovery of a small red dwarf star - Sirius C. This has now been confirmed, vindicating Temple's work.

Fig.2.7: The "emergence" of the Star of the Nommo, as drawn by the Dogon people. After Temple [1976, 1998]

The Dogon say that the *"spaceship"* of the visitors - the *Nommo* - looked *"like a new star"*, and that they will return one day, when *"a certain star will reappear"*, and there will be a *"resurrection of the Nommo"*. They also say that Sirius A and B *"were once where the Sun now is"*. The star will be invisible before it *"emerges"*, and is drawn with the rays inside the circle. It will only be *"formed when the Nommos 'ark' descends, for it is also the resurrected Nommos' 'eye' symbolically."* [31] Temple thinks this is Phoebe, Saturn's tenth moon, not to be confused with Phobos, one of Mars' moons that Scallion and others have predicted will soon break loose.

## Pueblo Native Americans: Fifth World in 2012

The Pueblo are those North American natives who live in stone or clay houses in central New Mexico and northeast Arizona. The term includes the Navajo, Hano, Hopi, Zuni, Acoma and Laguna people, who are all said to have descended from the Anasazi people who lived over 1000 years ago. It is unclear as to which tribe of Pueblo people the following refers to.

Speaking Wind, a Pueblo Indian from Northern New Mexico, has said that the Fifth World will start in December 2012. This conforms to Hopi prophecies, even though some have put the transition at 2011:

*"As I said, the final cleansing of Earth began in June 1998. In September 1998, the five brothers (planets) aligned themselves to usher in the cleansing energies of Earth. The chaos everyone has been anticipating, or the tearing away of the illusion and the lie, will begin between January and April 1999 and will continue to escalate until the nine brothers (planets) align themselves on the 5th May 2000. From that date, until the last day of the Fourth World, December 22, 2012, a date taken from our star calendars, everything living will undergo a purge. If mankind will not willingly let go of the illusion, and the lie, it will be stripped away. And we have only begun to feel the effect, since June 1998. The 23rd day of December 2012 is the first day of the Fifth World".* [32]

## Cherokee Calendar

In her book *The Cherokee Sacred Calendar*, [33] Raven Hail (a member of the Cherokee Nation of Oklahoma) describes a calendar system that seems to be a cross between the Aztec and Maya sacred calendars. It is a 260-day wheel with twenty day-signs, which have names very similar to the Aztec version. However, they use a numerical notation identical to the Maya notation. The ephemeris for finding your sacred calendar birthday is comparable to that given by Bruce Scofield in his book *Day Signs*, about the Aztec system, and both of these correlate to the True Count. Hail says that a World, or Sun, was approximately 5,200 years (in the Long Count of the Maya, the 13-baktun cycle lasts 5,200 Tuns, or 360-day years, which is about 5,125 solar years; the Aztecs

*Fig.2.8: The Cherokee calendar, as shown by Raven Hail. After Hail [2000].*

didn't have a Long Count, but only a concept of Suns, of which the current is the Fifth, but with varying accounts of how long the Suns were). Hail says that previous Worlds or Suns have ended in cataclysm, and this one, which is the *Sun of Heron* (which equates to the

*Sun of Movement* in the Aztec), will end in earthquakes, but nobody knows when.

However, the ephemeris, like Scofield's, lists the day-signs for the first day of each thirteen-day period from January 11th 1900, but where Scofield's ends on December 20th 2000, Hail's ephemeris goes on to December 18th 2012, and then lists the day three days later as *Four Flower* - December 21st 2012, where the ephemeris ends. The extra ephemeris section alone is quite useful, but there is something else that we need to take into account. On the page about this book at *Amazon.com* the book receives some very bad reviews, including one by someone called Tahlehquah, who says, *"As an official of the Cherokee Nation, let me advise the readers that the 'teachings' of 'Raven Hail' are not endorsed by the Nation, nor in fact, do they follow any Cherokee historical or cultural beliefs that I have ever heard."* [34]

### Cherokee Calendar Wheels

Dan Troxell, who is *"of Chickamauga Cherokee blood"*, has a website called *Mysteries of Trox.* [35] On the site, he tells of the Cherokee Calendar and how it was inspired by *"the 52 scales around the mouth of the rattlesnake"* and that it measures *"Time Untime"*.

He describes a system of interlocking wheels, and says sometimes the wheels were made from stone, and sometimes the wheels were formed on the ground using pebbles. These are often mistaken for Medicine Wheels. They represent the movement of *"the stars, the heavens and the universe"*. On the rings are *"glyphs and colours"*, the alignments of which give various meanings.

There are six rings - three visible (representing heavens) and three invisible (representing universe). One of the three visible wheels has 22 sections, each representing 52 years. The 22 sections are divided into two parts; the first thirteen are years of *Light* and the following nine are years of *Darkness*. The whole cycle is thus 1,144 years, and is called a *World*, consisting of 676 years of Light (13 x 52) and 468 years of Darkness (9 x 52). There is a transitional period from Light to Darkness and vice versa, called a *Crossing*. These Crossing points vary in length, from zero to 25 years, and are a collective struggle comparable to the birth and death transitions of the individual.

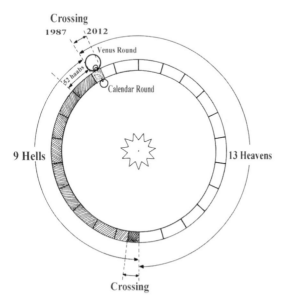

*Fig.2.9: A diagram based on a description of the Cherokee calendar by Dan Troxell.*

Here again, we have confirmation of a 25-year transitional period starting in 1987, since Troxell says that *"the Cherokee calendar ends in 2012"*.

Incredibly, Troxell says the Cherokee name for the Great Spirit Creator is *Yahowah*. This seems to back up the claim of the Mormons that one of the Lost Ten Tribes of Israel once lived in America. In fact, Tony Shearer (who I mentioned at the end of Chapter 1) thought that the 22 golden plates found by Joseph Smith, the founder of Mormonism, had come from Palenque, and that Mormon was Lord Pacal of Palenque. It was also Tony Shearer who first publicized the concept of the ending of the nine Hell cycles on August 16th - 17th 1987 (Harmonic Convergence). Dan Troxell's description is exactly like a diagram called *The Echo Wheel*, by Nick Armstrong on his website *2012 Unlimited*. [36] From the text with the diagram, it is obvious that the inspiration for Armstrong's version is the Shearer information; actually, it is almost identical to Shearer's diagram, which is also called *The Echo Wheel* (Shearer, 1975, p99). I can't help wondering if Dan Troxell was inspired by the same source, or even by Armstrong.

## The Seneca Indians
Seneca society's Wolf Clan Teaching Lodge *"teaches the wisdom, prophecy, and philosophy of Earth history"*, and Grandmother Twylah Nitsch [37] is a Seneca Elder of the Wolf Clan, who was chosen *"many decades ago"* to preserve the Wolf Clan teachings of her maternal grandfather, Moses Shongo, the last of the traditional Seneca medicine men:

*"The Seneca Grandfather Moses Shongo (died ca.1925) foresaw a 25-year period of purification, lasting until the year 2012 or so, during which the Earth will purge itself."* [38]

So, here we have a native prophecy concerning not only 2012, but a 25-year period of purification preceding 2012, and that means that the year 1987 was flagged long before the late Tony Shearer (in 1969 or 1970) told José Arguelles that August 16th-17th 1987 would be the end of the ninth Hell cycle (in the so-called prophecy of *Thirteen Heavens and Nine Hells*). This is the time that Arguelles called *"Harmonic Convergence"*. This also has a bearing on the Kalachakra prophecy (see Chapter 3).

## Zulu Prophecy: The Return of Mu-sho-sho-no-no
Credo Mutwa, an 80 year-old Zulu *Sanusi* (shaman) and elder from South Africa (and author of *Song of the Stars: The Lore of a Zulu Shaman*), gave a talk at the Living Lakes Conference in California on October 2nd 1999, which included the following:

*"Let me tell you two last things please. One, it is this, that I am told by the great storytellers of our tribes that fresh water is not native to our Earth, that at one time, many thousands of years ago, a terrible star, or the kind called Mu-sho-sho-no-no, the star with a very long tail, descended very close upon our skies. It came so close that the Earth turned upside-down*

*and what had become the sky became down, and what was the heavens became up. The whole world was turned upside down. The Sun rose in the south and set in the north. Then came drops of burning black stuff, like molten tar, which burned every living thing on Earth that could not escape. After that came a terrible deluge of water accompanied by winds so great that they blew whole mountaintops away. And after that came huge chunks of ice bigger than any mountain, and the whole world was covered with ice for many generations. After that the surviving people saw an amazing sight. They saw rivers and streams of water that they could drink, and they saw that some of the fishes that escaped from the sea were now living in these rivers. That is the great story of our forefathers. And we are told that this thing is going to happen again very soon. Because the great star, which is the lava of our sun, is going to return on the day of the year of the red bull, which is the year 2012."* [39]

We have heard about the Dogon of Mali, North Africa, with their astronomical knowledge and calendar connection to the Blue Star. There is a stone circle in South Africa, called *Timbavati*, which means *"the falling down of a star"* in Zulu language. It still has an equinox alignment intact. In 1997, a stone circle in the southern Egyptian desert was found to have an alignment to the Summer Solstice sunrise, and at 6,000 BC is the *"oldest astronomically aligned structure yet discovered anywhere on the planet."* [40] There is also a stone observatory at Nomoratunga in Kenya, connected with the *Borana Calendar*, based on rising stars and lunar phases. There are more stone circles in Ethiopia, Morocco, The Gambia, Senegal and Togo. The point is this; the Long Count has been traced to Izapa. Izapa has Olmec connections. The Olmec carved mysterious giant stone heads with African features. Could there be a calendrical connection between the Long Count and Africa? The 520-day eclipse calendar of the Berbers of Tenerife also suggests this.

## Maori Prophecy: Veil Dissolves in 2012

The indigenous people of New Zealand, the Maoris, have a creation legend in which *Rangi* (the Sky) and *Papa* (the Earth) were partners and were *"closely clasped together"*. They had a number of children, including a wind god, sea god, and war god, who lived in-between these two parents, squashed and without light. One day these children decided to push their parents apart so they could have room to move. They all tried and failed until one of the gods, *Tane*, pushed them apart, separating them - and then there was light.

There is a second, more secretive, legend that follows on from this that says that there will come a time when the *"children of Tane"* (mankind) are so busy, so distracted with fighting, greed and lust, so separated from our original parents that they - Rangi and Papa - will take that opportunity, while no-one is looking, to quickly come back together, destroying everything in the process.

Recent conversations between a young Maori [41] and the *kaumatua* (tribal elders) have revealed that they see the prophecy being fulfilled in the year 2012. When one elder said

"*Ka hinga te arai*," the rest nodded and agreed. Since "*hinga*" means "*to fall*" and "*arai*" means "*curtain*," the phrase was at first understood to mean "*the curtain will fall*," as in "*final curtain*" or the end of the world. However, the elder was one who retained knowledge of the "*tuturu Maori*," or "*original Maori*" language, and it turned out that the original meaning of the word hinga was "*to dissolve/to be removed/to fade*"; and the original meaning of the word arai was "*veil/thin separation*". Since, when people die, the Maoris say they have gone "*ki muri i te arai*," "*behind the veil*" or "*passed over*", the word arai actually means '*a separator*' between the physical world/plane and the spiritual world/plane.

So, in 2012, when "*ka hinga te arai*," the Maoris imply that there will be a "*dissolving of the veil*," or merging of the physical and spiritual planes.

# Chapter 3:
# Oriental/Asian Calendars

## Vedic Time Cycles

In the Hindu system of time cycles, inherited from the Vedic civilisation of the Indus Valley (now believed to date back to 7,000 BC), and preserved in manuscripts called the *Vedas*, the longest cycles last trillions of years, but at the shorter end of the cycle spectrum, we have the four *Yugas*, which are:

*Krita/Satya Yuga* (Golden Age): 1,728,000 years = 2,160 x 800
*Treta Yuga* (Silver Age): 1,296,000 years = 2,160 x 600
*Dvapara Yuga* (Copper/Bronze Age): 864,000 years = 2,160 x 400
*Kali Yuga* (Iron Age): 432,000 years = 2,160 x 200

Each Yuga is split into three parts: dawn, day and dusk:

*Krita/Satya Yuga*: dawn = 144,000; day = 1,440,000; dusk = 144,000
*Treta Yuga*: dawn = 108,000; day = 1,080,000; dusk = 108,000
*Dvapara Yuga*: dawn = 72,000; day = 720,000; dusk = 72,000
*Kali Yuga*: dawn = 36,000; day = 360,000; dusk = 36,000

If these numbers look familiar, that is because they are precessional numbers, in which a *Platonic Year* (an early term for the precession of the equinoxes, named after the Greek philosopher Plato), is equal to 25,920 years (12 x 2,160, or 360 x 72), or one complete precession of the equinoxes (or solstices); a Platonic month is equal to 2,160 years, or the precession of the equinox through one sign of the zodiac; a Platonic day is equal to 72

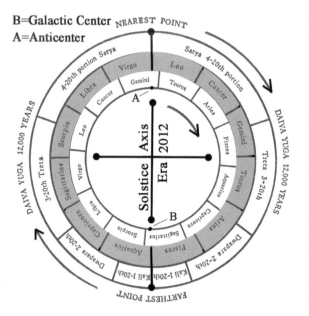

Fig.3.1: *John Major Jenkins' adjusted version of Yuktewar's yuga model. In this version, the ascending half of* Kali Yuga *starts on the solstice-galaxy alignment era of 2012 AD. From Jenkins [2002].*

years, or the precession of the equinox through one degree; two Platonic months are equal to 4,320 years; half a Platonic month equals 1,080 years; two Platonic days equal 144 years. These Platonic/precession numbers also occur in the Long Count system of the Maya: 360 days = 1 tun; 3 tuns = 1,080 days; 7,200 days = 1 katun; 144,000 days = 1 baktun; 7,200 tzolkins in the 13-baktun cycle.

The philosopher René Guenon and other sources say we are now nearing the end of Kali Yuga, although some sources say it only started in 3102 BC. In John Major Jenkins' recent book *Galactic Alignment*, [1] he goes into the Vedic yuga system in some detail, and studies the work of Hindu saint Sri Swami Yukteswar (born 1855), who discovered an oversight in the Vedas and went on to explain it. In one of the oldest Vedic writings, attributed to the god-man Manu, the four Yugas are said to add up to 24,000 years, but when they are enumerated they only come to 12,000 years. The *Krita/Satya Yuga* (Golden Age) lasts 4,800 years; the *Treta Yuga* (Silver Age) lasts 3,600 years; the *Dvapara Yuga* (Bronze age) lasts 2,400 years, and the *Kali Yuga* (Iron Age) lasts 1,200 years.

Yukteswar explained the enigma in a diagram that equates the 12,000 years to a *descending* half of the 24,000-year cycle, and another 12,000 years to an *ascending* half. Jenkins' Study of the Yukteswar analysis shows that Yukteswar was talking about the precession cycle, but basing it on a 24,000-year cycle, rather than the (approximate) 25,800-year cycle recognised by astronomy. The *"descent into darkness"* started when the Summer Solstice (June) Sun was aligned with the apparent, or visual, Galactic Centre around 10,800 BC, and the *"ascent back to light"* takes place now, when the Winter  Solstice (December) Sun aligns with the apparent Galactic Centre (Galactic Equator)circa 1998-2012.

## Galactic Alignment and the Vedas

In *Galactic Alignment*, John Major Jenkins has shown that not only was knowledge of the precession of the equinoxes encoded into mythology worldwide, but the ancients also knew that there are certain times during the cycle of precession when the Earth-Sun-galaxy relationship allows the influx of some kind of energy that triggers a transformational leap in mankind.

There are two points on the ecliptic where the solstices (Winter and Summer) occur, and the ancients knew these solsticial points as "gates". These celestial gates were described by Macrobius as the Gates of Capricorn and Cancer, and were seen as doorways through which the soul descends to be reborn on Earth and ascends following physical death.

In Joscelyn Godwin's book *Mystery Religions in the Ancient World*, [2] the gate of reincarnation is called the Silver Gate (Cancer), while the gate of ascension is called the Golden Gate (Capricorn), but he says that the Silver Gate is the "*Way of Reincarnation*", while the Golden Gate is the "*Way of the Gods*" and leads "*beyond the Circle of Necessity, i.e. to release from*

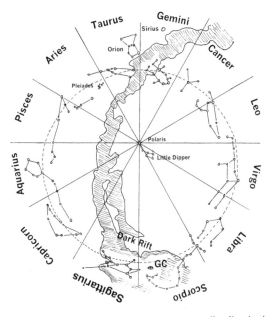

Fig.3.2: The 'celestial gates' are currently situated where the ecliptic (dotted line) crosses the Milky Way.

the round of birth and death. These are the two routes from which the soul can exit from the world at death, and the Capricorn gate is the one through which the gods descend to Earth." [3]

It is clear from both *Hamlet's Mill* [4] (see page 110) and from Jenkins' *Galactic Alignment* that these gates don't actually lie in Cancer and Capricorn, but the neighbouring constellations of Gemini and Sagittarius. This is because precession has moved, or *precessed*, the gates back into the neighbouring constellations. The Golden Gate lies at *Galactic Centre* in Sagittarius, and the Silver Gate lies at *Galactic Anti-centre* in

Fig.3.3: The Golden Gate and Silver Gate currently lie on the galactic equator.

Gemini (there will be more on this in chapters 7 and 8). Following the work of Oliver Reiser, Jenkins makes a convincing case that the alignment of the solstice Sun with the Galactic Equator (close to Galactic Centre), which is flagged by the end of the 13-baktun cycle in 2012, marks the time-window when the divine influences descend:

*"Precession changes our angular orientation to the larger magnetic field of the galaxy in which we are embedded. During regularly occurring eras in the precessional cycle, as indicated by the solstice-galaxy alignments (probably the equinox-galaxy alignments, too), the Earth's protective magnetic shield becomes unstable and oscillates. Without a complete field reversal being required, this oscillation allows greater amounts of mutational rays to strike the surface of the Earth. While this may result in mutations and a greater chance for 'evolution', of greater significance is the possible transformative effect on human consciousness during alignment eras, when human beings are exposed to higher doses of high-frequency radiation."* 5

Fig.3.4: The chakra system in the microcosm and the macrocosm (image on left: Darlene). From Jenkins [2002]

In other words, when the solsticial points (and possibly the equinoctial points) come into alignment with the galactic plane (the Galactic Equator), the celestial gates *"open"*.

Jenkins refers to Swami Sri Yukteswar's study of the Vedic Yuga system (that may have originated as long ago as 7000 BC), and shows how that system is also flagging the galactic alignment. He concludes that there is a Galactic Chakra system, with the base chakra at Galactic Centre, and the crown chakra in the direction of the Galactic Anti-centre. Earth is at the level of the fifth (throat) chakra, evolving towards the sixth (ajna or third eye):

*"The as yet unspoken message in this survey is that the galactic alignment opens a channel for the Kundalini shakti to flow through the Earth, cleanse (it) us, and excite it (us) into a higher level of being."* 6

Fig.3.5: Some interpretations of the galactic chakra system would have the base chakra at Galactic Anti-centre near the Gemini/Taurus boundary, and the crown chakra at Galactic Centre, near the Sagittarius/Scorpio boundary. After Timms [1980, 1994].

However, Jenkins also accepts that the alternative concept, in which Galactic Centre is seen as the crown chakra, and Galactic Anti-centre is seen as the direction of the root, or base chakra, may be equally valid. Douglas Baker suggests Sirius is the Galactic Third Eye.

## The Chinese Calendar

The Chinese calendar consists of 60-year cycles, which in turn consist of five twelve-year cycles. Each year is named after one of twelve animals, and one of five elements, with two consecutive years being named after each element: *Rat; Ox; Tiger; Rabbit; Dragon; Snake; Horse; Sheep; Monkey; Rooster; Dog; Pig.* These are sometimes called the Twelve Terrestrial Branches. The elements are Wood, Fire, Earth, Metal and Water.

Each element has a destructive manifestation followed by a constructive manifestation, making the Ten Celestial Stems. The current Chinese 60-year cycle started on 22nd February 1984 with the year *Wood Rat*, and almost halfway through the 60 years, on 23rd January 2012, the Chinese year *Water Dragon* will begin.

## The Tibetan Calendar

The Tibetan calendar is based on the Chinese system, and started in the year 1027, when the *Kalachakra* teachings were introduced to Tibet. However, this was the year *Fire Rabbit*, three years after the start of the Chinese 60-year cycle, so the current Tibetan 60-year cycle, or *Rab-byung*, therefore started on February 28th 1987. This is the seventeenth cycle of 60 years.

The twelve Tibetan animals vary slightly from the Chinese, and start with *Rabbit* rather than *Rat*, due to the three-year difference; the elements are thus listed starting with Fire, rather than Wood. [7]

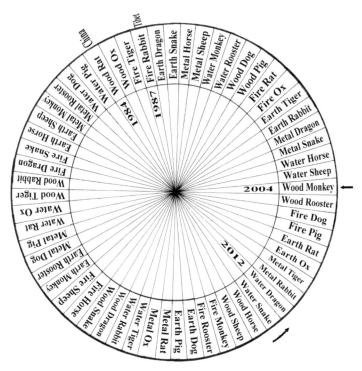

Fig.3.6: *The 60-year combination-cycle of "stems and branches," showing the Chinese and Tibetan start-points of the current cycle and the relative position of 2012.*

## The Tamil Calendar

The Tamil calendar of southern India also includes a 60-year cycle, which, like the Tibetan one, re-started in 1987 (but in mid-April, rather than February). It is a derivative of the old Hindu solar calendar and is based on the sidereal year. The 60-year cycles may be connected to the 60-year Jupiter-Saturn conjunction cycle, but the last conjunction was in May 2000, not close to the end/start of any of the above calendars. Each year has a name in the Tamil calendar, and 2012 is called *Nandana*, which means *delight*.

John Major Jenkins has discovered [8] that in Islamic and Indian astrology, the lunar nodes, which precess around the sky over 18.61 years, [9] are represented as the head and tail of a dragon. The lunar nodes are the points where the Sun and Moon's orbits intersect. When an eclipse occurred, the dragon was thought to be eating the Sun or Moon. According to an Islamic text, when the south lunar node (tail of the dragon) is at exactly 3° Sagittarius, it is *exalted*. This is close to Galactic Centre, and Jenkins points out that although the precise alignment of the Galactic Equator with the solstice Sun was in 1998, maybe eclipses could "*represent the quicker 'second hand' of the precessional clock*". [10]

There will be a total lunar eclipse on Winter Solstice 2010. So, if galactic alignment involving the Sun at the Galactic Equator was the "*hour hand*" at Winter Solstice 1998, and the lunar eclipse on Winter Solstice 2010 is the "*minute hand*," when the Moon becomes involved, then maybe the "*second hand*" involves the alignment of another body to Galactic Centre on the Winter Solstice of 2012.

One 'classic' degree of precession is 72 years; Winter Solstice 1926 heralded the year 1927 (see below), and was 72 years before Winter Solstice 1998; a sixth of that is twelve years (1998 to 2010); a sixth of that is two years (2010 to 2012). So the question is, what celestial body will appear in conjunction with Galactic Centre on Winter Solstice 2012? Could it be asteroid 2002AU4 or 1999NW2, both due on that day; perhaps a comet or meteor shower, EMP wave appearing as a blue star from Galactic Centre; Nibiru; Planet X; Mercury/Venus; Mars; a supernova in Sagittarius, or something else?

## Kalachakra: Tibetan Buddhist Prophecy

The Buddha (Gautama) gave the Kalachakra teachings just before his death (*Kala* means time and *chakra* means wheel, so Kalachakra means *wheel of time*). The first King of Shambhala was a witness to this (he was the first of a line of seven kings), and he took the teaching to *Shambhala*, a mythical kingdom in a hidden valley of the Himalayas. The eighth king founded a line of 25 kings (25 plus 7 = 32 altogether), and the prophecy says that the last of these will establish the Golden Age. Each king reigns for 100 years, so the Golden Age comes 3,200 (32 x 100) years after the death of Buddha. The reported dates of Buddha's death vary from 2422 BC to 546 BC, so the coming of the Golden Age is due between 779 AD and 2655 AD. [11]

The Kalachakra teaching was taken to Tibet in 1027 AD (1026 in some versions), and this is when the Tibetan calendar begins. Most sources agree that the 21st (28th overall) king assumed power in 1927, and will rule until 2027. So, the 25th and last (32nd overall) king would thus be due in the year 2327 AD. However, some lamas believe the 25th king, *Rudra Cakrin*, is ruling *now*, which would still fit in with the possible dates for the death of the Buddha. In fact, the *Nyingmapa*, or *"Ancient Ones"* - the oldest sect in Tibetan Buddhism - say that *Padma Sambhava* (Guru Rimpoche) brought Buddhism from India to Tibet *"around the eighth century AD."* So perhaps the 13th (20th overall) king started ruling around the eighth century, 300 years before the Kalachakra teachings were taken to Tibet, and it was the 25th king (32nd overall) who took the throne in 1927. If so, then his reign ends in 2027, and some time before then he will fight and win the last battle against the *"king of barbarians,"* inaugurating the Golden Age, which will last at least a thousand years.

## The Kalachakra-2012 Connection

In his 1975 book *The Transformative Vision*, [12] José Arguelles claimed that the sixteenth 60-year Kalachakra cycle that began in 1927, and was to end in 1987, was the *"last 60-year cycle of the Tibetan calendar"*, and he had already been told in 1969, by the late Tony Shearer, that the ninth and last Mexican *"Hell cycle"* would end in 1987. This seemed to be an amazing coincidence. Shearer's understanding of the *"present major cycles of Heavens and Hells"* developed from a conversation with a Mexican artist called Covarrubias, who had got the information from *"a sorceress in the jungle hotlands of Tehuantepec."* [13] Shearer worked out how the cycles correlated to the Gregorian calendar, and that information is published in his 1971 book *Lord of the Dawn*, [14] and

*Beneath the Moon and Under the Sun* (1975). [15] He found that the end of the ninth Hell would be August 16th 1987, which, according to a calendar correlation that is only one day away from the True Count, was *13 Ahau* - the last day in the 260-day tzolkin (in the True Count - the unbroken count still used by the descendants of the ancient Maya - 13 Ahau was the previous day). This seemed to be another amazing

*Fig.3.7: The emblem of Kalachakra, or the* Ten of Power, *combining ten syllables that express the essence of the teachings. The outer teaching includes the prophecy, the inner teaching deals with techniques of manipulating energy flow through the psychic centres in order to transform the body into "a vehicle of liberation," and the other teachings include the use of sacred symbols such as this one, which connects to the Kalachakra deity in a passionate embrace with his consort - the unity of male and female - compassion and wisdom, necessary for enlightenment.*

coincidence. Arguelles announced in his book *The Mayan Factor* (released in 1987) that August 16/17th 1987 would be Harmonic Convergence, inaugurating a 25-year period of *"phase shift,"* culminating in *"galactic synchronisation"* in 2012.

However, Arguelles and Shearer made several errors in their calculations. They said that Cortés landed on Good Friday April 21st 1519, and that this was the day 1 Reed in the year 1 Reed - the prophesied day for the return of Quetzalcoatl, the mythic saviour-god/man of the Aztecs (known to the Maya as Kukulcan). Exactly nine Calendar Rounds later (a Calendar Round is 18,980 days, or 52 x 365-day haabs, so nine of them would be 170,820 days), the nine Hells would, they said, end on Harmonic Convergence, 16th August 1987. Using the *"terminal year-bearer system"* where the year is named after the 360th day, 1519 was the year 1 Reed or *Ce Acatl*, but April 21st (Julian Date or JD) was actually a Thursday - Good Friday was April 22nd. That's only one day of error, but when we then investigate to find out when the day 1 Reed occurred, we find it was twelve days later, on 4th May (JD). When we then check to see when nine Hells after Good Friday 1519 (170,820 days) would be, we get January 7th 1987 (GD, or Gregorian date), 221 days before Harmonic Convergence. Nine Calendar Rounds after the day 1 Reed would be 20th January 1987 (GD), which is 208 days before Harmonic Convergence.

Considerable study has allowed a re-appraisal of Shearer and Arguelles' statements, so that they can be re-stated correctly. Since Shearer's information originated in Tehuantepec, and the Tehuantepec River is just south of Oaxaca, and the Teotitlan area is just north of Oaxaca, we could re-state the facts as follows:

The landing of Cortés at Veracruz occurred in the spring of 1519, which corresponded to the year Ce Acatl (1 Reed), dedicated to the principal god/hero of the ancient Mexicans, Quetzalcoatl. Furthermore, the ancient Mexican seers had prophesied that this particular year would mark the end of a "Heaven" period consisting of thirteen 52-year cycles, and the beginning of a major "Hell" period consisting of nine 52-year cycles, or 468 years. However, various districts of Mexico followed different variations of the 52-year cycle, and there is only one that ended in 1519. This is known as the Teotitlan Calendar Round, and the day 2 Reed, (2 Acatl or 2 Ben), June 13th (JD) 1519, marked the beginning of nine 52-year cycles that would terminate on 1 March 1987 (GD), the end of nine Teotitlan Hells. On this day, a 25-haab cycle of Purification would begin, ending on February 23rd 2012, which is just two days after the Tibetan Losar New Year.

The Tibetan calendar started in 1027 with the arrival of the Kalachakra teachings, and the sixteenth 60-year Rab-byung cycle of the calendar ended on February 28th, 1987 - just two days before the end of the nine Teotitlan Hell cycles. Amazingly, although the Losar New Year is governed by the lunar cycle, if we add 25 365-day haabs to the end of the sixteenth 60-year Rab-byung cycle in 1987, we arrive at the Losar New Year in 2012, which occurs on 21st February 2012, two days before the end of the Teotitlan-timed Purification period.

There is actually another significant fact about 1927 that Arguelles missed: The '21st king' of Shambhala assumed power in 1927, but some lamas believe this is actually the 25th (= 32nd overall) and last king who is ruling now (32 x 100 years after Buddha's death). This last King will be the tenth and final incarnation of Vishnu, who will return to vanquish Evil, put an end to the Age of Discord and inaugurate the Golden Age. The Hindu name for this king is *Kalki*, while the Tibetan name is *Rudra Cakrin*, and in the Golden Age, which will last at least 1,000 years, there will be no more work or fighting, and our lifespan will increase to 800 years, according to the prophecy.

## Hindu Prophecy: Kalki and the Critical Mass of Enlightened Ones

In *The Way to Shambhala*, [16] Bernbaum says that the Golden Age will come when the Sun, Moon and Jupiter all meet in the same quadrant as the Tishya constellation [17] (which is part of Cancer). The next time this happens will be on 26th July 2014, according to my astronomical software, [18] but here is a quote from *Dr Nelson's Website*, revealing that Kalki is already here and the Golden Age is coming in 2012:

*"About 15 million people around the world think of Kalki Bhagavan as the Supreme Being who will usher in a new age. This golden age was inaugurated on September 25, 1995, and will be fully realized in the year 2012. The Vishnu Purana and several other sacred texts consider Kalki to be the last incarnation/avatara of Lord Vishnu. He has descended nine times already (23 times in an unedited version), and the last one for this cycle will be at the end of Kali Yuga, the present degenerate age. Some Hindu thinkers put the beginning of Kali Yuga around 3102 BCE, and since it is supposed to last 432,000 years (according to one reckoning), many Hindus are not expecting Kalki anytime soon. Nevertheless some individuals have been identified as Kalki by their devotees."* [19]

On the *Skyboom* website, a page about this *"Avatar of the Golden Age"* explains the 2012 connection further:

*"Others would say that this is not possible, that the old calendars say that the Golden Age won't 'be here' for thousands of years. Currently there is heated debate in India, as some experts have claimed to have found errors in the ancient calendars. This puts the date of the Golden Age very close to the end of the Mayan calendar".* [20]

The *Golden City* website explains that Kalki only needs to enlighten 60,000 people in order to start a chain reaction, since he is a *Mukti-Avatar* (*"a divine Master through whom the Divine can transfer Enlightenment to any number of people"*):

*"Secondly, there are now very powerful spiritual energies engulfing the Earth coming from the centre of the Universe. These energies are meant to make mankind enlightened, but*

*somehow the process is not starting off as it was supposed to. So Kalki can give and transform these energies to anyone now, but only until 2012. If 60,000 have become enlightened before this, he can help man getting enlightened. If later, the negative powers will take over and we have missed this very rare chance. The future will not at all be nice if man will not transform fully in the near future".* [21]

In 1977, another teacher, Goswami Kriyananda (who is not from India, despite the name), told his student Ray Grasse that the period from 2010 to 2012 signified a *"potentially important window for open contact with non-human races"*. [22]

# Chapter 4:
# I Ching: Ancient Chinese Lunar Calendar

### Timewave Zero

The *I Ching*, or *Book of Changes*, consists of an arrangement of 64 hexagrams (six-line figures) made up from two types of line - yin and yang - and has been used for millennia as an oracle, in which coins or sticks are thrown, the combination of which signifies one or two hexagrams - the second hexagram represents the predicted change in situation from the first one. However, as I mentioned in the introduction to this book, in *The Invisible Landscape*, [1] Terence and Dennis McKenna make a case that the I Ching had originally been used as a lunar calendar in which the 64 six-line hexagrams - 384 lines in all - had represented the 384 days in a thirteen-month lunar year.

In 1971, the brothers made a journey down to the Amazon jungle, in which they had a shared hallucinogenic experience, furnishing information on the pattern behind the unfolding of events in the universe. They returned home, convinced that concealed in the I Ching lay a mathematical encoding of this pattern, and they proceeded to examine it closely.

They noticed that the two main numbers of the I Ching - six (lines in a hexagram) and 64 (hexagrams in the sequence) - when used as multipliers around a 384-day basic cycle, caused the following resonances:

**64** x **6** = 384 days -**13 lunations** / 1 lunar year
384 days x **64** = 67.29 solar years - **6 minor sunspot cycles**
67.29 solar years x **64** = 4,306 solar years - **2 zodiacal ages**
4,306 solar years x **6** = 25,836 solar years - **1 complete precession of the equinoxes**

An inspection of an early arrangement of the hexagrams, known as the *King Wen* sequence, showed beyond any doubt that the hexagrams were deliberately and carefully arranged into this order - for example, the second hexagram of each pair is either a complete reversal of the first (where each line changes to its opposite), or it is an inversion of the first (the whole hexagram is turned upside down). They then proceeded to apply a series of operations to the sequence in order to mathematically extract all the information and convert it into a *Timewave*.

*First Operation*: The amount of difference between sequential hexagrams (the number of lines that changed to their opposite) was first numerated, then graphed, and the graph was reversed and re-combined with itself to produce a *simple wave*. This was then analysed for *skew* in two directions, producing

Fig.4.1: *The* King Wen *sequence of the I Ching.*

two sets of 64 numbers that were then combined into one set. The simple wave was next analysed for *divergence, congruence* and *overlap* of the two components, and the resulting set of 64 numbers was combined with the skew set.

*Second Operation*: Next, the simple wave was recombined with itself at three levels, where six simple waves were laid end-to-end, representing the six lines of a hexagram; two larger versions were overlaid on the six, to represent two trigrams (half-hexagrams of three lines each, of which there are a total of eight that combine to make the 64 hexagrams), and finally, one still larger simple wave was laid on top to represent a whole hexagram. This *complex wave* has 384 positions (6 x 64) available for analysis, and the 64 final numbers from operation one can be recombined using the complex wave, into 384 *quantification values*, or the *number set*. When these 384 values are graphed, we arrive at a figure called The Eschaton. To get this far, the McKennas used what was then an advanced computer at a university, the printouts from which are the appendices of the first edition of *The Invisible Landscape*.

This Eschaton wave would be repeated at a series of levels, each 64 times greater than the one below, and combined into a "*modular wave hierarchy*". This later became known as the *fractal wave*, and is composed of 26 levels that govern all existing change from sub-quantum events up to the duration of the three-dimensional universe. The term 'fractal' had not even been invented at this point, however, and Peter Meyer's *Timewave Zero* computer software, incorporating all the fractal levels and first

Fig.4.2: Operation 1a: The graph of the numerated difference between each hexagram and the subsequent one. After McKenna, [1975, 1993].

Fig.4.3: Operation 1b: The Simple Wave. After McKenna [1975, 1993].

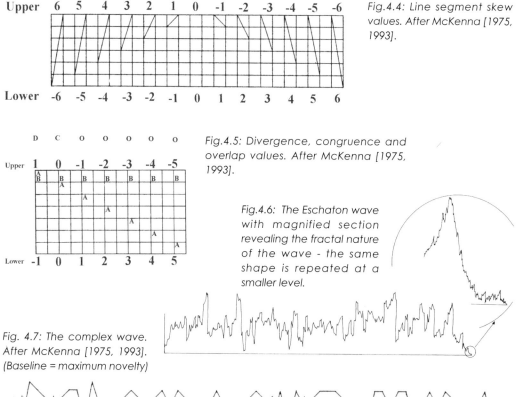

Fig.4.4: Line segment skew values. After McKenna [1975, 1993].

Fig.4.5: Divergence, congruence and overlap values. After McKenna [1975, 1993].

Fig.4.6: The Eschaton wave with magnified section revealing the fractal nature of the wave - the same shape is repeated at a smaller level.

Fig. 4.7: The complex wave. After McKenna [1975, 1993]. (Baseline = maximum novelty) developed in 1987, was still about thirteen years away.

The next step was to correlate the Eschaton wave with history, when history is expressed as a graph of novel events. The explosion of the atomic bomb at Hiroshima on August 5th 1945 (US time) was taken to be a sufficiently 'novel' event that it should correlate to a major peak on the wave. When we consider the acceleration of technology in the last 300 years, and look at the Eschaton wave as a 4,306-year cycle, it seems obvious where the Hiroshima bomb explosion should lie on the wave. When this is done, there is just one 67.28-year cycle left until novelty hits the baseline, on 17th November 2012. [2] This is the point where all the waves and sub-waves peak together, signifying the *"maximum ingression of novelty into spacetime"* - an evolutionary *Omega Point* (end point, named after the last letter of the Greek alphabet) and dimensional transition known as *concrescence* (originally a biological term meaning *"the growing together of related parts, tissues, or cells"*, adapted by philosopher Alfred North Whitehead to refer to the point of maximum novelty).

When Peter Meyer's software allowed the full fractal wave to be examined, the maximum novelty point moved away from 5th August 1945, due to the cumulative effect of all waves and sub-waves, but by then Terence McKenna had heard about the 13-baktun cycle of the Maya and its end point in December 2012 and had brought the termination point forward to coincide with it, and this was incorporated into the software. In 1996, the mathematics of Timewave theory came under criticism by a British mathematician named Matthew Watkins, but it was later re-calculated by another mathematician and nuclear fusion specialist, John Sheliak, using vector analysis. Sheliak confirmed that there was an error, but it was correctable, and the resulting fractal wave (sometimes called *TimeWave One*) was again hooked onto history at the Hiroshima event, thus restoring the meaning to the fractal wave. However, when the end-point is moved forward to coincide with the 13-baktun end-point on December 21st 2012, the novelty spike in 1945 moves on to September 8th (not back to the date of the Trinity test, when the first nuclear bomb was exploded, just prior to Hiroshima, as implied by Sheliak's commentary), [3] an unremarkable date, so perhaps the original November 17th 2012 date of maximum novelty really is the end of the Timewave after all.

McKenna admitted in 1975 that the *"best fit"* method was only one of the ways to determine the *"possible dates of a future concrescence."* [4] The second method, he said, *"is more subtle and takes account of the precession of the equinoxes."* He went on to suggest that the *"Winter Solstice node"* is approaching Galactic Centre, and that when that node eclipses Galactic Centre, it *"might be an event unusual enough to signal an onset of concrescence."* [5] He also pointed out that although the solstice node is currently *"only about 3° from Galactic Centre, a degree covers a large area in space, and the galaxy may be presumed to have a gravitational centre, a radio centre, and a spatial centre."* [6]

In other words, not only had McKenna's Timewave predicted the evolutionary pinnacle of this spacetime dimension would occur just 34 days before the end of the 13-baktun cycle, but he had also intuited the importance of the 2012 alignment of the Winter Solstice

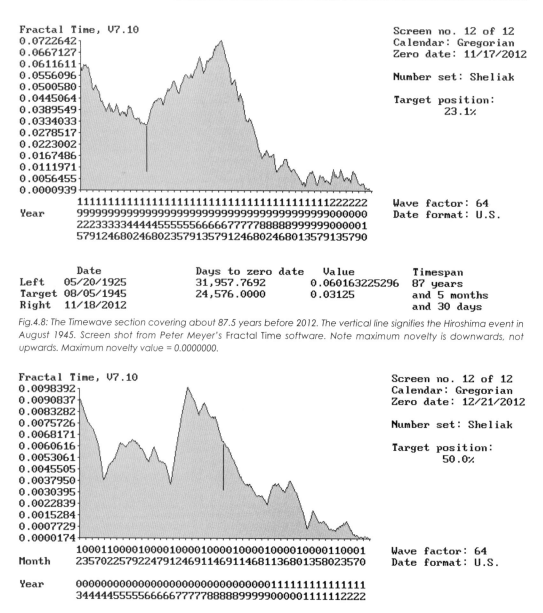

```
Fractal Time, V7.10                              Screen no. 12 of 12
0.0722642                                        Calendar: Gregorian
0.0667127                                        Zero date: 11/17/2012
0.0611611
0.0556096                                        Number set: Sheliak
0.0500580
0.0445064                                        Target position:
0.0389549                                             23.1%
0.0334033
0.0278517
0.0223002
0.0167486
0.0111971
0.0056455
0.0000939
           1111111111111111111111111111111111111111111112222222    Wave factor: 64
Year       9999999999999999999999999999999999999999990000000    Date format: U.S.
           2223333344444455555566666777778888899999900000001
           5791246802468023579135791246802468013579135790
```

|        | Date       | Days to zero date | Value          | Timespan      |
|--------|------------|-------------------|----------------|---------------|
| Left   | 05/20/1925 | 31,957.7692       | 0.060163225296 | 87 years      |
| Target | 08/05/1945 | 24,576.0000       | 0.03125        | and 5 months  |
| Right  | 11/18/2012 |                   |                | and 30 days   |

*Fig.4.8: The Timewave section covering about 87.5 years before 2012. The vertical line signifies the Hiroshima event in August 1945. Screen shot from Peter Meyer's* Fractal Time *software. Note maximum novelty is downwards, not upwards. Maximum novelty value = 0.0000000.*

```
Fractal Time, V7.10                              Screen no. 12 of 12
0.0098392                                        Calendar: Gregorian
0.0090837                                        Zero date: 12/21/2012
0.0083282
0.0075726                                        Number set: Sheliak
0.0068171
0.0060616                                        Target position:
0.0053061                                             50.0%
0.0045505
0.0037950
0.0030395
0.0022839
0.0015284
0.0007729
0.0000174
           10001100001000010000100001000010000100001100001    Wave factor: 64
Month      23570225792247912469114691146811368013580023570    Date format: U.S.

Year       00000000000000000000000000000000000111111111111111
           34444455555666667777788888999990000011111112222
```

|        | Date       | Days to zero date | Value          | Timespan |
|--------|------------|-------------------|----------------|----------|
| Left   | 12/22/2003 | 3,286.5912        | 0.009070767204 | 9 years  |
| Target | 06/22/2008 | 1,643.0000        | 0.006303699244 |          |
| Right  | 12/21/2012 |                   |                |          |

*Fig.4.9: The Sheliak wave 2003-2012. The diagram shows novelty peaks for the nine years leading up to 2012, with the end-point set to the Maya end-date of December 21st 2012. Screen shot from Peter Meyer's* Fractal Time *software.*

```
Fractal Time, V7.10                          Screen no. 12 of 12
0.0039246                                     Calendar: Gregorian
0.0039067                                     Zero date: 12/21/2012
0.0038889
0.0038710              September 11th 2001    Number set: HuangTi
0.0038531
0.0038352                                     Target position:
0.0038173                                          50.0%
0.0037994
0.0037815
0.0037636
0.0037458
0.0037279
0.0037100
0.0036921
            0100100102102102102102102102102102102102101011011   Wave factor: 64
Hour        0680680573573572462462462461351351340240240139139l   Date format: U.S.

Day         22222333000000000000000111111111111111122222222222
            77899011112334556778990112334556778990112334556
```

| | Date | | Days to zero date | Value | Timespan |
|---|---|---|---|---|---|
| Left | 08/27/2001 | | 4,134.2184 | 0.00377066098 | 1 month |
| Target | 09/11/2001 | 06:00 | 4,119.0000 | 0.003709316254 | |
| Right | 09/26/2001 | | 4,103.7815 | 0.003845878026 | |

*Fig.4.10: The Huang Ti wave showing a "target date" (where the vertical line is) of September 11th 2001. The end-date is set to December 21st 2012. When the end-date is moved on to 23rd December, the novelty spike will move to the right coinciding with the target date vertical line. Screen shot from Peter Meyer's Fractal Time software.*

```
Fractal Time, V7.10                          Screen no. 12 of 12
0.0468934                                     Calendar: Gregorian
0.0468755                                     Zero date: 12/21/2012
0.0468576
0.0468397              September 1st 1939     Number set: HuangTi
0.0468218
0.0468039                                     Target position:
0.0467861                                          50.0%
0.0467682
0.0467503
0.0467324
0.0467145
0.0466966
0.0466787
0.0466609
            0100100102102102102102102102102102102102101011011   Wave factor: 64
Hour        0680680573573572462462462461351351340240240139139l   Date format: U.S.

Day         11111222222222222222233300000000000000011111111111
            77899011223445667889001112334556778990112334556
```

| | Date | | Days to zero date | Value | Timespan |
|---|---|---|---|---|---|
| Left | 08/17/1939 | | 26,790.2184 | 0.04673941098 | 1 month |
| Target | 09/01/1939 | 06:00 | 26,775.0000 | 0.046678066254 | |
| Right | 09/16/1939 | | 26,759.7815 | 0.046814628026 | |

*Fig.4.11: The Huang Ti wave showing a target date of September 1st 1939, showing resonance to the 9/11 event in Fig. 4.10. As with Fig. 4.10, if the end-date is moved to 23rd December, the novelty spike moves on two days, in this case to September 1st 1939, when Hitler invaded Poland. Screen shot from Peter Meyer's Fractal Time software.*

```
Fractal Time, V7.10                          Screen no. 12 of 12
0.0098829                                    Calendar: Gregorian
0.0091236                                    Zero date: 12/21/2012
0.0083643
0.0076049                                    Number set: Sheliak
0.0068456
0.0060863                                    Target position:
0.0053270                                       50.0%
0.0045677
0.0038083
0.0030490
0.0022897
0.0015304
0.0007711
0.0000118
          0110000011000000110000011000001100000010000001   Wave factor: 64
Month     8021356801134679122457902235780213468911246791   Date format: U.S.

Year      0000000000000000000000000011111111111111111111
          6667777777888888888999999900000001111111222222
```

| | Date | Days to zero date | Value | Timespan |
|---|---|---|---|---|
| Left | 08/29/2006 | 2,305.3828 | 0.004884556867 | 6 years |
| Target | 10/26/2009 | 1,152.0000 | 0.002197265625 | and 3 months |
| Right | 12/22/2012 | | | and 24 days |

*Fig.4.12: The Sheliak wave: the resonance period of 6.29 solar years (6 x 384 days) leading up to the date of concrescence in 2012. Screen shot from Peter Meyer's* Fractal Time *software.*

```
Fractal Time, V7.10                          Screen no. 12 of 12
0.0411405                                    Calendar: Gregorian
0.0403805                                    Zero date: 12/21/2012
0.0396206
0.0388607                                    Number set: Sheliak
0.0381007
0.0373408                                    Target position:
0.0365808                                       50.3%
0.0358209
0.0350610
0.0343010
0.0335411
0.0327811
0.0320212
0.0312612
          000110000001000000110000011000001100000011000000   Wave factor: 64
Month     5780113468911246790223578021356801134679122 4579   Date format: U.S.

Year      3333344444444444444444444444444444444444444444
          9999900000001111111122222222333333344444444455555
```

| | Date | Days to zero date | Value | Timespan |
|---|---|---|---|---|
| Left | 05/11/1939 | 26,887.3828 | 0.036145106889 | 6 years |
| Target | 07/14/1942 | 25,727.7316 | 0.033454123169 | and 3 months |
| Right | 09/03/1945 | 24,580.6171 | 0.031265010126 | and 24 days |

*Fig.4.13: The 6.29-year period leading up to September 1945, encapsulating World War II, which shows an almost exact resonance (on the Sheliak wave) to the same time period leading up to 2012 (see Fig.4.12). Screen shot from Peter Meyer's* Fractal Time *software.*

Sun with a point near the Galactic Centre, not knowing that the Maya had foreseen this very event well over 2,000 years ago!

## 9/11 Resonance

Following the terrorist attacks on the World Trade Centre and other targets in the USA on 11th September 2001, Zyzygyz, the founder of the *Time Wave Zero 2012* [7] Internet discussion group, checked the *Timewave* software to see if there was a novelty spike on that day, but there was nothing obvious. When he looked for resonances on the Timewave, he found a partial resonance to the Nazi invasion of Poland on 1st September 1939.

When Zyzygyz mentioned this to Peter Meyer, he took a look himself and pointed out that there was an exact resonance using the *Huang Ti* numbers (see below) and the 23rd December 2012 end date. [8] The resonance is also exact using the 21st December 2012 end date, but both dates are on the bottom of a large novelty spike when the 23rd is used as an end-date.

Since Meyer had only calculated the Huang Ti number set to test Timewave theory, and the Huang Ti sequence has a dubious history, [9] plus the fact that this only works with the Lounsbury end-date (23rd December 2012), it started looking as if none of the existing number sets were quite right since they didn't show a novelty spike on the 9/11 event using the original end date in November 2012, or the Winter Solstice end-date of the Maya. However, this brought to light the fact that there is a very close resonance on Timewave One (the Sheliak wave) between the six years and one day of World War II, and the six years and one day leading up to 21st December 2012 (see colour page III). [10] This is partially explainable in terms of the resonances mentioned above. 6 x 384 days = 6.31 solar years (six lunar years), which creates resonances within the wave, but it is still quite disturbing considering a discovery by Michael Drosnin that World War III will start in 2006, according to the Bible Code (see next chapter).

## Franklin Timewave - Zyzygyz's Brainwave

Magic squares are grids of numbers which are arranged in rows and columns in a square in such a way that all columns, rows and diagonals add to the same number. Traditionally, there is a magic square associated with each planet - a 3 x 3 square is associated with Saturn; a 4 x 4 square with Jupiter; 5 x 5 with Mars; 6 x 6 with the Sun; 7 x 7 with Venus; 8 x 8 with Mercury; and 9 x 9 with the Moon. [11] Ben Franklin (who was almost certainly a Mason and so may have been privy to Maya calendrical information - see *The Eye in The Pyramid* in Chapter 8), one of the Founding Fathers of the American constitution, devised a different arrangement of the Mercurial magic square (an 8 x 8 square, consisting of the numbers from one to 64). However, the numbers in the Franklin Square add to the same number in so many ways (at least 75) [12] that the square has become a mathematical legend. When you take into account the fact that the numbers in the 8 x 8 Mercurial square add to 260 - the number of days in the Maya sacred calendar, or tzolkin, and also, the number of katuns in

*Fig.4.14: The Magic Square of Mercury, showing how rows, columns and diagonals add to 260. Any quadrilaterally symmetrical pattern of eight squares will also add to 260, e.g. two squares mirror-imaged in each corner.*

the 'macroscopic tzolkin' of the 13-baktun cycle - then we have the suggestion of a link between the Franklin 8 x 8 square, the I Ching (an 8 x 8 square of 64 hexagrams), and the Maya calendars.

This connection was discovered and published by José Arguelles in *Earth Ascending* in 1984, before he knew that Terence McKenna had used the I Ching to arrive at 2012 as the year in which the concrescence (evolutionary Omega Point) of the universe would be achieved.

Zyzygyz (without knowing that Arguelles had already published the Franklin-I Ching connection) figured that if the numbers in the Franklin 8 x 8 square were each replaced with the hexagram of that number (in the *King Wen* sequence), then the Franklin 8 x 8 square could be converted into a Timewave! Peter Meyer [13] helped out by generating the 384 number-set from Zyzygyz's 64 Franklin-hexagram numbers, and they found that a true Timewave was possible (this is not guaranteed - an earlier attempt to make a timewave from the earliest I Ching arrangement, the Fu Hsi sequence, wouldn't work [14]). The largest level of the wave could then be mapped against time, and Zyzygyz noted various correlations to events in the solar system, with peaks and troughs on the Franklin Timewave.

With help from Brendan Boerner, John Sheliak and myself, Zyzygyz persisted until he was able to generate a *Franklin Timewave* that would map the last seven billion years, but it doesn't answer all the questions after all. It doesn't show the rush into novelty that all the other waves (except Huang Ti) show between the late sixties and early nineties. It shows more resonance between World War II and the 2006 to 2012 period than the Huang Ti, Watkins, and Kelley waves, but not as much as the Sheliak wave, though it doesn't show a novelty peak for the Hiroshima date, or any of the first nuclear tests. It does, however, seem to show a resonance between Saddam Hussein's assumption of power in Iraq, and Sargon of Akkad's takeover of Mesopotamia (Iraq) in 2334 - 2279 BC.

*Fig.4.15: The Franklin square does everything that the Mercury square does, plus many more bilaterally symmetrical patterns such as these.*

Fig.4.16: *The Franklin wave showing the 67.29-year resonance period leading up to 2012. Saddam Hussein was made President on July 17th 1979, which is just to the right of the vertical line, at the top of the steep descent into novelty. Screen shot from Peter Meyer's Fractal Time software, adapted for the Franklin number set.*

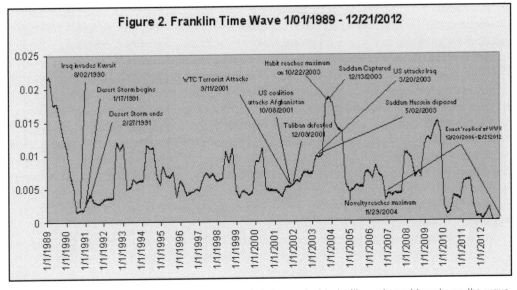

Fig.4.17: *The Franklin wave showing how recent events in Iraq coincided with peaks and troughs on the wave. Diagram by Zyzygyz.*

# Chapter 5:
# Abrahamic Religions

*Disclaimer: Before going any further, I need to point out that I do not subscribe to any of the judgemental or right-wing attitudes expressed on any of the literalist religious sites that I quote from; nor do I sympathise with any fanatical or tyrannical attitudes expressed on any websites. If there is any judging to be done, then I would suggest that our higher selves judge our lower selves as individuals; I also suggest that religion and race is irrelevant.*

## Christianity - The Rapture and 2012

There have been several Christian groups and individuals claiming on the Internet and in books that in 2012 the *Day of the Lord* will arrive. For instance, in a recent novel by Ivan and Dora Cain, *The Year 2012*, [1] "*Elbib Ehtdrow*" is a reporter in Jerusalem covering the descent of a hooded humanoid on a cloud in 2012. The person is taken to be the Messiah returned and calls himself "*Natas Reficul*", and starts putting the world in order. This is a predictable replay of the prophecies of the *Book of Revelation* - just reverse the spelling of names to get the plot.

There is also *Magic Music Myth* [2] - a rock opera, CD and live concert by *Alchemy* about the judgement of the Devil in 2012, and a proposed film, originally known as *Phantasm 2012 AD: The Mormon Mausoleum - Apocalypse and Hell on Earth*, now re-titled *Phantasm's End*. The more positive side emerges in the form of a music CD called *2012* by *Soul Rising*, who call themselves "*humble seekers of Christ.*" A fifth example of this Christian/2012 connection is the book *God's New Millennium*, [3] by Richard Henry Whiteside, and his website *Godsweb*, [4] which announces that the New Jerusalem is to be situated in central California and fully functioning by 2012. So, are these authors and groups just 'jumping on the bandwagon', or are there scriptural reasons for presuming that Christianity's *Day of Judgement* will happen in 2012?

Without getting into complex theological doctrines of premillennialism, amillennialism and postmillennialism, or pre-tribulational, mid-tribulational or post-tribulational positions, let's just see if we can find any reason why concepts such as *The Rapture, Second Coming*, and *Judgement Day* are being connected with 2012. The various approaches above can be summarised by saying that there are biblical reasons for expecting a seven-year period of *Tribulation* (troubled times), and that either before, after or halfway through this period, The Rapture will occur, when the 144,000 chosen ones will be taken up to heaven. Judgement Day (usually taken to be the Second Coming, though some refer to The Rapture as this), will then occur either at the end of the seven-year period, or after a further thousand-year period.

Fundamentalist preacher Jack Van Impe says that the Second Coming of Christ will occur between 2001 and 2012, [5] and gives some interesting clues as to the reasoning in the summary of his video *Left Behind*. [6] The clues point to a three-part answer. The first part is in the first three gospels (Matthew, Mark and Luke); the second part is in the *Book of Daniel*, and the third part is in the rabbinical lore of Judaism. The first two are covered in the next two sections; the third is covered under the Judaism section.

## Matthew, Mark and Luke

Many people assume that all the end-time prophecies originate in the *Book of Revelation* - the last book in the bible, accredited to apostle John - but there are many other references, including a *"mini-apocalypse"* in three of the four gospels - Matthew 24-25, Mark 13, and Luke 21. The first thing explained by the online authors [7] is that the first sections of the mini-apocalypses describing Tribulation are actually about the events that were predicted to lead up to the destruction of the Temple of Jerusalem in 68 -70 AD, *not* about Jesus' Second Coming. This initial reference to a mini-apocalypse was in answer to the first part of a question from the disciples, asking when the Temple would be destroyed. The second part of the question - *"and what will be the sign of your coming and of the close of the age?"* was answered next (the questions are fully listed in the Matthew version and the answers fully listed in the Luke version). In Luke's gospel, this question is answered in Chapter 21, v.24: *"...and Jerusalem will be trampled by the Gentiles until the times of the Gentiles are fulfilled."* In 68 AD (often put at 70 AD), when the Romans destroyed the Temple, the Jewish people had a further 1,900 years to wait until they regained control of Jerusalem during the Six-Day War in 1967, when the times of the Gentiles (non-Jewish people) were fulfilled. The verses of Luke 21, following verse 24, may describe the physical, religious and moral signs that would take place between the first sign, or *Pre-sign,* in 1967, and Jesus' return. Most theologians believe that these signs have now all been fulfilled.

## The *Book of Daniel*

Nebuchadnezzar, king of Babylon, had a dream of a statue with a head of gold, arms and chest of silver, a belly and thighs of bronze, and legs of iron. The feet were part iron and part clay. Then a boulder smashed into the feet of the statue and it crumbled to dust, leaving the stone, which *"became a mountain and filled the whole Earth"*. The prophet Daniel decoded the dream as follows: there would be four empires or world kingdoms, symbolised by gold, silver, bronze, and iron, and representing the Babylonian, Persian, Greek, and Roman empires. The last of these is followed by the Heavenly Kingdom of God... except that there is actually another empire in-between - iron mixed with clay - possibly referring to the *"empire"* of the Roman church. So, we have a similar version to the Maya and Aztec vision of a set of four or five

Gold — Babylon
Silver — Persia
Bronze — Greece
Iron — Rome
Iron/Clay — Vatican/Europe

*Fig.5.1: The statue of Nebuchadnezzar's dream, depicting four/five empires preceding the coming of the Kingdom of Heaven.*

eras, ending in a dramatic transition to a new state of being.

Before looking at the encoded numbers of years, we must first take note of the biblical code where "*a day*" represents a year. Earlier in his book, [8] Daniel speaks of "*seventy weeks of years*", which represents a 490-year period (70 x 7 days = 490 days) and gives us a clue about a day-year code. [9] There is, however, a direct connection to the words of Jesus, when Daniel overheard a "*holy one*" or angel ask how long the sanctuary would be "*trampled under foot*" (Daniel 8: v13-14), and the reply was "*For two thousand and three hundred evenings and mornings; then the sanctuary shall be restored to its rightful state*". Using the day = year rule, we find that 2,300 years after the invasion of the Greeks around 333 BC leads to 1967 AD! However, closer investigation reveals a discrepancy of up to two years, since the calculation fails to take into account the "*missing year zero*" between BC and AD dates, and although Alexander the Great invaded Israel in 333 BC, he captured Jerusalem in the following year, 332 BC.

In the last three verses of the *Book of Daniel*, it says the period preceding the end of days can be figured as 1,290 "*days*" or 1,335 "*days*": "*From the time that the continual burnt offering is taken away and the abomination that makes desolate is set up, there shall be a thousand two hundred and ninety days. Blessed is he who waits and comes to the thousand three hundred and thirty five days... the end of days*". The difference between these periods is 45 days, and using the day = year rule, this gives the 45 years between 1967 and 2012.

However, this begs the question, when was the burnt offering taken away, and what is the "*abomination of desolation*"? Jerusalem fell to Nebuchadnezzar around 597-602 BC, when the burnt offering would have been taken away. About 1,290 years later, the Dome of the Rock was built on Temple Mount in 691 AD - an obvious contender for the 'abomination' as far as the Hebrews were concerned. But the passage could be interpreted to mean that the burnt offerings ended at the same time that the abomination was set up.

I have heard a rumour that there was an earlier mosque on the site of the Dome of the Rock, with a suggested build date of 677 AD; 1,290 years after this would bring us to 1967, and then the extra 45 years would bring us to 2012. [10] However, this could be an attempt to manufacture evidence.

So, to summarise, the recapturing of Jerusalem by the Israelis in the Six-Day War of 1967 is a key date encoded in the words of both Jesus and Daniel, and starts off a 45-year period ending in 2012. The Second Coming will occur during this 45-year period, according to the beliefs of some Christians. There are many possible interpretations as to exactly what the Second Coming might be.

## The Fig Tree Parable

Some sources, which don't connect the abomination with Arabic mosques, have said the parable of "*the leaves of the fig tree*" [11] has a 2012 connection. This version is Luke 21: v29-33:

"*Look at the fig tree, and all the trees; as soon as they come out in leaf, you see for yourselves and know that the summer is already near. So, also, when you see these things taking place, you will know that the Kingdom of God is near. Truly, I say to you, this generation will not pass away till all has taken place.*" [12]

A biblical generation is threescore years and ten, or 70 years. [13] The nation of Israel was re-established by UN resolution in 1947, so the Second Coming would happen by the 69th year after 1947 (2016). If an "*abomination of desolation*" was to be set up at Temple Mount on 21st December 2012, then 1,335 days later would be 17th August 2016, which is 49 years or seven weeks of years after 1967 - that would then be the Day of Judgement.

## Revelation

The *Book of Revelation* repeatedly mentions a certain time period (five times), which comes straight from the *Book of Daniel*. In *Revelation*, the "*nations*" will "*trample over the holy city for 42 months.*" [14] This period is exactly 1,260 days (42 x 30 = 1,260), and also appears as "*a time, two times and half a time,*" [15] where it is based on a 360-day year (3 x 360 + 180 = 1,260) - this form appears in the *Book of Daniel* twice. [16] The third form is "*one thousand two hundred and sixty days*", which appears in *Revelation* twice. [17] Some researchers have connected this 1,260 figure with the *Feast of Trumpets* (*Rosh Hashanah* - the Jewish New Year) 2005, which starts at sundown on October 3rd that year (it is always on the day *1 Tishri* in the Hebrew calendar). There is an annular solar eclipse due on 3rd October 2005, and it is exactly 2,550 days before the day of Yom Kippur in 2012 (26th September 2012), also known as the *Great Trump* (there will be more on this in the *Judaism and 2012* section). 2,550 is the sum of 1,260 and 1,290.

However, the seven-year Tribulation, if taken as 360-day years, is two times 1,260 days, and *Daniel* and *Revelation* emphasise the halfway point as significant ("*a time, two times and half a time*"). Seven 360-day years after October 3-4th 2005 leads to August 27-28th 2012.

Following 25 years of study, Andy Alcon of Texas, USA has independently calculated that 4th October 2005 will be the date of the "*sign in the heavens*" indicated by *Revelation* 12:1:

*Fig.5.2: Tarot trump number three, The Empress, shows a woman with a crescent moon under her feet and a circle of stars above her head - some packs actually show twelve stars. The word "trump" is short for "trumpets of Armageddon", the last of which will wake the dead at Judgement Day, and the 22 Tarot trumps correspond to the 22 chapters of the* Book of Revelation. *From a deck designed by Oswald Wirth in 1896.*

*"And a great portent appeared in heaven, a woman clothed with the Sun, with the Moon under her feet, and on her head a crown of twelve stars; she was with child and she cried out in her pangs of birth, in anguish for delivery."*

The Moon will be at the feet of Virgo, one of the twelve constellations, with the Sun at her shoulders, and Jupiter and Mercury in her belly, says Alcon. [18] He expects a red comet to appear at this time, corresponding with the red dragon that *Revelation* mentions in the next verse. Alcon says this will be the start of the seven-year period of tribulation that will end on October 3rd 2012, which will be *"the start of the millennium and the end of this current age"* when there will be an alignment of Venus with the star Regulus, the *"foot"* of Leo - an alignment that corresponds to several biblical passages. However, this seven-year tribulation period is seven 365-day years plus two leap days, so does not relate directly to the 360-day years described in Daniel and *Revelation*. Another problem is that nowhere in *Revelation*, or in any of the biblical passages describing the Tribulation, is there a period of seven years mentioned. [19] It is a presumption based mainly on Daniel 9:24-27, which is actually about the timing of the *"first coming"* of the messiah. The idea is usually supported by the presumption that the seven seals, trumpets and plagues encode a seven-year period, and that the 1,260-day period describes the halfway point. Another problem is that when I checked 4th October 2005 on astronomical software (*SkyGlobe* and *Cybersky*), the Moon was with Jupiter and Saturn, and not beneath the feet of Virgo until 6th October.

*Fig.5.3: On 6th October 2005, Virgo will have the crescent moon beneath her feet, the Sun at her shoulders, and Jupiter and Mercury "in her belly". Image created using CyberSky software - http://cybersky.com*

The interesting thing about this is that Joel Keene independently pin-pointed October 3rd 2012 as being the day of the arrival of an electromagnetic pulse, which he calculated from the Nostradamus quatrain 1:16. He included this in his coincidence-inspired novel *Cosmic Locusts*, [20] (of which we shall say more in Chapter 11), and was amazed when Alcon contacted him to tell him of his own conclusions. As it happens, October 3rd 2012 will be in the middle of *Sukkott*, the *Feast of the Tabernacles* in the Jewish calendar, which celebrates the end of the harvest.

## Ezekiel

The *Book of Ezekiel* contains a precessional code, according to author Stephen E. Crockett in *The Prophet Code*, [21] but although Crockett interprets the code to signify that the precessional cycle ends in the year 2144 AD, when he says the vernal equinox precesses into Aquarius, the year 2012 still figures strongly in the code, as the years between 1944 and 2012 are *"the time of the end"*. The period between 1948 and 2012 is significant and the 2005 to 2012 period signifies a seven-year clean-up period from *"the destruction of Gog's military to 2012"*. The years 2000 to 2012 signify *"an extinction level event"*, but Crockett also claims that the third of the four *"horsemen of the apocalypse"* mentioned in the *Book of Revelation* is due between 2010 and 2012. This is the Black Horse that brings famine, and is followed by the Pale Horse of death between 2013 and 2016.

## Judaism and 2012

At the beginning of the *Book of Genesis*, which is part of the Jewish *Torah* (the first five books of the Bible), we are told that God created the world in six days, and on the seventh day he rested. The Jewish Rabbis had a specific interpretation of this, which shows a *"macrocosmic"* creation event extending through history, echoing the Maya belief, uncovered by Jenkins, of a forthcoming *Creation Day*:

*"The Rabbis taught that there were 7,000 years of time. They divided time into a 6,000-year segment followed by the 1,000-year Messianic Kingdom. They based this on Psalm 90:4, which says that to God a thousand years is as a day. What the Rabbis taught was that as the week of creation was seven days, that is seven 24-hour days, so each day stood for a thousand years, with the seventh day as a day of rest - the day of the Messianic kingdom."* [22]

*Fig.5.4: The Rabbinical (according to the Rabbis) interpretation of the Menorah, or seven-branched lamp holder, is that it represents the Seven Days of Creation as described in the* Book of Genesis, *but on a macroscopic scale, in which each 'day' lasts 1,000 years.*

The Jewish Calendar starts with the birth of Adam, and by Bishop Usher's famous analysis, in which he consulted all the male genealogies in the Old Testament (adding given ages of fathers at the birth of their first son, working back from the zero-point of Christ's birth, on which our Gregorian calendar is based), we find 4004 BC as Adam's birth date. Thus, we arrive at autumn 1997 as 6,000 years after the birth of Adam (the Jewish New Year, Rosh Hashanah, usually falls between autumn and winter). It seems that Usher made a three-year discrepancy, since the *Byzantium* [23] website says that the birth of Adam was 4,000 years before the birth of Christ, so Gregorian year 2000 should be the Jewish year 6000. However, Jewish year 5760 started on September 30th 1999, so this means there is a 240-year discrepancy between the Jewish and Gregorian calendars.

In the four-part online article on the *Prophecy and Current Events* website, *Rosh Hashanah - Is It The Rapture?*, [24] the author explains how the year 5760 is kabbalistically encoded into the phrase "*six days*" (of creation), thereby implying that Gregorian year 2000 is the end of the 6,000-year period. The article concludes that "*some Rosh Hashanah between 1999 and 2012, or shortly thereafter, might be the completion of the 6,000 years of man and the start of the millennium*". The seven years between Adam and Eve's creation and the picking of the apple from the Tree of Knowledge must be taken into account, bringing the start of the Day of the Lord to 2007 AD, but the author goes on to acknowledge that it could be "*as late as 2012*" due to "*the calendar reforms and modifications that have taken place over the years.*" This is really an admission that the case for 2012 sounds convincing, but no further details could be found to explain the discrepancy between the termination points of the seven days of creation and the 13-baktun cycle.

Rosh Hashanah starts at sunset, continuing to the following sunset, but it is also the start of a ten-day festival called *Teshuvah*, "*which means 'returning'. In the spiritual sense, Teshuvah means returning to the Creator of the universe, who we call HaShem. It means turning away from the secular, from the worldly way of life and turning back to His way of life.*" [25]

The definition of this return sounds very Gnostic:

"*The concept of Teshuvah as 'return' emphasizes the fundamental spiritual potential of every person. Chassidic thought teaches that within each of us resides a Divine soul, a spark of God. This infinite Godly potential represents the core of our souls, our genuine 'I'.*" [26]

In Judaism, there are three days that are heralded by a trumpet. These are *Shavuot* (First Trump), proclaiming God's betrothal to Israel; *Rosh Hashanah* (Last Trump), New Year and start of the ten-day *Teshuvah*, or "*return*"; and *Yom Kippur* (Great Trump), heralding the return of the Messiah to Earth.

Rosh Hashanah takes on even more significance when we see a full list of its titles:

1. *Teshuvah* (repentance)
2. *Rosh Hashanah* (Head of the Year, Birthday of the World)
3. *Yom Teruah* (the Day of the Awakening Blast/Feast of Trumpets)
4. *Yom HaDin* (the Day of Judgement)
5. *HaMelech* (the Coronation of the Messiah)
6. *Yom HaZikkaron* (the Day of Remembrance, or memorial)
7. The time of Jacob's trouble (the birth pangs of the Messiah)
8. The opening of the gates of Shomayim (Heaven)
9. *Kiddushin/Nesu'in* (the wedding ceremony)
10. The resurrection of the dead (rapture, natzal)
11. The Last Trump (shofar)
12. *Yom Hakeseh* (the hidden day)

In the year 2012, Shavuot falls on 27th May, Rosh Hashanah falls on September 17th/18th and Yom Kippur falls on 26th September. The conclusion is that the last trump is synonymous with Rosh Hashanah, when the Gates of Heaven will open and the *"righteous will enter in rapture"* on 17th/18th September 2012. However, Yom Kippur also has another title - *Closing of Gates*; the Gates of Heaven will therefore close on 26th September 2012.

As a chilling postscript, if we look at Chapter 7 (*Phobos Fly-By of Earth*), we find that Glen Deen's low-precision orbit model gave Earth an impact with Mars' moon Phobos on September 18th 2012! This is reminiscent of the Bible Code prediction (further on in this chapter), although some Bible Code scholars interpret it as Mars being crumbled by the Earth. However, there are new developments in Glen Deen's theory, and the latest one does not involve Phobos or September 2012 (covered in Chapter 7).

## Islam and 2012

Like Judaism and Christianity, Islam also expects *"the last days"* and a Day of Wrath (Judgment). They have *mala'ika* (angels), including Mikail (Michael) and Jibril (Gabriel). There is also an evil *jiin* called Shaytan. At death, the *ruh*, or spirit, leaves the body and waits in *barzakh* (purgatory), and returns to the body on *Yawm al- Ba'th*, the day of *"Rising From the Grave"*. The destination is then *Jinnah* (the Garden) - for Muslims only - or *Nar* (the Fire). They also expect an antichrist figure, called *Dajjal*, which means *"deceiver"*, and before the Last Day, Jesus (who is seen as a prophet) will re-appear and kill the Dajjal. Most Muslim sources regard prediction and prophecy as a bad idea (like the Bible, the *Qur'an* gives signs, but says only God (Allah) knows *sa'*, *"the Hour"*). However, some have stuck their necks out. According to John Whalen, who is quoted all over the Internet:

*"... Several Sufi sects have already declared 2076 as the Year of the Haj (end day), because it will coincide with the year 1500 in the Islamic Calendar. An article by Abdal Hakim Murad, Islam and the New Millennium, confirmed this, quoting Imam al-Suyuti, the*

*greatest scholar of medieval Egypt. At first, al-Suyuti believed the end of the world would occur in the year 1000 of the Islamic Calendar. He later changed his prediction to 1500 of the Islamic Calendar."* [27]

However, at *Islaam.com*, Safar Ibn `Abd Al-Rahman Al-Hawali, author of *The Day of Wrath*, says that he agrees with the Christian date interpretation I have already quoted above. Speaking of Jerusalem, he says:

*"When Daniel specified the period between its distress and relief, between the era of anguish and the era of blessing, he put it as 45 years! We have already seen that he specified the time of the establishment of the 'abomination of desolation' as the year 1967, which is what in fact occurred. Therefore, the end - or the beginning of the end - will be 1967 + 45 = 2012, or in lunar years 1387 + 45 = 1433."* [28]

From an Islamic perspective, the USA is Babylon, and the "*abomination of desolation*" was the gaining of Jerusalem by Israel in 1967. All three religions, Christianity, Judaism and Islam, see themselves as the ones who will be chosen and saved at Judgement Day.

## The Masonic Calendar

I recently bought some Masonic documents and discovered that they were dated in a Masonic calendar of *Anno Lucis*, or *Year of Light*. Anno Lucis 5950, the year in which one of the documents was produced, is also given as the Gregorian date AD 1950. Thus, the Gregorian year AD 2000 would equate to AL 6000 in the Masonic calendar. So, the Masonic calendar equates to the 'corrected' version of the Hebrew calendar. The capping of the Great Pyramid that was planned for New Year's Eve 1999 (but was cancelled by the Egyptian authorities), can now be seen as a symbol of the completion of *Man the Microcosm*, or as the descent of the New Jerusalem; the expected end of the Sixth Day of Creation, and the start of the Seventh Day, or Golden Age (see Chapter 8, *The Eye in the Pyramid*).

Further investigation showed that not all Masonic Brotherhoods use the Anno Lucis system. The Ancient and Accepted Scottish Rite, for example, use *Anno Mundi*, or the *Year of the World*, which equates to the current Hebrew calendar, and is 240 years behind ours. *Encyclopédia Judaica* [29] agrees that this discrepancy is due to an error, and that the Jewish year 6000 should coincide with our year 2000 AD (2000 CE + 4000 BCE = 6000). This still leaves unexplained the twelve-year discrepancy between the *Transition of Ages* marked by the Judaeo-Christian calendar, and that marked by the Long Count calendar of the Maya, apart from the seven years spent by Adam and Eve in the garden, which bring the date forward to 2007, for which we have corroboration in Ethiopia.

## The Ethiopian Calendar

The Ethiopian calendar, which originated from the Coptic Egyptian calendar, puts the Creation date at 5500 BC. However, they put the birth of Christ in the Gregorian year 7 AD. Since the Ethiopian calendar (like the Gregorian) uses the birth of Christ as a baseline, this means that the Ethiopian year 2000 will start on the Gregorian date, September 12th 2007 AD (this is the start of Coptic year 1724). Thus, although the Creation date is linked to Egyptian ideas, the Age-Transition point signified by the 2000th year after the birth of Christ is over seven years closer to the end-point of the Maya than is the same date in the Gregorian calendar.

The Ethiopian year starts on September 11th, except during leap years (which occur when the Ethiopian year number is the same as any Gregorian leap-year number), when it starts on September 12th. So, September 11th 2012 will be the start of Ethiopian year 2005. The first month in the Coptic year, which also starts on September 11th, is called Tout - from the Egyptian god Thoth, god of calendrical cycles, whose sacred number was 52, the same number that obsessed the Aztecs. [30] Although the Dogon people of Mali also currently celebrate New Year on September 11th, this is *not* the heliacal rise of Sirius, which currently happens on August 1st.

## The Bible Code

Michael Drosnin's book *The Bible Code* [31] tells the story of a code discovered in the original Hebrew version of the Old Testament of the Bible, which has now been verified by various mathematicians and code-breakers, and apparently predicts all major news items *"from the holocaust to Hiroshima"*. The discovery would have been impossible before the computer age, since special software is able to apply a skip-code to the whole text, skipping a certain number of letters, then extracting a letter, and repeating the process over and over in a matter of minutes - a process that would previously have taken many lifetimes.

Some recent events have been decoded before they happened, including the assassination of Israel's Prime Minister, Yitzhak Rabin, on 4th November 1995. Drosnin actually warned Rabin about the prophecy fourteen months before it happened, but the warnings did not avert the killing. The Hebrew year 5756, that would start in September 1995, was found with *"Rabin assassination"* and the name *"Yitzhak Rabin"* was also found with *"name of assassin who will assassinate."* It was only after the event that they found the name of the assassin, Amir, and the place, Tel Aviv, where it took place. The collision of the comet Shoemaker-Levy 9 with Jupiter in 1994 was decoded two months before the event, including the names of the astronomers who discovered it, and the date: *8th Av* (one of the Hebrew month names), which equates to July 16th. Although the astronomers had predicted this event a few months beforehand, the Bible Code apparently predicted it 3000 years before that, Drosnin points out.

The code also mentions the asteroid that wiped out the dinosaurs 65 million years ago, but Drosnin mentions no more comets or asteroids until the Shoemaker-Levy impact. Then

*Fig.5.5: A skip-code applied to the text from* Exodus *chapter 34 to* Deuteronomy *chapter 1 reveals the combination given here. Adapted from* Torah4U *software - http://exodus2006.com/torah4u.htm*

he found that the Hebrew year 5766 (Oct 4th 2005 to Sept 22nd 2006) was also encoded with the word "*comet*", plus the words "*Its path struck their dwelling*" and "*year predicted for the world*". Again in 5770, or 2009-2010, the word "*comet*" combines with the words "*days of horror*", plus "*darkness*" and "*gloom*". If this isn't bad enough, 5772 (or Sept 29th 2011 to September 16th 2012), combines "*comet*" with the words "*Earth annihilated*"!

Only three years are mentioned by Drosnin after this - they are; 5774, or 2014 (an encoded year which combines with "*the great terror*" and coincides with the predicted close passage of known asteroid 2003 QQ47); 5873, or 2113 (which combines with "*for everyone the great terror, fire, earthquake*" and "*desolated, empty, depopulated*"); and 5886, or 2126, the last date he mentions, which is encoded along with the word "*swift*" and the phrase "*in the seventh month it came*" (although this would refer to the seventh month of the Gregorian calendar, rather than the Hebrew one). Astronomers have, in fact, predicted the return of comet Swift-Tuttle to the solar system in July 2126.

This all sounds depressing, to say the least (and I *have* tried to say the least), and it all seems to back up the even more depressing *Book of Revelation*. However, Drosnin says that the finding of the code enabled mankind to alter fate, and the code implies that there are now at least five possible futures at any one time. Drosnin himself has been heavily involved in trying to alter the future by talking to Israeli and Palestinian politicians.

So, what of these cometary impacts? Well, the Earth can't be annihilated in 2012 because there are still people left to be terrified by the remaining events, but also because

"*2012*" and "*comet*" are encoded with "*It will be crumbled, driven out, I will tear to pieces*", which means the comet will break up like the Shoemaker-Levy comet. The pieces would thus hopefully be moved away from their collision course with Earth.

The Bible Code continues to be challenged; some think the codes are imaginary; some think they are real, but cannot predict the future; some just object for religious reasons. Many others object because it is just too depressing to contemplate seriously.

## Noah Predicts Flood

Further exploration of the Bible Code by Joseph Noah in his book *Future Prospects of the World According to the Bible Code* [32] revealed that the 9/11 tragedy was also encoded in the book of Exodus, along with the name *Bin Laden*. He goes on to find an explanation for the symbolism of the *Book of Revelation*, finding that the "*seven seals*" are the seven years from 2005 to 2012 (according to the Hebrew calendar; that is, October 2005 to September 2012). He also finds that Mars' moon Phobos [33] will be hit by an American missile in 2010 and break into seven pieces. The seven break up further into ten pieces - these are the seven heads and ten horns of *Revelation*. [34] Three of these ten collide with the USA in 2010. Another three hit Russia in 2011, and three more hit China in 2012. The final asteroid (*Wormwood* of *Revelation*) will hit the Gulf of Arabia in 2012, resulting in a world axis shift of 25°, the submergence of Japan, [35] the Philippines and the West coast of the USA.

Drosnin's second book, *Bible Code II: The Countdown*, [36] only goes up to 2006, since that is the predicted date for World War III (and this is very interesting in light of the resonance on the Timewave between World War II and the six years leading up to 2012), but...

Andy McCracken, webmaster of the *Exodus 2006* website, [37] using Bible Code software, has found that the same piece of code that Drosnin found, where "*comet*" is encoded with "*It will be crumbled... I will tear to pieces*", is also accompanied by words that imply the comet is a "*60-mile blunderbuss*" that splits up, part of it hitting Canada in 2012 and causing a huge earthquake.

## Final Word on Part One

For those of us indoctrinated with Christian dogma from an early age, who later broke free from the guilt and fear that has been used as a control mechanism for two thousand years, it thus comes as a bit of a shock to realize that the ancient Vedic system is also based on eras represented by metals in the same order as the metallic eras of Daniel; the oldest being gold, then silver, then bronze, then iron - the current age - except that in Daniel's version there is a fifth era of iron and clay. It is also a surprise to find that in the Hopi myths and some Maya myths, we also seem to be in the Fourth Era, or World, while in the Aztec and variant Maya myths, we are in the Fifth World, or Sun. The precession of the equinoxes (or solstices) is also a recurrent theme, even cropping up in a Gnostic text called *The Sophia of Jesus*, as well as in some Maya, Egyptian and Vedic myths, but the most amazing thing is that *all* these calendars and prophecies seem to culminate in 2012!

# PART 2:
## 2012 Theories

*T*he Creator, when he looked upon the things that happened, established his design, which is good, against the disorder. He took away error, and cut off evil. Sometimes, he submerged it in a great flood; at other times, he burned it in a searing fire; and at still other times, he crushed it in wars and plagues, until he brought ... (4 lines missing) ... of the work. And this is the birth of the world."

**The Nag Hammadi Library, Asclepius 21-29** [1]

# Chapter 6:
# Sunspot Cycles

## Cotterell's Magnetic Flip

Adrian Gilbert and Maurice Cotterell, in their book *The Mayan Prophecies*, [1] say that the end of the 13-baktun cycle is the culmination of a series of long-term sunspot cycles, which will flip the Sun's magnetic field and thus that of the Earth too, causing earthquakes and worldwide flooding. Moreover, the changing magnetic field will alter the endocrine-hormone production of the pineal and other endocrine glands. The book, which was a bestseller, makes some interesting points, and has caused serious fright to a lot of people. However, when I studied the text more closely, I could not see how the many pages of graphs and calculations related to the end of the 13-baktun cycle. I was beginning to think that some vital parts of the manuscript must have been omitted, when I discovered that I was not alone in my misgivings.

John Major Jenkins had also found fault with *The Mayan Prophecies*, and in an online review he detailed many errors in the book:

*"Cotterell's theories as they relate to Mayan astronomy and calendrics require major adjusting, correcting or even abandonment. The sunspot cycle information in itself was interesting to learn about, but the subsequent argument for 'field reversals', even when carefully read, is unconvincing. Even less convincing is the implication of conscious intent on the part of the Maya in calculating these things."* [2]

The detailed graphs of the cycles do not actually show significant termination points at the end of the 13-baktun cycle, so even though Cotterell's original theory of a sunspot cycle-driven astrology postulated in Part One of his first book, *Astrogenetics* [3] (1988), was quite feasible, the mistakes he made in trying to apply it to the Maya calendrical systems in *The Mayan Prophecies* (1995), means it is convincing only if you don't dig too deeply into the reasoning. The theory is then repeated in his follow-up books. In *The Supergods* [4] (1997), *The Tutankhamun Prophecies* [5] (1999), *The Lost Tomb of Viracocha* [6] (2001), *The Terracotta Warriors* (2003) and the proposed *Celtic Chronicles* (2005), we can see a pattern emerging... every two years he publishes another book that applies the whole theory to another lost culture, examining archaeological relics and finding connections to his theory, often by examining detailed jewellery and counting the spots, lines, and markings until he finds a number that fits into his sunspot theory. We can thus presumably expect more of the same in 2007, 2009 and 2011.

To summarise very briefly, the theory examines the different rotation periods of the Sun's polar magnetic fields and its equatorial magnetic fields - 37 and 26 days respectively, according to Cotterell [7] - that drive the 11-year sunspot cycle. When a third variable of the Earth's position is added, a 187-year sunspot cycle emerges. Further extrapolations seem to

**Equatorial fields**          **Polar fields**

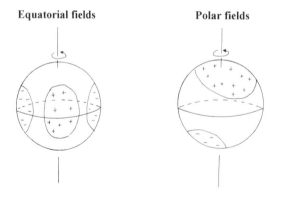

*Fig.6.1: The four equatorial magnetic fields of the Sun rotate faster than the two polar fields. This causes the intertwining field lines that erupt as sunspots every 11.3 years on average. After Gilbert and Cotterell [1995].*

imply a set of five larger cycles of either 3,553 years or 3,740 years duration. He correlates these to the five eras or Suns of the Aztecs. Since the 3,740-year period amounts to 1,366,040 days, which Cotterell says is *"close to"* a number that appears in the Dresden Codex, this shows that the Maya were tracking sunspot cycles. However, the period in the Dresden Codex is 1,366,560 days, which is a difference of 520 days. Since the Dresden Codex contains Venus tables, Cotterell suggests that since 2,340 Venus cycles of 584 days equal 1,366,560, the Maya must have been using Venus as a calibrator to adjust the 1,366,560 figure back to 1,366,040.

However much of this number juggling we do (and *The Mayan Prophecies* has a 100-page appendix full of it), the fact remains that it doesn't explain what will happen in 2012. The reader's mind is numbed by the complexity of the theory, so that he/she just has to take the authors' word for it that the world will be destroyed in 2012 by a full solar magnetic reversal that causes the Earth's magnetic field to reverse polarity.

*Fig.6.2: Increasing solar activity gives an upward trajectory when graphed. Adapted from several Internet sources.*

Even though this theory is seriously faulted, it is a fact that the scientifically accepted records of sunspot activity do seem to be heading for a climax in the near future, and there has been some research that indicates the existence of megacycles (longer overall cycles). Geomagnetic reversals do occur, and we are overdue for one, but *The Mayan Prophecies* has led many authors and researchers into an irrelevant maze. Those who found the book convincing would be well advised to read John Major Jenkins' review. [8]

## Change in the Solar Maximum

The sunspot cycle reaches its maximum approximately every eleven years, and then sunspot activity switches to the opposite hemisphere of the Sun. The recent maximum was due in March to April 2000, and the following one was therefore expected in 2011. However, the maximum didn't actually occur until February 2001, so the following one is now expected in 2012. Some people have suggested that this is evidence of a sunspot megacycle, possibly connected with the end of the Maya 13-baktun cycle, but the recorded cycle length has varied between eight and fourteen years in the past, so the lengthened sunspot cycle may not be so significant in itself. Having said that, we have also seen a continual escalation of solar activity over the last fifteen years, with ever-larger X-ray flares, record-breaking coronal mass ejections, and solar storms that have caused the northern lights to descend further and further south. When the last cycle finally peaked in 2001, George Withbroe, Science Director of NASA's Sun-Earth Connection Program said, *"This is a unique solar maximum in history. The images and the data are beyond the wildest expectations of the astronomers of a generation ago."* [9]

After the solar maximum, the activity continued, with a record-breaking X-20 solar flare on 2nd April 2001 (some reports said it was an X-22, since the dial only goes up to X-20 and the needle was stuck up against the end). The northern lights, or *aurora borealis*, are an aerial display of shifting coloured light patterns usually only visible from the Arctic Circle, and caused by the interaction of solar wind, the Earth's magnetic field and the upper atmosphere. In April 2000, a solar storm had caused the Aurora to be seen as far south as North Carolina in the USA, but in June 2001, a solar storm caused a geomagnetic effect that pulled the aurora down as far as Mexico! In 2002, there was the most complex Coronal Mass Ejection (CME) ever recorded. A CME happens when the gas envelope of the Sun explodes outwards. In 2003, we had a record-breaking nine major solar eruptions in the space of twelve days, and then, on 4th November 2003, there was the largest solar flare ever recorded, estimated at the time to be between X-28 and X-35, but now known to have been even bigger. Some scientists are now saying the Sun is more active than it has been for a thousand years - we shall return to this later. [See Chapter 12 and also colour pages.]

## Australian Ham Theory

Kev Peacock is an Australian amateur radio operator, or 'ham', who set out to study how Earth's atmospheric and weather conditions affected his radio signal. He became immersed in a detailed investigation of the sunspot cycle, solar flares, and the solar wind. He noticed that the graphs of solar activity show a clear incline over the last few hundred years since records began in 1611 AD, and that geomagnetic and seismic (earthquake) activity is also increasing. In fact, there is a direct correlation between the peaks and troughs of all three graphs. Peacock concluded that in July-August 2011 there is a possible coincidence of four factors that could, if they occur at the same time, endanger the Earth. These are the four factors:

1. The height of summer in the northern hemisphere in June 2011 (Summer Solstice is June 21st), when the Earth's magnetic North Pole is closest to the Sun.

2. There will be three eclipses that occur between 2nd June 2011 and 1st July 2011 (two solar and one lunar), causing geomagnetic effects (in the same way that a major earthquake in Turkey followed the eclipse in August 1999).

3. The solar maximum is due at this time (see page 75), when the Sun's magnetic field reverses (every eleven years on average).

4. The peak of a solar megacycle, or long-term sunspot cycle, indicated by the incline in graphs of solar activity may coincide with the solar maximum.

The combination of aligned Sun, Earth and Moon with the eleven-year sunspot cycle maximum, and the Earth's north magnetic pole pointing to the Sun hasn't happened for 65 million years, according to Peacock, who says the result of the above four factors coinciding will cause the Earth's magnetic field to collapse and reverse, the "*resulting earthquake and volcano activity bringing about the end of our civilization by the end of 2012*". [10] A new ice age would probably follow, due to a global temperature drop as volcanic ash cuts out sunlight.

As for Peacock's solar maximum calculations, he devised this theory when the solar maximum was still due in 2011, but since it has now shifted to 2012, these factors will only coincide in 2011 if the current sunspot cycle is around ten years and four months in length. Even so, his discovery of the coincidence of the peaks and troughs of the seismic, geomagnetic and sunspot graphs could be very significant (see colour page IV).

## Mass Telepathy in 2012

Jazz Rasool gave a talk at the *Mysteries of the World* conference in Marlborough, UK in 2001, in which he pointed out that we are currently experiencing the most active solar cycle since records began, and that the eleven-year sunspot cycle has just jumped forward a year, so that the current phase will terminate in 2012 instead of 2011. The fact that the Schumann Resonance (electromagnetic waves in the cavity between the Earth's crust and the ionosphere) is said by some researchers to be rising in frequency (see Chapter 9), combined with recent discoveries by the Japanese scientist Hiroshi Motoyama that the frequency around psychics increases to a level of 17 Hertz, leads Jazz to the conclusion that these environmental factors will lead to a "*switching on*" of some of the massive amount of genes with officially unknown function (so-called 'junk DNA'), which he calls "*Species DNA*", leading to mass telepathy and telekinesis. This will be the birth of a new species: *Homo spiritus*. [11]

## Pi in the Sky

Michael Poynder says in his book *Pi in The Sky* [12] that the Stone Age priesthood used to work with and manipulate the Earth's magnetic energy grid. They knew about the 22-year binary sunspot cycle, and they used the value of Pi (the ratio of the circumference of a circle to its diameter), approximated to 22 over seven, in the layout of many sacred sites. The sunspot part of the theory was inspired by Maurice Cotterell's first book *Astrogenetics*, as Poynder has now confirmed to me. [13] However, Poynder seems to have been one of the first to look for, and find, astronomical meaning in ancient jewellery and artefacts. Having found a sixteenth century German silver chalice with built-in gnomon (a rod, the shadow of which moves with the Sun) that threw a shadow onto the inside surface, acting as a sun-dial, Poynder suggested that the ninth century Irish Derrynaflan chalice and paten (communion plate) were designed to act in a similar way, but would allow *"differential dialling of the Sun's magnetic fields and of the equinoxes, solstices and quarter days, i.e. the 'pattern' of the Druidic year."* [14]

This book is like a missing link between Cotterell's *Astrogenetics* and Cotterell and Gilbert's *The Mayan Prophecies*. Cotterell had suggested in Part Two of *Astrogenetics* that the 260-day Tzolkin of the Maya is based around the coincidence of the solar polar and equatorial magnetic fields (they coincide at 262+ days, according to Cotterell's figures, but after 260 days the equatorial field has made exactly ten revolutions - however, these figures are wrong). [15] He had also suggested that the *"Mayan collapse"* (when they abandoned their cities) was due to a decline in fertility caused by the proposed magnetic field reversal of 672 AD (Jenkins argues that this is far too early). [16] In 1988, Cotterell didn't mention the Long Count calendar, or 2012. Meanwhile, in 1992, Poynder must have asked permission to use the sunspot graphics, bringing Cotterell's attention to *Pi in the Sky*, in which Poynder finds sunspot knowledge encoded in ancient artefacts, and concludes that the ancients were tracking the sunspot cycle in preparation for 2012. Then, in 1997, Cotterell launched *The Mayan Prophecies* and its sequels, attempting to show how sunspot knowledge was encoded into ancient artefacts as a message to future mankind about 2012. However, in the Cotterell version it was as a warning of catastrophe.

Having established in his book that *"Stone Age Man"* dowsed earth energies, showing many examples of pendulums, Poynder traces a series of earth energy lines and *"Earth stars"* covering the globe. He takes a close look at Newgrange, one of the Irish passage graves, the major structures of which *"were completed sometime between 3200 and 3700 BC"* according to Martin Brennan. [17] The inner chamber is illuminated by the Sun every Winter Solstice. Poynder demonstrates how Newgrange was designed around the *Golden Mean* (Phi), and quotes Cotterell as saying *"the Golden Mean is the solar radiation frequency."* [18] Poynder's conclusions can be summed up as follows:

In or just prior to 3113 BC, at the end of the last 13-baktun cycle, the *"Shining Ones"* (Priests of Light) of Irish mythology entered the stone chambers, never to re-emerge. The Winter Solstice Sun entered the cairns through polarising crystal skylights, accelerating the

*Fig.6.3: The auric body of a cairn becomes a UFO [Poynder, 1992].*

"*auric body*" of the cairn through the speed of light, when it massifies into a "*vehicle of electromagnetic resonance*", or an extra-dimensional UFO. The priests, who were out-of-body and whose subtle bodies melded with that of the cairn, have time-travelled in their UFOs to the present time, to communicate the message that we should raise our consciousness for 2012, which will be the start of a New Age of Enlightenment. In 2004, Poynder published a follow-up book called *Lost Science of the Stone Age: Sacred Energy and the I Ching*.

# Chapter 7:
# Astronomical Claims

### Astronomical Phenomena
Astrologer Raymond Mardyks has pointed out five unusual astronomical phenomena that are due to occur in 2012. [1] They are listed below, followed by a list of relevant comments and observations:

1. A transit of Venus, in which Venus will pass directly in front of the Sun (from our perspective on Earth) - something *he* says only happens every 120 years.

2. A solar eclipse, in which the Sun and Moon conjunct the Pleiades, on 20th May 2012.

3. A second solar eclipse, in which the Sun and Moon align with the head of the constellation Serpens, the serpent (held by Ophiuchus, the Serpent Handler, who stands with one foot on the body of the Scorpio constellation and the other on its stinger, right next to Galactic Centre).

4. The alignment of the solstice Sun with the Galactic Equator, which he says started in 1986 [2] or "*around the time of Harmonic Convergence in 1987*" [3] and will finish in 2012 (he also puts the mid-alignment point, when the centre of the Sun is on the Galactic Equator, as 1998-2001).

5. From an Earth perspective, Venus "*returns to the same area of the sky every eight years,*" and each time is getting nearer and nearer to the Pleiades constellation. In 1972, Venus

was one degree from Alcyone, the central star of the Pleiades, but in 2012 Venus will be so close to Alcyone that it will be closer to it than some of the other stars in the Pleiades constellation. He then connects this to the 2012 termination point of the 13-baktun cycle, since *"the Pleiades were very important to ancient Mayan astrologers and calendar keepers."* Mardyks sees the Pleiades as a kind of transformer that steps down energy and information from Galactic Centre and transmits it to Earth in a less potent form. After 2012, he says the Pleiades will no longer act as a galactic transmission centre for Earth - we will *"receive energy and frequencies direct from Galactic Centre."* [4]

Comments:

1. Some sources *have* said that Venus transits (or alternatively, "Venus Passages") occur once per century, but this is a little misleading. They do occur once per century, but in a pair, eight years apart. In other words, they occur twice per century (but not necessarily every century, since there were none in the twentieth century). They occurred in 1761, 1769, 1874, 1882 and 2004, and one will take place in 2012. Here are the approximate 120-year intervals (113 and 130 years in this case - the total is 243 years) mentioned by Mardyks, but between *pairs* of transits. The first of a pair occurred on June 8th

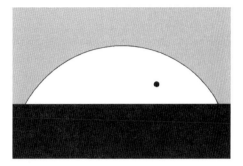

*Fig.7.1: This is how the 2012 Venus transit will appear through a filtered telescope.*

2004, and the second will occur on June 5-6th 2012, shortly after 10.00 PM Universal Time on 5th June (Universal Time is five and a half hours behind GMT, so it will be 3.30 AM on 6th June 2012 GMT), continuing until about 4.45 AM Universal Time on 6th June).

2. The May eclipse which conjuncts the Pleiades is also a rare conjunction of the Pleiades with the zenith passage of the Sun (May 20th 2012), the event which John Major Jenkins says is being pointed out by the Pyramid of Kukulcan at Chichen Itza (see Chapter 8; *A Precessional Alarm Clock*). The conjunction will happen at a local time (at Chichen Itza) of noon.

3. The second of these solar eclipses is on November 13th, one day before the day of the Aztec New Fire ceremony, which took place every 52 years - a Calendar Round - and (thanks to John Major Jenkins' book *Tzolkin*) we know there is a Maya Calendar Round that ends in 2012; in the Tikal Calendar Round series, it falls on April 2nd 2012. The Serpens constellation that Mardyks says will be aligned with this eclipse is not actually on the ecliptic, where the Sun and planets travel, but its head is about the width of a zodiac constellation away from the ecliptic.

4. The alignment of the solstice Sun with the Galactic Equator was astronomically exact in 1998-1999, and since the Sun is a half-degree wide, and precession moves at about one degree every 72 years, that means it takes 36 years for the Sun to cross the Galactic Equator. In other words, the process started in 1980-81 and will finish in 2016-17. Jenkins has shown that the Maya were targeting the end of the 13-baktun cycle onto this galactic alignment process. Mardydks' attempt to connect the 1987 Harmonic Convergence with galactic alignment is incorrect. [5]

5. The synodic revolution of Venus occurs five times in eight haabs (365-day years). These five points where Earth is overtaken by Venus (which orbits the Sun in only 224.7 days), or Earth-Venus inferior conjunctions, are called *retrograde loops*, since Venus appears to reverse its direction, from our perspective, for about a month. After the eight-haab-period, it returns to the same part of the sky, as seen from Earth (though its position actually precesses round the zodiac by about 2.4° every eight haabs [6]). The period from one loop to the next averages out at close to 584 days (583.92 days), the Venus period closely watched by the Maya; 5 x 584 = 2,920; 8 x 365 = 2,920. We will have more to say about the Venus-Pleiades conjunction shortly.

Swedish Maya calendar researcher Carl Calleman says there is a Mayan prophecy that "*the new world of consciousness will be born*" during the Jun 5-6th 2012 Venus transit. [7] He doesn't give a reference for the prophecy (but as we shall see later, this was his own spin on Hebrew prophecy as a "*solution*" to the Maya calendar) and has sometimes changed his focus to 2011, since his own theory seems to require a 2011 end-point (see *The Calleman Solution* in Chapter 19). Yet he has recently re-stated the importance of the 2012 transit.

   There will also be two lunar eclipses in 2012. [8]

## Venus Transit Theory

Researcher Will Hart, author of a recent book called *The Genesis Race*, [9] remarks that since some sources say the current 13-baktun cycle began on the "*Birth of Venus*" (page 83), and since it will conclude in 2012, which is the same year as one of the rare Venus transits mentioned above, then it must have something to do with the meaning of the forthcoming end-point. Looking back at the past Venus transits, Hart notes that the 1518-1526 pair corresponded to the landing of Cortés in Mexico, and the following transit-pair in 1631-1639 was followed by the *Maunder Minimum* when there were no sunspots seen for 70 years; the 1761-1769 pair he connects to the birth of the American Revolution. He points out that the Earth has been slowly warming up since the last ice age ended 13,000 years ago, and we are now nearing the end of an interglacial period. He also notes how solar activity has been increasing for the past 300 years. Although sunspot numbers reached their highest so far in 1960, solar activity is still much higher than predicted, with record-breaking temperatures in August 2003, and solar storms causing an electrical failure across USA and Canada, affecting 30 million people. Following 1960, there has been a steady increase in earthquakes and volcanic activity. Since the next predicted solar maximum has now shifted forward to 2012, Will Hart concludes that *"the Maya knew that the Venus transit acted like a circuit breaker switching off the sunspot cycle and impacting the Sun-Moon-Earth-Venus system."* [10] He predicts that the increased volcanic ash in the atmosphere will start a cooling of the planet that will be the end of the Fifth Sun of the Aztecs and the start of the Sixth Sun, between June and December 2012.

Carl Calleman has pointed out that previous Venus transits seem to have coincided with jumps in global communications. The 1518 transit coincided with Magellan's plans for the first circumnavigation of the globe; the 1631 and 1639 transits coincided with the first postal services; the 1761 transit inspired a co-operation of astronomers all over the world; and the 1874 transit coincided with the laying of the first transatlantic telegraph cable and Bell's first plans for a telephone. Calleman thinks the Venus transits of 2004 and 2012 will somehow trigger the first major outbreak of human telepathy, resulting in a kind of global brain, as Gaia, the Earth goddess wakes up. Peter Russell put this concept forward in his 1982 book *The Awakening Earth: The Global Brain* [11], though not in connection with Venus transits, but human population numbers (see Chapter 12).

## Venus-Pleiades Conjunction

Raymond Mardyks said above; *"Venus returns to the same area of the sky every eight years, and each time is getting nearer and nearer to the Pleiades"*. He points out that in 1972 Venus was 1° from Alcyone, the central star of the Pleiades, but in 2012 Venus will be right next to Alcyone. Venus and the Pleiades were both very prominent in the Maya time-keeping systems, so I decided to do some investigation, using Cybersky software. [12]

Fig.7.2: The Pleiades star cluster, which is located in the shoulder of Taurus. The large central star is Alcyone.

The first thing I discovered was that Venus is very close to Alcyone on 3rd April 2012. This is connected to the retrograde loops of Venus, as mentioned above, when Venus 'loops' every 584 days and completes a pentagram of five loops around the zodiac every eight years; but this return is actually 2.4 ° away from its original position eight years previously. It takes 243 years for Venus to return to the exact point where it started, which equals 152 of the 584-day cycles (the true average is around 583.92). This is equal to 30.4 pentagrams, or 30 pentagrams plus two extra 584-day cycles (or two points of a pentagram), bringing it

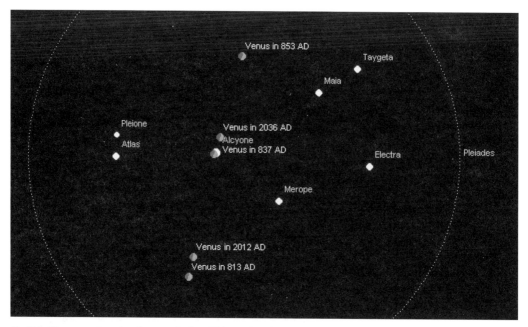

*Fig.7.3: Diagram showing the proximity of Venus to Alcyone, the central star of the Pleiades star cluster on 13th March 813 AD; 15th March 837 AD; 16th March 853 AD; 3rd April 2012; 4th April 2036 AD. An amalgamation of five screen shots from CyberSky software - http://cybersky.com*

into alignment with the original five points. This is not a complete revolution of the pentagram, but a 72° revolution. It takes more than a multiple of the eight-year pentagram, because the constellations have also precessed over 243 years, by about 3.3°. One complete revolution of the pentagram takes 1,199 years.

The astronomy software enabled me to reverse the movement of the planets and stars by 1,199 years; the time it takes for the entire Venus pentagram to get back to its start point. This took me to the year 813 AD. However, further research showed that the 1199-year cycle of Venus' proximity to the Pleiades runs from 837 AD to 2036 AD. Venus moved further away from the Pleiades at each eight-year interval, remaining closer to Alcyone than its 2012 position until the year 853 AD. Then it continued moving further from Alcyone until about 1436 AD, when it started to move back towards Alcyone again. After the 1,199-year cycle completes, in 2036 AD, Venus is at its closest to Alcyone again.

The conclusion is that in 2012, although Venus will be closer to Alcyone than it has been since about 853 AD (1,159 years), it continues to get closer to Alcyone until 2036 AD, so the conjunction does not seem to be overly significant to 2012 after all.

## Birth and Death of Venus

In his book *Worlds in Collision*, [13] Immanuel Velikovsky has said that the Birth of Venus occurred when Venus was *"born"* from Jupiter. A cosmic collision caused a part of Jupiter to burst out, becoming a comet, and leaving the famous red spot where it emerged (just as some cosmological theories say that the planets were thrown out of the Sun and later solidified). This is clearly illustrated in the Greek myth of Athene, who sprang from the head of Zeus (Fig.14.4, page 164), making Mount Olympus tremble and stirring the sea (Athene, reasons Velikovsky, is the planet Venus, and Zeus is the planet Jupiter). Velikovsky dated this event as contemporary with the Exodus of the

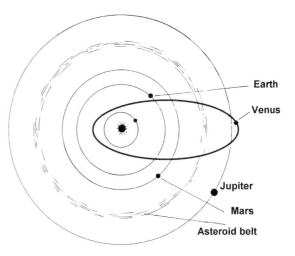

*Fig.7.4: The early orbit of Venus, according to Velikovsky. After O'Brien [1998].*

Israelites from Egypt, explaining the plagues and parting of the Red Sea. Several Maya and Aztec myths were also cited as evidence, including the fact that Quetzalcoatl, which means feathered serpent, is the well-known name for the planet Venus, also called *"the star that smoked"*. Velikovsky quotes from Brasseur's *Histoire Des Nations Civilisées du Mexique*:

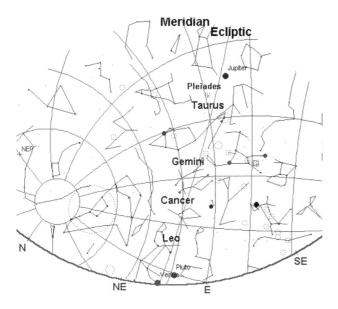

*"...The Sun refused to show itself and during four days the world was deprived of light. Then a great star ... appeared; it was given the name Quetzal-cohuatl ... The sky, to show its anger... caused to perish a great number of people who died of famine and pestilence... It was then...*

*Fig.7.5: This is the sky on 12th August 3114 BC, with the Pleiades on the meridian and Venus just appearing on the horizon. Adrian Gilbert believes this represented the 'Birth of Venus'. Screen shot from CyberSky software - http://cybersky.com*

*that the people* [of Mexico] *regulated anew the reckoning of days, nights, and hours, according to the difference in time.*" [14]

In *The Mayan Prophecies*, Adrian Gilbert says that he used astronomical software called *SkyGlobe* to look at the sky as it appeared at dawn on 12th August 3114 BC (where he dates the beginning of the 13-baktun cycle). He found that as the Pleiades were positioned on the meridian, the rising Sun was preceded by Venus as the morning star. This he took to be the mythical Birth of Venus associated by Velikovsky with the start of the new calendar implied by Brasseur. However, whereas Velikovsky dated the event at around 1500 BC (coincidentally when Izapa, the origin point of the Long Count calendar, was first inhabited), Gilbert associated it with the start of the 13-baktun cycle in 3114 BC. According to Gilbert's previous book, *The Orion Mystery* (with Robert Bauval), [15] in ancient Egypt the dawn rising of Sirius heralded the flooding of the Nile and the beginning of a new year, and the meridian transits of Orion correlated to the *First Time* and *Last Time* of Osiris (see Fig.8.7, page 98). In a similar way, Gilbert reasoned that to the Maya, the meridian transit of the Pleiades announced the Birth of Venus as it rose over the horizon.

Gilbert used *SkyGlobe* to check the sky on 22nd December 2012 (where he dates the end of the 13-baktun cycle), and found that just before sunset, as the Pleiades rise over the eastern horizon, Venus sinks below the western horizon. This, he thinks, is the symbolic "*Death of Venus*," indicating the start of a new precessional age.

Chris Morton and Ceri Louise Thomas have repeated this conclusion in *Mystery of the Crystal Skulls* (see Chapter 19), and have also supplied a Death of Venus sky chart, which Gilbert had not included in *The Mayan Prophecies*. They have also adjusted the start and end dates of the 13-baktun cycle by one day to the True Count correlation - dates that Jenkins has confirmed.

However, Jenkins has checked the sky chart for 12th August 3114 BC on *SkyGlobe* and two other astronomy packages, and found that Gilbert had omitted to double-check his findings, since Venus actually "*made its last appearance as the morning star almost two weeks before the Long-Count zero-date*". [16] I have looked at the *SkyGlobe* [17] and *Burden of Time* Maya calendar software, [18] which gives Venus phases, and found that on 12th August 3114 BC, Venus was approaching the end of its 263-day period of visibility and was five days away from its heliacal set when it disappeared into the glare of the Sun. [19]

So, Adrian Gilbert saw on the *SkyGlobe* program that Venus was close to the Sun at the start of the 13-baktun cycle, and concluded that it was at heliacal rise, when in fact it was close to heliacal set, which happened about six days later. This means that the sinking of Venus below the horizon while the Pleiades are on the meridian (as found by Morton and Thomas) on the Winter Solstice of 2012, loses any significance as a 'Death of Venus'.

## Nibiru

As we have noted, Velikovsky dated the astronomical event correlating to the Birth of

Venus at around 1500 BC with the Jewish Exodus, but Graham Phillips has also convincingly explained the events of the Exodus as side effects of the eruption of the volcano Thera. [20] Nigel Appleby has unified both these ideas with that of *Nibiru*, the tenth planet. [21]

The existence of Nibiru was postulated by Zecharia Sitchin in his book *The Twelfth Planet* [22] (twelve planets, counting the Sun and Moon), since his interpretation of Ancient Sumerian mythology implies that

*Fig.7.6: An Akkadian cylinder seal, apparently showing a star with eleven planets around it.*

there is a large planet - Nibiru - on an elliptical orbit, which enters the solar system every 3,600 years (peopled by the *Annunaki*, who are the biblical *"Sons of God"* (*Genesis*, chapter 6), and who are called *"The Watchers"* in the *Book of Enoch*). Velikovsky and Sitchin actually used the same Sumerian myth as part of the evidence for their respective theories (the Marduk and Tiamat myth), so they can't both be completely right. According to Sitchin's chronology, the next return is due in 3400-3600 AD.

Appleby suggests that it was Nibiru that caused the disasters of the Exodus as it *"shunted both Mars and the Earth dangerously close to each other's orbit..."* [23] and that it was this that triggered the eruption of Thera. However, Velikovsky didn't say Mars was involved in the original Birth of Venus incident, but two later incidents around 700 BC.

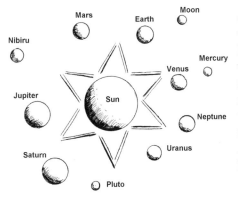

*Fig.7.7: According to Zecharia Sitchin's interpretation, the orbs on the cylinder seal correspond to the Sun and nine planets, plus the Moon and Nibiru. Pluto appears out of sequence, since it is shown in its previous position as a moon of Saturn.*

Nonetheless, the theory does provide the mechanism of a large passing body to interfere with Jupiter and cause the ejection of Venus. In addition, it would mean that Nibiru is due to return soon (1500 BC to 2000 AD = 3,500 years); Appleby suggests that the next return of Nibiru is due between 2012 and 2036, as we shall see.

If there is anyone who is still in favour of correlating the Birth of Venus incident to 3114 BC, despite the errors of the Gilbert interpretation, then it would follow that the 13-baktun cycle is measuring the period of return of some other huge planetoid (as suggested by Willaru Huayta, Credo Muttwa and the Bible Code) due in 2012.

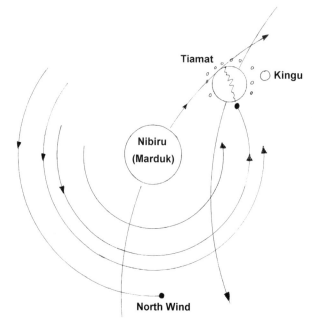

*Fig.7.8: Sitchin's interpretation of the Marduk and Tiamat myth is a series of collisions between the moons of Nibiru and the planet that once orbited between Mars and Jupiter - Tiamat. The moons of Tiamat became comets, the shattered half of Tiamat became the asteroid belt, the other half became the Earth, and Tiamat's main moon, Kingu, became our Moon. Appleby thinks Nibiru also lost some mass in these collisions, becoming a similar size to the Earth. After Sitchin [1976, 1978].*

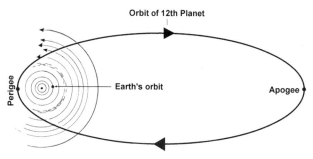

*Fig.7.9: The eventual orbit of Nibiru. After Sitchin [1976, 1978].*

## The Return of Nibiru

Appleby quotes the Washington Post (30/12/83), that "*a heavenly body possibly as large as the giant planet Jupiter*" [24] has been spotted by the IRAS satellite in the direction of Orion and, says Appleby, this is Nibiru and it is due to "*become visible to Earth and appear as a new star, sometime between 2012 and 2036.*" [25] However, Appleby says it is now near the size of the Earth, since it broke in two, as described in Babylonian myths (this somewhat contradicts the statement from chief IRAS scientist Gerry Neugebauer about it being the size of Jupiter!). Thus, any cataclysms as it comes close to Earth again will be less severe than previous ones.

There is a possible connection here to Egyptian and Greek mythology. According to Murry Hope "*The Eye of Ra, which was the exclusive weapon of Sekhmet, is described as a bright and burning object (a planetessimal or comet perhaps?)... we are seeing Ra in terms of the Sirian System, and Sekhmet as his daughter...*". [26]

Typhon, the father of Orthrus (Sirius) is shown in *The Twelfth Planet* as a winged serpent, like Quetzalcoatl (who promised to return) and was "*a kind of comet*", which was invisible. [27]

If we take a detailed look at the zodiac of Dendera, it seems as if the Eye of Ra has just come out of the Square of Pegasus, between the fish of Pisces (see Fig.8.1, page 93). In the epic book on astro-mythology, *Hamlet's Mill*, there is a collection of myths, which together imply that Nibiru/Marduk (identified as either "Jupiter", "*a comet*" or "*the ark*") entered the Pegasus square, which is said to be the "*entrance to the abyss.*" [28] Channeller Jelaila Starr claims to have received messages from "*the Nibiruan Council*" saying that an anomalous NASA photo of an object "*near the vicinity of EQ/Pegasi in the Pegasus star system*" is actually Nibiru! [29]

Finally, researcher Barbara Hand Clow connects these threads by saying that Nibiru's 3,600-year orbit takes it near Sirius! [30]

*Fig.7.10: Zeus and Typhon. After Sitchin [1976, 1978].*

### Phobos Fly-by of Earth

In an article by James van der Worp [31] about the fly-by of Mars by comet 76P, on June 5th 2000, evidence was presented that the orbit of Phobos (see colour pages) was affected, resulting in it being shunted towards Earth's orbit, on a collision course, with a projected impact time around September 12th 2000. An Internet discussion ensued between van der Worp and Glen Deen, involving complex astro-physics calculations, and Deen came to the following conclusion:

*"My low-precision orbit model gave Earth impact of Phobos on September 18, 2012 with an escape velocity of 3.99731 Km/s..."* [32]

However, Glen Deen later modified his theory. He has since said it was not loosened in 2000, but in 2001 (by comet 75P Kohoutek), and has also stated that "*Planet X*" could impact Mercury circa March 2nd 2012, and Mercury could impact Venus circa June 6th 2012, resulting in a rendezvous of Venus/Mercury with Earth on 11th December 2012, [33] like a game of cosmic billiard balls, which sounds very unlikely.

### Behemoth and Leviathan

*E.Din Land of Righteousness* [34] is a massive work by El (a.k.a. Elliott Rudisill), with over 350 pages of very small print. The author has used the Bible, as well as the Dead Sea Scrolls, the *Book of Enoch*, the *Book of Jubilees* and other apocryphal works, combined with the works of Zecharia Sitchin, to form his interpretation of human history. He also lists the Popol vuh, Bhagavad Gita, Ramayana, Talmud, Upanishads, Kabbalah and Koran in his list, as well as some of the most influential modern books on 2012.

The planet Nibiru is said by the author to have passed through the solar system around 5100 BC (no reference is given), and is predicted to return around 2012 AD, possibly as the

"*New Jerusalem.*" [35] The *Book of Job* is analysed in detail, since Rudisill is convinced that the family of Job was killed by a meteor in the form of "*fire from heaven*" and accompanying "*great wind*", and that the two biblical "*monsters of the deep*" mentioned in the book, *Behemoth* and *Leviathan*, are actually huge asteroids swimming in the sea of space. *Daniel*, *Psalms* and *Enoch* all mention these monsters too, and, when cross-referenced with St. John's *Revelation*, their consistency and route can be surmised.

By combining the Great Pyramid timeline, the "*Enochian Jubilee Calendar*" and the 13-baktun cycle of the Maya, the author came up with a "*Galactic Calendar*" at the root of them all [36] and was able to plot an unfolding, if now outdated, scenario. That scenario was as follows:

Between autumn 2004 and spring 2005, an asteroid or comet would impact the Earth and penetrate the crust. [37] Then a star would appear in Pisces. This was Leviathan, and its apparent route was mapped through the sky towards Orion. [38] Around the same time that Leviathan appeared in Pisces, Behemoth would travel another route from the "*southern constellations*" starting at Hydras, and its apparent route would also take it towards Orion. [39] Since Behemoth is "*the one that hides*", it might remain hidden until it got to Orion. Behemoth has "*ten horns*" and Leviathan has "*seven heads*", but when meeting in Orion, "*somewhere in the middle of 2008 CE*" (CE or Current Era = AD), they would combine to become the "*seven-headed ten-horned 'Red Dragon'*" of the *Book of Revelation*. The Red Dragon would be "*cast into the pit*" around summer solstice 2008; [40] or the Leviathan part at least, while the Behemoth component would by-pass Earth, but return in 2012 due to being thrown off orbit by the galactic super-wave that Paul LaViolette has predicted (see below).

Thus as 2012 approaches, Mercury (Archangel Michael) collides with the Red Dragon (Leviathan), and Venus and Jupiter may also be hit, but the Moon will take a severe hammering and may blow apart, with the pieces hitting Earth along with Leviathan. [41] Three and a half years later (42 months or 1260 days), Behemoth will return, becoming Osiris reborn, or the re-born *First Father* of the Maya. [42] The galactic superwave will come into view in Sagittarius, where Galactic Centre is located, appearing as a blue star, or the eye of God, "*shortly before the winter of 2012 CE*," [43] and will arrive at the same time as Behemoth and as Nibiru, which will be the "*descent of the New Jerusalem*". [44]

## Waffle Straining

A detailed review of *E.Din* was posted on the *Diagnosis 2012* website and Rudisill responded, posting a reply and corrections at his own website. [45] Among several problems with the book, I noticed that the diagrams show the timing of the Winter Solstice 2012 event to an accuracy of one second, while a four-year error due to the Jubilee calendar being neglected during the time that the Israelites were in Egypt, is called "*a calculated error*" that is "*close to exact*." [46] A 40-year error is said to be more accurate than the Great Pyramid, and the 1,260-day period from the *Book of Revelation* is miscalculated by 384 days, which displaces the whole impact scenario by the same period, from mid-2008 to July 2009. [47] Rudisill agreed in his reply and corrections page that most of the points I raised were valid, but he didn't mention this 384-day error. Unfortunately, *E.Din* provides no references or index, so checking out the information is very tedious, but having performed that drudgery, we find that the complex theory is error-riddled, reducing it to an interesting but unsubstantiated idea. The full review is posted online, at *www.diagnosis2012.co.uk/new4.htm#leviathan*, where there is a link to the author's reply and corrections.

## Obliquity Harmonics

Keith Hunter is the author of several articles posted on the Internet at *www.2near.com/edge*. In the first of these, *Earth Pole Shift 2012 13.0.0.0.0.*, [48] Keith theorised that a pole shift is coming that will reinstate the Earth's 360-day rotation period and eventually restore it to its original spherical state, raising the consciousness of mankind in the process. In the second essay, *Sacred Geometry, the Earth, and the Mayan Calendar 'End-Date' of 2012*, [49] he continued the theme, explaining the harmonic relationships he had discovered between the Earth's oblateness (ratio of its equatorial diameter to its polar diameter) and the angle of the Earth's obliquity of the ecliptic (the tilt of the Earth's axis).

Following a request from Hunter to comment on his theory, I informed him of some problems I found with it. After this communication, Keith removed his original essay, *Earth Pole Shift 2012*, and made several alterations to his second essay, *Sacred Geometry*, so I will only comment on the second version of the second essay. Hunter says that the Earth's axis tilt angle, or obliquity, is diminishing every year and he calculates that in 2012 it will be in a harmonic relationship to its oblateness. However, it is plain that the numbers do *not* have a harmonic relationship to each other, in the same way that (for example) the numbers 85 and 1085 do not have a harmonic relationship (see note [50] for the actual figures). When I pointed this out to Hunter, he said, "... *it is not important that they are not harmonics. They are obviously related. Just to look at them, this is obvious*". [51] Another problem emerged when I checked more than ten Internet sources on the polar and equatorial measurements of the Earth. None of the resulting oblateness figures were anywhere near Hunter's figure, but his explanation was even more perplexing than the previous one. He said that his figures were "*not based upon the actual physical dimensions of the Earth that we measure*". [52]

Details of several other errors were e-mailed to Hunter, so he might post corrected versions, or remove the essays... or he might not. A more thorough critique, including the figures with seven decimal places, can be found at *www.diagnosis2012.co.uk/new3.htm#kh*.

## Galactic Core Explosion

Astrophysicist Dr Paul LaViolette's book *Earth Under Fire* [53] combines recent scientific data with myth and legend to rediscover the reason why ancient civilizations tried to warn us of impending disaster. LaViolette has an impressive list of achievements; he lists twelve groundbreaking discoveries that he made, which were later vindicated by other researchers.

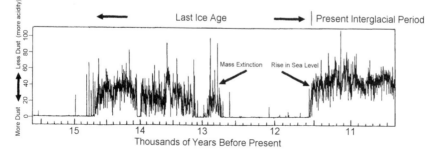

*Fig.7.11: A graph showing changes in acidity around the close of the last ice age, deduced from the Greenland Summit ice core. Adapted from LaViolette [1997].*

LaViolette's new model predicts that the core of our Milky Way galaxy is not a black hole, but a massive object that explodes periodically. These *"galactic core explosions"*, he says, happen approximately every 26,000 years, *"with the possibility of a 13,000 year recurrence interval"*, [54] sending out a *"galactic superwave"* of cosmic rays. He theorises that the superwaves could have entrained Earth's cycle of precession into its approximate 26,000-year pattern. [55] This is especially likely if a wave arrived when the Earth's polar axis was facing Galactic Centre, as it was around 12,850 years ago. This is very close to the 12,700 years BP date (Before Present; by convention before 1950 AD) indicated for the superwave, by ice core information (see diagram and Chapter 10), and also to the date at which the Greeks set the beginning of the Platonic Year (cycle of the precession of the equinoxes), which was *"when the vernal equinox was just about to enter the constellation of Leo, i.e. around 10,800 BC"* [56] or 12,750 years BP. This was also the

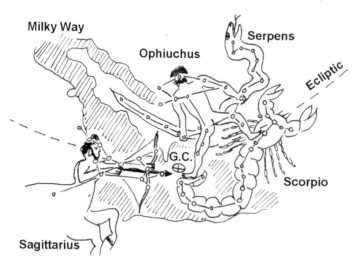

*Fig.7.12: The arrow of Sagittarius and the sting of Scorpio, as well as the foot of Ophiuchus, the Snake Handler (see page 93), all define the position of Galactic Centre. After LaViolette [1997].*

approximate date that Bauval, Gilbert and Hancock found encoded at the Giza plateau in Egypt (see next chapter), and LaViolette follows up on this, showing that not only Giza, but also the zodiac and the Tarot were all time capsule systems encoded with information about the last galactic superwave, which swept through the solar system, ending the Ice Age about

*Fig.7.13: The club of Orion and the horns of Taurus define the Galactic Anticentre, which is the direction in which the Galactic Superwave departed. After LaViolette [1997].*

13,000 years ago. This knowledge may be preserved in the myths of the *Eye of Ra* and *Eye of Horus*, which were sent to punish mankind.

Geologist Gregg Braden (see Chapter 9) predicts a geomagnetic reversal linked to a 13,000 year cycle, and LaViolette confirms that at that time "...*the intensity and declination of the Earth's magnetic field underwent major variations in step with the eleven-year sunspot cycle. The amplitude of these cycles was hundreds of times larger than modern geomagnetic solar cycles, suggesting that solar flare activity at that time was also hundreds of times more intense, approaching levels normally observed in T Tauri stars.*" [57]

T Tauri stars have a mass similar to the Sun (though expanded between two to five times that of the Sun), but have collected a large amount of dust along their equatorial planes, which causes them to emit most of their radiation in the infrared part of the spectrum and exhibit constant flaring, in which the flares are between 100 and 1,000 times larger than typical flares on the Sun.

## Electromagnetic Pulse Wave

I recently discovered an online fictional work called *Galactic Tsunami*, [58] in which it becomes apparent to the characters in the story that the event that governed the timing of the 2012 termination point of the Maya 13-baktun cycle was the arrival of an "*EMP wave*". In the story, this wave is said to be due every 500 years, and currently overdue by 200 years. Although this is fiction, it is based on the discoveries of astrophysicist Paul LaViolette (see above). The emphasis of *Earth Under Fire* was on a galactic core explosion that happens at intervals of 13,000 and 26,000 years, and sends out a "*galactic superwave*" of cosmic waves that bring dust and cause solar activity to increase, while blocking out the sunlight and causing major geomagnetic variations.

However, when I re-read pages 334-335 of LaViolette's book, I found that he did say smaller EMP events happen on average every 500 years. The following is a quote from an online essay by Paul LaViolette:

"*Galactic superwaves may also produce an intense electromagnetic pulse (EMP) whenever a cosmic ray front happens to strike the Earth's atmosphere. Galactic superwaves such as those that arrived during the last ice age could have generated pulses delivering tens of thousands of volts per meter in times as short as a billionth of a second, comparable to the early-time EMP signal from a high-altitude nuclear explosion.*

*Galactic Centre activity occurs frequently between major superwave events. Astronomical observation indicates that during the last 6,000 years, the Galactic Centre has expelled fourteen clouds of ionised gas. These outbursts may have produced minor superwave emissions with EMP effects comparable to those of major superwaves. About 80% of these bursts took place within 500 hundred years of one another. With the most recent outburst occurring 700 years ago, there is a high probability of another one occurring in the near future.*" [59]

Nevertheless, the diagram in *Earth Under Fire* reveals that, although the average may be 500 years, there was one period of almost 2,000 years without a wave, and the pattern certainly doesn't look predictable.

*Fig.7.14: The timing of minor Galactic core explosions over the last 6,000 years, and consequent cosmic ray pulses that would have caused an electromagnetic pulse through the Earth's atmosphere. Adapted from LaViolette [1997].*

# Chapter 8:
# Alternative Archaeology

## The Dendera Zodiac
Astrologer John Lash gave a lecture at the Alternative Egypt Questing Conference at the

Logan Hall of The Institute of Education, London, on 23rd October 1999, in which he claimed that there were originally thirteen signs in the zodiac, the thirteenth being the *Snake Handler*. Instead of splitting the ecliptic into twelve equally sized sections, there were thirteen sections of different sizes, depending on the sizes of the constellations. Once this is taken into account, Lash says that the Sun's vernal equinox will not transit from Pisces to Aquarius for another 700 to 800 years.

The circular zodiac on the ceiling of the Temple at Dendera in Egypt shows the twelve signs, the Snake Handler without the snake, several other constellations, the five visible planets, and the 36 decans. The Egyptologist R.A. Schwaller De Lubicz has shown that the Dendera Zodiac demonstrates that the Egyptians knew about the precession of the equinoxes. [1] The axes marked on the zodiac show the movement of solstices and equinoxes through the constellations

Fig.8.1: *The circular zodiac on the ceiling of the temple at Dendera, Egypt, with the zodiac constellations shaded. It seems that the current era is encoded into the carving. After Lucie Lamy.*

between the foundation of Egypt and the time of the building of the Dendera Temple. Sirius appears twice - once on the true north-south axis, above the horns of the "cow of Isis", and also on the axis of the temple, as Horus on a papyrus stem. The light of the star would illumine the inner temple on New Year's Day, at the heliacal rising, when the temple was built. In that era, this would have coincided with the Summer Solstice in Cancer, which is why Sirius also appears aligned to Cancer on the north-south axis.

John Lash points out another axis on the Dendera Zodiac, which goes from the four rams' heads, through Pisces, across the pole to the star Spica, which is being held by Virgo. This, he says, is pointing out the position of the vernal equinox today. The line goes through the Square of Pegasus, which has writing on it - "*the Programmes of Destiny*". At exactly 90° to this axis, another line can be drawn through the tip of the arrow of Sagittarius, which points to Galactic Centre, where the solstice alignment will occur in 2012.

## Crustal Displacement

In his book *Fingerprints of the Gods,* [2] Graham Hancock suggests that an unusual planetary alignment at the end of the 13-baktun cycle will cause a gravitational effect on the crust of the Earth, which is top-heavy with polar ice. The crust will slip, wiping out most of the life on Earth as a result of colossal tidal waves. However, this planetary alignment is actually due on 24th December 2011, which is the date given by Frank Waters in *Mexico Mystique* as the end of the 13-baktun cycle. Since the end-point has now been confirmed as 21st December 2012, then if we are due for crustal displacement, this planetary alignment will probably not be the trigger. However, Hancock finds convincing evidence that the event that triggered the flooding at the end of the Ice Age, around 13,000 years ago (he puts it at 10,500 BC), is connected to the precession of the equinoxes, and is due again around about now.

As we have already mentioned, it seems that Frank Waters got the December 24th 2011 end-point from Michael Coe's 1966 book *The Maya*, but in later editions and other works, Coe used the *Lounsbury Correlation* that fixes the 13-baktun end-point (13.0.0.0.0) at 23rd December 2012. This correlation is second only to the final Goodman (GMT-2) correlation in popularity - the one that supports the True Count, and it is this GMT-2 correlation that ends on the Winter Solstice of 21st December 2012.

## The Hall of Records

In his 1998 book *The Gods of Eden,* [3] Andrew Collins has followed up legends of an undiscovered underground complex at the Giza plateau in Egypt, and by a study of the much overlooked *Edfu Texts* has concluded that the complex takes the form of twelve chambers surrounding a thirteenth.

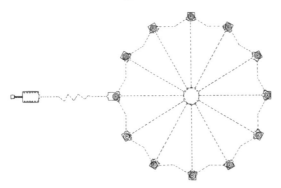

He calls the complex *The Chambers of First Creation,* and says that in each of the twelve chambers were kept "*Iht-relics*", and in the central 13th chamber was the "*Bnnt-embryo*", also known as a "*seed*", or "*egg of creation*". [4] Collins imagines the embryo to be "*a large conical-shaped omphalos or benben stone, plausibly a crystal-like structure...*" and the Iht-relics, "*smaller, hand-held sacred stones, or crystals...*" [5] This is such a similar idea to the 'Ark' of the Native Americans (see *Crystal Skulls* in Chapter 19), that it implies a 2012 connection, and this connection has been made by Nigel Appleby.

*Fig.8.2: Andrew Collins' plan of the probable arrangement of the Chambers of First Creation, based on the Edfu texts and books of the duat. Drawing by Bernard G. From* Gods of Eden, *Collins [1998].*

Nigel Appleby simultaneously came to the same conclusion as Collins did, after studying the Edfu Texts, though he differs in his prediction of the Hall's location. There has been some controversy about Appleby's book *Hall of the Gods*, as several authors accused him of plagiarism, but since it was published at the same time as *The Gods of Eden*, this probably doesn't apply to the following.

As the Giza pyramids in Egypt correspond exactly to the layout of the Belt of Orion, [6] if the image of the Orion constellation was superimposed onto the pyramids, the position of Sirius,

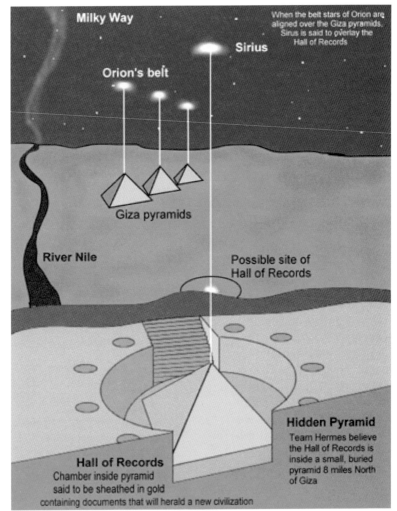

Fig.8.3: The location of the lost Hall of Records, according to Nigel Appleby and the Operation Hermes team.

argues Appleby, would overlay the Hall of Records. From his study of the Edfu Texts, Appleby concluded that the Hall of Records is a central chamber surrounded by twelve others, and even conjectured that the central chamber contains a small pyramid, as opposed to just a pyramidion, or capstone. Inside should be information concerning the history of mankind, and, says Appleby, crucial information to prepare mankind for the coming of the "*Fifth Age of Man*", which will begin in 2012.

Fig.8.4: *The Phoenix or Bennu bird. After Bauval and Gilbert [1994, 1995].*

## The Return of the Phoenix

The Phoenix myth relates to the periodic reversal of the Earth's magnetic field due to the long-term sunspot cycle that culminates in a solar magnetic reversal, says Appleby. This magnetic reversal is due in 2012. Here, Appleby has obviously been influenced by Cotterell and Gilbert's *The Mayan Prophecies*. Appleby refers to Michael Mandeville's self-published book *The Return of the Phoenix*, [7] which predicts the *Fifth Flight of the Phoenix* as a movement of the Earth's lithosphere, in which it "*takes flight*", moving as much as 30° of latitude. This is otherwise known as crustal displacement or crustal slip (as predicted by Hancock above), and Appleby

says, "*If Mandeville is correct, then it will fly again on 22 December 2012*". [8] Thus it was a surprise when I found on Mandeville's website [9] that he said the Fifth Flight will be most likely to occur in the years 2000 or 2001 (after Edgar Cayce). More recently, I looked at his site, and now that we have passed 2001 and the Fifth Flight failed to happen, he says that it cannot be predicted ("*except by those with 'otherworldly' connections*") and denies that the Maya calendar could be connected with it. However, Mandeville has seemingly misunderstood the whole concept of the galactic alignment process, associating the alignment with the Spring Equinox of

Fig.8.5: *At vernal equinox, 10,500 BC: the Sun in Leo lines up with the Sphinx, while Orion's belt culminates at the meridian - a pattern mimicked on the ground by the three pyramids. After Robert Bauval and R. J. Cook in Bauval and Hancock 1996.*

2012, rather than the Winter Solstice.

Swedish scientists have, says Appleby, determined that the date of the most recent magnetic reversal, or shift (but not a *"full reversal"*), occurred in 10,500 BC. [10] This happens to agree *"with extraordinary exactness"*, according to Appleby, with the date that Edgar Cayce's visions revealed as the time the Great Pyramid was built (10,490 BC). It is also the date that alternative Egyptologist John Anthony West [11] and geologist Robert Schoch have determined as the construction date of the Sphinx. Thus the Sphinx and Pyramid may have been designed as clues to last 12,500 years and help warn us of the coming changes in 2012, and lead us to the Hall of Records. [12]

According to Appleby, [13] the Sphinx was designed as a Phoenix (man + bull + lion + eagle), and is aligned to a point on the horizon that gives us a clue as to the meaning of the Phoenix legend. The Sphinx, as pointed out by Bauval and Hancock, [14] faces the point on the horizon where the sunrise on the vernal equinox was in the constellation of Leo, while Orion was at its lowest point in the

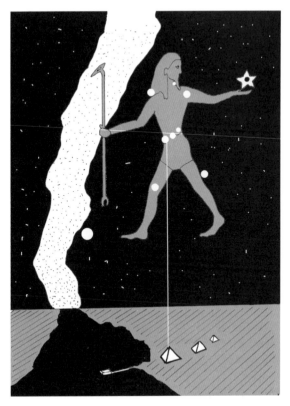

*Fig.8.6: Orion's belt and the Giza pyramids. The star Al Nitak aligns to the southern shaft of the King's chamber of the Great Pyramid. After Robin Cook in Bauval and Gilbert [1994, 1995].*

sky. This occurred in 10,500 BC, and is known as *Zep Tepi* - the *"First Time"* of Osiris (Orion). The *"Last Time"* of Osiris will occur when Orion is at its highest point in the sky, and Bauval and Hancock gave it variously as 2450 AD [15] and 2500 AD. [16] Appleby gives it as 2012 AD. Having checked, I have found reason to agree with him. [17] In order to arrive at this conclusion, he needed to place Zep Tepi around 500 years before Bauval and Hancock's Zep Tepi date, thus bringing their projected date for the Last Time back 500 years. However, he placed Zep Tepi at 11,500 BC, [18] but does not seem to realise that this means the Last Time would have happened around 1400-1500 AD, which is half a precessional cycle later (around 12,900 years).

Appleby also says that at the time of Zep Tepi, the planet Venus performed a retrograde loop over the top of the Orion constellation: *"This phenomenon only occurs once every 12,500 years, and the next time it will occur happens to be in the year 2012"*. [19] However, as

*Fig.8.7: The pyramids at Giza represent the belt of Orion around 10,500 BC, the First Time of Osiris according to Bauval, Gilbert and Hancock, and Orion is currently approaching its highest point - the Last Time of Osiris. After Robin Cook in Bauval and Gilbert [1994, 1995].*

we shall see, this information on the retrograde loops of Venus was supplied to him by Gino Ratinckx and Patrick Geryl, and on closer examination, turns out to be totally misleading. But more than that, the date which Geryl and Ratinckx gave for the retrograde loop was actually 9792 BC, not 10,500 BC or his revised Zep Tepi date of 11,500 BC. This is an error of 1,708 years, but as we shall see when I look at Geryl and Ratinckx's claims, they also made an error, and the best match for the 2012 loop happened in 9389 BC according to the results I got with the *SkyGlobe* software, so this brings Appleby's error up to 2,111 years. It is a pity that he tried to incorporate the Venus loop into his theory (which is mostly irrelevant, as we shall see), since it has obscured the point that we are now in the Last Time of Osiris.

### The Pyramid of Kukulcan; a Precessional Alarm Clock

When the Toltec people from northern Mexico moved down to Chichen Itza, on the Yucatan peninsula, they merged their own zenith cosmology with the Maya system, and the result was the Pyramid of Kukulcan. This has been designed so that every year, on Spring Equinox, the afternoon sun causes a shadow play so it appears that a huge serpent is descending from the sky, down the pyramid. However, John Major Jenkins shows that the pyramid is much more than an equinox indicator. It is a *"precessional clock with its alarm set for the twenty-first century"*. [20]

Jenkins says that Kukulcan (the Maya name for Quetzalcoatl, the plumed serpent) was the symbol of a Sun-Pleiades-zenith conjunction. The zenith passage of the Sun takes place over Chichen Itza on 20th May, around 60 days after the Spring Equinox. The Crotalus rattlesnake, whose pattern is constantly used in

*Fig.8.8: Quetzalcoatl, the feathered serpent.*

Mesoamerican art, has a marking on it which is identical to the Solar Ahau glyph of the Maya, and its rattle was called *tzab*, which is the same word in the Yucatec-Mayan language used for the Pleiades star cluster, a small cluster of seven stars in the Taurus constellation (see illustration).

Fig.8.9: In Egypt, the Sun was depicted as a feathered snake.

The moving snake on the Pyramid is an annual reminder of a conjunction of the zenith Sun with the Pleiades over Chichen Itza, but this conjunction is an event that will only occur during a 72-year time window, from 1976 to 2048. Right at the centre of this time window is the year 2012, when the 13-baktun cycle ends. On 20th May 2012, the zenith passage of the Sun will combine with a solar eclipse, on the tzolkin day *10 Chicchan*, which means *serpent*.

Thus, John Major Jenkins has discovered the meaning of the Toltec New Fire ceremony, [21] which was bequeathed to the Aztecs. Every 52 years, when the combination of haab and tzolkin calendars - the Calendar Round - approached its end-point, the priests would wait to see if the Pleiades reached the zenith at midnight. They were actually measuring the precessional movement of the Sun-Pleiades conjunction towards the zenith on the zenith-passage day that occurs exactly six months later. The conjunction was calculated at night, six months previously, since the Pleiades are not visible in daylight.

Fig.8.10: The shadow-play occurs 60 days before the Pleiades-zenith Sun conjunction in 2012. From Jenkins [2002].

## The Rattling of the Pleiades

In his book *Gateway To Atlantis*, [22] Andrew Collins has amassed a collection of evidence that the civilization of Atlantis was destroyed by a tidal wave following the collision of a comet (known to geologists as the Carolina Bays comet), and that Cuba is a remnant of the landmass. The proximity of Cuba to Mesoamerica would explain the Aztec and Maya fascination with cataclysm. The *Chilam Balam of Chumayel*, Collins tells us, "*spoke of an almighty cataclysm during which the 'Great Serpent' was 'ravished from the heavens together with the rattles of its tail' so that its 'skin and pieces' of its bones 'fell here upon the Earth'*". [23] The Calina Carib tribe in Surinam, South America, still have myths of a fiery serpent that came from the Pleiades and "*brought the world to an end*" with "*a great fire and a deluge*". [24]

Fig.8.11: The serpents on the rim of the Aztec Sunstone have the seven stars of the Pleiades on their snouts, according to John Major Jenkins. Adapted from Roberto Sieck Flandes.

There is also a Hebrew legend, says Collins, that "*the Great Flood was caused after 'the upper waters rushed through the space left when God removed two stars out of the constellation Pleiades'*". [25] Collins has pointed out that the Pleiades were seen as the rattle of a celestial snake, as indicated by John Major Jenkins, but Collins also adds that the Pleiades as the snake rattle, "*warns its potential victim of an imminent strike.*" [26] Collins thinks this may have come from the direction of the Pleiades.

Astronomers call Earth-crossing asteroids "*Apollo objects*". This brings to mind Philip K. Dick's enigmatic statement in *Valis* that "*the Head Apollo is about to return*". [27]

## The Eye in The Pyramid

On Raymond Mardyks' website *Galactic Astrology Centre*, [28] he decoded the Great Seal of America, which appears on every dollar bill. The Seal shows a thirteen-step pyramid with the date 1776 in Roman numerals on it. Just as the Pyramid of Kukulkcan has 91 steps on each of the four sides, making 364 in all, plus the top level, giving the number 365, the Great Seal pyramid also has an encoded calendrical meaning. Like some Maya pyramids, it has a date on it, but in the Gregorian calendar, and four sides of thirteen levels gives 52, which is the number of weeks in our year. However, thirteen and 52 are also the key numbers in the Maya calendar systems.

The thirteen baktuns of the 13-baktun cycle

Fig.8.12: The Great Seal of America, as found on every dollar bill.

consist of twenty katuns each, and each katun consists of twenty tuns, so there are 5,200 tuns in the 13-baktun cycle. There are also 52 haabs in a Calendar Round. Some Maya groups named cycles after end dates rather than beginning dates. They also used a 13-katun cycle known as the Short Count. 1776 was not only the year that the American Declaration of Independence was signed (on 4th July), but was also a special year in the Maya Long Count calendar. Just as the last katun in the 13-baktun cycle could be called *"katun 2012"*, the first katun in the cycle of thirteen katuns, would be called *"katun 1776"*. In fact, the katun ended 33 days before the signing of the Declaration.  So 1776 is the bottom level of the pyramid, where the date is actually inscribed - the top of the pyramid is therefore 2012.

The top would also be 2012 if each level represented one of the thirteen baktuns in the 13-

Fig.8.13: The Great Seal as an encoded single cycle of the Short Count calendar. The 13-katun Short Count continued to be used after the Long Count and its 13-baktun cycle fell into disuse. Adapted from Mardyks.

baktun cycle, with 3114 BC at the bottom. The top of the Great Seal pyramid shows an eye-in-triangle, which has been associated with Sirius, God, the pineal gland, and the Illuminati. Mardyks goes on to point out that not only was the Egyptian calendar based on the rising of Sirius, but that *"the Sun is astrologically conjunct Sirius every year on July 4th, for the birthday of the United States of America"* (this means they are plotted on the same degree of the same zodiac sign, even though Sirius is some way off the ecliptic). Also, some Maya groups in the Yucatan froze their New Year to July 26th, *"when Sirius rises in that part of the world"* (after its period of invisibility). On January 1st at midnight, Sirius culminates, reaching its highest point in the sky at the only time of year when it is visible all night long, according to Mardyks (about 12.30 AM according to SkyGlobe).  It is thus also a key marker in the Gregorian calendar.

Sirius was of great calendrical importance to the ancient Egyptians, since its heliacal (first dawn) rising marked the New Year and the annual Nile flood. In 2004, Robert Bauval and Graham Hancock released their book *Talisman - The Sacred Cities and The Secret Faith*, concerning Masonic secrets about Sirius, which were encoded into the design of Paris and Washington (Masons were behind the gaining of American Independence and the French Revolution; Ben Franklin, George Washington and Napoleon Bonaparte were all known Masons).

Paul LaViolette's 13,000-year cycle would also fit the Great Seal pyramid on the dollar bill, as would Adrian Gilbert's *Age of Adam* (see the penultimate item in this chapter). With each level as 1,000 years, 2012 would still be on the top.

## Great Pyramid: Calendar in Stone?

An essay by Paul White, *The Secrets of Thoth and The Keys of Enoch*, which can be found all over the Internet, and seems to have been copied from an original at *Rense.com*, includes the following:

*"According to the 'calendar in stone' of the Great Pyramid, which describes the so-called 'Phoenix Cycle' of our galactic orbit, the present time period ends (converted to our present calendar) in the year 2012 AD. The Greek word PHOENIX, derived from the Egyptian word PA-HANOK, actually means 'The House of Enoch.'* [29] (See note for Paul White's source on this).

J. J. Hurtak, who is mentioned in the article, and who wrote *The Keys of Enoch*, does not mention 2012 as far as I know (I have searched his book and webpage, www.keysofenoch.org). In fact, Hurtak's book says that the Keys *"were given on January 2/3, 1973, to prepare mankind for the activation of events that are to come to pass in the next 30 years of 'Earth time'"*. [30] Those 30 years expired in January 2003. We have already established that Michael Mandeville could not be the source of the Phoenix-2012 connection; at least not the current version of his website, but what about Appleby's claim that Mandeville's 1997 self-published book stated that 2012 was the end of the Phoenix cycle? The way Appleby worded it, he could have meant that *"If Mandeville is correct"*, then according to Appleby's interpretation of Mandeville, *"the Phoenix will fly again on 22 December 2012"*. [31]

Since the earliest posting of this essay that I could find dates to October 1999, it could have been inspired by Appleby's *Hall of the Gods*, which came out the previous year (albeit only for six days before it was withdrawn due to accusations of plagiarism; I managed to get myself a copy during those six days). I wondered if the information could have come from Howard Middleton-Jones or James Wilkie, who work together on the *Ambilac* website, but the 2012 prediction from Ambilac comes from an analysis of the whole Giza plateau, not just the Great Pyramid.

## Star-Map-to-Ground Correlation at Giza in 2012

Howard Middleton-Jones showed a sky map for December 21st 2012 at his lecture at The Glastonbury Symposium in 1999, saying that the satellite pyramids at Giza reflect the positions of the planets at the end of the Maya 13-baktun cycle. Here is an extract of an article on his website, *Archaeology - Archaeoastronomy - Ancient Civilizations*:

*"Are we going to have a new neighbour (Sun giving birth?) on 21st December 2012... A satellite pyramid of Khufu will be the centre point for the complete Giza alignment on 21st December 2012 at a precise time (22.00 hrs, 18 mins, 13 secs, local Cairo time) [sic] and Venus will be completely aligned  - connections will be made to our previous civilization on Mars, and our Sun, which was born of Alcyone in the Pleiades, our nearest relatives."* [32]

I spoke to Middleton-Jones on the phone shortly after the 1999 Symposium, and he said that the alignment in 2012 would involve a planet or body currently beyond Pluto, which had just been discovered.

Struggling to find an astronomical justification for this, instead I asked astrologer Paul Wright to calculate an astrological chart for Cairo on 21st December 2012. He prepared a chart for early afternoon, which coincides with dawn in Mexico, and although there are no obvious conjunctions, Mercury and Venus are both in Sagittarius, with the Sun rising just after them. However, this is the position in the tropical Zodiac, as used by astrologers, based on the zodiac as it was 2,300 years ago, since the constellations were chosen to represent twelve partitions in the seasonal year. The zodiac has precessed through many degrees since then, so that in

Transits 21 Dec 2012
Natal Chart
21 Dec 2012
13:00  EET −2:00
Cairo > Al-Qahirah
30N03 031E15
*Geocentric*
*Tropical*
*Placidus*
*True Node*

*Fig.8.14: An astrology chart for Cairo on 21st December 2012, according to the tropical zodiac. Chart prepared by Paul Wright, Orionstar Charts.*

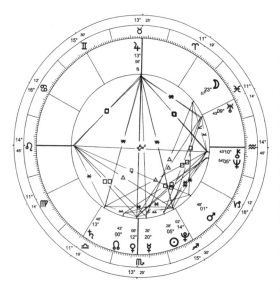

*Fig.8.15: The sidereal zodiac for Cairo on 21st December 2012. Chart prepared by Helen Sewell.*

the sidereal zodiac - the positions of the constellations as they are now - Mercury and Venus will be in Scorpio, with the Sun rising just after them.

Since *the* event that occurs on this date is the conjunction of the Solstice Sun with Galactic Equator, close to Galactic Centre, also in Sagittarius, I suddenly remembered that Zecharia Sitchin predicted that when Nibiru returns, it would reappear "*in the regions of the constellation of Sagittarius*".[33] Could this be the new planet that Jones predicts will be "*born of the Sun*"? Comet Hale-Bopp was discovered in Sagittarius in 1995, having an orbital period of 3-4,000 years. Some people suggested that it was Nibiru, but it was too small. However, Appleby believes that Nibiru has fragmented - could Hale-Bopp be a forerunner of Nibiru, on the same orbit?

## Giza-Genesis

When I had a look at James Wilkie's *Ambilac* website [34] and Howard Middleton-Jones' *Archaeology - Archaeoastronomy - Ancient Civilizations* website, [35] I found the information so complex and convoluted that it was hard to know where to start. When Jones and Wilkie finally produced a book, *Giza-Genesis: Best Kept Secrets,* [36] I was relieved that the confusion would finally be over and I could follow the whole story logically from start to finish. I followed the story, but there was nothing logical about it!

In the book, the characters of the Old Testament have been converted into a star chart using their age at fatherhood, and age at death, where the age at death is divided by 360 - then the result is multiplied by age at fatherhood to arrive at an angle. The same is done for the son, and so on, for six generations, and the points are joined together by equal-length lines. After the first six generations, there are four remaining generations until Noah, but the formula results in an angle over 360° for the first of these - Enoch. Instead of continuing around the circle to get an acute angle, the authors decide to go back to the "*Adam point*" and draw the line from there. The logic breaks down further at this point, and eventually the reader has to take their word for it that this diagram represents the Giza plateau and helps locate the hidden Hall of Records. Noah's Ark is then mixed up with the Ark of the Covenant to find that the biblical recipe for these are really the instructions for building the Great Pyramid, and there is a secret room accessed from the Grand Gallery, leading to a giant crystal underneath one of the Queen's pyramids of Khufu. [37] Further contortions lead to the conclusion that the Giza plateau is a map of the sky on 21st December 2012, when everything goes inter-dimensional.

Somehow, Wilkie and Middleton-Jones have got the idea that the Great Pyramid is misaligned from true north by almost 4°, and even give the figure to seven decimal places, but in *The Complete Pyramids*, [38] Egyptologist Mark Lehner reveals that the misalignment is close to a mere three *minutes* (or a twentieth of a degree) from true north! [39] Wilkie and Jones' Giza alignment on 21st December 2012 is calculated using their supposedly super-accurate, but in fact totally inaccurate, number, which means that the whole theory is invalidated. Even their diagrams of the Giza pyramids show the Khufu, or Great Pyramid, as being smaller than the Khafre pyramid! The Giza-Genesis theory is thus a prime example of pyramidiocy and unworthy of any further discussion. A better title would have been *Giza-Genesis: Best Kept a Secret!*    For a more detailed review, see *www.diagnosis2012.co.uk/new2.htm#giza-gen*

## The Re-Birth of Osiris

In an e-mail debate between Rush Allen and James Wilkie, posted on Allen's *SiLoaM.net* website, [40] in which Allen challenges Wilkie to explain himself and Wilkie fails, Allen claims that although he sees the *Ambilac* articles as disinformation, they are right in their conclusion [by some miracle] that the Hall of Records will be opened on December 21st 2012 at 10:18:13 PM local Cairo time (22:18:13). However, he says the opening of the Hall of Records is a kind of mass illumination of mankind. He concludes that Wilkie and Jones must have got the actual time by intuitional methods, since their reasoning is impossible to follow, while Allen himself found the time by astronomy and astrology.

Rush Allen found that:

*"The zenith meridian at Giza runs through Jupiter at the Hyades in Taurus. The metaphor for this alignment is that the kingdom (Jupiter) will be restored to Egypt (Taurus) at that precise moment. Thus, Osiris, the Bull of Egypt, will return from the dead at 22:18:13 on December 21, 2012."* [41]

## Secrets of the Alchemists

In 1926, an enigmatic alchemist called Fulcanelli published a book called *Le Mystere des Cathedrales*, or *Mystery of the Cathedrals*, [42] which explains how Gothic cathedrals have hermetic and alchemical secrets encoded into their architecture and sculptures. In 1957, a second edition appeared and included an extra chapter on the significance of a monument in the town of Hendaye in the Pyrenees. The monument - an engraved pedestal with a pillar and engraved cross - was built around 1680 (see colour pages). Fulcanelli said that on the cross is encoded a warning of an imminent trial by fire for the northern hemisphere.

More recently, in Kenneth Rayner Johnson's 1980 book *The Fulcanelli Phenomenon*, [43] Paul Mevryl contributed the afterword, an essay called *The Cyclic Cross of Hendaye*. Mevryl suggests several possible interpretations of the cross. These scenarios include solar flares triggered by the Grand Cross planetary conjunction of August 1999, which didn't happen, or the approach of an elliptically orbiting planet between Sirius and our Sun. The second scenario will crop up later in this book, apparently independently, and it is somewhat incredible that Mevryl should have come up with this, considering that he makes no mention of Robert Temple's *The Sirius Mystery*, which had been in print for four years when this book came out. When I saw the drawings of the cross, I noticed that on one of the panels on the pedestal there is a quincunx with central large angry Sun, reminiscent of the Aztec Sunstone and its five eras. However, Fulcanelli had said that only four ages of the world were represented on the cross, but these can be correlated to the four Worlds of the Hopi and Maya.

In 1999, Jay Weidner and Vincent Bridges published a thorough exposition of the hidden meaning encoded into the Hendaye Cross; *A Monument to the End of Time, - Alchemy,*

*Fig.8.16: The four sides of the base of the Cross of Hendaye. The shield-like design faces south, the star faces east, the Sun faces west and the Moon faces north. From The Mysteries of the Great Cross of Hendaye by Weidner and Bridges [2003], used by permission. Photos (C) Darlene, 2004.*

*Fulcanelli and the Great Cross.* [44] The authors traced the alchemical thread back to Egypt, to the first Gnostic groups, and re-exposed the fact that behind alchemy there lies a triple transmutation; of the inner, of the outer and of time. The inner transmutation is the refining of the psychosexual energies and fluids; the outer is using the inner change to transmute physical states; the third is the same transmutation applied to the whole Earth, changing the Age of Iron to the Age of Gold. The four ages - Gold, Silver, Bronze and Iron relate to the 26,000-year cycle of precession, say the authors, with the *"Fall"* occurring when the *Tree* (the celestial axis, or Earth's rotational axis) points *away* from the centre of the galaxy. *"Resurrection"* or *"redemption"* occurs when the Tree points towards the centre of the galaxy. This is the point when the *"sparks of light"* - our souls as fragments of God - return to the source; *"... the Gnostic concept of the Great Return of the lesser lights to the Light."* [45]

The thread is traced from ancient Egypt to the Coptic Church, the Gnostics, the Hebrews, Islam (the Sufis), the Order of Sion, and the Knights Templar, the grail romances, the Tarot, and, with increasing persecution of heretics, the engraving of cathedrals, and finally, the Rosicrucian movement.

The four engravings on the pedestal are found to refer to the four Tarot trumps; The Star, The Moon, The Sun and Judgement. The pillar represents the *Djed*, or Earth's rotational axis (Moira Timms has already pointed this out in her essay, *Raising the Djed* [46]). The two 'X' engravings refer to the winding of the ecliptic and equinoctial points, plus trump number 20 - Judgement. The authors decode the meaning of the engraving *"ocruxaves pesunica"*, which means *"... the secret concerns a cross and a snake which somehow measures the twelfth part"*. [47] When these clues are combined (along with

Fig.8.17: *The Star, the Moon, the Sun and the Last Judgement represent the four faces of the Hendaye cross. From The Mysteries of the Great Cross of Hendaye by Weidner and Bridges [2003], used by permission. Illustration (C) Darlene, 2004.*

clues from the kabbalistic Tree of Life, the 22 paths of which correlate to the 22 Tarot trumps), the authors conclude that half a precessional cycle ago, the Spring Equinox fell on the cusp of Leo/Virgo; 12,960 years later, in 2002, the Autumn or Fall Equinox would be in the same position. The planetary attributions of the Tarot trumps, combined with the orientation of the faces of the monument, confirm that 23rd September 2002 was the date in question. Trump 14, Temperance (Alchemy), correlates to the direction of Galactic Centre, while Trump 21, The World, correlates to the opposing Galactic edge.

Fulcanelli implies that the cross at Hendaye signifies a *"fatal period"* of a *"double catastrophe"*. If autumn equinox 2002 is the mid-point of a twenty-year period (the XX engraving implies this), this may imply the last katun of the 13-baktun cycle, since this is the nearest Autumn Equinox to the katun mid-point (12th February 2003, Long Count date: 12.19.10.0.0.). [48] The authors were stunned to discover that Paul LaViolette has been warning the world of just such a double catastrophe, in the form of the galactic core

*Fig.8.18: The Latin inscription means "Hail, O Cross, the Only Hope", but also conceals anagrams. From The Mysteries of the Great Cross of Hendaye by Weidner and Bridges [2003], used by permission. Photo (C) Darlene, 2004.*

explosion, which he already tentatively linked to the 2012 end-point. The first effects would be *"electromagnetic shifts... crustal torque, pole shifts, tidal waves and high winds"*. The second catastrophe would be *"an explosion of the Sun's corona caused by the influx of cosmic dust pushed by the galactic superwave"*. [49]

Fulcanelli also said that the inscription *"ocruxaves pesunica"* revealed a place of refuge. By clues from Fulcanelli, the authors arrived at two anagrams: *Inca cave, Cusco, Peru* and *Hail to the Cross at Urcos*. The authors were again amazed to find not only caves at Cusco (Cuzco), but also a nearby town called Urcos with a cross. Sadly, the original cross had been destroyed, but they concluded that the place of refuge may be either the caves at Cuzco, or the legendary tunnels under the Andes, if someone finds an entrance.

The authors suggest that we should learn to *"weave [our] Bardo or transitional body into nicely fractal flows of self-awareness"* [50] simply by meditating on compassion, as suggested by the work of Itzhak Bentov. [51] We shall thus be ready to be *"harvested"*, to become a soul inhabiting a star, like the pharaohs of Egypt. [52] *The Paris Papyrus* (an Egyptian magical text discovered following Napoleon's conquest of Egypt) gives some clues that the transformational process may be triggered by the light from the glow of the exploding galactic centre, triggering a cerebro-chemical outpouring, which fuels an internal light that externalises as *"the shining light or star body of imperishable quality"*. [53]

## Descent of the New Jerusalem Cube

*A Monument to the End of Time* concludes that the Cross at Hendaye encodes information on the formation of a *"cube of space"* over the twenty-year period between 1992/93 and 2012. This cube is formed by the alignment of three axes, which are the ecliptic axis, the galactic axis and the *"planetary equinox axis"*. On each equinox, an Earth cube is formed:

*"As the equinoxes precess backward against the fixed stars, the Earth cube slowly rotates. The fixed locations of the Cube of Space form a space/time constant with which the Earth cube comes into alignment once every 13,000 or so years"*. [54]

The mid-point in the alignment of these cubes, when they are perfectly coordinated, was on the autumnal equinox of 2002. The twenty-year period ending on Winter Solstice 2012 is the "*eschatological moment when the New Jerusalem descends to Earth*", [55] as described in the *Book of Revelation* (which does describe it as a cube, but with sides of 12,000 stadia or 1,500 miles, [56] though 12,000 is probably symbolic). The process must be aided by a ceremony every equinox, in which the kabbalistic Tree of Life is "projected onto *the Celestial Sphere*", [57] a technique developed by the Hermetic Order of the Golden Dawn during the late 1800s. The method is combined with the Enochian magical system devised by Sir John Dee in Elizabethan times. Both of these have geometrical connections to these nesting cubes, described as the "*Gnosis Gnomon*", like the throne of Osiris. The results of a failure would be "*dire*":

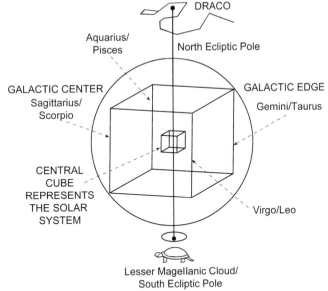

Fig.8.19: The alignment of the Cubes of Space - the solar cube is inside the large galactic cube. From The Mysteries of the Great Cross of Hendaye by Weidner and Bridges [2003], used by permission. Illustration (C) Darlene, 2004.

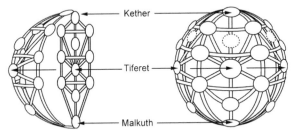

Fig.8.20: Projecting the Tree of Life onto a sphere, with Kether corresponding to the North Pole. From The Mysteries of the Great Cross of Hendaye by Weidner and Bridges [2003], used by permission. Illustration (C) Darlene, 2004.

"*The New Jerusalem Cube is the switch box, and, to follow the analogy, if it is wired wrong or not at all, then it explodes when the juice is turned on. The current is already running, and the sparks are popping all over the planet*". [58]

Success would mean:

"*New Jerusalem then becomes the unitary model which allows the Earth cube and the solar hyper-cube to nest within the higher dimensional flow coming from galactic central. It would mediate the centropic to entropic collapse of light into matter by stabilizing the oscillation between 3 and 4-D, in other words, a virtually eternal reality constructed from mind mirroring matter with its own light. It will connect celestial & terrestrial grids allowing 4-D existence."* [59]

The *"Enochian transformer cube"* had to be resonant by 2002, when it would start crystallising. If not, it would start to fragment over the ten years to 2012.

On 23rd September 2002 in Cairo at 5.30 AM, Nicki Scully and those on her Shamanic Tour of Egypt performed the Raising of the Djed ceremony in front of the Sphinx in Egypt, thus effectively starting the cube crystallisation process. The *Diagnosis 2012* website had been an important catalyst in bringing about this event, with an essay contributed by astro-mythologist Rush Allen, which commented on the website coverage of *A Monument to the End of Time*, inspiring Weidner and Bridges to write an article [60] that culminated in the ceremony at Giza. My friend Ian Crane was independently on the Giza plateau at that time and said, *"... the alignment of Sirius, Orion and the full Moon was absolutely spectacular, with Orion's belt aligned directly over the pyramids at dawn. I have never before experienced quite such a vivid enactment of 'As above, so below'."* [61]

Fig.8.21: Osiris as the Orion constellation, carved on the pyramidion (capstone) of the pyramid of Amenhemet III in the Cairo Museum.

## Signs in the Sky

Adrian Gilbert's book *Signs in the Sky* [62] explores biblical prophecy and traces Christian origins to Egypt, to try and find an answer to the question of what exactly the prophesied *"signs in the sky"* preceding the end of the age will be. Gilbert has been influenced by de Santillana and von Dechend's epic work on mythology, *Hamlet's Mill*, which finds most mythology to be cosmologically or astronomically based. In support of Paul White's statement above, Gilbert does conclude that Giza is a *"map of time"*, and that *"this position of Orion's Belt could therefore symbolize the idea of the returning phoenix at the end of one age and the beginning of another"*. [63]

Building on his discoveries in *The Orion Mystery*, Gilbert has discovered that the Orion cult has spread into Turkestan, with the Sabian *"star-worshippers"* and the Sarmoung brotherhood, of which the spiritual teacher Gurdjieff was a member. Many biblical stories contain coded astronomical and astrological messages revealing connections to Egyptian beliefs, which came out of Egypt with Moses, says Gilbert.

We know about the alignment of the Winter Solstice Sun with Galactic Equator, between Sagittarius and Scorpio, which John Major Jenkins has identified as the 2012 end-point of the 13-baktun cycle of the Maya. This is caused by the approximate 26,000-year precession of the equinoxes, except that the Maya were measuring *"precession of the* solstices", which is the same cycle, but measured from a different point - the precession of the Winter Solstice, as opposed to the Vernal (Spring) Equinox. What Gilbert seems to have discovered is an Egyptian knowledge of the precession of the Summer Solstice, and the consequent encoding of this knowledge in the Bible. The Vernal Equinox, as we know, is precessing from Pisces to Aquarius, at the same time as the Winter Solstice precesses from Sagittarius to Scorpio, but at the same time, the Summer Solstice precesses from Gemini to Taurus.

To recap on part of Chapter 3; the ancient Greeks, who received much of their knowledge from Egypt, believed that souls reside in the Milky Way between incarnations, and that there are two 'gates' on the Milky Way. These are the Silver Gate of Gemini, through which souls descend to Earth, and the Golden Gate of Sagittarius, through which souls ascend. Other versions say

*Fig.8.22: Osiris holding the ankh, or key to the star, or door. After Robin Cook in Bauval and Gilbert [1994, 1995].*

the souls of men can ascend by either gate, but that the Silver Gate leads to reincarnation and the ancestors, and the Golden Gate leads beyond reincarnation. The Golden Gate is also that through which the Gods descend.

The Silver Gate is just above the 'hand' of Orion, who the Egyptians associated with Osiris, and they depicted him holding a star in his hand. In *The Orion Mystery*, Bauval and Gilbert presumed this to be the star Aldebaran. Now, Gilbert has found that the Egyptian word for star, *s'ba*, also means 'door', so Osiris is holding a star-gate. In some depictions, Osiris is holding an ankh towards the gate, so this must be the key that unlocks the star-gate.

After studying bible prophecies, visiting Israel and computing star and planet positions on his *SkyGlobe* software, Gilbert came to the conclusion that the astronomy of Summer Solstice 2000 [64] represents the beginning of the Apocalypse, when the Silver Star Gate opens. This is the "*Omega position*" of Orion, rather than 2380 AD, when "*the Belt of Orion will reach its most northerly position*". [65] It is the end of a 13,000-year cycle that Gilbert calls the *Age of Adam*, or the *Age of Orion*. [66]

In August 2012, says Gilbert, Venus (symbolizing Isis and Mary as "*Bride of Heaven*") will be "*stationary in the hand of Orion*". He is talking here about the infamous retrograde loop of Venus mentioned by Appleby. Orion, as he has explained convincingly in the book, symbolizes Christ, and this is his mystic marriage (there is a hint that we should be prepared with our "*wedding garment*", which to the Egyptians was a "*stellar, Sahu body*" that needed to be "*crystallized*"). [67] This could also be the return of Quetzalcoatl, since he was connected with Venus, and thereby the sign preceding a "*second coming*".

Gilbert's interpretation of biblical prophecy, using the fig tree parable (see Chapter 5), and the return of the Jews to Israel in 1948, indicates that all prophecies would be accomplished by 2018. This also happens to be, according to John Major Jenkins, the year that the Winter Solstice Sun will definitely clear the Galactic Equator, having spent 36 years crossing it in the other Star-Gate. [68] But as we have already seen in Chapter 5, if we take the UN resolution that created the State of Israel in 1947, the fig tree parable indicates 2016 as the accomplishment of the prophecies, and this is the last year of galactic alignment, if 1998 is taken as the exact halfway point in the process. Gilbert calls the Silver Gate the Gate of Hades, which suggests that there may be a few *"Years of Hell"* coming up, before the opening of *"Heaven's Gate"*! There are some remarkable parallels here to the work of Weidner and Bridges, with a twelve-year countdown from Summer Solstice 2000 to 2012, as opposed to a ten-year countdown from Autumn Equinox 2002 to 2012. Both approaches involved a ceremony at the Great Pyramid; both ceremonies connect to the start of the Descent of the New Jerusalem [69] of the *Book of Revelation*, and both mention the necessity to prepare our *Bardo* body (as in the Tibetan system) or *Sahu* body (as in the Egyptian system) for 2012. One thing that Gilbert missed is that just above the hand of Orion is situated the Galactic Anti-centre, as we saw at the end of Chapter 7.

*Fig.8.23: The path of Venus during its retrograde loop in 9792 BC, according to Geryl and Rattinckx, is actually the loop that occurred in 9696 BC, according to SkyGlobe. Shown on CyberSky software - http://cybersky.com*

## The Orion Prophecy

In November 2001, Belgian authors Patrick Geryl and Gino Ratinckx published a book that follows on from Gilbert and Cotterell's *The Mayan Prophecies*, and has also been influenced by Gilbert and Bauval's *The Orion Mystery* - hence the title: *The Orion Prophecy*. [70] Like *The Mayan Prophecies*, Geryl and Ratinckx say that a sunspot megacycle is due in 2012 and will cause a global catastrophe. They say they have found evidence in the *Egyptian Book of the Dead* that in 9792 BC a very similar catastrophe occurred (resulting in the sinking of Atlantis), and that an astronomical sign of the imminent return of the catastrophe is a retrograde loop of Venus that happens above Orion and near Gemini.

However, I checked and re-checked the authors' claims using astronomical software, and they just don't add up. There are twelve retrograde loops of Venus that occur over Orion, between 1924 and 2012 (see colour pages), and of these, the best match to the 9792 BC position shown by Geryl and Ratinckx (in which Venus slows and changes its apparent reverse direction to resume forward motion above the hand of Orion), happened in 1940. You can check them on the shareware program *SkyGlobe*. I wrote a detailed review of the book and posted it online at *Diagnosis 2012*, [71] but the authors failed to address the points raised.

Not many astro-software programs go back as far as 9792 BC, but *SkyGlobe* does the job nicely. I had not tried *SkyGlobe* when I wrote the review, but now that I have checked on it I have found that the shape and position of the 2012 loop agrees with the one shown by Geryl and Ratinckx, but the 9792 BC loop differs considerably. The loop

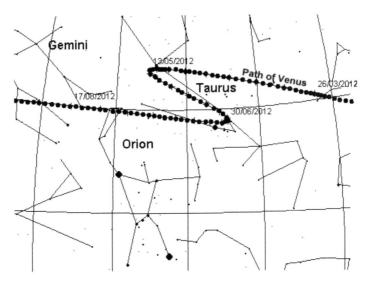

*Fig.8.24: The path of Venus during its retrograde loop in 2012 AD is actually a perfect match for a loop that occurred in 9389 BC, according to SkyGlobe. Shown on CyberSky software - http://cybersky.com*

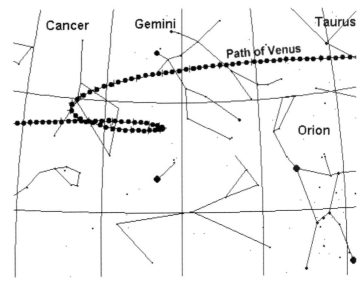

*Fig.8.25: The actual Venus loop pattern in 9792 BC, according to SkyGlobe, which has an exact match in 1609 AD. Shown on CyberSky software - http://cybersky.com*

they show for 9792 BC looks most like the one that *SkyGlobe* shows for 9696 BC, 96 years later. This just adds to a long list of problems with their theory. In fact, the Venus retrograde loop of 9792 BC, as shown on *SkyGlobe*, has an exact match in the year 1609 AD. After much searching with the software, I found that the exact match for the 2012 loop actually happened in 9389 BC. [72]

We are told by the authors that if a star-map featuring Orion is laid onto a map of the Giza pyramids, with the belt stars aligned to the three Giza pyramids, then other stars align to other pyramids. [73] In particular, they suggest that Aldebaran, in the star group called the Hyades (in the Taurus constellation) would overlay the pyramid of Amenhemet III at Hawara. Since astronomers call the Hyades *The Labyrinth*, this could indicate the location of the long-lost massive astronomical building also called The Labyrinth! They were convinced that it needed to be found urgently since it contained knowledge of the events that led to the Atlantean flood.

This was quite easy to check on, using the map in Mark Lehner's book *The Complete Pyramids*, and I expected a slight error. However, when I aligned the belt of Orion to the Giza pyramids, I found that while Hawara lies about 15 miles in a south-south easterly direction from Giza, Aldebaran overlaid an area just over a mile to the south-west of Giza! This is a massive error. However, although *The Orion Prophecy* is seriously faulted, it did bring up some interesting points.

At the start of the book, Geryl was about to look for an answer in the zodiacs of

*Fig.8.26: When the celestial belt of Orion is lined up with the terrestrial one at Giza, Egypt, the celestial labyrinth is nowhere near the terrestrial one! Adapted from a map in Lehner [1997].*

Dendera Temple in Egypt. The rectangular zodiac particularly interested him, since he thought it contained coded information about the catastrophe that ended Atlantis, and how to calculate when the cycle would recur. It was at this point that Ratinckx showed him a rare copy of Frenchman Albert Slosman's translation of the *Egyptian Book of the Dead* (*Le Livre de l'Au-dela de la Vie*) and Geryl was so amazed by what he read that he forgot all about the Dendera Zodiac. This is a shame, since David Pratt has published information on the Dendera Zodiac (see his *Poleshifts: Theosophy and Science Contrasted* webpages [74]) that finds evidence of three previous world catastrophes encoded (just as Slosman had discovered by decoding the *Egyptian Book of the Dead*). As we have seen, John Lash also found 2012 encoded in the round Zodiac of Dendera. Pratt also quotes S. A. Mackey as saying that the design of the Labyrinth showed three pole shifts. A full, detailed review of *The Orion Prophecy* can be found at www.diagnosis2012.co.uk/orp.htm

# Chapter 9:
# The Geomagnetic Field

## Magnetic Field Reversal

Geologist Gregg Braden has pointed out that Earth's magnetic field has dropped 38% in the last 2,000 years (equivalent to an average of 1.9% per century), and that the rate of decline has risen to an average of 6% over the last 100 years. [1] In other words, the global magnetic field is dropping at an accelerating rate towards a "*Zero Point*" at which the polarity of Earth will reverse. [2] Geological surveys of the mid-Atlantic ridge show that this has happened many times before in the history of the Earth. Braden says that the declining magnetic field is causing the *Schumann Resonance* of the ionosphere to increase, and that it is currently resonating at between 8.6 - 9 Hz (at the time that he wrote the book which was first published in 1993), and will level out at 13 Hz - the next number in the *Fibbonacci* series. [3] The whole process is connected to the Maya calendar, says Braden, the largest increase being recorded in 1987, which is when the Harmonic Convergence occurred. He says the last polar reversal was 13,200 years ago - close to half a precession cycle. [4]

In order to adapt, we must allow our bodies to alter their resonant frequency to match that of the Earth. The process of adaptation is blocked by negative emotion, so we must

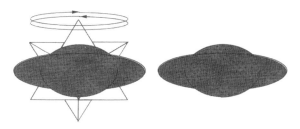

*Fig.9.1: The Mer-Ka-Ba, with counter-rotating tetrahedrons, appears as a UFO according to Gregg Braden. From Braden [1993-1997].*

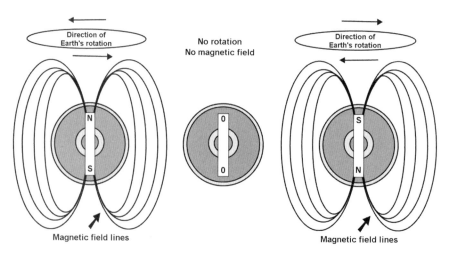

No rotation
No magnetic field

*Fig.9.2: According to Braden, the Earth's rotation slows until it stops, when the geomagnetic field drops to zero. Then the rotation starts in the opposite direction, with a reversed geomagnetic field. Adapted from Braden [1993-1997]*

become compassionate and generate unconditional love, says Braden. Shortly before *Earth Shift*, or *Zero-Point*, some people may achieve resonance in advance of the mass of humanity, and their "*Mer-Ka-Ba fields*" - counter-posed tetrahedronal fields - will counter-rotate and merge to form a saucer-shaped "*light body*", carrying those people into the Fourth Dimension. [5] This is *The Rapture*, according to Braden. He also claims [6] that many sacred sites were designed for initiation, including the Great Pyramid, and are places with a low magnetic field, allowing an easier alteration of frequency, so we should visit them. [7]

*Fig.9.3: In some accounts, the astral body is connected by a cord from its head to the physical body's head. Adapted from W. G. Watts in Muldoon and Carrington [1929].*

Some information originating in a completely different field may help illuminate the low magnetic field-spiritual body connection. Bob Monroe, a pioneer of techniques to induce out-of-body experiences (OOBEs), states that when an OOBE is occurring, the body's polarity or electromagnetic field reverses itself. This polarity reversal has been witnessed by consciousness-researcher Michael Hutchison [8] while observing experiments at the Monroe Institute in Virginia, USA, and this begs the question, "*If the Earth's magnetic field reverses, would this trigger the mass of humanity to have an out-of-body-type experience?*"

## One-Baktun Geo-Dynamo

In 1996 it was discovered that the Earth's core revolves faster than the crust. According to the *Outline of Historical Geology*, an online publication by bio-geologist Ellin Beltz:

"*The speed of the core's independent spin is between 0.4 and 1.8 degrees a year, which works out to a full lap, relative to a fixed point on the surface, about every 400 years. The leading suggestion for the cause of the independent motion is an interaction between magnetic fields generated by fluids moving in the Earth's outer core, which is molten iron, and the inner, [which is] solid crystal. The implications of differential rotation between the core and the surface are hot topics at professional meetings and in various physical and geophysical journals. The iron crystal in the core is longer from north to south, but it does not exactly match Earth's poles. As a result of the core's orientation and rotation, 'magnetic north' moves over time. The physical pole of the planet also wobbles over time, a process called 'precession of the equinoxes.'*" [9]

The length of a baktun (of which thirteen make up the cycle that terminates in 2012) is 144,000 days, which is 400 tuns (or 360-day "years") - about 394 tropical years. Could there be a connection to the 400-year core rotation period? Several sources, including Gregg Braden, have suggested that the end-point of the Maya may be connected with an imminent magnetic pole shift; Ellin Beltz says that the 400-year differential rotation of the core causes the magnetic poles to wander (polar wander is now known to be accelerating). Other sources have connected it to geomagnetic reversal, and some scientists have started saying we are due for geomagnetic reversal soon!

## Imminent Reversal

On 17th April 2002, *Telegraph.co.uk* (website of Telegraph Group Limited, who publish the *Daily Telegraph* newspaper) reported that the previous week a paper had been published in the scientific journal *Nature*, concerning new discoveries about the Earth's magnetic field:

"*Dr Gauthier Hulot of the Institut de Physique du Globe de Paris and colleagues at the Danish Space Research Institute in Copenhagen used magnetic field measurements taken by the Danish Oersted satellites and compared them with similar readings made in 1980 by the American Magsat satellite... The results, published in Nature, confirmed that the Earth's magnetic field is getting weaker. If it continues to weaken at its current rate, the dipole field will have vanished in 2,000 years. But Dr Hulot and his team also found a large area of 'reversed magnetic flux' - where the magnetic field runs counter to the rest of the world's field - below South Africa and the Southern Ocean. Normally, lines of field move from the south to the north. But in this 'reversed flux' area, the magnetic field lines loop backwards and head south. Under this area, the columns of moving liquid iron in the core may be rotating a little differently than they are in the rest of the core, locally weakening and reversing the magnetic field.*" [10]

The same article points out that computer simulations of the magnetic field performed in the mid-1990s [11] had already predicted not only that a magnetic field reversal would be preceded by a decrease in magnetic field intensity, but also that areas of reversed magnetic flux would appear prior to reversal.

In November 2002, the online version of the newspaper *The Observer*, reporting on Dr Hulot's results, added that;

*"...the magnetic field seems to be disappearing most alarmingly near the poles, a clear sign that a flip may soon take place... Using satellite measurements of field variations over the past twenty years, Hulot plotted the currents of molten iron that generate Earth's magnetism deep underground, and spotted huge whorls near the poles... Hulot believes these vortices rotate in a direction that reinforces a reverse magnetic field, and as they grow and proliferate, these eddies will weaken the dominant field: the first steps toward a new polarity, he says."* [12]

The article also points out that although ancient lava beds show that some reversals lasted thousands of years, some researchers say *"some flips may have lasted only a few weeks."* [13]

The Canadian government funds a research group called *Geolab*, which tracks the movement of Earth's north magnetic pole. Previous measurements showed that between 1831 and 1904 it did not move much, but during the 70 years after that, it started a slow movement northward. Then it started to accelerate so that in March 2003 the BBC reported that Dr Larry Newitt of Geolab said it is currently moving four times faster than it was during the 70-year wander. In the same report, David Kerridge of the British Geological Survey, when asked about the geomagnetic field, is quoted as saying that *"there is strong evidence that the field is decreasing by about 5% per century"*. [14]

So here we have some strong confirmation that Gregg Braden's prediction of a geomagnetic reversal is quite likely to happen; the articles above confirm many of his points, including the fact that the Earth's magnetic field has been declining for the last 2,000 years.

## A 100,000-Year Cycle

We have already mentioned ice cores in the section on Paul LaViolette's galactic superwave. The first ice cores were taken from Camp Century, Greenland, and Byrd Station, Antarctica, in the early 1960s. LaViolette undertook the first ice core study to look for cosmic dust levels in 1981 and 1982, using the Greenland sample. The results were supported by a later beryllium-10 study of the Greenland cores, and of the later Vostok (Antarctica) cores, and LaViolette interprets the resulting graphs as indicating a 26,000-year period between cosmic ray and cosmic dust peaks, with an occasional "*13,000 year half-cycle recurrence interval*". [15]

In 1999, a paper on the Vostok ice-cores was published in *Nature*, [16] showing graphs of temperature levels, methane levels, carbon dioxide levels, marine oxygen isotope levels and solar output levels. They all show an approximate 100,000-year cycle with a high degree of correlation. Thus, each of these 100,000-year cycles would equate to about

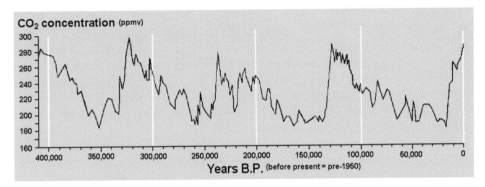

Fig.9.4: *Carbon dioxide concentration over the last 410,000 years as recorded in the Vostok ice core. Adapted from Petit, Jouzel, et al [1999].*

Fig.9.5: *Temperature change over the last 410,000 years as recorded in the Vostok ice core. Adapted from Petit, Jouzal, et al [1999].*

four 26,000-year precession cycles.

In the journal *Science* (29th March 2002), the AIST (National Institute of Advanced Industrial Science and Technology) announced a discovery of a 100,000-year cycle in the Earth's magnetic field:

*"Using a high-sensitivity magnetometer to measure remnant magnetization of marine sediments, we obtained a continuous record of variations in strength and inclination of magnetic field that have occurred in the past 2.3 million years. Frequency analysis of this record has led to the discovery of a long-term periodic component of 100,000 years... The 100,000-year period of variation corresponds with variation in the eccentricity of Earth's orbit and the period of the glacial/interglacial cycles. Therefore, magnetic field changes must be understood within the context of variations in the Earth system."* [17]

Then, two months later, on 6th June 2002, in a paper called *Variations in Solar Magnetic Activity During the Last 200,000 Years: Is there a Sun-Climate Connection?* by Mukul Sharma, Assistant Professor of Earth Sciences at Dartmouth College, it was announced [18] that he had just discovered a 100,000-year solar activity cycle. He apparently did a combined study of the ice core results and the marine sediment results mentioned above, and concluded that the solar magnetic field had a 100,000-year cycle linked to Earth's cooling and warming cycles - the ice ages.

This has led to renewed discussion of the controversial Milankovitch theory, which was postulated in the 1940s and suggested that:

*"... the cyclical variations in the Earth's orbit around the Sun result in the Earth receiving varying amounts of solar radiation that, in turn, control the climate. This explanation is under dispute because the variations of the solar energy in relation to the changes in orbit are very small"*. [19]

However, the fact that it was already known that the Earth has a 100,000-year cycle of eccentricity (deviation from a circular orbit) means that these recent findings are probably more than coincidence!

# Chapter 10:
# Ice Cycles

## The Celestial Ice Clock

A book by Dr William A. Gaspar, *The Celestial Clock*, [1] claims that the 5,125-year 13-baktun cycle is exactly one eighth of a 41,000-year cycle of conjunctions of Neptune and Pluto - a period which is also the sum of a 23,000-year *"truncated precession cycle"*, and an 18,000-year *"solar magnetic reversal"* cycle.

The 23,000-year period is a *"dominant ice volume collapse cycle"*, and every 11,500 and 23,000 years, there is a major polar axis shift, causing severe earthquakes and flooding, according to the Gaspar Theory. The Earth goes through warming and cooling cycles, which are a result of increased heat and carbon dioxide, but independent

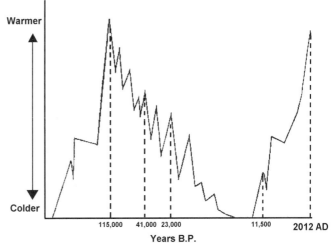

Fig.10.1: Gaspar's take on the Milankovitch cycle was summed up in this distorted graph. After Joan Hultman in Gaspar [1999].

from mankind, says Gaspar. The *"black hole"* at the centre of the galaxy exerts a cyclic gravitational pull every 23,000 years, when *"the North Pole Axis aligns with the centre of the Milky Way galaxy"*, [2] resulting in friction between the magma and Earth's crust, which produces heat and melts the ice-caps. This can also happen at the half-period of 11,500 years, when the axis *"may be shifted back into position at every 11,500 years at its 'half cycle' alignment"*. [3]

Dr Gaspar is a medical doctor, and has taken on a very difficult job here, trying to unify the complex cycles of the Milankovitch theory with the 18,000-year solar reversal cycle of the Sun's *warped neutral sheet*, as calculated by Maurice Cotterell, plus astrological cycles, Peter Noone's ice theory that predicted an ice age following the 5/5/2000 *"planetary alignment"*, and the catastrophe theory of Allan and Delair. He also brought in John Major Jenkins' essential interpretation of Maya myth and calendrics in the theory of galactic alignment.

In Allan and Delair's book *When The Earth Nearly Died*, [4] a scholarly attempt was made to date Noah's flood and find a plausible agent that may have caused it. The massive amount of geological evidence that they supplied leads to the conclusion that the flood occurred 11,500 years ago. [5] Gaspar's theory is quite hard to follow, but he certainly raises some interesting points. It is remarkable, though, that he doesn't mention directly that the 41,000-year cycle is also the period known as the variation of the obliquity of the ecliptic, or the variation of axis tilt cycle.

## Milankovitch Cycle

There are several websites that give a clear summary of the Milankovitch theory, which lies at the base of Gaspar's book, and on them you will find described a minimum of three long-term cycles that affect the climate. There is a good but simple explanation called *Milankovitch Cycles* and *Glaciation*, which describes a 100,000-year "*eccentricity*" cycle, a 41,000-year "*axis tilt*" cycle, and a 23,000-year precession cycle (precession is usually said to be 25-26,000 years - we shall return to this point). Since most of Earth's landmasses are in the northern hemisphere, the combined effects of the three varying cycles can trigger glaciation:

"*At times when northern hemisphere summers are coolest (farthest from the Sun due to precession and greatest orbital eccentricity) and winters are warmest (minimum tilt), snow can accumulate on and cover broad areas of northern America and Europe.*" [6]

However, "*at present, only precession is in the glacial mode, with tilt and eccentricity not favourable to glaciation*". [7]

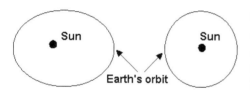

*Fig.10.2: The Earth's 96,000-100,000-year cycle of eccentricity.*

On the NOAA Palaeoclimatology Program site [8] (NOAA - National Oceanic and Atmospheric Administration of USA), there is a similar explanation, except that precession is given as 22,000 years! A more thorough explanation is given on the *US Naval Observatory* site, [9] and mentions the three cycles above, plus a one-year cycle and a 21,000-year cycle. The basic

climate cycle is, of course, the yearly cycle of the seasons. This is caused by the 23.4 - 23.5° tilt of the Earth's axis, and on one day each year, the northern hemisphere is at its coldest, when tilted away from the Sun. This is on the Winter Solstice. The Earth's orbit varies in eccentricity every 21,000 years, and it just so happens that perihelion (closest orbital point to the Sun) is currently very close to Winter Solstice. "*It turns out that the proximity of the two dates is a coincidence of the particular century we live in*". [10] (The 100,000-year cycle modifies the 21,000-year one).

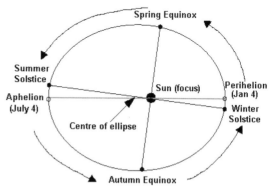

*Fig.10.3: The Earth's variation of eccentricity cycle. The elliptical orbit rotates in a counter-clockwise direction once every 21,000 years.*

The 22,000 or 23,000-year precession cycle used in the Milankovitch theory results from the combination of the 26,000-year precession of the equinoxes, in which the axis of the Earth rotates in a clockwise direction (if viewed from above the North Pole), and the 21,000-year variation of eccentricity cycle, in which the Earth's elliptical orbital path around the Sun itself rotates in a counter-clockwise direction. Thus, the combined cycles mean that the proximity of the Earth's North Pole to the Sun goes through one cycle every 22,000 - 23,000 years. [11] Gaspar speculates that the precession cycle is truncated due to sudden axis shifts, related to the changing magnetic field of the Sun. His graph of global warming shows a peak 115,000 years

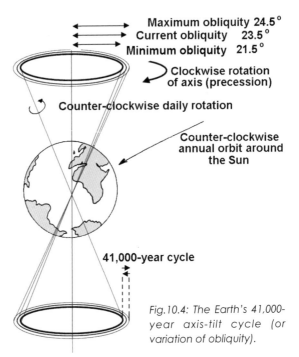

Fig.10.4: The Earth's 41,000-year axis-tilt cycle (or variation of obliquity).

ago, which is made up of 5 x 23,000-year cycles. The 41,000-year variation of obliquity (tilt) cycle is also clearly visible, and is comprised of a 23,000-year cycle, plus an 18,000-year cycle, according to the Gaspar Theory (however, this 18,000-year cycle is the one proposed by Maurice Cotterell in *The Mayan Prophecies*, and we have seen that this

theory is faulted). At the peak of warming, the ice caps melt, causing flooding and constant rain, which washes the carbon dioxide out of the atmosphere into the sea, leading to *sudden* cooling and glaciation. We are currently at a warming peak of the same magnitude as that of 115,000 years ago, preceding the onset of the last ice age, and the 41,000-year cycle, which is clearly visible in ice core studies, is exactly divisible by the 5,125-year 13-baktun cycle that ends in 2012.

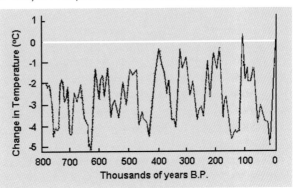

Fig.10.5: Data from Greenland/Antarctica ice cores, ocean, lake and bog sediments and tree-rings is combined in this graph, the last section of which is the basis for Gaspar's distorted rendition (Fig.10.1). After UWDAS (University of Washington Department of Atmospheric Sciences).

Gaspar's key graph that connects 2012 to the ice theory (see Fig. 10.1) differs from those taken from the results of the Vostok ice core studies (see Fig. 9.4 and 9.5), which he also reproduces in his book, and it is also distorted, with the dated peaks at disproportionate distances to each other. The source from which Gaspar generated his key graph is shown in *The Celestial Clock* on page 36 of his book (see Fig. 10.5). After a search, I found the origin of the graph on the website of the University of Washington's Department of Atmospheric Sciences. [12] The webpage explains that the graph was generated using a combination of palaeoclimatic data from Greenland and Vostok (Antarctica) ice cores, plus ocean sediment cores, cross-referenced with insects and pollen found in lake sediments and bogs, and tree-ring data. It shows the 100,000-year warming cycle even clearer than the Vostok ice-core graphs.

For the 'icing' on the Gaspar cake, there is a paper by E. C. Njau of the University of Tanzania, which studies global warming and Milankovitch cycles, and predicts an imminent climate change between 1997 and 2012! [13]

# Chapter 11:
# 0.0.0.0.0

## Flood at 3113 BC

Egyptologist David Rohl has ruffled a few feathers in the Egyptological and archaeological communities with his revised chronology of Egyptian, Old Testament and Mesopotamian timelines. Rohl is currently completing a doctoral thesis at University College, London, and is Britain's most high-profile Egyptologist, following his 1995 documentary TV series *Pharaohs and Kings: A Biblical Quest*, and his two books *A Test of Time* and *Legend*.

In an article called *Mountain of the Ark*, [1] published in *The Express* newspaper in 1999, Rohl re-examines the evidence for the biblical flood. The flood story originated in a Sumerian legend called *The Epic of Gilgamesh*, in which the original Noah was called *Utnapishtim*. Rohl shows that the eleven-feet-deep layer of silt found at Ur (where Abraham originated, probably bringing the legend with him) by Sir Leonard Wooley between 1928 and 1934, can not only be dated to around 3100 BC, but he also reasons why later conclusions were wrong, since other, later-dated silt deposits were found to be only localised floods.

Then he supplies some evidence that the biblical dating was also faulty, and that when rectified it supports his new archaeological date for the flood:

*"The Greek and Aramaic versions of the Old Testament (both of which are older than the earliest surviving Hebrew copy of the Bible) suggest that the Flood took place up to eight hundred years prior to the date calculable from the Massoretic (Hebrew)text (c. 2300 BC)*

*from which the Latin and English translations of the Old Testament derive. A date of around 3100 BC is therefore quite possible if we take into consideration these earlier sources. It is also reassuring to note that the Mayan tradition places the Great Flood in Mesoamerica at precisely 3113 BC, according to their recently deciphered calendar". [2]*

Thus we have evidence that the Sumerian (biblical) flood was contemporary with the start of the 13-baktun cycle. Most of the conflicting Mesoamerican accounts that remain regarding previous eras include an era that ended in flood. One of the Aztec versions (the *Leyenda de los Soles*) says that it was the Fourth Sun that ended in flood (we are now in the Fifth Sun). If the five eras of the Aztecs are each 5,200 years in length, as suggested by Gordon Brotherston, [3] and this is a remnant of the original 5,200 tuns (about 5,125 years), then this means that the previous era, which closed in 3114 BC, ended in a flood. However, most of the Mexican accounts, and the Popol vuh of the Maya, indicate that it was the first era that ended in a flood.

## Comet Explosion: 3114 BC

David Furlong, author of *Keys to The Temple*, [4] has pointed out that around 3100 BC, [5] not only did Stonehenge phase one appear, but also the great stone circles of Castlerigg in Cumbria, Stennes Stones in the Orkneys, and Newgrange in Ireland, while the building of long barrows ceased at this time. Dynastic Egypt was also founded at this time, while the Maya, in a third area of the world, dated the beginning of the 13-baktun-cycle of their Long Count calendar from 3114 BC. Geo-climatologists have found a climatic change around this time, called the *Piora Oscillation*, which resulted in a "*sulphate deposit*" in the Greenland ice cores. This implies volcanic eruption or cometary impact, and there is evidence of flooding in Mesopotamia (as Rohl has now pointed out), and also in the Navajo district of America. A rise in sea level also occurred at this time on the coast of Brittany, and at the Dead Sea in Israel, plus there was a sudden drying up of the Sahara area. Furlong then goes on to connect these events to the sinking of Atlantis, bringing the proposed date forward 6,400 years from Plato's 9500 BC to 3100 BC.

On his website *Evidence for Astronomical Aspects of Mankind's Past and Present, and of Recent Climate*, [6] Timo Niroma of Finland has independently observed several anomalies around 3100 BC. There was a methane peak (caused by fires); a cold spell, according to the tree-ring record of ancient bristlecone pines; and the coastal menhirs in Brittany suddenly appeared. Niroma also lists several of the events spotted by Furlong above. Niroma suggests that a "*huge meteorite swarm*", possibly from the "*break-up of a great comet in the inner parts of the solar system*", caused tsunamis and an atmospheric dust blanket. Two small craters have been discovered from this period. Niroma points out that Stonehenge phase 1 was purely astronomical - the later phases included ritual uses (though some of the 56 'Aubrey holes' were re-dug later to receive human cremations). The wave of stone circle building, he says, was to study the celestial phenomena and try to predict repetitions.  He goes on to make the "*outrageous suggestion*" that the meteorites responsible were the Taurids, and, in particular, Comet Encke, which is associated with the Taurids. The path of Encke has been tracked back to an Earth intersection about 5,000 years ago. However, further investigation showed that another comet - Comet Oljato - had a trajectory that was virtually the same as that of Encke about 9,500 years ago, and this seems a more likely candidate than Encke for the 3100 BC episode. The final suggestion is that a comet or asteroid 100 kilometres across disintegrated in 9500 BC, into three main fragments - Oljato, Swift-Tuttle and another. The third fragment is what rained on Earth in 3114 BC.

Support for this connection between the Long Count and comets comes from a book called *Exodus to Arthur - Catastrophic Encounters with Comets,* [7] by Mike Baillie. Baillie is a dendro-chronologist (tree-rings and climate studies), and establishes correlations between tree-ring anomalies and comets, taking into account history and mythology. Comets are repeatedly referred to as flaming serpents and dragons throughout history. Gods and demi-gods such as Lug, Merlin, Phaethon, Typhon, Quetzalcoatl, Michael, Gabriel, and even Jesus, have comet connections. When Baillie asked atmospheric physicist Gerry McCormac what would happen if a comet approached very close to Earth, he replied:

"*If it came within the Earth's magnetosphere it would probably be spectacular... the sky would go purple or green, particles from the comet would spiral down the lines of force, and it is likely that you would have amazing auroral displays and coloured streamers...*" [8]

Baillie replied:

"*Oh... you mean like Quetzalcoatl, the Central American sky serpent with his feather arrangement represented as flames of fire?*" [9]

There is also accumulated evidence that a comet this close would produce an *audible hissing sound!*  Comets can often appear to be brilliant white, and were once known as "bearded stars" - is this why the myth of Quetzalcoatl (like that of Jesus) speaks of a white bearded man who promised to return one day?

The ancient Egyptian *Book of the Celestial Cow* describes the myth of Ra getting angry with his subjects and sending his eye out to punish them, in the form of Hathor/Sekhmet/Amit, which E. P. Grondine on the *Cambridge Conference* site [10] says represents the fragments of comet Encke that fell to Earth in 3114 BC. He also cites the work of Dr Lonnie Thompson's team from Ohio State University, whose recent ice cores from Peru

*Fig.11.1: A comet appearing as a bearded star. From Helvelius, Cometographia (Danzig, 1668).*

and earlier ones from Mount Kilimanjaro in Tanzania show "*a climate collapse circa 3200 BCE, with dating determined by radio carbon dating*". [11]

## The Eyes of Ra and Horus

The myth of the Right Eye of Ra says that in the first universe (world) made by Ra, the people began to plot against him, and he hurled his Divine Eye at them, in the form of the goddess Sekhmet. Murry Hope says that this Eye was a "*bright and burning object*" [12] and may represent a comet or planetissimal that fell to Earth, causing devastation. Ra then departed into the sky and created the current world. The Eye of Ra became the Uraeus snake at the centre of the pharaonic headdresses, and we have already discussed the snake-comet connection. However, there is another myth of Ra that may be connected here. Ra's wife, Nut, offended him by cohabiting with her brother, Geb. Ra then forbade Nut to give birth on any of the 360 days of the year. She appealed to Thoth, Lord of Time, who then played a game of *senet* (an Egyptian board game, similar to draughts) with the Moon and won "*a seventy-second part of her light*". One 72nd part of 360 is five (360/72 = 5), and so Thoth won five days on which Nut gave birth to the five "*epagomenal neters*" - Osiris, Horus the elder, Set, Isis, and Nephthys. Murry Hope says this means that,

Fig.11.2: The pharaonic headdress with the Uraeus snake - the right eye of Ra.

"*... a change in the Earth's orbit involving the Moon, which precipitated a change in the Earth's axis, was responsible for the five extra days we now have in our calendars...*" [13]

Since all five of these epagomenal gods or neters have associations with Sirius, Hope sees Sirius as playing some part in the drama. The presence of a right eye implies the involvement of a left eye, and the left eye was the lunar eye, or Eye of Horus, who, like Ra, was also depicted with the head of a hawk.

The Eye of Horus - the *Oudja* or *Utchat* - was a left, or lunar eye, and represents a *hekat*, which was a unit of volume used for the measurement of grain. It was seen as a measurement of time and volume. It is made up of several components, each of which represents a different fraction; there is a quarter, half, eighth, sixteenth, 32nd, and 64th. When they are all added together, they total 63/64. This is very close to the ratio of the *Pythagoras Comma* of music theory, which is the difference in ratio between octaves and fifths, and amounts to about 1.0136, while 64/63 is about 1.0158. Pythagoras was primarily a

Fig.11.3: *The left eye of Ra, or the eye of Horus and its component fractions of volume and time.*

mystic, and the ratio has been seen to represent the difference between the imperfect mortal state and the perfected immortal state. It is also close to the ratio between solar and lunar years (1.0307), [14] which is the ratio between the lunar left eye and the solar right eye. However, while the Jewish Sadducees kept time by the Sun, and the Pharisees kept a lunar calendar, the Pharisian lunar calendar was not 354 days in length, as in twelve lunar months, but was actually 360 days in length, the same as the tun of the Maya. The ratio between the solar year and a 360-day year (1.0146) is much closer to the Pythagoras Comma and to the Horus Eye ratio - in fact it lies halfway between them.

So, encoded in the myths of the solar and lunar eyes, we have a suggestion of a past astronomical event that *"altered the length of the year"*, and (since our right eye is connected to our left rational hemisphere and our left eye is connected to our right intuitive hemisphere) there was a *"fall"* from an intuitive right-brain state of consciousness to a rational left-brain state. The galactic alignment process signals the activation of the pineal eye (Eye of Horus in a triangle) that lies between the hemispheres and will allow whole-brain consciousness. We shall return to this idea in Part 4.

## Keene on Comets

In 2002, Joel J. Keene published a book called *Cosmic Locusts*, [15] connecting comet impact to 2012, following a series of personal synchronicities. Joel's birth date is, astrologically, on the cusp of Scorpio and Sagittarius, which is the celestial position of Galactic Centre, and even more accurately, the Galactic Equator. When he heard that the 13-baktun cycle of the Maya was designed to terminate when the Winter Solstice Sun converges on this very point, in 2012, and concurrently found that the biblical *Book of Joel* (also his own name) seems to describe Earth's future passage through the tail of a comet, Joel became aware of a clustering of more synchronicities around himself. He started to write it all down in a fictional format, because it was all so incredible, but Keene found that the synchronicities were continuing. For example, he had written of a 2012-convergence of a burst of energy from Galactic Centre, and the return of the shattered remains of a comet, only to find that astro-physicist Paul LaViolette had already said that we are overdue for a burst of energy from Galactic Centre, and tentatively connected it with the end-point of the Maya. Then he found that dendro-chronologist Mike Baillie had discovered evidence that an ancient shattered comet became associated with the mythology of the Birth of Venus (Quetzalcoatl), which is also associated with the start of the 13-baktun cycle. Finally he found that the series of prophecies of the end-times given to the children at Fatima by an apparition of the Virgin Mary

*Fig.11.4: A comet appearing as a sword. From Helvelius, Cometographia (Danzig, 1668).*

spoke of the *"birth of the planet Venus"* being responsible for the forthcoming ascension of mankind, as well as mentioning the flaming sword of St. Michael (sourced from *Fatima Prophecy* by Ray Stanford). The coincidences are still continuing. [16]

# Chapter 12:
# Fringe Science

## Naked Singularity

A 1999 essay called *Awakening to the Omega Point,* [1] by Bob Buck, notes that the planets are losing their magnetic fields; Jupiter's red spot changed its direction of rotation in 1986-87 and the Sun is losing its polarity. In addition, he says that there has been a shifting of the spectrum in the auroras and rainbows, like a red shift, but in the other direction - a kind of violet shift. A powerful magnetic field is the cause, says Buck (the auroras or light displays are caused by the interaction of the solar wind and Earth's magnetic field). Buck describes the unknown magnetic field that we are approaching as the *"naked singularity"*, and says that it will probably upset the *Oort cloud* (a spherical cloud of material including billions of comets, believed by some astronomers to surround the solar system at a distance of one light year), and cause more comets to divert from their usual orbits. He thinks that every 13,000 years Earth goes through one of these naked singularities, which he sees as a merging of dimensions, but also thinks a 23° axis shift of the Earth, back to its position perpendicular to the ecliptic, may be possible. He predicted that the encounter would happen sometime between 2003 and 2012.

In an update, Buck says that due to reading a book called *The New Gravity* by Kenneth G. Salem, he now thinks that the speed of light is accelerating at a rate of 2.8 Angstroms per second, and will do so until it reaches a critical point, when a *"phase change"* will occur, shifting the whole universe to a higher frequency. He quotes from an article by Linda Moulton Howe, telling of a recent discovery that one of the heavier atomic particles - the *muon* - is not behaving the way it has been for the last 30 years. Buck predicts that other, less heavy particles will change next, and so on, until photons and other weightless particles are affected and the phase shift occurs (by 2012), but he says that this will affect the whole universe - not just this solar system.

## Shift of the Ages

David Wilcock's online book *Convergence* has now been re-written as *The Shift of the Ages* [2] (it seems it was originally changed to *Convergence II*), and is an attempt to find the science and philosophy behind the 13-baktun cycle using Cotterell's sunspot theory as a key part of the puzzle. In *Convergence*, Wilcock had concluded that the end-point should be 2039, following Maurice Chatelain's reinterpretation of the Maya Calendar, which was based on the conjunctions of Jupiter and Saturn, but as he explained to me by e-mail, *"now I know that the 2012 date fits in much better, though the Jupiter/Saturn conjunctions are definitely still important."* [3]

   *The Shift of the Ages* covers many subjects, such as Earth changes, Superstring theory, sacred geometry, The Philadelphia Experiment, Bruce Cathie's Earth grids, and Richard Hoagland's planetary geometry observations, and it forms an introduction to the more scientifically-orientated follow-up, *The Science of Oneness* [4] (previously called *Convergence III*). However, these books are not just fringe science, because Wilcock believes himself to be a reincarnation of Edgar Cayce (an American clairvoyant, who died in 1945 and whose photo shows similar facial features to Wilcock), and has been channelling Ra. The Ra material was first channelled by Carla Rueckert and is the source of much of the cosmological information in the books. What makes Wilcock different from most channellers, though, is that he manages to unearth obscure scientific papers that confirm many of the points that were channelled from Ra. But it turns out that Ra also indicated the importance of 2012:

*"Without any reference from either side to the Mayan Calendar, Ra independently stated that the cycle change would come between 2011 and 2013..."* [5]

...and accordingly, Wilcock's website, *Ascension2000.com*, now states its objective is to scientifically prove that *"a dimensional shift is to occur on Earth on or before 2012"*. [6]

   The follow-up book to *The Science of Oneness* leaves channelling behind and is called *The Divine Cosmos*. [7] It is a bold attempt to re-write the current scientific paradigms, using cutting-edge international scientific research findings. However, it is advisable to first read *The Science of Oneness* as an introduction. *The Divine Cosmos* covers subjects including aether theory, zero point energy, the amazing work of several Russian scientists, Earth changes, solar developments and changes on other planets in the solar system, tornados and vortexes, and plasmatic phenomena (a plasma is an electrically-charged gas, or, as the Concise Oxford Dictionary puts it, *"a gas of positive ions and free electrons with an approximately equal positive and negative charge"*).

   In *The Divine Cosmos*, Wilcock claims that he has found the *"'smoking gun' to prove that an energetic transformation process is culminating in December 2012"*, [8] particularly in his Chapter 8, and even more so, the supplement that follows at the end of Part 1. Here, he describes remarkable papers from Russian scientists, which certainly warrant a closer look.

## Solar System Changes

Dr Alexey Dmitriev is a professor of geology and mineralogy, and the chief scientific member of the United Institute of Geology, Geophysics and Mineralogy within the Siberian department of the Russian Academy of Sciences, in Novosibirsk, Siberia.

In a paper entitled *Planetophysical State of the Earth and Life,* [9] Dmitriev discusses recent changes on the Sun, the Earth and the other planets of the solar system. He notes the upward trajectory in the amount of solar activity since the *Maunder minimum* (when sunspots were very scarce) in the late 1600s (see Fig.6.2, page 74), and the increased frequency of X-ray flares. Wilcock extends this information in *The Divine Cosmos*, giving accounts of recent solar storms, X-ray flares that caused power-grid collapses and alteration to Earth's magnetic field, coronal mass ejections and the increasing speed of the solar wind. The records are constantly being broken as the Sun gets ever more active, lending support to the idea that we are approaching the end of a solar megacycle.

Dmitriev also points out the Earth's magnetic anomalies, weakening field and accelerating movement of magnetic poles (discussed above) as evidence that a "*geomagnetic inversion*" is taking place. He mentions the increasing temperature and climate changes that are currently causing concern, and then shows that extreme weather and seismic phenomena such as floods, hurricanes, earthquakes and landslides are also on the increase, having gone collectively up by 410% from 1963 to 1993 (Wilcock

*Fig.12.1: The lower graphed line (NEIC) is generated from the figures gathered in April 1999 by Michael Mandeville when he did a laborious catalogue search on the National Earthquake Information Centre database, searching for global earthquakes of magnitude 2.5+ from 1973 to 1999. The upper line (ANSS) is generated from a similarly laborious search performed by the author in 2004 through the Advanced National Seismic System Catalogue database. The information is more complete and up-to date on the upper graph line, but supports Mandeville's conclusion.*

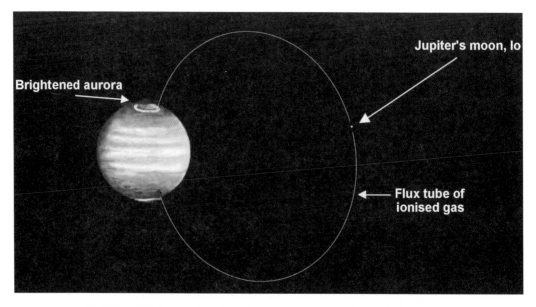

*Fig.12.2: Artist's impression of the flux tube going from Jupiter to its moon Io.*

says the figure is now around 600%). Wilcock again provides back-up information here (sourced from Michael Mandeville), with evidence that volcanic activity has increased by 500% since 1875. However, official sources in Western Europe and USA say that increased reports of earthquakes are explained by advances in seismic detection technology and increased numbers of monitoring stations around the world, while an apparent rise in numbers of volcanic eruptions is due to the population explosion, with more people living near volcanoes and reporting the eruptions via the improving communication network.

The other planets in the solar system are also showing changes, says Dmitriev, including a change in atmosphere, brightening, and the appearance of dark and light spots on Venus, plus "*a sharp decrease of sulphur-containing gases in its atmosphere*" and a sodium (or natrium) atmosphere or "*tail*" forming around the Moon. The atmospheric density of Mars was twice as thick as it should have been, causing damage to NASA's *Mars Surveyor* satellite in 1997. There has also been warming on Mars, causing the melting of the Martian ice caps, plus a "*cloudy growth in the equator area and an unusual growth of ozone concentration*". Jupiter's magnetic field intensity has doubled, and the planet has developed a visible one million amperes flux tube of ionised gases from its magnetic poles to the moon Io. Dmitriev also mentions that Jupiter has had an "*appearance of radiation belt brightening*" and "*large auroral anomalies*", but these are thought to be an aftermath of the collision with comet Shoemaker-Levy-9 in 1994. On Saturn, the brightness has increased, along with the appearance of polar auroras. Uranus and Neptune have both had recent polar shifts, and the magnetosphere of Uranus has made a sudden leap in intensity, while Neptune has had *"a change in light intensity and light spot dynamics"*. Pluto has also had *"a growth of dark spots"* (first photographed by the Hubble Space Telescope in 1994 and released to the public in 1996). In fact, in July 2003 it was announced on the BBC news website [10] that astronomers have been baffled to find that Pluto's atmosphere has thickened over the last fourteen years (deduced by calculating the dimming of background stars as Pluto passes in front of them). Wilcock also adds that a new thin atmosphere on Mercury has recently been observed, [11] and he has also updated the planetary observations (since Dmitriev's essay was written in 1997 and updated in 1998), showing that these changes are an ongoing process. [12]

Dmitriev says that there is one root cause for all these Earth changes, solar changes and changes to the other planets, and they can all be attributed to the fact that the solar system is moving into a new energetic area.

## Magnetized Band of Plasma
The Russians have been studying the *heliosphere* boundary since the 1960s, and have observed that the thickness of the 'shock wave' at the leading edge has increased ten-

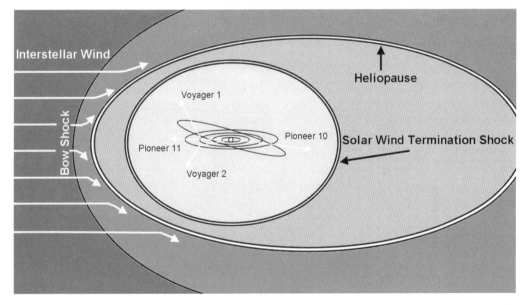

*Fig.12.3: A cross-section of the heliosphere showing US mission trajectories that sent back some of this information. As the solar system moves through interstellar space, the solar wind continues out past all the planets, until it slows to a stop. This boundary is called the* termination shock. *This is comparable to the hull of a ship moving through the sea. The interstellar wind is like the sea, and there is a layer surrounding the termination shock that is comparable to a bow wave. The whole solar system, including termination shock and surrounding shock wave, is called the* heliosphere, *and the edge is called the* heliopause. *The leading edge of the heliosphere is called the* bow shock.

Distance from Sun in AU (astronomical units)    NOT TO SCALE

*Fig.12.4: A close-up of the heliosphere boundary, showing the incoming interstellar plasma build-up (the thickening layer of deflected plasma) and how other particles interact with the boundary.*

*Fig.12.5: The heliosphere travels into the magnetized plasma band.*

fold (1,000%) since then! That is, it has gone from about four Astronomical Units (AU) to about 40 AU. This is because the solar system is moving through a magnetized band of plasma that is sticking to the edge of the heliosphere, *"which has led to a plasma overdraft around the Solar System, and then to its breakthrough into interplanetary domains"*. [13]

It is this plasma, seeping into the solar system, that is causing the alterations, says Dmitriev, and the solar changes are reinforcing the changes on the planets described above. On Earth, there is a build-up of new plasma in the ionosphere (about 60-100 miles above the Earth), affecting our weather processes, and the solar changes are adding to these, causing the geomagnetic reversal. Dmitriev mentions the *"vacuum domains"*, or tornado lights that he has studied [14] (the lights occur in the vacuum at the centre of a tornado, and the term *vacuum domains* also includes phenomena such as ball lightning, poltergeist lights, earthquake lights, and the *elves* and *sprites* in the ionosphere that we shall return to later), and concludes that these vacuum domains are not only on the increase, but they cannot be explained by modern branches of physics. A version of the ether-model (nowadays called zero-point energy) is used to try and understand them:

*"Because these non-homogeneous vacuum domain objects display not-of-this-physical-world characteristics such as 'liquid light' and 'non-Newtonian movement', it is difficult not to describe their manifestations as being 'interworld processes' ... Such disturbances cause and create energy and matter transfer processes between the ether media and our three-dimensional world... Hundreds of thousands of these natural self-luminous formations are exerting an increasing influence upon Earth's geophysic [sic] fields and biosphere. We suggest that the presence of these formations is the mainstream precedent to the transformation of Earth; an Earth which becomes more and more subject to the transitional physical processes which exist*

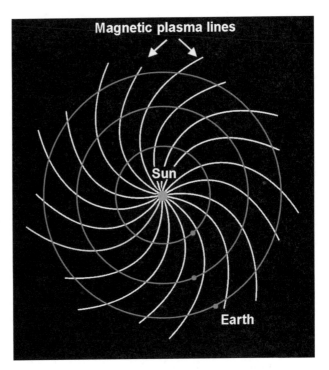

*Fig.12.6: The Parker Spiral - magnetic plasma lines in the solar system.*

*within the borderland between the physical vacuum and our material world."* [15]

In other words, Dmitriev sees the solar system changes as soon culminating in an evolutionary change that involves interaction with something beyond the three-dimensional world.

Wilcock has extended and supplemented the Dmitriev paper, suggesting that the magnetized plasma bands are part of a galactic version of a known solar system structure called the *Parker Spiral* (Fig.12.6, page 135). This is a series of magnetic plasma lines that spiral out from the Sun across the solar system in curved paths, radiating out like a Catherine wheel in slow motion. Wilcock proposes that the area that the solar system is entering is a macroscopic version of this, with the lines radiating from Galactic Centre.

Other scientists have interpreted the solar system changes as the approach of Planet X, [16] or as the effects of the hypernova explosion of the star *Eta Carinae*, [17] but these theories are much less convincing than Dmitriev's one. Wilcock claims that, at the climax in 2012, we are due for a *"matter transmutation"*, and thinks our entry into the plasma beam is through ripples spaced out by *phi*, the *Golden Ratio*. Also known as the *Golden Mean*, or the *Divine Proportion*, phi is defined as the ratio that results if a line is divided into two sections so that the ratio of the smaller segment to the larger segment is the same as the ratio between the larger segment and the whole line. It can be calculated to many decimal places, but is approximately 1.6180339. It is a ratio that appears throughout nature; for example, in the proportions of the human body, animal bodies, plants and DNA. The orbital periods of some of the planets in our solar system are related by phi, and the rings of Saturn are spaced by phi. In the twelfth century, Leonardo Fibonacci discovered a number series related to phi, which starts with a 0 and 1, then continues by adding the two previous numbers to get the next one (0, 1, 1, 2, 3, 5, 8, 13, etc.). The ratio of any two successive numbers in the series

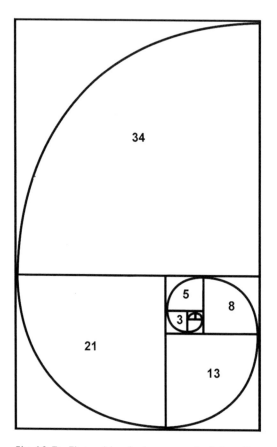

*Fig.12.7: The phi-spiral generated by the Fibonacci series.*

gets nearer to phi, the further along in the series it is. The ratio can be used to generate a spiral, and that phi-spiral is found in places as diverse as pinecones, pineapples, the shell of a Nautilus and the spiral form of a galaxy. The golden ratio also occurs in the musical scale and in classic works of art. [18] Wilcock says:

*"I believe that we are moving into a new zone of aetheric energy, and that such zones have 'ripples' surrounding them in either direction that are spaced out by the phi ratio. The closer that we get to the new zone (actually like a spiral-cut piece of pie when seen from an overhead view of the galaxy, similar to the structure of the Parker Spiral magnetic field in the solar system), the more rapidly we move through these threshold points. Each one of them creates a sudden spike in the level of ambient aetheric energy moving through our Sun and planetary systems. This in turn creates a sudden spike in the pressure of luminous plasma energy at the Earth's core. These pressure surges are released as earthquakes... The pressure surges also are related to the sudden increases in consciousness, since torsion waves are the carriers of consciousness."* [19]

The supplement to *The Divine Cosmos*, Part One, is the "*smoking gun*" to which he referred, and is called *The Ultimate Secret of the Mayan Calendar - an imploding cycle of energy increase, culminating in 2012-2013 AD*. [20] It attempts to explain, in layman's terms, a paper by Sergey Smelyakov. Smelyakov's original 64-page paper is called *The Auric Time Scale and The Mayan Factor*.

## The Auric Time Scale

The full title of the paper written by Sergey Smelyakov and Yuri Karpenko is *The Auric Time Scale and The Mayan Factor: Demography, Seismicity and History of Great Revelations in the Light of the Solar-Planetary Synchronism*. [21] Sergey Smelyakov is a professor of mathematics at Kharkov University, Ukraine, Russia, with an interest in astrology, and he has found that the Golden Section, or phi, governs the movements of the asteroid belt and the cycles of solar activity, as well as all the planetary orbits in the solar system, including comets. He has also found that phi governs the stock market and population growth, and by applying the same phi harmonics to the 13-baktun cycle, he has, according to Wilcock, found a phi spiral that seems to spiral in on itself on December 21st 2012 - a kind of time implosion, or final "*point of bifurcation*".

I read through the 64-page, equation-drenched online paper, and found that the authors had based their theory on a start-date of 6th August 3113 BC, taken as a Gregorian historical date, as given by José Arguelles in *The Mayan Factor*, when in fact the start date 0.0.0.0.0 was actually 11th August 3114 BC, as we now know. As a result, the authors had shifted the end-date forward to 2013. I contacted Sergey Smelyakov, [22] wondering whether or not the theory would survive the news, and was relieved when he replied, [23] telling me that "*several numerical conclusions might be slightly changed*", but that the theory was not seriously damaged by the modification. This meant that Wilcock's smoking gun was still smoking - or would be after a re-load!

Smelyakov had realized there was a discrepancy in *The Mayan Factor*, since the given start and end-dates (3113 BC and 2012 AD) did not allow for the 1,872,000 days to elapse between them, being a year short. He had correctly guessed that the error was to do with the so-called *"missing year zero"*, which has to be accounted for when counting years from BC to AD or vice versa (remember, there was no year zero, since the year following the hypothetical day of Christ's birth was 1 AD, and the year directly before it was 1 BC). However, he presumed that Arguelles' start-date was a Gregorian historical year, and that the finish date was a year early, so he moved the end-date forward a year to 2013. Actually, he placed the end-point at 19th November 2013, due to a calculation using the Julian Day Number, but confused it with the Julian Date. I also brought this matter to his attention in the first email, referring to several online Julian Date and day calculators that he could use to check the calculation, showing that the true end-point is December 21st 2012. [24]

In a further communication, Smelyakov said that the revised figures for the second version of The Auric Time Scale, rather than detracting from the theory, enhanced it:

*"However, if we take the year of 3114 BC for the starting point, even more intriguing results follow; e.g. the separating epoch of 1997 comes to 1996 - the year of comet Hale-Bopp."* [25]

## BIFURCATION POINTS (B.P.s) AND B.P. INTERVALS

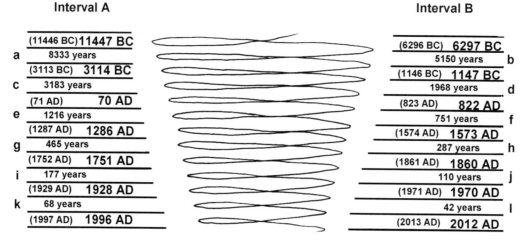

Fig. 12.8: An explanation of how the bifurcation points are generated for the Auric Time Scale ('auric' comes from the chemical abbreviation for gold - Au, after the Golden Section or the Golden Mean).

This was looking good, but just then I discovered something else about The Auric Time Scale, which did not bode well for the theory. The Auric Time Scale is a series of *"bifurcation points"* that are generated by *"phi harmonics"*, and form a time-spiral, as I already mentioned above. Smelyakov had calculated the two bifurcation points that occurred in 6296 BC and 11,446 BC, before the start of the 13-baktun-cycle. The further back in time you go, the further apart the bifurcation points get. However, at the other end of the spiral, the last two points he gave were 1997 and 2013, so theoretically the bifurcation points could be calculated on past his original 2013 termination point, all the way to the centre of the spiral, where they would converge on one point in time. I continued the calculation forward in time, and found the phi spiral whorls into itself, with time speeding up to infinity, on 11th June 2037 AD. This was an approximate calculation, and alternative calculations resulted in this 'end-of the-whorl' point being projected anywhere between May 2036 and November 2038, depending on the criteria used in the calculation (such as re-calculating from 11,447 BC; from 3114 BC; projecting from December 2012; and on how many decimal places were used). However, the main point is that the centre of Smelyakov's spiral is over twenty years after the end of the 13-baktun cycle.

I wrote to Smelyakov [26] to tell him my findings, and he replied, saying that he wasn't trying to say that 2012 was the end of the world, but just that the 13-baktun cycle was resonating to The Auric Time Scale. Even so, he said I had made a valid point:

*"... your suggestion as to forward continuation of this series might also be significant. Frankly speaking, I did not think of it... Now, I am surprised that this idea had not come to me..."* [27]

David Wilcock was certainly under the impression that the spiral whorls in on itself in 2012, as he says in his introductory *"smoking gun"* essay to The Auric Time Scale, entitled *The Ultimate Secret of the Mayan Calendar*:

*"Here, it is important to remember that the entire cycle decreases to a certain final moment at the end of the cycle. Even though the phi-based series F can theoretically extend infinitely in either direction, when you are dealing with a series that is exponentially decreasing in duration, the cycle does converge on one end-point, simply representing smaller and smaller intervals of time in that moment. This would be the same as how the central point of the spiral on a seashell is theoretically infinite in its imploding 'recursiveness', yet you nevertheless can clearly define where the end of the seashell's spiral is."* [28]

In October 2004, over two years after the communications above, Smelyakov sent me his modified theory. However, the modification only extended to altering the dates of bifurcation points, when the 13-baktun start point was corrected by shifting it a year to 3114 BC (Gregorian historical). The continuation of the spiral to its implosion point was not addressed, but there are indicators that the implosion point should have been incorporated into the modified Auric Time Scale theory.

## Critical Mass

Pierre Teilhard-de Chardin was a palaeontologist, but also a Jesuit priest. His study of the development of early hominids and the increasing size of brain cavities led him to a conclusion that was unpopular both with the church and with other palaeontologists.

He developed the law of *Complexity Consciousness*, which indicates that "*the greater the complexity of brain and nerve apparatus, the higher the form of consciousness*". He saw the primary function of his religion - Christianity - as a mechanism to prepare humanity for a profound evolutionary event in its future that he called the "*Omega Point*". He described the Earth as a lithosphere (solid crust) covered by a hydrosphere (watery layer) and then an atmosphere or gaseous envelope. Within the hydrosphere and atmosphere is the biosphere, or "*layer*", of living organisms, and he thought that the purpose of evolution was to develop a self-reflective consciousness that could build up a *Noosphere*, or mind-layer around the planet. Mankind is the species that has started the process, and it will culminate in a direct telepathic communication between people, which would be the birth of the *ultra-human*. This would finally cause the Noosphere to become an awakened Noosphere, or *Christosphere*, an event that will happen "*at the apex of the cone of spacetime*" - the Omega Point.

In *The Awakening Earth*, [29] Peter Russell has built on the ideas of De Chardin, and says that as world population approaches the critical number of ten thousand million ($10^{10}$), we could suddenly find ourselves functioning on a new level, as cells in a "*global brain*". Since there are $10^{10}$ atoms in a neuron and $10^{10}$ neurons in the human cortex, Russell theorises that when the numbers of living units approach the "*critical mass*", they start to behave like parts of a larger organism. World population is currently well above $10^9$ (one thousand million), at about six billion (six thousand million, or $6 \times 10^9$), so we are definitely "*in the ball-park*".

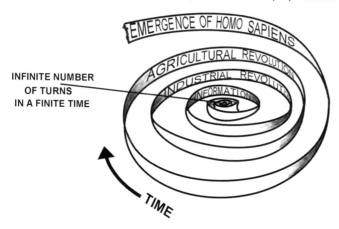

INFINITE NUMBER
OF TURNS
IN A FINITE TIME

In *The White Hole in Time*, [30] Russell analyses the acceleration of human knowledge, at first comparing it to an ever-steepening curve, but then he observes that the evolution and history that has led to the present time can be seen as a spiral, and that, "*paradoxically, although such spirals go on forever, they have a finite length*". [31] Immediately after this, he

*Fig.12.9: The White Hole in Time is at the centre of a spiral converging on a point in time that seems to be around 2012 AD. After Russell [1992].*

discusses the similarity of McKenna's Timewave Zero [32] to the spiral of time, with ever-shortening epochs and accelerating change, converging on a point of maximum novelty. He calls this *"compression"*, and notices the coincidence between the end of the 13-baktun cycle and the end of McKenna's Timewave, seeing 2012 as the centre of the spiral, and a likely consciousness shift-point. He compares the process to the evolution of a star that becomes more compressed until it becomes a singularity, or black hole. This is what lies at the centre of the spiral - what Russell calls a *"white hole in time"*. As we approach it, *"we will be experiencing an ever-accelerating spiral of inner awakening"*. [33]

## Information Doubling

Robert Anton Wilson's 1982 book *Right Where You Are Sitting Now* [34] included an analysis of history entitled *The Jumping Jesus Phenomenon*. [35] In a 1973 study by French Economist Georges Anderla of the Organisation for Economic Cooperation and Development (OECD), a basic unit was used to represent the scientific knowledge of humanity in the year 1 AD. Calculations were then made to determine how long it took for that information to double. Tongue in cheek, Wilson re-named the unit *"one jesus"*, after a certain *"celebrated philosopher"* who was born that year. Then he charted the time it took for the knowledge to double, to the level of two *"jesuses"* (2 j), and again, how long it took to double again, to 4 j, and so on, illustrating his account with historical examples.

So, starting at the estimated start of the species Homo sapiens, it took until 1 AD to arrive at the basic unit of 1 j; that is about 40,000 years if we take 40,000 BC as the start of the species. It took 1,500 years for the next doubling, then 250 years for the next, then 150 years, then 50, then ten, then seven, and then six. That takes us to the date Anderla's study was completed in 1973. In 1982, when Wilson published *Right Where You Are Sitting Now*, he estimated that the next doubling happened in 1978-79, and that in 1982 it doubled again to a level of 512 j.

By 1990, when Wilson wrote another article on information doubling, *Gaia - The Trajectories of Her Evolution* (part 4), [36] he said that information was then doubling every 18 months. Further investigation had caused him to modify the earlier figures slightly, so that it took 40,000 years to reach the first unit of knowledge, which was now placed in the Bronze Age. A further 3,000 years then led to the first doubling at *"the Roman Empire"*, around 1 AD. The name of the knowledge unit was thus no longer relevant, though Wilson didn't bother to replace it, just referring to them as *"doublings"* (I would have changed the name to *"merlins"* if it was up to me). The other times of doubling remain as in Anderla's study. Wilson shows the acceleration process by comparing the Agricultural Revolution, which took thousands of years to transform society, to the Industrial Revolution, which happened about ten times faster, to the Computer Revolution, which is happening ten times faster again. He goes on to say that it seems to be *"a fractal process, with some quantum jumping included"*, and then points out the similarities to the fractal Timewave of McKenna, and its acceleration of novelty:

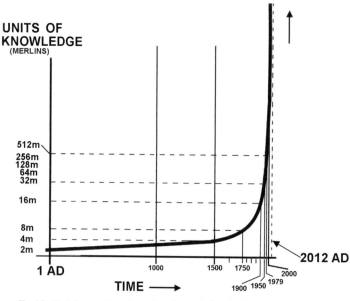

UNITS OF
KNOWLEDGE
(MERLINS)

512m
256m
128m
64m
32m

16m

8m
4m
2m

1 AD

1000    1500    1750    2000

1900  1950  1979

**2012 AD**

TIME ⟶

*Fig.12.10: Information doubling time. Adapted from Wilson [1983].*

"*[McKenna] predicts that by 2012 we will pass through major quantum jumps in information/ power every day, at the beginning of the year, and eventually every second, in the winter, climaxing when the evolutionary break-throughs start coming in nanoseconds*" [37]

Wilson continues:

"*I have never quite succeeded in explaining to myself why I find that scenario unbelievable. I do find it lovely, mathematically; I find it intuitively appealing; I admit it fits most of the data of my own survey of history, but... I evidently have my own conservative streak. I cannot imagine socio-evolutionary quantum leaps accelerating to the rate of 1,000,000 per second.*" [38]

So, even though a graph produced in Wilson's 1983 book *Prometheus Rising* [39] shows the information doubling as an asymptotic curve showing an exponential growth that goes vertical just after the year 2000, it is only Wilson's "*conservative streak*" that stops him saying any more, except that he agrees with Peter Russell in *The Awakening Earth* that Gaia (a name used for Earth as a living being, originally an ancient Greek Earth goddess),

"*... has eighteen of the nineteen traits of a living organism, as formulated in General Systems Theory. The one and only trait of a living creature missing in Gaia, Russell points out, consists of ability to reproduce...*" [40]

Wilson thus sees future space colonies as seeds that will lead to the reproduction of Gaia, when Earth will exist as a living being. However, if we think of human children, they cannot reproduce until they have finished developing, but they have the *potential* to reproduce.

Although no references are given, P. M. H. Atwater claims, in her book *Future Memory*, [41] that information doubling has now been scientifically projected to 2012:

*"It has been estimated by some scientists, that by the first six months of 2012, global information could double each day. During the second six months of that year, they claim that global information could double each hour. If these scientists are right, come 2013, the doubling of global information could well be each and every second."* [42]

## Quantum Awakening

On 27th December 1978, Ken Carey was in bed with a cold and high temperature, when he experienced what sounds at first like an auditory hallucination. When he realized the importance of what he was hearing, he grabbed a typewriter and began to type it out. He kept on typing for eleven days, well after the cold had passed. He felt as if *"something enormous"* was looking through his eyes, that he interpreted variously as angelic, extraterrestrial, or even as *"informational cells in a Galactic organism"*. He is convinced that it was not channelling since there was no trance, loss of consciousness, or voice change.

The information he received reads like a schedule for the awakening Noosphere described above. He was told that there was a series of three waves of transmissions of telepathic awareness. The first had taken place between 1967 and 1969; the second was happening then, between 1977 and 1979, and the third wave would be between 1987 and 1989, which was verified ten years later when Carey found himself receiving another set of transmissions. The transmissions were to help prepare humankind for the *"first unified movement of the awakened planetary organism"*. [43] Carey says that this will be a *"birth"*, when *"the Star Maker will consciously awaken in all systems capable of sustaining universal awareness"*, and that *"the Earth has a due date sometime during the second decade of the twenty-first century"*. [44]

Even the nineteenth trait of a living organism, the ability to reproduce, is foreseen to occur in the millennium following *"Quantum Awakening"*. [45] The transmissions also seem to confirm the connection to the critical mass of world population levels, since population levels at the moment of Quantum Awakening are predicted to be around eight billion ($8 \times 10^9$), [46] and afterwards will level out around eleven billion. [47] There is also a description of time cycles that is very reminiscent of Timewave Zero:

*"The curves of every cycle since the beginning of time - cycles short and cycles long - will crest together in a single moment soon after the turn of the Third Millennium AD."* [48]

As with Timewave theory, the event is not just local to this solar system, but in this version will coincide with the time when *"the universe reaches a point of maximum expansion"*, [49] and we presumably wouldn't know that was about to happen because the further we look into the universe, the further into the past we look (because of the time light takes to travel).

Carey says that the *"return of the gods"* was pinpointed by the Maya at Winter Solstice 2011 AD, [50] but as we know, the end of the 13-baktun cycle correlates to Winter Solstice 2012 in the Gregorian calendar. So, is this Carey's conscious mind clouding the transmission with misinformation he may have got from Michael Coe or Frank Waters? [51] If the transmission is pure, then how did this error creep in? It is now agreed amongst most Mayanists that the 13-baktun cycle will end in December 2012, though some say 23rd December instead of the 21st. Yet the transmissions repeat the 2011 date through all three books, written over a period of nine years. [52] If the awakening event was actually due in 2011, and the Maya had been a year out, then the transmission should have been worded differently. Unfortunately, this makes me suspicious of the transmissions, and I notice that the first *Starseed* book was copyrighted in the same year that Russell's *The Awakening Earth* was published - 1982. However, Carey's description of the Quantum Awakening process is still a fascinating possibility:

*"There will be a great shift then, a single moment of Quantum Awakening. In this moment, the smallest interval of time measured in these dimensions - the interval that occurs in every atom between each of its billions of oscillations per second - will be lengthened unto infinity. An interval of non-time will expand. Through that expansion eternity will flow. Some will experience this moment as minutes or hours, others as a lifetime. Still others will experience this flash of non-time as a succession of many lives, and some few will, in this moment, know the Nagual itself, the great nameless Presence that exists before and after all these worlds.*

*In the expanse of the non-time interval, human beings will have all the time they require to realise, experience and remember full consciousness of their eternal spirits, and to recall the origin of their individuality in the primordial fields of being. All will have ample time to recharge their form identity and its biological projection with the awareness of who they are, why they have individualized, and why they have chosen to associate with the planet's human expression. Each one will have the choice to return to biological form or to remain in the fields of disincarnate awareness.*

*Those who choose to return to human form will do so fully aware of who they are. No longer will they be but partially incarnate; they will resume biological residence with the full memory and consciousness of their eternal natures, sharing the creative capacities of the Star Maker, whose reflective cells they will then know themselves to be."* [53]

# PART 3:
## Beyond the Veil

*T*he fragment of the *Paris Papyrus* suggests that the original light which shines in is the light of the Sun. But what if there is a special kind of light, such as the glow of an exploding galactic centre, which triggers this transformation, whether we are prepared or not? In addition to the physical disaster, we could also be faced with a spiritual or psychological disaster in which the transformational process is triggered automatically, creating havoc among those who are not prepared for the astro-alchemical transmutation.

**Weidner and Bridges, *A Monument to the End of Time*** [1]

# Chapter 13:
# Shamanism

## Holy Flesh

The Spanish historian Sahagún recorded that the Aztec people consumed certain intoxicating mushrooms. In the Nahuatl language these mushrooms were known as *Teonanácatl*, which means *"flesh of the gods"*. The Maya shamans and kings are known to have used a mushroom called *k'aizalah okox*, or the *"lost judgment mushroom"* to produce visions and to travel to the underworld - *Xibalba*. They also used the venom of a poisonous toad called *Bufo alvarius*, which was probably dried and then smoked. [1] The mushrooms are varieties of the Psilocybe species, probably *Psilocybe mexicana*, or *Psilocybe cubensis*, and contain the hallucinogens psilocin and psilocybin, which are both tryptamines (4-hydroxy-DMT and 4-phosphloroxy-DMT). The toad venom contains 5-methoxy-DMT, and Bufotenine. [2]

*Fig.13.1: Mushroom use, depicted in the Codex Vindobonensis of the Mixtecs.*

It was Psilocybe cubensis [3] that the McKenna brothers ingested on their trip to the Amazon, combined with the smoking of the bark of another hallucinogenic plant called *Banisteriopsis caapi* (which is better known as *Ayahuasca*, after which the now-famous hallucinogenic brew is named). This combination provided the 34 day experience, including communication with an insectoid being, that resulted in the I Ching-based Timewave Zero theory. In fact, Terence McKenna later stated that when pure DMT (N-N-dimethyltryptamine) is smoked, it facilitates communication with extra-dimensional life-forms that he calls *"self-transforming machine-elves"*, and that they told him that the *"laws of physics will be transformed around 2012"*. [4]

I recently found another user of the sacred fungus, whose experience seemed to verify what McKenna said:

*"Our Awakening... My partner and I took some Magic Mushrooms, and what should have been a fun trip turned into a vision of the future. It woke us up and pulled us out of the Old World for once and for good... We also received a date, like a programmed ending point, or beginning... 2012. This is the moment where time and therefore also space will fall apart, and we will remain with only our spirit (energy). And it isn't anything dramatic, because at that point you will realise the body is only a blockage, it cannot deal with the speed, and you will want to be released from it..."* [5]

In June 2004, I received more confirmation on the mushrooms/2012 connection, when a web surfer known as *Unborn Mind* wrote to tell me about the experience of a friend a few weeks previously. The person in question was inexperienced in the use of psychedelic mushrooms, and he ate four to five grams of them with the sole intention of becoming intoxicated:

*"He has no knowledge of religion or prophecy.  What followed after was described by him [as] 'the ripping away of everything as we knew it' and he was very adamant about the year this would happen (you guessed it, 2012).  I just think it is very interesting coming from someone with absolutely no knowledge of what a Mayan even is."* [6]

## The Spirit Molecule

So, the Maya shamans ingested psychedelic mushrooms and toad venom containing methylated tryptamines. As we know, they (or the Olmecs or Izapans) also devised a calendar consisting of 260 katuns that terminates in 2012 AD. Terence and Dennis McKenna, while in the Ecuador rainforest, ingested the very same methylated tryptamine-containing mushrooms that the Maya had used, plus they smoked the beta-carboline containing Ayahuasca bark. They then de-coded the 26-level temporal hierarchy of Timewave Zero from the I Ching, and found that the termination point was in 2012 AD.

The pineal gland is a small gland in the centre of the brain, the function of which we are only just beginning to understand. Descartes said it was the *"Seat of the Soul"*; others call it 'the third eye', but it now seems that among its many functions, it can, under certain circumstances, produce *both* types of hallucinogen above - methylated tryptamines *and* beta-carbolines!

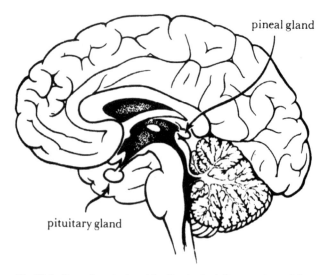

*Fig.13.2: The pineal gland is situated at the centre of the brain. From Baker [1977].*

We have known since 1967 that a hormone found in the pineal gland [7] is actually identical to 6-MTHH, [8] which is a hallucinogen found in Virola and related species, and sometimes used in the Ayahuasca brew. It is a beta-carboline synthesized from melatonin, and at least two other beta-carbolines have also now been reported as being synthesized in the pineal gland. [9] One of these is known as Pinoline, first identified in 1961, [10] and we will have more to say about it later. In addition, I have just discovered there is also evidence that the pineal gland

Fig.13.3: *A comparison of tryptamine molecules that occur in plants. Adapted from McKenna [1975, 1993].*

produces 5-meo-DMT, [11] and we now have new evidence that it also produces DMT itself.

Between the 1960s and 1970s, it was found that the hallucinogen DMT (N-N-dimethyltryptamine) was synthesised in human lungs, blood, and brain (known as *endogenous DMT*, or DMT made inside the body as opposed to exogenous DMT that is taken into the body from outside), but more recently in 1990, Dr Rick Strassman (then Associate Professor of Psychiatry at New Mexico University's School of Medicine in Albuquerque) succeeded in getting funding for a five-year study into DMT, and found substantial evidence for *"an essential function in DMT production and assimilation"* [12] in the pineal gland. His book, *DMT: The Spirit Molecule*, [13] which sums up the five-year study, was published in 2001 and makes fascinating reading.

Strassman finds evidence that the pineal gland manufactures DMT in certain circumstances, and that these include birth, death, near-death experiences (NDEs) and other mystical states, including 'close encounter' incidents, as detailed in the work of Harvard psychiatrist John Mack, who worked with over a hundred abductees before his untimely death under the wheels of a drunk driver in 2004. Caroline Taylor wrote a review of *DMT: The Spirit Molecule* exclusively for the *Diagnosis 2012* website, and has included a dialogue between Rick Strassman and herself, in which she asks his opinions regarding McKenna, the Timewave, and John Mack's work. She summarises her impressions of the book:

*"The 'spirit molecule' is, for Dr Strassman, essentially a kind of chemical 'vehicle', enabling disembodied consciousness to be carried to other realms of existence. If McKenna and the Mayan Calendar creators were right, it may be that we will be needing this vehicle - en masse - in the near future. Rather than a redundant organ like the appendix (as it was once thought), the*

Fig.13.4: *The 'spirit molecule' - pure dimethyltryptamine, or DMT, apparently made naturally in the pineal gland as well as the lungs and the blood, according to Dr. Rick Strassman's findings. After McKenna [1975, 1993].*

*pineal gland may in fact be a FUTURE ORGAN. Upon this little pine-nut of an organ could rest a new model of brain and mind - indeed a whole new paradigm."* [14]

At the end of her review, Caroline asks a very interesting question of Rick Strassman, and gets a very interesting reply:

**Caroline Taylor:** *"Put more specifically; do you feel that endogenous DMT could have a role to play in some future scenario, involving mass major trauma of some kind? [Do you agree] this would be followed, potentially, of course, by a sudden evolution of consciousness to a happier state, for some/all of our species... in other words, a biologically-based eschaton? Such a scenario could be the result of some major environmental collapse, of course - or some harder to imagine one, involving the final timewave 'concrescence' in 2012. In either case, do you agree with my feeling that endogenous DMT could, figuratively speaking, be waiting in the wings right now for its star performance as a vehicle of mass transcendence, or purveyor of large amounts of human (and animal?) consciousness to some other dimension? (I hesitate to say 'higher', for it could also be called 'deeper', or 'fuller'.) In any case, the pineal gland (body) could be both the 'port' of this vehicle, and possibly a vital 'future' organ."*

**Rick Strassman:** *"I have been nursing a theory along these lines for some time. Briefly, that the N-methylating enzyme responsible for DMT production turns on in everyone across the planet at the same time, thus ushering in the eschaton, messianic age, non-corporeal consciousness, or what have you. This could take place any number of ways; one way is a common cold virus gets a bit of DNA implanted into it that is inserted into all of us, which is programmed to turn on at some specific time, unleashing the N-methylating enzyme effects. This time would be an astrologically determined event, such as solar flare, particular constellation alignment, etc. Of course, along the lines of your interest in John Mack's work, that stimulus for enzyme activation could come from 'them'."* [15]

## The Psi Molecule

In her book *Where Science and Magic Meet*, [16] parapsychologist Serena Roney-Dougal has studied the endocrine system and compared it with the *"yogic"* system of chakras. It has been known for many years that the seven power-zones that lie along the spine between the perineum and cranium correlate to the positions of glands in the endocrine system, but her study makes some important new connections. The central channel that connects the chakras is called the *sushumna*, and this is analogous to the central nervous system, while the other interweaving channels are called *ida* and *pingala*, which relate to the sympathetic and parasympathetic parts of the autonomic nervous system. A study of the definitions of the chakra functions, as given by Satyananda (Swami Saraswati Satyananda is a modern yoga teacher, of the Bihar School of Yoga, Bihar, India), shows a

PINOLINE

6-METHOXY-TETRAHYDRO- BETA-CARBOLINE

6-MTHH

6-METHOXY-TETRAHYDRO-HARMAN
(ADRENOGLOMERULOTROPINE)

HARMINE

(TELEPATHINE)

*Fig.13.5: Two beta-carboline molecules (on the left), which occur naturally in the pineal gland, compared with the harmine molecule that is found in the bark of yage/caapi/ayahuasca and in Syrian rue (Peganum Harmala). Pinoline occurs in Virola and related species of plants, as well as in the pineal gland of humans.*

correlation to the biological functions of the related endocrine glands, and this includes the *ajna* or eye chakra, since the pineal is like a vestigial eye, and governs hormonal output according to how much light is received by the retinas of the eyes. It is responsive to the daily solar cycle, the monthly lunar cycle, the seasonal variation over a year, and even the 11.3-year (average) sunspot cycle, but in the case of the Moon and sunspot cycles, they are detected via the changing geomagnetic field. The ajna is a *"command"* chakra, just as the pineal is the biological clock that functions as an *"off switch"* for hormones, while the pituitary is the *"on switch"*.

Roney-Dougal says:

*"... together with serotonin and melatonin in the pineal gland and retina, there is another class of compounds called beta-carbolines, which are produced by the pineal gland, our third eye, and which are chemically very similar to the harmala alkaloids, which are potent hallucinogens. The pineal gland is therefore involved in altering our state of consciousness to a potentially psi-conducive state."* [17]

The pineal is involved in timing the onset of puberty, at which time it calcifies, and it has now been established that there is a relationship between poltergeist cases and puberty and adolescence. Roney-Dougal goes on to say:

*"... young children have no sense of direction until about age 11, and then girls become really remarkable in their accuracy, while boys remain inept".* [18]

It has been established by Indian researchers that a change in the geomagnetic field of about twenty nanoTeslas is enough to *"lower seizure thresholds and precipitate convulsions in people who suffer from epilepsy"* [19] (in tribal societies, these people would be trained as shamans, and taught to control the condition and use it to advantage), but following solar storms or flares, the geomagnetic field can change by as much as 500 nT. [20] Roney-Dougal thinks that the calcification at puberty allows the pineal to become sensitive to electromagnetic fields, and there is evidence (after dowser Bill Lewis detected a spiral of energy around a standing stone that was later verified by a physicist from Imperial College, London, using a gauss meter) that water dowsers are responding to changes in the geomagnetic field. [21] As Paul Devereux (co-ordinator of the Dragon Project, which measured energies at ancient sites) puts it, "*... it is certain that many living organisms can sense variations in the geomagnetic field directly, and it is highly probable that human beings have such sensitivity as well*". [22]

A correlation has now been established (by Michael Persinger) between ghosts and *sudden increases* in geomagnetic activity, and the same for poltergeists, [23] while another correlation has been established between *quiet* geomagnetic activity and successful remote viewing and telepathy experiments. [24]

Knowing, as we do, about the changing geomagnetic field and its trend towards inversion, we could speculate that a sudden change of geomagnetic field on that kind of scale could be enough to trigger a pinoline-activated leap in psychic abilities. As the general electromagnetic field intensity drops (i.e. quiet geomagnetic activity), there may be a tendency towards increased telepathy and clairvoyance, but at the time of sudden jumps (i.e. sudden increases in geomagnetic activity) due to increasing solar storms and flares, there could be outbreaks of poltergeist activity and apparitions. In fact, harmine was actually called *telepathine* when it was first extracted from B.caapi, due to its effects; then it was found that the same alkaloid had already been extracted from Syrian Rue

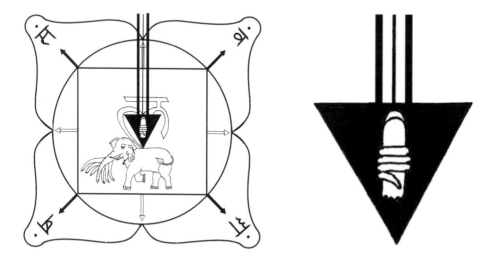

*Fig.13.6: The base, or* muladhara *chakra, located at the base of the spine. In the centre of the symbol for the base chakra (close-up on right), we can see the Kundalini Fire-Snake coiled three and a half times around the Shiva line of force that descends from above. Adapted from Scott [1989].*

(Peganum harmala) and named *harmine*. Another possibility is that the geomagnetic changes will cause Kundalini, the Fire-Snake, to involuntarily awaken from its slumber in the base chakra and rise up the spines of humans, hopefully causing enlightenment, or *Samadhi*. This is a scenario predicted by several researchers, based on the legend of the Return of Quetzalcoatl, the Feathered Serpent.

## Bicycle Accident

In 1985, a Dutch boy (with a Swiss-Norwegian lineage), Ananda Bosman, had a bicycle accident while living in England. It was during puberty when he was about fifteen years old, before the calcification of his pineal gland. The trauma triggered off a seven-year process in which the pineal eye was progressively opened, allowing an alternative neurochemical process to begin, in which endogenous (made in the body) pinoline and DMT were being synthesized and secreted into his system:

*"This increased especially during the night, when more melatonin was available to be synthesized into Pinoline, and hence allowing 5meo-DMT"* [25]

The boy had an out-of-body experience (OOBE) at this time, in which he met *"non-localised quantum selves"*. These beings were beyond extraterrestrial or even ultraterrestrial, defining themselves as *"InterUniversals"* and collectively calling themselves *"Emmanuel"*. One individual identified himself as *"Salvana"*. After the accident, Bosman witnessed multiple UFOs during a visit to England, and the following year one of the InterUniversals appeared to him while he was awake, with his eyes open, and Ananda later says he was *"alerted by 'Emmanuel' in 1989 to the significance of 2012."* [26]

Over the next few years, he was given all sorts of information, and developed several projects to help humanity prepare for the forthcoming Omega Point by developing a method to bring about *"the translation of our biological body back into its vacuum hyperspatial Original Light Body form"*. [27] Part of this process involved a fourteen-day *"dark-room retreat"*, in which melatonin floods the system;

*"Once there is a threshold of melatonin, then pinoline results. After some four to seven days, 5-meo-DMT awakens. One can see in three-dimensional Holon pictures, as the thoughts behind language..."* [28]

A *Holon* is something that is simultaneously a whole and a part - something seen from a holistic perspective.

*"After some 10-12 days, one starts to see in infrared and ultraviolet, one can actually run across the room and touch a person, by seeing their heat patterns. The Holon images exteriorise and one is walking in a virtual reality... the DNA language, macro uploaded and interactive"*. [29]

The dark-room retreat is combined with a tryptophan-rich diet to give the pineal gland the raw ingredients it needs (tryptophan is destroyed by cooking). The diet must also avoid dairy products, alcohol, drugs, and many everyday foods that interfere with the process. [30]

Ananda reveals what may be news for Rick Strassman; Dr Callaway of the University of Kuopio, Finland, already "*conclusively demonstrated that the Near-Death Experience,*

**TRYPTOPHAN**                         **MELATONIN**

*Fig.13.7: Tryptophan is the raw material from which the pineal synthesizes melatonin and tryptamine. From tryptamine is synthesized DMT, and from melatonin comes pinoline and 6-MTHH. Adapted from McKenna [1975, 1993].*

*Out-Of-Body Experience, and death itself (by blood plasma spinal tap readings), are based on pinoline, DMT, and 5-meo-DMT release*". [31] This work was published in 1991 and 1993, [32] so it was being done at the same time as Strassman was doing his research. Callaway had also demonstrated that lucid dreams are induced by DMT, and this is something that will be relevant later. [33]

Ananda also claims that that the Gnostics and Alchemists used a combination of Syrian Rue (which contains harmine or *telepathine*) and Acacia (Acacia contains DMT) as a kind of Western Ayahuasca, and should soon be publishing a book on this, *The Soma Conspiracy*, along with several other books, including one called *The Rig Veda*, in which he identifies the Rig Veda (or Vedas, a collection of ancient Hindu holy writings) as the source for the "*Apocalypse code*" of The *Book of Revelation*. [34]

In 2002, seventeen years after his first contact with Emmanuel, Ananda was reading the Vedas (which some claim are as much as 7,000 years old), when he was "*thunder-struck*" to realise that they mention a deity or *Manu* named *Salvana* - the same name as one of the Emmanuel group that contacted him. More than this, he was said to be "*one of the central Manus from the seven Alpha-Omega Manu couples that overwatch and influence the species development*" and, according to Ananda, is also "*the Omega Manu of our cycle, into which our reality is emerging*". Ananda claims that the Vedas also time this "*emergence*" as coinciding with the galactic alignment process, and he identifies Salvana with the Noosphere:

"*The Vedas conveyed such an emergence to be astronomically marked by the precise alignments of our astrophysical back garden that accurately took place in 1998 and will again in 2012 - an emergence we are amidst. The Omega Manu, in hadron physics jargon, acting as a kind of Macro Irreversible Coherent Noosphere of our Age.*" [35]

## Syrian Rue

In the online *Diary of a Psychonaut*, [36] I found an account called *Time Stop* by someone known by the webname *Copehead*, who had combined Syrian Rue, mushrooms and laughing gas (nitrous oxide):

*"Let me add a little disclaimer here. I am not a follower of Terence McKenna. I do not subscribe to his theories, although I have read both* Food of the Gods *and* True Hallucinations, *as well as much of the material online. His ideas are definitely entertaining, but I have a hard time lending much credence to them. Having said that, here is the message I received, reconstructed from my messy notes as best as possible: 'Time stops in 2012. Please be ready. The work must be finished. This is the moment all the great books of history have been written about. This is the birth of religion.'"* [37]

The next account, *Mushroom Love*, follows ingestion of Psilocybe cubensis:

*"Again I received the idea that something monumental was to happen in 2012. I was seeing images of McKenna, along with things like '2012, are YOU ready?' I was told that we make our own reality [and] that no one needed to be unhappy. When I asked if the 2012 thing were real, I was told (the voice was now present) again; 'We make our own reality. It is as real as you want it to be'. I knew suddenly that this could happen. I realized that 2012 is just a date and that I could transform my own consciousness by then if I wished to do so. I decided right there to do so, and to help as many others to do so as I could. It was a very religious feeling."* [38]

In the third relevant account, *Monkeys in Space*, the author writes:

*"I had a vision of the universe, containing itself. I saw a series of calendars, clocks and other time measuring devices, the most perfect/accurate of which seemed to be the Mayan calendar. Again I experienced the 'time stop' phenomenon as well as the mushroom voice. Again it told me many strange and wonderful things. Here are a few of those things:*
    *The mushroom, mankind and several other species on this planet (including dolphins) are all collaborating on a colossal project, the ultimate nature of which was somewhat elusive to me. Most of humanity is completely unaware of their participation in this project, but the majority of the other players are fully aware of their own parts in it. This project will reach completion in the year 2012. It has something to do with time, consciousness, and perhaps leaving the planet or returning it to a pristine state."* [39]

So, what all this seems to mean is that tryptamines and beta-carbolines enable contact with some information-source that is trying to get us to prepare for 2012, but does this happen with only these molecules?

## Salvia Divinorum

*Salvia divinorum*, or *Diviner's Mint*, is widely thought to be the 'divine plant' of pre-conquest Mexico, known in the Nahuatl language as *pipiltzintzintli*. The Mazatecs still use it today. I have encountered several people who have received information about 2012, following the use of this sacred plant. As I write, it is still legal, as far as I know, in most places except Australia. Charlie Sabatino, who lives in Mallorca, Spain, wrote:

*"I took some strong drugs (Salvia divinorum) and 'heard' that I was to write a screenplay called 2012 (I'm a writer). I grabbed a pen and then started scribbling whatever came into my mind; it was like taking dictation..."* [40]

The notes extended for six pages and subjects included the Maya calendar, UFOs, standing stones, telepathy, visions and dreams. Charlie concluded:

*"Geoff, I was a really normal guy once. Italian butcher's son from the Bronx, NY. I didn't ask for any of this... I blame my wife."* [41]

Someone called *Damaeus* also had a vision of 2012 with Salvia:

*"Concerning Salvia divinorum and 2012, I gather from my experiences with Salvia that none of us will ever see the destruction of the Earth. We will hear the calling before it ever happens and our consciousness/spirit/soul will simply float away, leaving our physical bodies to be destroyed with the worldwide earthquakes or whatever other disasters nature has in store."* [42]

SALVINORIN A

*Fig.13.8: The Salvinorin A molecule.*

A web-surfer called *Canul* includes the following comment about his first experience with Salvia:

*"In my first experience I felt and saw things of this reality that made me think of 2012. I had a perception of reality that is commonly described in Salvia divinorum literature: experiencing two different realities in parallel. One reality was the one that habit tells me [is everyday reality], the other one was 2012 nearby. I don't attribute this to the enthusiasm I have over 2012. It was authentic. I am reminded of the scene in the movie Artificial Intelligence, where the boy runs away with the other A.I. models from the 'robot gatherers.'"* [43]

Another psychonaut, *Shivasix*, says, "*Salvia divinorum is a powerful plant helper sent to ease our transition at the end of time*", [44] which he correlates with the end of the 13-baktun cycle in 2012.

And the final anecdote on 2012 information via exogenous molecules comes from *Tomorrowlander* and his girlfriend, who had a large dose of a rather dangerous cough mixture and touched their foreheads together (pineal area), when an audible angelic voice said, "*In the year 2012, we will come...*" [45]

# Chapter 14:
# Other Altered States

## Near-Death Experiences

I have recently discovered several apparently independent accounts in which people undergoing a near-death experience (NDE) have been given access to information about 2012. The most detailed account I found is that of Cassandra Musgrave, which happened in 1992:

"*I feel that my near-death experience was a real gift. I feel it was a real blessing. It really awakened me. I was water skiing in northern California and when I fell down by some freak accident, the rope twisted around my left arm and dragged me behind the boat. And I found myself being pulled at a very rapid speed and unable to get any air. And my friends, who were goofing off, didn't stop the boat because they weren't paying any attention.*" [1]

As Cassandra began to drown, she entered into a dream-like state that was the start of her NDE:

"*All of a sudden, I was out of my body watching myself being pulled along and thinking 'This is really incredible. This is really quite amazing.' On an inner level, I was being pulled through a very dark tunnel. I didn't feel afraid at all. All of a sudden, I found myself coming into a wide open space with stars all around, like out in the universe.*" [2]

It was here that Cassandra received a prophetic vision:

"*Basically, I saw that there was a twenty-year period from 1992 to 2012. Things will be greatly accelerated on Earth. All these things will be manifest by great Earth changes: earthquakes, floods, tidal waves, great winds. I also saw there were certain areas that would be particularly affected - the areas of the east coast [of America], which will be surprised regarding earthquakes. I remember very clearly Japan slipping into the ocean. I was shown there was going to be something akin to three days of darkness. I don't feel it is from a nuclear war. To me, it was more of a feeling of natural Earth disasters with smoke from volcanoes that would block the Sun. We are all going to be on a roller-coaster ride, and yet it is not forever. If we have darkness for three days, it will pass. We will always have the light."* 3

Ken Kalb's book *The Grand Catharsis* 4 is a history of consciousness from 1987 to 2012, weaving together many bodies of knowledge to focus on the real issues for the new millennium, and was based on a lucid vision gained during a near-death experience in 1969. However, Dannion Brinkley is a more famous case, since he had an NDE that lasted 28 minutes. This was the longest clinically documented NDE ever recorded up until that time (I have since heard of a case that lasted over an hour and a half, from 1982). 5 His experiences during these 28 minutes are related in great detail in his bestseller, *Saved by the Light,* 6 as summarised by Mike Pettigrew:

Fig.14.1: Entrance to the Celestial Paradise by Hieronymous Bosch. Many near-death experiencers describe travelling through a tunnel into a bright light.

*"On September 17, 1975, Dannion Brinkley was talking on the phone during a thunderstorm. A bolt of lightning hit the phone line, sending thousands of volts of electricity into his head and down his body. His heart stopped, and he died, but in the process, he had a near-death experience. When Brinkley revived in the morgue after 28 minutes of death, he had an incredible story to tell."* 7

Briefly, he found himself floating above his body and went down a spiralling tunnel into a brilliant light, where he was approached by a glowing silver being that radiated love. He then re-experienced his life (which had been one full of aggression, including a spell in the marines). He judged himself, feeling the pain he had caused others, and also the positive effects he had caused. He was taken to a crystalline city of light. He saw a group of twelve beings representing the signs of the zodiac, plus a thirteenth being that presided over the other twelve:

*"Dannion was approached by each one of these beings with what looked like a small box. Each time this happened the box opened up*

*to reveal what looked like a small TV screen. Scenes showing events from the future appeared on the screen that would grow in size until Dannion found himself inside the scene. These were major world events that would take place in the future. There were over 300 of these scenes. 117 of these were major world events that Dannion was told would take place in the future (1975 to 2012). Dannion was immersed in events ranging from the nuclear accident at Chernobyl, the break-up of the former Soviet Union, the Gulf War, changes to our Earth's climate, breakthroughs in technology and many other things. Now [in 2002], about 100 of these very specific global events have already occurred."* [8]

After getting instructions for the building of special centres, Brinkley was sent back to his body which had already been issued with a death certificate, and was cold and covered in a sheet (and, in this version, just about to be taken to the morgue). Following a lot of pain and paralysis, Dannion found he had telepathic and precognitive powers. His predictions are said to be coming to pass with astounding accuracy - 100 out of the 117, according to Mike Pettigrew in 2002.

Regarding 2012, when asked by an interviewer *"How bad will it get, Dannion?"*, Brinkley then replied:

*"Or how good will it get? I think it will get really bad geographically and topographically, but in spiritual consciousness it is going to grow in leaps and bounds. Oh, I wouldn't miss it for the world! This Earth is changing as the entire universe is changing, because between 2004 and 2014, more precisely between 2011 and 2012, we will experience the return of an energy system that existed here a long time ago. You can call it a spiritually uplifting consciousness, the Second Coming, or the birth of the Aquarian Age.* [9]

*In closing, this is my hope, rather than a prophetic prediction: as all the Earth changes, both subtle and massive, come to pass one by one, and most especially with the occurrence of the electromagnetic polar Earth shift (between 2012-2014), I hope we all will seize the opportunities for growth, which will undoubtedly present themselves to promote our inner development of spiritual virtues".* [10]

Phylis Atwater (also known as P. M. H. Atwater) underwent *three* NDEs, *and* a Kundalini experience (when the serpentine energy that lies dormant at the base of the spine is activated and moves up through the seven chakras or power-zones on its way to the Crown chakra). As a result, she became a researcher into near-death experiences (and author of eight books). In her research into child NDEs, she found that many of the children were reporting predictions of Earth changes, and she has correlated the timing of the culmination of these to December 2012, which she says will not only be the start of the Fifth World of the Maya, but also the *"final blossoming and fruition"* of the *"fifth root race"* [11] in the Theosophical scheme. The *fruits* would be the first manifestation of the next evolutionary stage, the sixth root race (the Fifth World of the Maya is The Sixth Sun of the Aztecs). These forerunners of the next phase are becoming familiar as the gifted and psychic children known as 'Indigo Children'. [12]

An Australian woman called Jackie, who experienced two NDEs in 1979, says that she received an important message from *"the angels"*, but couldn't quite remember what it was. Ever since, she has been looking for cues to jog her memory. While attending a Vancouver NDE conference, she got the cue she needed during a talk by P.M.H. Atwater, following which, she said:

*"It's all come back. It started yesterday in the experiencers' session. Then this morning - I already knew everything that woman said! In her talk she informed us that NDErs are, in effect, God's new chosen people. They're sent back to life with extraordinary powers to pave the way for the consciousness revolution that will transmute our planet, beginning in 2012."* [13]

Pam Reynolds of Atlanta, Georgia, also had a near-death experience involving a vivid vision of 2012:

*Fig.14.2: Some out-of-body experiencers report that their astral body is attached to the physical body via a silver cord that connects to the solar plexus (though others report the head connection already depicted in Fig.9.3).*

*"This happened about ten years ago when she was dying from a brain tumour... She saw future events like Earth changes, a breakthrough in physics and a consciousness change near 2012. She didn't see the end of the world, just changes."* [14]

## OOBEs (OBEs)

Christopher Bache is a professor of philosophy at Arizona State University, and does research into self-induced out-of-body experiences (they are called OBEs in America, since they are less likely to confuse them with the British medal of honour).

*"In one of his OBEs, he was told by a number of points of light (he assumed they were spirits) that around 2012 the world would go through a global crisis unparalleled in human history (apocalypse?). They did not tell him what would happen. Because he is a scientific thinker, he began look for what this crisis could be."* [15]

He has now concluded that it will be an environmental disaster largely caused by humanity. Coincidentally (or not), 2012 is the target date for the world to get its greenhouse gases under control. This is known as the Kyoto Protocol, and infamously the USA has been *"dragging its heels"*, avoiding signing the treaty.

Native American J. Reuben Silverbird (a half Apache and half Cherokee - or half Navajo by some accounts) was born blind, and up to age five he learned to travel out of his body, at which time he miraculously regained his sight. At the age of seven (sometime before 1960), he says:

*Fig.14.3: The ba, or Egyptian conception of the astral body, visiting its mummy. It is holding the symbol of eternity. Adapted from the Papyrus of Ani.*

*"... Just two years after my wonderful miracle of sight, I had another, most horrifying vision that will remain with me until the day the Creator decides I am ready to go to the mountain and join my dear parents, Sun Bear and Thomas Banyanca. The experience conceived [sic] the year 2012 and my death and bringing back to life by a spiritual, almost Holy Stranger. This story and the one about my blindness is too long and will be a part of my book Spiritual Healing Words of Wisdom."* [16]

## Lucid Dreams

When a dreamer becomes aware that they are dreaming, the whole dream becomes very realistic and the dreamer can then control the dream. This state is known as 'lucid dreaming'. Lucid dream researcher Stephen LaBerge, of the Lucidity Institute, says, *"OBEs are actually variant interpretations of lucid dreams,"* [17] and to support this position he cites a laboratory study. [18] However, other researchers such as Keith Harary disagree, citing other laboratory studies as evidence:

*"... The OBE and the lucid dream are not one and the same. Though the two are often confused with each other, laboratory studies show they are psychologically and physiologically distinct. For one thing, you don't have to be asleep to have an out-of-body experience. For another, the brainwave and eye movement patterns that have emerged from OBE studies in the laboratory are quite different from those associated with dreams."* [19]

Since techniques have been developed to induce an OOBE from within a lucid dream, some researchers such as Dean Walker believe *"OBEs and LDs to be part of a continuum of experience with considerable overlap between them".* [20] Whichever position we take, the fact is that we have already seen that OOBEs are a source of 2012 prophecies. It is also a fact that there are some accounts of lucid dreams featuring 2012.

Nick Cumbo, alias *Explora*, runs a website called *Dreampeace*, [21] which includes a forum called *Sea Life* that *"aims to bring together a large circle of dreamers, collaborating in mutual dreaming adventures..."* In 2002, Cumbo had a dream that included the following:

*"Suddenly, my attention is drawn to a large object in the sky. Looking up, I am stunned to see the words '2012, it is their last superstar' printed on a large banner. The banner is huge, but seems to be moving away. It is attached to an amazing spaceship, a white and blue ship, with bright flashing lights, which are travelling away quite quickly. I am amazed by the reality of the ship and its message, and continue focusing on what the banner says. As I do this, the words change to '2012, it is their next superstar'".* [22]

Since then, in March-April 2003 and March-April 2004, the *Sea Life* group has attempted a collective induction of dreams about 2012. [23]

The imagery from another lucid dream at the *DreamImages* site implies the advent of *"electrical changes"* and invisibility, just prior to a general *"ascent on an escalator"* that is labelled *"2012-2025"* in surroundings that look like New Zealand. [24]

In a precognitive dream of Paul Vigay, which he dates as *"sometime between 1998 and 2012,"* and that *"almost became a lucid dream"*, he witnessed a decloaking of extra-dimensional UFOs in the East Kennett area (near Avebury, Wiltshire, UK). [25] For more 2012 dreams, see the *Great Dreams* website at *www.greatdreams.com*. [26]

## Meditation

Gloria Karpinski gave a workshop in 2003 titled *Who Shall I Say Sent Me? - Rediscovering Our Power Before 2012*, in which she explained the significance of the subtitle, as reported by the *Women and Wisdom* website:

*"'I was 'getting' that year in meditation long before I knew why,' Gloria told the September workshop participants. Indeed, it was Gloria who first mentioned the year 2012 to us at the original* Women and Wisdom *group in New York, 25 years ago. 'I had no idea that year was pinpointed in the Mayan Calendar as the end of a 25,000 year cycle,' she explained. 'The last time this kind of cycle ended was, of course, before recorded history. So we don't know what form it took then or will take this time.'"* [27]

The implication is that it was before 1978 that Gloria first picked up the significance of 2012 while meditating. In her book *Barefoot on Holy Ground - Twelve Lessons in Spiritual*

*Craftsmanship*, [28] she reveals that this was not just an isolated event, but one that kept on recurring:

*"The first few times that I received the number 2012 in a meditation as a significant date, I took it with a big dose of cosmic salt. Like the contents of Pandora's box, the prophecy pot has been overturned and the contents have poured out into the collective for anybody to pick up and interpret. I asked myself: Is this a truth I have been shown or have I simply picked up on an arbitrary date because so many people have energized it that it is accepted as truth? But I realized that this date had been showing up in meditations before I knew anyone else was getting it. Then, as I read various prophecies, learned the unusual astrological line-ups of that year* [Gloria may be referring to galactic alignment, but see page 196 for other possibilities] *and talked to others around the world who had received the same information, I realized that if I was off, then lots of us were off at the same time."* [29]

She goes on to explain that she doesn't see 2012 as a date of catastrophe, but as the end of a period of purification and chaos.

## Past Life Recall

Randolph Weldon visited a regression hypnotist who hypnotically regressed him so far into the past that he re-experienced memories from several former lives. These previous lives included an Egyptian potter who had apparently lived through the disasters that occurred at the time Moses led his people out of Egypt. The potter witnessed the cyclone, earthquakes and clouds of red dust that turned the rivers *"red with blood"*, as described in the *Book of Exodus* in the Bible. Then came a hail of large stones, one of which crashed through the roof and killed his mother-in law. With his remaining family he joined the people stampeding out of the city, and saw a rain of burning oil. Weldon says that many Egyptians joined the Exodus of the Israelites, since Moses had threatened that his god would bring about the destruction of Egypt if the Israelites were not freed. Weldon's former self then witnessed the *"pillar of cloud"* that the people followed by day, that appeared as a *"pillar of fire"* by night, and the close pass of a *"huge, dazzling, fuzzy yellow ball"* that caused the waters of the Red Sea to part, while most of the refugees crossed to the other side. The potter and his family were at the back of the crowd, with the Egyptian chariots behind them, when a massive bolt of electricity flashed from the comet-like object to the ground and the waters crashed in and ended his incarnation.

The vision precisely matched Velikovsky's interpretation of the Exodus, which he put down to the 'Birth of Venus', as described in Chapter 7, in which a cosmic collision - with a passing planet or star - had pulled out a portion of Jupiter, which became a comet with a 52-year period that eventually cooled and became the planet Venus. Velikovsky dated the event at around 1500 BC, though astronomers might argue Venus couldn't possibly be that young.

However, in his book *Doomsday 2012*, [30] Weldon relates the regression above, and its

*Fig.14.4: In the Greek myth, Vulcan cured Zeus (Jupiter) of his headaches by splitting his head open with an axe - and Pallas Athene (Venus) was born. Atlanta Fugiens by M. Maier, Oppenheim, 1618.*

correlation to Velikovsky, and by combining the results of a similar past-life regression, concludes that we are due for a repeat visit from the huge celestial object that triggered the Venus events, and that this visit is due in 2012. Weldon found that in Barbara Hand Clow's book *Eye of the Centaur*, she describes a past life as a Minoan priestess (in Knossos on Crete) called Aspasia, who received a warning that a massive comet was coming which would cause Thera (a huge volcano, the remains of which is now the island of Santorini in the Mediterranean Sea) to erupt. Aspasia was also informed that the comet returns every 3,500 years. Clow later recalled the experience of the passage of the comet and the resulting earthquake in which her life as Aspasia ended.

As also mentioned in Chapter 7, Graham Phillips has already connected the events of the Exodus to the explosion of Thera, and Nigel Appleby has connected the giant planet Nibiru (usually said to be on an approximate 3,600-year orbit) to the same event, and predicted its return in 2012 (3,500 years later), but Weldon does not refer to Sitchin, Phillips, Appleby or even Nibiru.

Amazingly, Weldon seems not to have read Zecharia Sitchin's *The Twelfth Planet*, but refers to another book called *The Genius of the Few* by Christian O'Brien (Turnstone, 1985), who, like Sitchin, is one of the few people who can translate Sumerian cuneiform script. O'Brien comes to many of the same conclusions as Sitchin. Weldon concluded, using Barbara Hand Clow's figure of a 3,500-year-comet cycle, added to Velikovsky's date for the Venus incident, that a *"Death Star"* that contributed the matter that became the embryonic Venus (pulled out *by* Jupiter, rather than coming *from* Jupiter as Velikovsky argued), was due to return around the turn of the millennium. It would be red in colour, to fit in with the past-life memories, and would therefore be either a red dwarf star, an infrared dwarf or possibly a smaller Jupiter-like planet. It couldn't be a red giant as that would be the size of the Earth's entire orbit. The minimum size of a red/infrared dwarf is between a tenth and twelfth the size of the Sun, according to Weldon, but another possibility is a 'proto-sun' like Jupiter (which some consider to be a failed star), but with a minimum scale of two times the size of Jupiter (or 600 times the size of Earth). On p.173, Weldon says that the IRAS satellite (Infrared Astronomical Satellite) should have detected any infrared dwarf out there when it scanned the entire sky in 1983, but it failed to pick anything up. He obviously didn't know about the article in the *Washington Post* (to which I have already referred in Chapter 7), in which an announcement was made that the IRAS satellite *had* actually picked up a planet the size of Jupiter, which may be part of our solar system.

It is ironic that Weldon used a past-life memory of Barbara Hand Clow to make his case for an imminent 2012 cataclysm, since Clow has since written a book called *Catastrophobia*, [31] which argues that the current obsession with imminent catastrophe is a kind of mental block in the unconscious mind of the species caused by a racial memory of a catastrophe in 9,500 BC (as posited by Allan & Delair in *When the Earth Nearly Died* [32]). She says 2012 will be a leap in consciousness.

The predictions of seers, including Cayce and Nostradamus, of cataclysmic events around the turn of the millennium, served to add fuel to Weldon's fire, but the fact that they have not yet come true has led to the conclusion that the Maya and Hopis must have got it right at 2012, and the other predictions are all about twelve years out.

Weldon says that the difference between the coming event and the previous visits of the Death Star is that this time we have over 500 nuclear installations, millions of gallons of radioactive waste and thousands of nuclear bombs that will all be unleashed in the mayhem, leading to a double catastrophe, the smattering of survivors all dying of radiation poisoning. That's the bad news!

The good news, says Weldon, is that life will continue in the astral planes and that it is up to us to use our remaining time to try and clear our karmic debts, otherwise we will end up on the lower astral, in the "*House of Hopelessness*" or the slightly better "*Plane of Illusion*", both of which the author claims to have visited during his nocturnal projections with his guides. He believes we should actually seek out adversity for ourselves in order to help balance up any nasty behaviour in this life or any previous ones.

It is intriguing that Weldon comes to the same conclusion as Appleby (though with more emphasis on the catastrophic), but using completely different sources. However, his principle evidence for the 3,500-year period is Barbara Hand Clow, who obviously doesn't agree regarding the recurrence of a catastrophe in 2012. It also turns out that Weldon's regression hypnotist is the same person that regressed Clow (Gregory Paxon), and he reported that a third client of his also "*recounted life as a young seer-priestess on that island, and died in the same apocalyptic disaster*". When these things are taken into account, plus the possibility that Weldon's prior knowledge of Velikovsky and some of the millennium prophecies had tainted his regression, we may be able to relax a little. There was actually nothing in Weldon's book to tie this event specifically to 2012, except that it is a supposed date of prophesied disaster that is close to the Cayce and Nostradamus predictions. Velikovsky's date of 1495 BC, plus Clow's 3,500 years, gives the year of catastrophe as 2006.

**Future Life Pre-call**

In September 2003, the *Hindustan Times* [33] reported that *"an eminent film and TV personality, Smita Jaykar"* underwent *"future progression"* under the guidance of Dr Kondaveti Newton and reported that only one fourth of the world's population would survive to see 2012:

"'I could see the Earth enveloped in a golden light. Everything was in absolute peace and though the world was sparsely populated, all the inhabitants looked like highly enlightened beings,' *says Smita while describing life on Earth as it would be by the year 2012. The Marathi actress was talking about her belief in the concept of past and future lifetimes."*

So, what would it be - earthquakes, volcanoes, floods or the Third World War?

"'Natural calamities yes, but the major part of destruction would be caused by a war, no doubt,' *she says empathically.* 'It was quite a few years back that Dr Newton had carried me to the future and I couldn't quite believe what all [sic] I saw, but now I can see signs of it all coming true,' *Smita adds."* [34]

This again is not a good outlook, but 25% survival is certainly an improvement on Weldon's 0%!

# Chapter 15:
# UFOs and ETs

**UFO Waves**

A 'UFO wave' (or 'UFO flap') simply means a concentration of reports of unidentified flying objects in a certain area at a certain time. The world's biggest ever UFO wave started in Mexico in 1991 at the time of that year's total solar eclipse, and continues to this day. This has helped focus world attention on the Maya calendar and prophecies. A recent UFO wave over Arizona may also point to the Hopi prophecies, just as an Israel wave highlights the biblical prophecies. In a similar way, during the total solar eclipse of 1999, the eclipse shadow passed over Turkey and appeared to trigger not only an earthquake but also a UFO wave that is still continuing.

Following the 1991 wave in Mexico, a series of three videos were released [1] showing nearly 200 video clips of Mexican UFOs from 1991 to 1996, and stating in the commentary that the 1991 eclipse had been predicted in the Dresden Codex (one of only three surviving codices, or books, written by the Maya). The editors of the video, Lee and Britt Elders, and Jaime Maussan (the Mexican TV commentator covering UFOs), had concluded that the 1991 eclipse was the start of the Sixth Sun - the event that is usually associated with 2012.

I have looked into this question and found that errors were made; there is good reason to deduce that the original UFO was actually Venus, appearing during the darkness of the eclipse, [2] but that doesn't alter the fact that there has been a massive wave of UFOs in Mexico since 1991, as shown in the other videos and on Mexican TV. They are seen disappearing behind buildings, flying in groups and 'buzzing' (harassing) commercial and military aircraft.

However, the eclipse was *not* predicted in the Dresden Codex after all! I found Mayanist Mike Finley's website *The Real Maya Prophecies: Astronomy in the Inscriptions and Codices* [3], which explains that, in order to use the Dresden Codex for eclipse-prediction, the periods must be *"recycled"*, or extrapolated into the future. In other words, it may be possible to find the 1991 eclipse date by extrapolation, but the actual (Maya equivalent of July 1991) date is not recorded in the Dresden Codex. So, this is one area in which

Fig.15.1: *Two Aztec priests adjust a calendrical device. The National Stone, Museum of Anthropology, Mexico City.*

the video editors have made misleading statements. Another point made by Finley is that the accuracy of the charts fails after a few recyclings, due to accumulated error, and so a correction factor must be used over the 38 recyclings necessary to bring the eclipse table forward to cover 1991. I wrote to ask Mike Finley if he thought the 1991 eclipse could have been predicted using the GMT correlations. He took a detailed look at the problem, and his reply is posted at the *Diagnosis 2012* website [4] for those interested, but he summed up as follows: *"Conclusion: The table isn't even close to the mark!!!"* [5] Therefore, there was no reason for concluding that 1991 was the start of the Sixth Sun of the Aztecs (equal to the Fifth Sun or World of the Maya and Hopi Indians). This event is still scheduled for 2012.

## Contact

Jon King, editor of the late, great *UFO Reality* magazine, had several *"contactee"* experiences between 1980 and 1984, in which he encountered humanoid ETs in a parallel dimension. When asked if he had been taken aboard an alien craft, Jon said:

*"Well, I wouldn't call it an 'alien craft'. But for lack of a different way to describe it, I suppose that's what I'm saying, yes."* [6]

He was asked if he had been abducted by aliens, and replied:

*"No, I'm not saying that at all. I'm definitely not saying that. There was never any time I felt that I'd been abducted. Quite the opposite. It was as if the experience came in response to an inner need in me, a need to discover the truth about life. And this experience, once I'd processed it, satisfied that need. It was as if I called the experience to myself. Of course, I say all this with hindsight. At the time, it was very confusing to say the least. I went through hell; my life changed dramatically. From being a fairly successful musician, I virtually became a monk overnight! And all because of that experience."* [7]

## THE SCHEDULE

**Schedule - Phase 1:**
**Primary Data Interactive/Contact**
**Timegate 1977 - 1989**

**Schedule - Phase 2:**
**Primary Landings/Resonance Shift**
**Timegate 1989 - 2001**

**Schedule - Phase 3:**
**Primary Decloaking/Colonization**
**Timegate 2001 - 2013**

\* \* \*

**Primary Designated Landing Area**
**x-vis-Barbury Grid Coordinate**
**Wiltshire, England**

**Primary Earth Time Landing Coordinate:**
**Northern Hemisphere Sirius Alignment**
**[Stardate 13/20] circa July 17 - Aug 17 1998**

**5D World Wide Web**
**[Strategic Free Domain/Web Site Station]**
**Deployment Timegate: 1998 - 2004**

**4D-5D Migration Timegate: 2004 - 2010**

**5D Harmonic Interface Timegate: 2011**

**Domain HQ Decloaking Timegate: 2012**

**Earthshift: 2013**

*Fig.15.2: The schedule that was received by Jon King during his contact experiences. Adapted from UFO Reality, issue 4.*

The beings he encountered were from *"a different or parallel world rather than another star system"*, [8] or alternatively, *"the next kingdom in nature, or the next dimension of reality"*. [9] They told him, telepathically, about a schedule that was unfolding between 1977 and 2013. The schedule is split into three phases or *"timegates"*. Phase One is *Contact* from 1977 to 1989. Phase Two is *Landings/Resonance Shift* from 1989 to 2001. Phase Three is *Decloaking/Colonisation* from 2001 to 2013. Each phase is designed to bring about *"specific effects and changes in global consciousness"*. [10] Within Phase Three, by the end of 2004 (i.e. by now), a *"5D World Wide Web"* should be in position, synchronised with the Earth's geomagnetic grid; there will be *"Web Site stations"* and *"Strategic Free Domains"* at the Earth's *"grid cells"*. The 'D'(1D-5D), refers to the following kingdoms; minerals, plant, animal, human and *"alien"* (ultra-terrestrial).

Jon was told that a large triangular area of southwest England, centred on Barbury Castle hillfort, near Swindon in Wiltshire, UK, would be receiving *"energy codings"* (which sound remarkably like the crop circles which would soon proliferate in that area - see the next chapter) to prepare humanity for ET contact between 1998 and the dimensional shift, or *"Earthshift,"* around 2013. I spoke to Jon King on July 29th 2000, and he told me that, at the time he had his contact experiences, he had *never heard* anything about the Maya Calendar, Terence McKenna, or 2012. That removes any possibility of subconscious interference, and makes this an independent source of information on 2012 (although it seems that the later fictional TUMI column in *UFO Reality*, in which Jon King introduced the subject and presented the schedule, was influenced by J. J. Hurtak's *The Keys of Enoch* [11]).

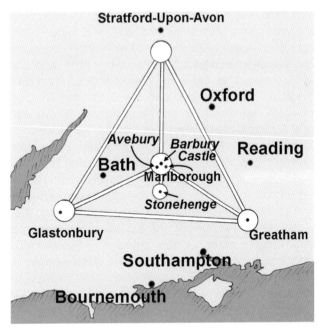

Fig.15.3: *Jon King's 'Aquarian Triangle'. Adapted from UFO Reality, issue 7.*

### Alien Telepathy

In the first issue of *UFO Reality*, [12] a UFO contactee called John Craig describes the appearance of a UFO following his cry for help on May 16th 1992. The sighting lasted half an hour and was also witnessed by his family. He started writing a book with his wife (who is Japanese), called *Merging Point*, which *"detailed the acceleration of evolving consciousness to a point in 2012 AD, when we would transmute our 3D consciousness to become truly multidimensional, galactic beings"*, [13] but the book seems only to be available in Japanese. On May 16th 1993, the anniversary of the contact event, Craig received a telepathic message leading him to a deserted beach where he witnessed another UFO, and he began to chant in an unknown language. The phrase *"Echan Deravy"* kept recurring, and he eventually realized that this was to be his new name. After this, the UFOs appeared *"as if on command"* in front of witnesses, and telepathic communication continued. Deravy stated:

*"These were not objects in a 3D sense. They were 'real apparitions', behind which some enormously-evolved consciousness seemed to be at work. Which is why I now say they are not separate from us. They do not come from another planet, but rather from hyperspace itself - from the place all shamans come and go to."* [14]

In a 1998 interview with *UFO Magazine* (UK version), Pam Hamilton described how, while she was growing up in Indiana, USA, she experienced close encounters that began at a very early age, before she could walk. These earliest memories were with the *Greys*, which are the ET-type familiar to us from television and films. When she was three years old, in 1951, she had her first encounter with a tall, pale being with fair hair. Ufologists now know this race as the *Nordics*. Like the Greys, the Nordics communicated telepathically and became Hamilton's constant companions. Unlike the Greys, there were identifiable males and females, "*sometimes even materializing when she was with other people*". This is a clear sign that the beings were not of the same density as our reality, and only visible to Hamilton at the time, according to *UFO Magazine*:

"*In subsequent contacts, the creature imparted specific dates into her mind, along with images associated with those dates. For example, she remembers him telling her that '2012 would be very important to me. I would be leading people through the mountains. What mountains? I have no idea. He said as I grew I would know certain things'. Yet, in her conversations with other abductees, she's learned that her experiences are not unique. There is a sense among people who've been abducted that they have something inside of them that will 'switch on' at some point...*" 15

Since Pam was told by military personnel that they knew she had implants in her eye and ear, the implication is there that perhaps these implants will be activated around 2012. However, since the military then said they had to "*adjust*" the implants so they could tell what the ETs were up to, perhaps they put them there in the first place.

**The Assessment**
Robert O. Dean, retired command Sergeant Major, who had "*Cosmic Top Secret security clearance*", apparently the highest possible security clearance in NATO, was posted in Paris at SHAPE headquarters (Supreme Headquarters Allied Powers Europe) in 1964, when a very secret document called *The Assessment* was published:

"*It was a military study that had been undertaken over a period of three years, and it concluded that although we were being monitored by extraterrestrial intelligences, there was no apparent extraterrestrial threat. It concluded that what was going on had been going on for a very long time, and that we are dealing with not one, but several extraterrestrial intelligences.*" 16

Bob Dean retired in 1976, and at that time four types of "*extraterrestrials*" had been identified by the military: 17

"*But it was not simply that we were being visited by interplanetary visitors, or interstellar visitors, or even intergalactic visitors. When I retired in '76, many people in the military, government and science knew we were not really dealing with those issues. Rather, we were dealing with an intelligence that apparently had a multidimensional source. Now I'm not enough of a physicist to explain to you exactly what that means, or even what another dimension is. But I think there's an analogy to be found in death. I've always suspected that death is simply a journey to another dimension, another reality. I think we've come from there, we incarnate here, we live our lives, and we go back there. I've concluded that there are other levels of reality. And in a different way, the SHAPE study concluded something similar."* [18]

Bob forsees an imminent *"transcendent transformation"* into another realm of reality that will be *"so unbelievable that you can't even imagine it"*. [19]

However, it seems to Bob there is at least one *"ET"* race that, along with governments and other powerful people, hope to thwart the process, and that humanity has failed to make the transition many times in the past. At the end of his presentation at the first *World UFO Congress* in Lima, Peru in August 2003, Bob mentioned that the end of the Maya calendar (13-baktun cycle) in 2012 could well be the crucial time.

Singular avistamiento de ufólogos en el Centro Cívico de Lima

*Fig.15.4: Some of the speakers at the* World UFO Congress *in Peru, 2003. Back row L-R: Geoff Stray, Salvador Freixedo, Haktan Akdogan. Middle row L-R: Brian O'Leary, Daniel Munoz, Bob Dean. Front: Marcia Schafer.*

In the late 1990s, Bob told Chris Carter, the producer of *The X-Files* TV show:

*"You're not kidding me. Don't tell me that you're getting all these story ideas out of your own head. You're getting some input from someone on some of these ideas, because I know how accurate they are."* [20]

### The X-Files

The final episode of what may be the final series of *The X-Files* TV show was shown in the USA in May 2002, and on British TV on 16th March 2003. The famous slogan started by *The X-Files*, *"The Truth is out there"*, was finally explained. This show was called *The Truth*, and in it, Fox

Mulder finally discovers the ultimate secret. The secret is that the final alien invasion is scheduled for 22nd December 2012 AD, and that the Maya designed their calendar to end in 2012 for this very reason.

However, as Bob Dean said:

*"When people talk about alien invasion ... I mean ... it's all gone on for so long now. If they had wanted to invade us, they would have done so a long time ago."* [21]

Dr Richard Boylan, a research behavioural scientist and cultural anthropologist, or, alternatively, psychotherapist and clinical psychologist, has been saying for years that sources in the US government have told him that they have agreed to join the Extraterrestrial Federation of Planets:

*"This federation is made up of beings of all types, from Whitley Streiber's Greys to non-corporeal, thought essences. From gasbag beings to intelligent insect races. This federation is a non-monetary, non-violent, telepathic coalition of beings from numerous planets. The Federation has already greatly affected our physical and spiritual evolution throughout history and even before."* [22]

They will supply us with all their technology, and train us in telepathic expertise:

*"Dr Boylan says the Mayans knew this would be taking place. By the end of the Mayan calendar [in] 2012, Earth and all of Humanity will be wholly integrated into this extraterrestrial federation."* [23]

# Chapter 16:
# Crop Circles

### Barbury Castle

The first recorded cases of crop circles appear to go back hundreds of years, the cause sometimes put down to fairies or demons, as with the 'mowing devil' event of 1678 in Hertfordshire, England. From the 1950s, crop circles were connected with UFO appearances, and sometimes called *UFO nests*. The most famous of these appeared in the mid-1960s, in reedbeds at Tully, Australia. From the mid-1960s to the early 1970s, there was a UFO flap in Warminster, Wiltshire, UK, which included several crop circles (still seen as UFO nests). From the late 1970s through the 1980s, they were thought by many to be a weather phenomenon, but were getting more complex, appearing in pairs, then threes, then as quincunxes. They were also increasing in numbers. In 1990, they were strung out into long 'pictograms' of connected glyphs and reached record-breaking figures across England, with the biggest concentration in Wiltshire. In 1991, another jump in complexity occurred and it clearly seemed as if the phenomenon was evolving. Then a popular newspaper ran an article in which two old men, Doug Bower and Dave Chorley, claimed to have made all the crop formations as a joke. So the bubble was burst, and

*Fig.16.1: The Barbury Castle pictogram, 17 July 1991. Photo: Richard Wintle/Calyx Photo Services.*

nobody had to worry about reconstructing his or her reality tunnel any more. The fact that Doug and Dave contradicted each other, changed their minds about which formations they had made, and failed to make any convincing demonstrations, went un-noticed. [1]

Jon King says he was totally unaware of crop formations when he had his contactee experiences between 1980 and 1984 (see previous chapter), but they certainly fit his prediction of "*energy codings*", since they cluster in the "*Aquarian Triangle*", which has actually been the centre of crop circle activity, though the focus is thought to be Avebury or Alton Barnes, rather than Barbury (three and a half, and six miles away respectively). However, on 17th July 1991, a field at the base of the Barbury Castle hill-fort hosted a stunning triangular formation that looked like Jon King's diagram of the Aquarian Triangle, and had appeared in the landscape right at the centrepoint of it. It was later described by Brian Grist as "*an alchemical Mandelbrot Set*", due to its similarity to alchemical diagrams that also represent chaos and order. [2] The Mandelbrot Set is a fractal - the pictorial

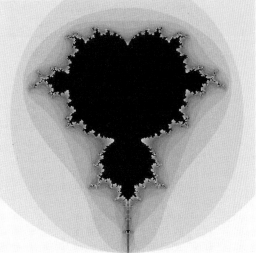

*Fig.16.2: The Mandelbrot Set. A representation of this shape appeared as a crop formation in 1991. Produced by David E. Joyce's Explorer Applet - http://aleph0.clarku.edu/~djoyce/julia/explorer.html*

Fig.16.3: Common Mexican forms of quincunx.
After Séjourné [1957, 1978].

BELOW: Fig.16.5: Crop formation at Overton,
Wiltshire, 13 July 1996 - note the resemblance to
parts of the Hunab Ku (below). Photo: Lucy Pringle.

ABOVE: Fig.16.4: A quincunx crop formation
that appeared at Everleigh Ashes, Wiltshire, 19
July 2000. The central circle is a bronze age
round barrow. Photo: Andreas Müller

BELOW: Fig.16.6: The crop formations at
Etchilhampton, Wiltshire, 1 August 1997. The grid
has striking correlations with the Maya
calendar, while its companion may represent
the six magnetic fields of the Sun.    Photo:
Werner Anderhub

Fig.16.7: Symbol adopted
by many to represent Hunab
Ku, from the works of Zelia
Nuttall. From Jenkins 2002.

representation of a complex equation from Chaos Theory, in which the whole picture is contained within itself at varying degrees of magnification.

Within a month, on 12th August 1991, the Mandelbrot Set itself appeared at a field near Ickleton, in Cambridgeshire. The original fractal discovered by Benoit Mandelbrot, it describes a system with a hierarchy of repeating patterns. So, these formations imply the significance of 2012 via Jon King, since his schedule predicts that "*Domain HQ*" will be situated at Barbury Castle, and is due to de-cloak in 2012, just prior to "*Earthshift*". In addition, they remind us that McKenna's Timewave Zero is also a fractal (originally called a *modular wave hierarchy* in 1975, before Mandelbrot had coined the term *fractal*) that terminates right at the end of 2012. There is even a rumour that McKenna claimed the Timewave is a Mandelbrot fractal, [3] but I have found no corroboration either that McKenna said this, or that the Timewave is a Mandelbrot Set.

## Quincunxes

A quincunx is defined as "*an arrangement of five things at the corners and centre of a square*". [4] Apart from simple circles, the quincunx is the most enduring crop formation design, some versions of which [5] are almost identical to some of the Mexican forms. [6] In his book *The Secret History of Crop Circles*, Terry Wilson reveals [7] that the first known appearance of the quincunx was in the 1950s in Heytesbury, Wiltshire, about the time of the first recorded crop circle in Mexico (in maize). Mexico also had its own quincunx crop formation in Milbaheta in 1977. In *Mexico Mystique*, Frank Waters describes the meaning of this figure:

"*It symbolises the four previous Worlds, or Suns and the present Fifth Sun as their unifying centre. But reconciliation of the bi-polar opposites during this era must take place within the human heart. So the quincunx also symbolises Quetzalcoatl, who by penitence and self-sacrifice made a final ascent out of matter into spirit, and was transformed into Venus.*" [8]

The quincunx can be seen at the centre of the Aztec Sunstone (see Chapter 1), where the four previous Suns surround the Fifth Sun, in which we are living now, usually interpreted as the Sun of Movement, indicating that the cycle's end will be marked by an earthquake. Some researchers think the five Suns represent a series of five 13-baktun cycles, of 5,200 tuns each, adding to 26,000 tuns (one full Precession of the Equinoxes), meaning that 2012 will be the end of the last of the series, and the end of a full cycle of 25-26,000 years. The Aztecs had forgotten about the Long Count and its 13-baktun cycle, but this possibility implies there may be some forgotten knowledge hidden in the Sunstone. [9]

## Calendrical Crop Codes

The crop formation at Overton, Wiltshire, 13th July 1996 (page 174), suggests a symbol often referred to as *Hunab Ku*, based on a design found by Zelia Nuttall. It incorporates the 'G' symbol, which represented Galactic Centre for the Maya, according to Yucatan daykeeper, Hunbatz Men. [10] If this interpretation is correct, then the attached crescent - a symbol interpreted in the later 1999 formations as the eclipsed Sun - may represent the eclipse of Galactic Centre by the Winter Solstice Sun, the event which John Major Jenkins has argued corresponds to the end of the 13-baktun cycle on 21st December 2012. In later photos of the formation, the small outlying satellite circle in the foreground has a tail and looks more like a comet, suggesting the return of Quetzalcoatl, but in the earlier images such as here, the tail is missing, so presumably that must have been a path left by a visitor.

On 8th/9thAugust 1997 at Etchilhampton, Wiltshire, two crop formations appeared next to each other. One was in the form of a grid, 30 by 26 squares, and the other was a six-pointed whirling star. Crop circle researcher Michael Glickman noticed that the grid was laid down *boustrophedon* style, or '*as the ox ploughs*' (in other words, the direction of lay alternates from line to line). He also pointed out that as there are 26 weeks in six months, and these are multiplied by 30 in the grid, the formation was signifying a time fifteen years in the future, which is the year 2012.

On further study, I found other 2012 indicators in the Etchilhampton formation. The tzolkin, or 260-day Maya sacred calendar, is a grid of 13 x 20 squares, and the 780-squared grid is divisible by exactly three tzolkins. In fact, a 780-day cycle was important to the Maya (in the Dresden Codex there are tables giving multiples of 780 days), because it is the synodic orbital period of Mars (the synodic periods of Mars were actually specifically demonstrated in an earlier formation which appeared at Titchbourne, Hampshire in 1995). The number of units could also be taken as 781, if one includes the large rectangle that contains the grid. 781 is the number of "*bits*" in Maurice Cotterell's 187-year sunspot cycle, which Cotterell has related to the 13-baktun cycle ending in 2012 (although he actually failed to do this convincingly). The six-pointed whirling star accompanying the grid could then represent the six rotating magnetic fields of the Sun (two polar and four equatorial) that cause the sunspot cycle.

## Solar Prediction

In the November/December 1998 edition of *SC* (*Sussex Circular*) [12] journal, amateur astronomer Jack Sullivan analysed a crop formation that had appeared at West Stowell, Wiltshire, on 23rd July 1994. The formation included a collection of standing clumps of cereal crop combined with three rings and a crescent. Sullivan reasoned that the clumps probably represented visible stars, and the rings were planets, while the crescent was the Moon. To cut a long story short, he found an exact match for the clumps in the constellation Cetus, which lies near Pisces on the ecliptic (or path of Sun and planets). Using astronomical software, he found the formation was depicting a conjunction of Saturn, Mars and Jupiter in the Cetus constellation. The date of the conjunction was 6/7th April 2000, which was six years in the future. Then Sullivan checked the position of the Moon, and found to his amazement that at midnight, not only was it in the exact position shown in the formation, but it was also four days after the New Moon, and would therefore

LEFT: The Aztec Sunstone. [See Chapter 1 and following page]

RIGHT: The Palo Volador of the Maya is a ritual that dates from pre-conquest days, in which a tall wooden pole represents the Maya World Tree - Earth's rotational axis. Four "angeles" (hanging by one leg) spin to the ground, representing the journey of the Hero Twins of the Popol vuh as they descend to the underworld - Xibalba - to battle with the Lords of Death. The four men spin through thirteen revolutions each, a total of 52, representing the 52-year Calendar Round. This is when the New Fire ceremony was performed by the Toltecs and Aztecs in order to stop the world from ending, but 52 is also symbolic of the 5,200-tun 13-baktun cycle that ends in 2012. [See Chapter 1]

*The Aztec Sunstone with colour restored, by Roberto Sieck Flandes.  It is possible that the original design was devised as a working calendar, with moving parts, recording the passing of eras, including the Long Count.  Theoretically it could record a unique date combination for each day over a period as long as 10,250 years.  [See Chapter 1]*

LEFT: Painting of the three cosmic ages according to artist Joachim de Fiore (circa 1130-1202). The first age is the Age of the Father at the bottom of the picture. The second age is the Age of the Son, and the third is the Age of the Holy Ghost at the top. These can also be called the ages of Law, the Word, and Spirit. [See Chapter 2]

ABOVE: The symbolism of The Star in the Tarot, especially this version by Lady Frieda Harris circa 1943, is suggestive of the Blue Star prophecy. The card is ruled by Aquarius (the coming Age), and was painted according to a design by Aleister Crowley, head of the AA (Argentum Astrum), the Order of the Silver Star - Sirius, according to Crowley's executor, Kenneth Grant. [See Chapter 2]

RIGHT: Zyzygyz's diagram showing how the 1939-1945 and 2006-2012 periods relate on the Timewave. [See Chapter 4]

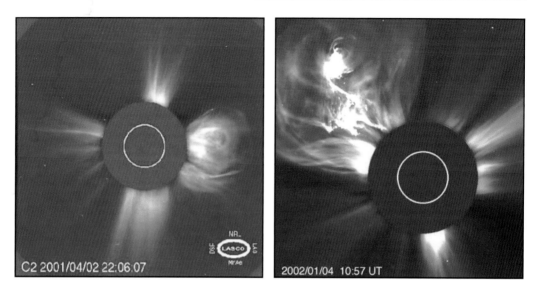

ABOVE: On 2nd April 2001, this record-breaking X-22 solar flare occurred. Photo courtesy of LASCO/NASA.

ABOVE: On 4th January 2002, the Sun provided the most complex CME (coronal mass ejection) ever recorded. Photo courtesy of NASA.

LEFT: This flare was released on 4th November 2003 and is now known to have been an X-45 - more than twice as large as any previously recorded flare (see Chapter 20). Photo courtesy of NASA.

BELOW: Kev Peacock's diagram showing the upward trend of earthquakes, geomagnetic activity and solar activity, and the clear correlation between peaks on all three graphs.

Earthquakes

Geomagnetic activity

Sunspots

[See Chapter 6 for details on the solar activity shown on this page.]

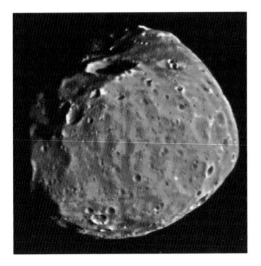

ABOVE: Mars' moon, Phobos. Some have predicted this may be dragged from its orbit and into a collision course with Earth in 2012. Photo courtesy of NASA. [See Chapter 7]

ABOVE: Computer model of the asteroid Toutatis, another celestial object some believe threatens our planet. Image courtesy of Scott Hudson and Steven Ostro, JPL and NASA. [See Chapter 18]

RIGHT: Some hold that a 'retrograde loop' of Venus occurring above Orion and near Gemini will herald a 'solar megacycle' catastrophe. Here, the twelve retrograde loops of Venus between 1924 and 2012 are shown on CyberSky software - http://cybersky.com [See Chapter 8]

ABOVE: *The Pyramid of Kukulcan at Chichen Itza, with Moon rising. Photo: Lee Anderson. [See Chapter 8]*

ABOVE: *The Hendaye Cross. Does this monument, built around 1680, encode a warning of "an imminent trial by fire for the northern hemisphere"?  Image from* The Mysteries of the Great Cross of Hendaye *by Weidner and Bridges [2003], used by permission. Photo (C) Darlene, 2004. [See Chapter 8]*

LEFT: *'Anamnesis' - intense mental download from Galactic Centre... The Diagnosis 2012 - or Dire Gnosis - website logo.  See www.diagnosis2012.co.uk, the most comprehensive website on 2012 predictions...*

BELOW: Examples of 'expulsion cavities' found by the author in the East Kennett grid crop formation (see right), indicating that the stems have been rapidly heated. Photo: Melissa White of The White Studio, www.thewhitestudio.co.uk

ABOVE: The 20 x 20 'grid' crop formation at East Kennett, Wiltshire, 2 July 2000. This can be interpreted as a calendrical grid representing three cycles from the Maya Long Count system. Photo: Francine Blake.

BELOW: Crop formation at Milk Hill, Wiltshire, 12 August 2001. 409 circles, 800ft in diameter... but do the 13 main circles in each arm represent the Maya 13-baktun cycle? Photo: Janet Ossebaard.

[See Chapter 16 for details of all the crop circles on this page]

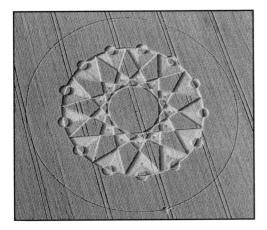

LEFT: Crop formation at Huish, Wiltshire, 20 July 2003, demonstrating the Maya 13-baktun cycle, as depicted by José Arguelles. Photo: Bert Janssen.

ABOVE: *This photograph was taken by Roz Savage at the annual festival of Snow Star or Qoyllur Riti, held just below the glacier on the sacred snow-peak of Mount Ausangate in Peru. There were 30,000 pilgrims in attendance. The festival celebrates the emergence of "the shining ones who will lead Peru and the world into a new era of peace". Roz Savage is the author of a forthcoming book,* Three Peaks in Peru *(website - www.rozsavage.com). [See Chapter 21]*

LEFT: *A 'Bronze Age calendar-priest king and queen' standing in front of Newgrange megalithic passage tomb in the Boyne valley, Ireland. The golden hats and collars are real and are recent archaeological finds made in Switzerland and Germany. Covered in thousands of Sun and Moon symbols, the hats record ancient time cycles. They are around 3000 years old. [See Chapter 22]*

appear as a crescent, as depicted. Jack Sullivan found that two other formations from 1994 also showed the same conjunction of April 2000.

Andy Thomas, then editor of *SC* journal (who now runs the *www.swirlednews.com* website and is also author of the crop circle 'bible' *Vital Signs* 13), was driving through Wiltshire, near the very spot of the original formation, around midnight on the night of 7th April 2000. He noticed that the sky had strange red patterns in it, and wondered why, having forgotten that this was the very time predicted by the crop formation six years before! It was only the following day that he realized the fact, and also heard what caused it. This is how Andy reported it in the 2002 edition of *Vital Signs*:

*"On 6/7th April 2000, one of the largest solar storms in a century erupted on the Sun, flooding the Earth's ionosphere with particles and creating the widest sighting of the aurora borealis across the UK and parts of Europe for many years, usually being restricted to more northern regions (hence its more common name of 'northern lights'). I was lucky enough to witness this effect as a strange shifting curtain of red light above Alton Barnes."* 14

The aurora was also seen as far south as North Carolina in the USA. Here we have a strong suggestion that crop formations may be linked to solar changes in particular, as well as being able to predict - incredibly - astronomical events and changes to the geomagnetic field.

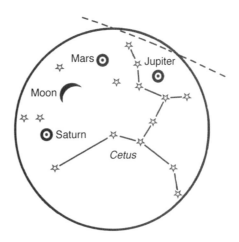

Fig.16.8: *The 'galaxy' formation at West Stowell, Wiltshire, 23 July 1994, seen with a diagram of the astronomical configuration which occurred in the sky at midnight GMT on 6th/7th April 2000. The diagram is shown here 'upside down' from normal protocol (the dotted line is the ecliptic plain) for clearer comparison with the crop circle image. Photo: Werner Anderhub.  Diagram adapted from Andy Thomas' Vital Signs [S B Publications 1998, 2002].*

## Venus Transit Prediction?

More recently, Jack Sullivan made another significant discovery concerning the 'missing Earth' formation, which appeared at Longwood Warren, Hampshire, on 26th June 1995. At the time it appeared, the design was widely interpreted as having catastrophic implications for our planet, since it seemed to show the Sun and the orbiting inner planets of the solar system as far as the asteroid belt, but although the orbit of Earth was depicted, unlike the other inner planets (marked as small rings), our own was absent from the chart. In 1995, Jazz Rasool said that the formation depicted the position of the planets at the time the formation appeared. However, this was only true if the solar system was viewed from 'below', whereas the astronomical protocol is to view it from 'above'. It did not explain why the Earth was missing, either.

In *SC* journal, issue 84 (May/June 1999), Jack Sullivan pointed out that the formation was a much more accurate rendition of the solar system from 'above' on 16th January 1998. This showed the *inferior conjunction* (during the retrograde loop) of Venus, when Venus is directly between the Earth and the Sun, in a plan view of the solar system. The formation was also an accurate rendition of the positions of the inner planets on 4th June 2004. This, again, was during the retrograde loop of Venus, and only four days before the *Venus transit*, where Venus passed directly between the Earth and Sun (in horizontal and vertical planes).

Thus, the Longwood Warren formation had a double connection to Venus and its 584-day (or 583.92-day) retrograde loop cycle. The Maya followed this loop cycle closely and it was tracked and recorded in the Dresden Codex over a period of 312 *vague years* (haabs). This is equivalent to three Venus Rounds of 104 haabs each (and three Venus Rounds is equivalent to one Mars Round or 146 Mars cycles of 780 days each); each Venus Round consists of 65 of the 584-day cycles. As if in confirmation of this connection, we find 65 'asteroids' depicted in the outer belt of the formation as varying-size small circles. The Venus Round is also equivalent to 146 tzolkins, or 13 Venus pentagrams (8 haabs each), and each of the Venus pentagrams is equivalent to 146 uinals.

There are 146 uinals between the Venus transit that occurred on 8th June 2004 (four days after the date encoded by the crop glyph) and the Venus transit due on 6th June 2012.

*Fig.16.9: 'Solar system' formation at Longwood Warren, Hampshire, 26 June 1995 - the Earth is famously missing from the chart, but Venus appears to be the main subject. Photo: Werner Anderhub*

The Venus transit in 2004 was the day 6 *Ik* in the tzolkin, and *Ik*, which means *"wind,"* is the equivalent sign of the Aztec god Quetzalcoatl, who is associated with Venus! In 2012, the Venus transit on June 6th will also be an Ik day (*1 Ik* in the True Count).

## 'Mayan' Crop Glyphs

On 4th May 1998, a crop formation of 33 revolving lozenge shapes appeared near West Kennett Long Barrow, opposite Silbury Hill, Avebury, Wiltshire, UK. It became known as the *"Beltane Wheel"*. There was soon a rumour circulating that the crop glyph was the same as the Maya Sun glyph. Since the Maya Sun glyph is called *Ahau*, and doesn't look like the crop formation, I wondered where the information came from. I eventually found that the source was Aluna Joy Yaxk'in, a New Age

*Fig.16.10: The 'Beltane Wheel' formation (in oilseed rape), Silbury Hill, Wiltshire, 4 May 1998. Photo: Andrew King*

speaker and author who works with *"the Mayan calendar"* (the Arguelles version). Aluna (whose website is called *Centre of the Sun* [15]) stumbled upon the formation on the day it appeared, while in the UK to attend the 1998 Mayan Dreamtime Festival in Glastonbury. She predicted finding a *"Sun"* crop circle shortly before seeing it, and has since said it connects to the Maya calendar, since there are *"33 solar petals"* on the formation, and the Maya tzolkin uses a combination of thirteen numbers and twenty day-signs (33 in total), which she calls *"Sun glyphs"*. [16]

On 23rd May 1999, at Avebury Trusloe in Wiltshire, a 'fried egg' appeared, containing eighteen 'sperms'. Around the edge were twenty smaller circles. This could be seen to represent the three basic cycles of the Long Count: a tun, or 360-day year, which consists of eighteen uinals of twenty kin (days) each.

In the following year, 2000, a 20 by 20 'waffle' grid appeared at East Kennett (see colour pages), in which I personally found many examples of expulsion cavities. An expulsion cavity

*Fig.16.11: The 'one-tun,' or 'fried egg,' at Avebury Trusloe, Wiltshire, 23 May 1999. Photo: Andrew King.*

is a hole that can be found on stem nodes, which are formed when the stalk is heated rapidly for a microsecond, and all the moisture collected there turns to vapour and bursts out. The effect has been demonstrated by using an industrial strength microwave oven, but apart from that, has only ever been observed in crop formations. Many other anomalies have been found, such as a high density of melted meteoritic particles, microscopic pit-holes in the stems and growth abnormalities in seeds from crop formations (a thorough scientific investigation of these effects can be found at *www.bltresearch.com*). This second grid could be interpreted as a calendrical diagram again, representing three cycles from the Long Count. Each square is a tun; each row of squares is twenty tuns, or one kaktun; twenty rows of one katun each are equal to one baktun (consisting of 400 tuns or 7,200 uinals or 144,000 kin). See colour page VII.

*Fig.16.12: Diagram of crop formation at Silbury Hill, Wiltshire, 25 August 2002. This remarkable design appears to embody both the cycles of Venus and precession. Diagram by Rob Seaman.*

On 12th August 2001, a huge six-armed 800ft diameter formation appeared on Milk Hill near Alton Barnes, Wiltshire. It had thirteen major circles in each arm (six thirteen-baktun cycles?). On 25th August 2002, a five-pointed star (pentagram) appeared at Silbury Hill, near Avebury, Wiltshire. It had thirteen 'scales' between each pair of arms, which makes 65 altogether. There are 65 Venus cycles (approximately 584 days each) in every Venus Round (Aztec and Maya), which is 104 haabs long (haabs are 365-day years). Venus makes a pentagram around the zodiac every eight haabs, so in the 104 haabs there are thirteen pentagrams. Also, there are 65 baktuns in five eras or 13-baktun cycles, making up a total of 26,000 tuns, or one cycle of precession. On 20th July 2003, the first-ever thirteen-fold star arrived at Huish, in Wiltshire (see colour pages), looking like a clock-face where each segment represents one baktun, combining to form a 13-baktun cycle (consisting of 7,200 tzolkins of 260 days each). The formation is uncannily similar to a diagram of the 13-baktun cycle that appears on page 47 of José Arguelles' *The Mayan Factor*. In April 2004, a crop formation was reported that turned out to be the 'ghost' of the Huish formation, where the shape had been transferred to the new crop (oilseed rape) via bare patches where the stems had originally been laid down the year before, presumably through some unusual effect on the soil. In 2004, a huge 'wheel' formation arrived opposite Silbury Hill utilising Maya symbolism around its edge. 2005 saw similar examples. So, every year now there are crop formations with connections to the Maya calendrical systems.

## The 'Aztec Pizza'

I have already mentioned my animation of the Aztec Sunstone in Chapter 1. The initial idea for the project happened around the turn of the millennium and, following three months solid work on it, I completed the animation (apart from the proposed soundtrack) on Friday 1st June 2001. On that very day, unbeknown to me at the time, a crop formation appeared at Wakerley Woods, Barrowden, Northamptonshire, UK, and was almost immediately nicknamed "The Aztec Pizza" by crop circle researcher Karen Douglas. There

*Fig.16.13: The so-called 'Aztec Pizza' which appeared at Wakerley Woods, Northamptonshire, 1 June 2001. Photo: Nick Nicholson*

was a general resemblance to the Sunstone, in that there were concentric rings of glyphs, but the Sunstone has a ring of twenty day-signs, surrounded by a ring of 56 quincunxes, surrounded by a ring of 104 'eagle-feathers', within a ring formed by two 'fire-serpents' of twelve segments each (see colour pages). The Wakerley Woods crop formation, on the

other hand, had a ring of eighteen inward-pointing isosceles triangles (that actually do look like inverted versions of the 'solar rays' on the Sunstone), surrounded by a ring of nine wider triangle glyphs, surrounded by a ring of eighteen 'G' glyphs, which is the Maya symbol for the Milky Way galaxy.

The thing that impressed me about the formation was the fact that it arrived on the same day that the animation was completed, and it displayed the numbers 9 and 18, which were the numbers involved with the discovery of the 'Secret Dial' that made the whole animation possible. Nobody had ever found the Long Count in the Sunstone before, because the number 18 could not be found on it, and since there are twenty days in a uinal and eighteen uinals in a tun, it was an essential requirement. I had spotted what looks like a visible segment of

*Fig.16.14: The Secret Dial - found by cutting and pasting nine double-quincunx sections together on a photograph of the Aztec Sunstone.*

a hidden ring, showing two quincunxes. I then electronically 'cut and pasted' eight copies of the suspected segment, each turned by multiples of a 40° angle, put them together, and found a perfect ring made from the nine segments of two quincunxes each, revealing the missing eighteen uinals! This does not work on some of the colour paintings of the Sunstone, since the angle varies by up to 2° on each side of the visible segment, and this can result in a twenty-quincunx ring. However, it works perfectly on a photo of the real thing. As a result, an animation showing the passing of the 5,125 years of the 13-baktun cycle can be shown on the Sunstone, starting in 3114 BC and ending on 21st December 2012, when the Solstice Sun conjuncts the equator of the Milky Way. It also happens that there are eighteen years in a quarter-degree of precessional movement, and since the Sun is half a degree wide, it will take eighteen years for the Sun to complete the second half of its crossing of the Galactic Equator, from 1998 to 2016. This is the event flagged by the Maya at 2012.

So, in 1999 we had a tun represented in the 'Fried Egg' crop formation at Avebury Trusloe, and in 2000 we had a baktun represented in the 'Waffle' crop formation at East Kennett. In 2001 we had a secret knowledge of the 13-baktun cycle represented in the 'Aztec Pizza' crop formation at Wakerley Woods. On the other hand, perhaps we just had an egg, a waffle and a pizza. [17]

## Nibiru Crop Code

Robert Boerman, a Dutch crop circle researcher, has written a book called *Crop Circles, Gods and Their Secrets*, [18] in which he analyses crop formations and discovers a kabbalistic code. The code gives hints about Nibiru, the planet on a huge elliptical orbit, which, according to Zecharia Sitchin's translations of cuneiform tablets from Sumeria, returns to our solar system every 3,600 years, and houses the "*gods*" who cross-bred our ancestors by genetic engineering. Boerman was constantly finding precessional numbers in his analysis of crop formations - by counting the number of circles and taking measurements, in yards, feet and inches (which *are* very ancient, as John Michell has pointed out [19]). To understand how Boerman arrived at 2012 as the return of Nibiru, we must go to his primary source on this - Alan Alford's *Gods of the New Millennium*, which states that Nibiru itself would not return until circa AD 3400, [20] but suggests 2012 as a date for the "*return of the gods*". [21]

Alford's calculations are convoluted and complex, and his reasoning murky, but he actually made two errors in his calculation of 2012. Boerman used Alford's "*return of the gods*" calculations for the return of Nibiru. This is simple, but not very effective, since he has duplicated Alford's two errors. Using Alford's figures, the correct calculation gives 2014, not 2012. [22] If we also take into account that if the current rate of precession has been slowing down from what it once was at the supposed time of the flood, as implied by Alford, then there could be up to another 42 years or so to add on to 2014, bringing it on to 2056! [23] We must therefore conclude that the evidence for a return of Nibiru in 2012, at least via Alford and Boerman, is rather questionable.

# Chapter 17:
# Secret Government

## The Montauk Project

In 1979, Charles Berlitz and William Moore published a book called *The Philadelphia Experiment*, [1] describing a wartime attempt by the US Navy to make a destroyer (the *USS Eldridge*) invisible to radar by using a very powerful magnetic field. The result was said to be the teleportation of the ship from its dock in Philadelphia to its other dock in Norfolk, Virginia, where it became briefly visible, then teleported back again to Philadelphia. The surviving crew were reported to have been fading in and out of visibility in the aftermath of the experiment, or to have permanently disappeared, or gone insane. Some were said to have died. The original source of the information, Carlos Allende, alias Carl Allen, said the experiment took place in October 1943, but investigation of naval records by Berlitz and Moore found that Allen was at the Norfolk, Virginia dock in October and the *Eldridge* was at sea. However, further investigation revealed that Allen stayed in Philadelphia on the weekend of 13-15th August 1943, just before joining his ship, the *S.S Andrew Furuseth* on 16th August. It finally emerged that the *Eldridge* was in the Philadelphia docks at this time, and the experiment must have taken place between 20th July and 20th August. The test with the most drastic side-effects probably occurred just prior to the reported public vanishing of two sailors that happened on 12th or 13th August. [2] Also mentioned is the claim that the Philadelphia Experiment resulted in contact with *"UFO occupants"*. [3]

An even more unbelievable sequel has arisen in recent years. Two American seamen are alleged to have jumped off the *Eldridge* during the Philadelphia Experiment on 12th August 1943. They found themselves not in the harbour, but on Long Island, New York, on 12th August 1983. They had time-travelled to a point where the government was conducting a similar experiment, The Montauk Project, connected by planetary magnetic fields that peak every 20 years on 12th August. The scientists working on the project have allegedly been able to time-travel through some kind of hyperspace loop between the experiment dates, but for some reason can't go beyond 2012. The source of this story is Al Bielek, who claims to be Edward

*Fig.17.1: The* USS Eldridge. *From the National Archives.*

*Fig.17.2: The author's old garage door (!) was a copy of the 'Time Tunnel' crop formation that appeared at Cissbury Ring, West Sussex, 15 July 1995. It is similar in appearance to the fictional time-travel device featured in the 1960s TV series* The Time Tunnel *- which is in turn similar to the description of the time-travel device supposedly used at Montauk.*

Cameron - one of the two seamen who jumped off the *Eldridge* (the other was his brother, Duncan Cameron).

Steven Gibbs is an inventor from Kansas USA, who apparently makes time-travel machines called *Hyperdimensional Resonators*, and a simpler version called the *Sonic Resonator*, and sells them. [4] On the *futurehorizons.net* website, he says:

*"We can say that the machine seems to induce out-of-body experiences in most users almost immediately. When out of your body it is possible to travel in time and space with your astral body and witness or experience events in time. This technology is real and has been experienced by hundreds of people worldwide".* [5]

Gibbs has been studying the time travel concept since 1981 and has spoken to someone called Bruce Perrault, who gave him information on the equipment that was on board the *Eldridge*. He says that when a hyperdimensional resonator is activated over a "*natural grid point*" or power spot, then physical time travel is possible. He claims several people who have bought his device have time travelled, but they were unable to return to their own time (surely cause for a refund?!). When asked about the future, he said:

*"When they sent some scientists from the Montauk Project into Earth's future, they hit a barrier in the year 2012. When they tried to go past the barrier from 2012 to 2013 they couldn't go through, they could only go around it. But after they went around it they found that all life on this planet had been wiped out... everything. Cities were all in ruins and there was no life found anywhere... at least they couldn't find any. They concluded that everything had been wiped-out".* [6]

However, Frissell and Bielek have a slightly less bleak interpretation of the same report. In *Nothing in This Book is True, But it's Exactly How Things Are*, [7] Bob Frissell says that the reason they couldn't go beyond 2012 was that the last time travel experiment will be in 2012, and all the experiments are interconnected. Frissell says they could also travel into the past, but not beyond one million years ago, since this was the date that the alien race known as the Greys did their first time-travel experiment (New Age guru Drunvalo Melchizedek was the source of Frissell's information). An unnamed interviewee that is presumably Al Bielek, in an on-line transcription of part of a nine-hour series of interviews, gives another version. Bielek says [8] that beyond 2012, time travellers have found *"a dreamlike reality"* that continues until 10,000 AD, although in the same interview he says there is *"a very abrupt wall there, with nothing on the other side"*. He says that humanity survives, but the future is just blocked from view. This is because of a change in vibratory rate: the end of third density and the start of fourth density. People will still have physical bodies, but be in a state of compassion, love and understanding:

*"It also relates to the realisation that one is not separate from the creator. It is that kind of spectrum which has been called by the Christians as [sic] the 'Second Coming'. The Second Coming is a state of being, not an individual arriving and establishing a power hierarchy."* [9]

### Remote Viewing and 'The Discontinuity'
Remote viewing is a technique used by the military to gather information, and was originally known as *psychic spying*. It is a disciplined form of clairvoyance, and has had some amazing results. Ex-military remote viewers have set up their own training schools, and this is now becoming a fairly widespread technique. On the *2013.com* website, [10] I found a statement that remote viewers have said *"nothing can be 'seen' beyond the year 2012"*. [11] The explanation given on the site is that humanity's perception of time will no longer be so *"linear and absolute"*:

*"'After' the year 2012, there is no lapse in time between a thoughtform and its corresponding 3D eventform. So, if a remote viewer in 1997 cannot see beyond 2012, it is to a large degree because the world(s) beyond 2012 have not been conceived of yet, or we are just perceiving/creating them now... THAT is the nature of the new time."* [12]

Ed Dames was in charge of a US Defence Intelligence Agency team of remote viewers. He became head of his own remote viewing company (Psi Tech), claiming that his company's remote viewing findings were 100% accurate; he is now executive director of the Matrix Intelligence Agency (but has been criticised on some message groups for making predictions that don't come true). In an online transcript of a radio interview with Art Bell in 1997, [13] Ed Dames answered a question about this 2012 block, saying that the in-house term for it is *"The Discontinuity"*:

*"... Remote viewers run up against a point where things change dramatically and globally... and it's all at once. I can give you my best guess about what that is... We have explored it, its geophysical parameters, biophysical parameters, trying to discern what the heck is happening, and we have a working hypothesis now, and the working hypothesis (and it's that only, by the way... it may be something that is truly beyond our ken), is that*

*time changes. That there is an event that is global, that something happens to the world that makes all the event timelines change."* [14]

He goes on to say that it seems to be a spiritual event that happens at one point in time, and affects all subsequent experience:

*"You appear to be somewhere else, and, in fact, you've leapt onto a different event trajectory, a different time... parallel time, if you will."* [15]

# Chapter 18:
# Nostradamus

### King of Terror

Michel de Nostredame was born in 1503 in Provence in France, and studied medicine and astrology. He had a natural talent for prophecy and used a bowl of water to aid his visions, in a similar way that a crystal ball would be used (as a 'screen' on which visions would appear). He used astrology to determine the time sequence of the prophecies. Being Jewish, and living in a culture of enforced Christianity, his prophecies were influenced by kabbalistic thought and prophecies from the Old Testament and the New Testament. To avoid persecution as a witch or heretic, he deliberately obscured the prophecies and re-

*Fig.18.1: Michel de Nostredame 1503-1566.*

arranged their sequence. He became quite renowned, and the Queen of France, Catherine de Medici, hired him. Nostradamus specialists [1] say that he predicted the Great Fire of London, the Second World War and the assassination of the Kennedys, but the prophecies are easily misinterpreted (both the allies and the Nazis in World War Two used the prophecies as propaganda). There are 1000 prophecies, written in Old French, in the form of four-line poems called *quatrains*. They are grouped in ten lots of 100 quatrains each, called *Centuries* (but Century Seven is incomplete, having only 42 quatrains), and when a prophecy is quoted, the Century is given first, then the quatrain number.

Nostradamus only made one unambiguous prediction in which he clearly identified the year in question. It is the oft-quoted 10:72, which is usually translated something like this (alternatives in brackets):

*In the year 1999 and seven months ["sept mois"]*
*from the sky will come the great King of Terror*
*He will bring back to life the great king of the Mongols.*
*Before and after, Mars [war] reigns happily [by good fortune]* [2]

If there is any substance to Nostradamus' prophecies, then surely this quatrain *must* be a major key. However, when nothing happened in July 1999, some said the prophecies were of no use. Others said that *"sept mois"* meant the original seventh month - September. Nothing happened then either. One Nostradamus site, now unavailable, suggested that the prophet was predicting the timing of a war, and that fortunately (since it would make it worse) Mars would reign before and after, but not *during* the war:

*"... When the Kingmaker Saturn leaves the sign of Mars' rulership on April 10th 1996, and returns to a sign of Mars' rulership in Scorpio, in the year 2012. This scenario would time this war as starting sometime after the year 1996, and ending sometime before the year 2012."* [3]

This interpretation gets *"war"* and the planet *"Mars"* from the same word (Mars), which may or may not be valid, but another questionable technique of interpretation is mentioned here:

*"Sometimes in the numbering of the quatrains Nostradamus gives us a further clue. Very often he gives us at least two numbers of the date an event happens and, in some cases, he gives us three numbers of the date. This quatrain is numbered 10-72. So here, he could be giving us three numbers, 1, 0 and 2 - this could very easily refer to the date 2001 or 2012. The 7 could be a clue as to the '7th month.'"* [4]

## John Hogue

Prophecy scholar John Hogue, in his book *Nostradamus - The Complete Prophecies*, [5] finds six quatrains to have a possible connection to the year 2012. Some of these connections are made as in the suggestion above, which links the number of the quatrain to the date of the prophecy. In prophecy 1:52, *"the two evil influences in conjunction in Scorpio"* are said to be a conjunction of Mars and Saturn in the constellation of Scorpio, and Hogue links this to October 2012, when such a conjunction will occur. He links prophecy 2:12 to 2012 via the quatrain number. Prophecy 5:78 mentions a thirteen-year period that Hogue connects to either the appearance of Halley's comet in 1986, or that of comet Hale-Bopp in 1997, which, when thirteen years are added, render the years 1999 and 2010, which is *"closer to the end of time as we know it"* (2012). In prophecy 6:24, a conjunction of Mars and *"the sceptre"* (Jupiter - in Cancer?) means April-May 2011, says Hogue (*"near the end of the Mayan calendar"*). Prophecy 9:12 links to 2012 via the quatrain number. In prophecy 9:55, a conjunction of Mercury, Mars and Jupiter again refers to April-May 2011. I don't find these very convincing; if 2:12 and 9:12 link to 2012, what about prophecies 1:12, 3:12, 4:12, etc.? The quatrains referenced to 2012 by Hogue concern the end of the Catholic Church, the coronation of a new king who will bring peace to the Earth, and a war followed by disease. However, the quatrains that are obviously based on the *Book of Revelation* are not included.

## Toutatis

In the *Book of Revelation* there are at least five meteorite showers, [6] four comet or asteroid strikes [7] and four earthquakes [8] seemingly described. Nostradamus also mentions a comet (or "*bearded*" or "*burning star*", or meteor) in nine quatrains, [9] meteorite showers (or "*stones from the sky*", "*red hail*" or "*fire from the sky*" etc.) in ten quatrains, [10] and earthquakes in five quatrains. [11] Some of these are clearly based on St. John's *Book of Revelation*.

Quatrain 1:69 describes a "*great mountain*" of size seven stadia (about seven eighths of a mile) that is "*rolling along*", and Michael McClellan's *New Prophecy Almanacs* say:

"*Every four years an asteroid named Toutatis passes uncomfortably close to the Earth. This elongated rock - which measures nearly a mile across - also possesses another feature of interest: it rolls end over end in a tumbling motion. It is the only near-Earth planetoid that behaves in this manner, eerily similar to the 'mountain' that 'rolls along' in Quatrain 1.69... If Toutatis is the asteroid predicted by Nostradamus, it will smash into the Aegean or Ionian sea part-way through the reign of Hieron (anagram of Chiren) [sic] ... Evidence in the* Epistle to Henry II *and the quatrains place Chiren's rule as king and later as emperor in the 2002 - 2012 period.*" [12]

Although Toutatis was very close to Earth in 2004, it does pass again in 2012. McClellan also finds evidence in Nostradamus' quatrains that China will abandon communism in December 2012, and Prince Edward will be made second emperor of Europe.

More and more Internet sites are interpreting various Nostradamus prophecies as describing events between 1999 and 2012, but they are not very convincing. Many state the conclusion without giving the evidence. For example, on a site called *Nostradamus 1999-2012 AD*, a fundamentalist Christian - Pastor Harry of the Church of Philadelphia - says Nostradamus was "*Satan's Prophet*":

"*... [He] seems to show us a Window of Time SEPT 1999 -2012 AD when The RAPTURE will happen so He can bring forth Antichrist onto the world scene.*" [13]

Another site, *King Of Terror*, quotes the 10:72 quatrain (see above), then says:

*"So warns Nostradamus in quatrain X.72, and thus heralds in the commencement of a window of prophecy originating from many cultures, religions and traditions, which runs 1999 - 2012."* [14]

There is a book out in German, by Manfred Dimde, the title of which translates as *Nostradamus: The Apocalyptic Decade*, with the extra subtitle *The Crucial Years Until 2012*. [15] Unfortunately, my ability to read German is phrasebook level, so I don't know if he's actually found anything convincing. Is everyone desperately trying to find a way of decoding a 2012 prediction from Nostradamus' quatrains, or are we still missing something?

## Phobos Revisited

After the seventh month of 1999 came and went, some realized that although the prophecy mentioned the seventh month, the calendar has since been adjusted by eleven days (when it was converted from Julian to Gregorian), which brings the date forward from 31st July 1999 to 11th August 1999, the date of the total solar eclipse (as seen over Cornwall in the UK). In fact, Nostradamus is said to have explained in a letter to Henri II of France that he was talking about an eclipse. Some said that since Phobos means 'Terror', one of the moons of Mars - the one called Phobos (see colour pages) - would be released from its orbit by the supposed gravitational effects of the eclipse and the Grand Cross conjunction a week later on 18th August 1999. *The Millennium Group* (TMG - the online forum and repository for scientific research into the current transformation of Earth's systems and astrophysical environment) hosted an article by TMG team members Ray Ward and Gary Goodwin in 2001, *The Four Horsemen of the Apocalypse*, which asked the question, *"Where has Phobos gone?"* The article suggested that during a CNN (*Cable News Network*) video clip taken from Turkey during the solar eclipse of 11th August 1999, *"Shadows* [were] *also seen crossing the face of the Earth at a nearly right angle to the Moon's shadow"*. [16] They suggest, with supporting photographs, that this was Phobos, and hint that perhaps Comet Lee had loosened it from its orbit in June 1999, so that it could be seen from Earth during the 1999 eclipse, as apparently predicted by Nostradamus.

In July 2000, James van der Worp and Glen Deen had suggested that the fly-by of comet 76P on June 5th 2000 shunted

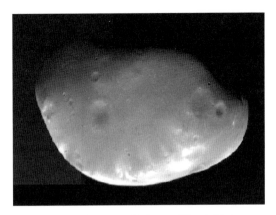

*Fig.18.2: Mars' moon, Deimos ("Panic"). Image courtesy of NASA, JPL and the Viking Project.*

Phobos out of orbit and onto a collision course with Earth. In fact, Ward and Goodwin also pursued this 76P-Phobos connection in their 2001 article, before concluding that Phobos had been loosened from its orbit in 1999. Deen calculated September 18th 2012 as the projected time of impact, but then changed the theory to the 'Planet X Cosmic Billiards Theory', as we saw in Chapter 7, which includes Phobos being loosened by comet Kohoutek in 2001.

According to Ward and Goodwin, there is a connection between two very public failed Mars missions and the fly-by of comet 76P, which they say triggered solar flares and dust storms on Mars. The last public pictures of Phobos and Deimos (the Greek names of two moons of Mars, sometimes translated as *Fear* and *Panic*) are from August 1998, and, to cut a long story short, there is evidence that they are already orbiting Earth, say Ward and Goodwin. [17] This includes a collection of photographs from various satellites and from the ground showing anomalous dots. The moons are only ten miles and five miles in diameter, respectively, and are said to have been asteroids originally captured into a Martian orbit, now transferred to ours. Ward and Goodwin suggest there is a covert operation being mounted to blast the "*Martians*" out of the sky. [18]

You may recall the Bible Code prediction that there will be a collision between a "*comet*" and Earth in 2012, and that the comet will be "*crumbled*". At the *Chapel Perilous* site, [19] they have found that the code also conceals a previously undiscovered element, which they call "*The Mars Code*". Until now, it sounded fairly nonsensical, because the author concludes that the "*comet*" is actually the planet Mars! Thus, it will be "*Mars*" that is destroyed in 2012 when it passes near the Earth.  However, in light of the information above, "*Mars*" could just as easily refer to one of the small Martian satellites, Phobos, or Deimos (if you think it's possible that amateur astronomers could miss this for so long, and NASA could keep a lid on it!).

## Nostradamian Fundamentalism

There is a site called *An Ancient Prophecy Revealed for 1999* (or its duplicate site, *The New World Order and Antichrist: The Years 2002-2012*), [20] which makes the outrageous claim that the UK's heir to the throne, Prince William, is the "*Once-and-Future King*", or King Arthur, who is also the "*Great Beast of Revelation*" (who "*was and is not and is to come*") and the Third Antichrist of Nostradamus' prophecies. The whole concept is supported by the prophecies of Nostradamus, and, preposterous as this sounds, if you spend some time looking at the material, you could end up feeling more than a little paranoid. When I discovered the site, it was just three weeks before the first of a series of prophecies were due to be fulfilled. It was predicted that Prince William would be crowned king of England on Summer Solstice 2002, and the royal family would be wiped out by a meteor strike just beforehand.

The timeline of predictions went from the predicted 2002 royal cometary wipe-out up to the destruction of the Antichrist at Armageddon on 21st December 2012. Of course, when the events didn't happen, the entire timeline prediction was changed and given much more leeway, so that most events on the timeline have between a three and ten year window to occur, and now all events include 2012 as a possible date. However, the final destruction of the Antichrist is now scheduled for 19th November 2021 [21] (don't ask me why). At least that should save on website updates! Obviously this is just another case of Nostradamus being used as propaganda.

## Nostradamus Meets Mother Shipton

So, going back to the *King of Terror* quatrain, 10:72, if we go down the page to quatrain 10:74, we find:

> *The year of the great seventh number accomplished*
> *it will appear at the time of the games of slaughter*
> *not far from the age of the great millennium*
> *when the dead will come out of their graves.* [22]

Remembering that Nostradamus was Jewish, think back to the Judaism section of this book, and think about the Jewish calendar, which starts with the birth of Adam - year zero; remember also the importance of 1,000-year periods, which are the same as a day for God. So if year zero is the year of the great first number, then year 6000 (2000 AD) is the year of the great seventh number. As for the games of slaughter, the Olympic games started in Greece as a festival of athletics, but the Romans replaced the athletic games with violent gladiator contests. So, not long after 2000 AD, *it* will appear, and this will be shortly before the start of the millennium (the 1,000 years of peace, Golden Age, Day of the Lord, or seventh Day of Creation), when the dead rise (as described in *Revelation* 20). After 2000 AD, there are Olympic games scheduled for 2004 (which passed without mishap), 2008 and 2012, so that gives us three possible years. This may sound tenuous, but most interpretations of Nostradamus are!

As to what *it* is that appears; when we glance up the page to the "*Great King of Terror*" that was loosened in 1999, we see that the quatrain in-between (10:73) is about judgement, which may connect the quatrain above and below it. In 1999, various people were saying that Comet Lee was the King of Terror (e.g. Howard Middleton-Jones reported that Comet Lee "*fragmented on its trip round the Sun*," and "*three anomalous objects were observed during the solar eclipse on August 11th 1999*" [23]), but how could this have been the King of Terror, as most people never heard of it? Perhaps there is another contender for the title that links 1999 to 2012 and is more believable than Phobos...

Now is a good time to bring in Mother Shipton, who was born in 1488 in Yorkshire, England, and made many prophecies that came true, including the Great Fire of London (also predicted by Nostradamus). In Shipton's *The Last Prophecy*, there are also clear references to the *Book of Revelation*, and verses three, four and five of the eighteen are especially significant:

*For those who live the century through*
*In fear and trembling this shall do*
*Flee to the mountains and the dens (Rev. 6:16)*
*To bog and forest and wild fens*

*For storms will rage and ocean roar*
*When Gabriel stands on sea and shore (Rev. 10:2)*
*And as he blows his wondrous horn*
*Old worlds die and new be born*

*A fiery dragon will cross the sky (Rev. 12:3)*
*Six times before the Earth shall die*
*Mankind will tremble and frightened be*
*For the six heralds in this prophecy*

The inference here is that these three verses describe the same events as those described between chapters six and twelve of *Revelation*. On a webpage called *Myrddin's Warning*, [24] these verses have been shown to act as a key to *Revelation* and Nostradamus. The first line of *The Last Prophecy* mentions the year 1926, so the events in question happening to "*those who live the century through*" must therefore happen just after the end of the 20th century. The third verse is interpreted to indicate six passes of a Near-Earth Object (NEO), and it so happens that Toutatis was discovered in 1988, and has a four-year orbit, which means that it will have passed six times and be on its seventh observed pass of Earth when it comes by on December 12th 2012! It passed in 2004, and will come again in 2008 and 2012 - the same years as the Olympic games ("*games of slaughter*"?). But there is more...

The sixth chapter of the *Book of Revelation* describes the opening of the seven seals, and when the sixth seal is opened, as Myrddin suggests, a solar eclipse is described ("*the Sun became black as sackcloth*"), [25] followed by a partial lunar eclipse ("*the Full Moon became like blood*"), [26] followed by a meteor shower ("*and the stars of the sky fell to the Earth*"). [27] Incredibly, there is a solar eclipse due on 13th November

*Fig.18.3: Mother Shipton: facsimile of her portrait from the cover of the 1686 edition of her prophecies.*

2012, followed by a "*partial*" eclipse according to Myrddin (but it will actually be a penumbral eclipse - see below) on 28th November 2012, followed by the Geminids meteor shower on 6th December 2012.

Chapter eight of the *Book of Revelation* contains details of two apparent further meteorite showers and three meteor strikes; one of these is undoubtedly the one that Nostradamus referred to as the "*great mountain*" in Quatrain 1:69, and another is the famous fallen star, "*Wormwood*". Myrrdin also brings our attention to Quatrain 2:30:

> One that shall cause the infernal gods of Hannibal
> to live again, the terror of Mankind
> there was more horror not to say ill days
> did happen or shall to the Romans by Babel

Myrrdin explains that when Hannibal called on the Celts of Gaul to help him fight the Romans, any captured Romans would have been sacrificed to the Celtic god, Toutatis, Lord of the World, after which the asteroid is named. The Quatrain also brings in a connection to the *King of Terror* quatrain (10:72), which implies that something happened in 1999 that will affect the orbit of Toutatis - and Toutatis is the Gallic equivalent of the Roman god Mars.

Myrddin differs by two days in his dating of the solar eclipse - he says it will be on 15th November 2012, and my two references say 13th November; [28] he also says that the end of the 13-baktun cycle has been "*recalculated by several experts*" to be 12th December 2012. The real reason some people are saying this is simply that they are confused. [29] A third error is that the "*partial*" lunar eclipse will actually be a *penumbral* eclipse, when the Moon only passes through a semi-shadow just beyond the main shadow of the Earth, and this kind of eclipse is hardly discernible, since the brightness of the Moon is only slightly impaired, so it will *not* go red. These three errors do not destroy the theory, but the fact that prophecy expert Peter Lemesurier says of Mother Shipton that "*not a single one of the blood-curdling world predictions so often attributed to her is actually to be found in the earliest edition of her*" [30] might thankfully mean that this theory, though ingenious, is wrong. If that is the case, then we are left to wonder why Toutatis is also known as *Lucifer's Hammer*. I can actually answer that question. In 1977, Larry Niven and Jerry Pournelle published a science-fiction novel called *Lucifer's Hammer*, about a dark star companion to the Sun called Lucifer that knocks a comet out of its orbit, sending it on an Earth-crossing trajectory with catastrophic consequences. Stephen Miller made the connection when he saw an animation of Toutatis (since it is a very odd shape, like a tumbling dumbbell) and put up a webpage about it, entitled *Lucifer's Hammer*, on his *www.mkzdk.org* website. [31]

# Chapter 19:
# The New Age

## The Next Precessional Age

In his book *Gods of the New Millennium*, Alan Alford made a study of ancient Babylonian and Sumerian mythology, and concluded that the gods of Babylon each ruled for one precessional age, which is a twelfth of an entire precession of the equinoxes. Combining "*the latest scientific estimates*" of the length of a precessional age (2,148 years, as quoted by archaeo-astronomer Jane Sellers) with biblical and Babylonian information, Alford concludes that the precessional age of Marduk began in 2284 BC. The next one began 2,148 years later, in 135 BC. Counting forward another 2,148 years, says Alford, brings us to the next one in 2012.

Alford does not think the planet Nibiru will return in 2012 as some have speculated, but predicts it around AD 3400. He does, however, see the start of the next precessional age as a likely time for the "*return of the gods*". This implies that they are lurking somewhere in the vicinity of the solar system, as predicted by Robert Temple in the latest edition of *The Sirius Mystery*. As mentioned already, there is an error of between two and 44 years in Alford's calculation, but that could just mean that his date for the flood is out by that much.

## Aquarius Now

Most astrologers place the junction between the Age of Pisces and the Age of Aquarius between 2060 AD and 2160 AD, but recently, with the popularity of the New Age movement, it has been brought back by many to the year 2000 or thereabouts. Many have simply stated that the Age of Aquarius has recently arrived, but don't give any references that can be checked up on. The problem is that there are two ways of measuring the boundaries between the signs of the zodiac; one is by agreeing that each of the twelve signs of the zodiac is an equally sized 'slice', in which the zodiac is split into twelve slices of 30° each; the other is by agreeing that the boundaries of the signs vary according to the size of the constellations. Since the Age starts when the Spring Equinox Sun enters the sign of Aquarius, we find that another problem, even if using the 'equal slices' version, is agreeing on exactly when and where one of the boundaries between the constellations (the 'cusp') is. Since there is so much disagreement as to exactly where the Pisces/Aquarius boundary is, a logical approach is to use astronomical software to reverse the Spring Equinox back through time, until it coincides with a more obvious constellation boundary, and then wind it forward in time, counting 2,160 years per sign. However, we also have the problem of agreeing on the length of the cycle of precession and, therefore, how long one twelfth of it would last for. As we have seen with Boerman and Alford, it is usually taken as 2,160 years per sign, though it is probably now nearer to 2,148 per sign. Weidner and Bridges used the Spring Equinox on the cusp of Leo-Virgo in

10,958 BC to work forward half a precessional cycle to 2002. This presumes six equal-sized ages of 2,160 years each.

The Aquarian Age Network [1] have now put out a statement explaining why they are now declaring that the Age of Aquarius started on Spring Equinox March 20th 2000 AD. [2] In layman's terms, this translates as:

"... *The point of the Spring Equinox (once being between the constellations Gemini and Taurus, on the Galactic Equator) already has moved more than 90° from this point on the Galactic Equator, which is opposite the centre of our galaxy... The 90° relates to three constellations, each 30°, and therefore the constellation Aquarius enters the Spring Equinox dawn and the New Age arrives.*" [3]

A Christian magazine called *Testimony* has actually modified this by twelve years, so that the Age of Aquarius is due on Spring Equinox 2012:

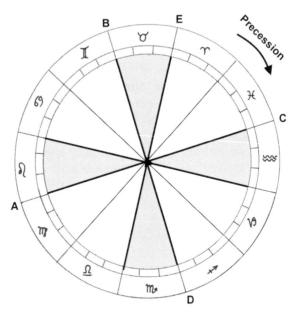

Fig.19.1: *The Precessional cross displayed on the astrological zodiac (signs arranged clockwise). A: Virgo/Leo cusp - Spring Equinox circa 10,958 BCE and Autumn Equinox today. B: Gemini/Taurus cusp - Spring Equinox 4480-4468 BCE and Summer Solstice today. C: Pisces/Aquarius cusp - Spring Equinox today. D: Scorpio/Sagittarius cusp - Winter Solstice today, 2000-2012. E: Taurus/Aries cusp - start of the Age of Marduk, Spring Equinox 2284 BCE.*

"*We now need to consider the concept of the meridian. This is an imaginary line running from the horizon due north of an observer through the heavens to the horizon due south of an observer. The meridian at the vernal equinox is called the Zero Meridian, and it runs through the constellation of Pisces in which the Sun is situated. At the time of the birth of Jesus Christ, the nearest visible star in Pisces to the Zero Meridian would have been that designated Alpha. However, due to the slow movement of the Sun through the zodiac, mentioned above (the precession of the equinoxes), the nearest star in Pisces to the Zero Meridian, in fact the nearest of all the 1,800 brightest stars as listed in a star catalogue, is now that designated Omega. It is calculated that it will be exactly on the Zero Meridian early in 2012.*" [4]

## The Great Conjunction

On a website called *Audrey's Ancient Egypt*, [5] Audrey Fletcher explains how she used the *Narmer Palette* from First Dynasty Egypt, plus *SkyGlobe* software, to work out that the Age of Aquarius starts on December 21st 2012 AD.

She first ascertained that the transition between the Age of Gemini and the Age of Taurus was in 4,468 BC, then, by working forward in 2,160-year jumps (since, in a Platonic Great Year of 25,920 years, each Zodiacal Age lasts 2,160 years), she found that the Age of Aquarius would start in 2012. Since the Great Year is made up of four Great Seasons, and the Gemini-Taurus junction was exactly a quarter of a Great Year ago, and represented a Great Autumn Equinox, it followed that the Great Winter Solstice would be in 2012.

Audrey calls Winter Solstice 2012 *The Great Conjunction*, since *SkyGlobe* reveals that six of the planets plus the Sun and Moon will all be in the same 180° section of the sky. However, the May 2000 conjunction, when four planets plus the Sun and Moon were aligned, was widely expected to bring massive changes, but none occurred. Astrologer Helen Sewell acknowledges that the 'Yod' (or 'finger of God') configuration in December 2012 of Saturn and Pluto, with Jupiter (spiritual enlightenment) as its central focus, could be a significant pointer to any events which occur at this time, especially as the Sun also enters Capricorn (the sign most associated with manifestation) at precisely 11:11 Universal Time, 21st December 2012. However, she says this does not constitute a 'Great Conjunction'.

I asked Audrey, "... *you don't mention the Maya - is it the Mayan Long Count end-date that led you to 2012 as the dawning of Aquarius, or did you deduce it independently?*" She replied, "*Yes the dating for the beginning of the Age of Aquarius is the same as the Mayan forecast, but I did arrive at that date independently...*" [6]

Barbara Hand Clow, in her book *Catastrophobia*, [7] has also used the Narmer Palette to deduce the date of the Gemini-Taurus transition, but she dates it at 4480 BC, which is twelve years before Audrey's date. [8] This results in a dawning of Aquarius in the year 2000, but on the Spring Equinox. The Pisces-Aquarius boundary is very vague, so to get a reliable calculation, one must go back to a time when the boundary is less disputable. Weidner and Bridges found the Leo-Virgo boundary to fit the bill:

"... *We discovered that the ancients had a very precise delineation between the two, one that has been maintained, pretty much the at the same point, into modern usage. With the help of* Voyager II *and our local planetariums, Chapel Hill and Boulder, we determined the point when the ancient Leo/Virgo cusp point fell on the Spring Equinox, March 22, 10,958 BCE. We used that as our marker and looked for the moment when it fell on the Fall Equinox, which turned out to be September 22, 2002.*" [9]

This also means that the Spring Equinox of the year 2002 would fall six zodiac boundaries away from the Autumn (Fall) Equinox (since the Sun moves through six constellations during half its annual journey, over six months), which means that the Pisces-Aquarius boundary coincided with Spring Equinox in 2002, by this calculation.

## Crossing the Threshold

In the summer of 2002, I heard philosopher Stanley Messenger give a talk about Rudolph Steiner's prediction of "*mankind crossing the threshold at the end of the century*". Stanley said that all the people who have completed a struggle towards enlightenment through the ages have formed a 'critical mass' that will allow the majority of mankind to cross this threshold together, that Steiner foresaw this, and that the time is now. Stanley sees the event as reaching its climax by 2012, and sees a connection to the crop circle phenomenon. [10] Although some feel it is unfair that the masses should reap the benefits of the sacrifices of a few, it would seem to be a natural process, like Rupert Sheldrake's 'Morphic Resonance' theories, or the 'hundredth monkey' phenomenon, in which an entire species somehow miraculously gains a behavioural attribute when a certain 'critical' percentage of individuals pioneer it. [11]

## Period of Justification

Robert Gilson has described an experience in January 1992, in which, after attending a week-long intensive course for spiritual growth in Phoenix, Arizona, he was "*zapped by the Michael energy*" (in a similar manner to the *Diagnosis 2012* image on the index page of my website - see also colour pages). In a state of heightened awareness, Robert was informed intuitively that there was to be a "*period of justification*" lasting twenty years, before the advent of a new consciousness occurred for humanity. During this time, people should start to sort out all their personal issues and emotional problems (or "*get our hearts in order*"), to prepare to receive the new energy, "*in order to make the shift gently, rather than in a mad panic*". [12] Twenty years from 1992 is, of course, 2012, but Robert knew nothing of the significance of 2012 at the time. [13]

Although there is no direct connection, this happened at the same time as the '11:11' events, when worldwide meditations were performed to open a "*Doorway*". The Doorway is an opportunity to evolve along with the Earth, and will stay open for twenty years from 11th January 1992 to November 11th 2011, according to *Solara*, [14] who started the movement. Solara claims that she is not a channel, but she "*simply embodies her vastness*", or in other words, she just *knows* and we should take her word for it. She says that the sign of 11:11 is "*a pre-encoded trigger placed into our cellular memory banks prior to our descent into matter*" and that this is why so many people responded to the idea. It aroused a lot of interest around 1992, when various people started seeing the number combination 11:11 all of a sudden (for example, in crop formations, or 11:11 being the exact clock time of synchronicities occurring). The Doorway consists of eleven gates, and the first is the *Healing of the Heart*, after which it "*seems to expand*", according to accounts on the official 11:11 website *www.nvisible.com*. One thing that many of the 11:11 enthusiasts have missed is that not only (in the tropical zodiac) does the Sun enter Capricorn at 11:11 on 21st December 2012 (see previous page), but Winter Solstice the same day will also occur at exactly 11:11 Universal Time, according to the US Naval Observatory. [15]

## Galactic Synchronization

In his 1987 book *The Mayan Factor*, José Arguelles says that the 5,125-year "*Great Cycle*" (13-baktun cycle) marks the end of Earth's passage through a "*resonant frequency synchronisation beam*", which will prepare Earth and humanity for an ascension, or evolutionary leap, to the next dimension. This book has been an inspiration to many people, and was responsible for bringing the Maya calendar to the attention of the world at large. In it, Arguelles synthesized Ben Franklin's 'Magic Square' (see Chapter 4), the I Ching, sunspot cycles, the tzolkin, Long Count and the Complexity Consciousness ideas of Teilhard de Chardin. The galaxy is seen as an immense living being that communicates with its organs - the solar systems - by pulses of energy sent from *Hunab Ku* (galactic centre). The Sun receives the pulses and transmits them via the 22-23-year binary sunspot cycle to the planets and lifeforms in order to cause a harmonic resonance that will allow a progressive evolution towards global, then solar, then galactic consciousness. This is achieved via the evolving Noosphere, which Arguelles calls the planetary memory program, or *Psi Bank*, which is situated at the Van Allen radiation belts surrounding the Earth.

The 13-baktun passage through the beam is the gestation time for the creation of a planetary light body that takes the form of a dodecahedron-shaped etheric geomantic grid [16] on the surface of the Earth. UFOs are defined as:

"*... Unified Field Organisers, an intelligent release of galactically programmed, psychically active, radiant energy simultaneously attracted to and emanated by Earth's resonant etheric body.*" [17]

The period from 2007 to 2012 sounds very similar to Jon King's 1998 to 2004 *5D World Wide Web* positioning and synchronisation, and, having compared King's fictional *TUMI* column in *UFO Reality* to *The Mayan Factor*, the influence seems obvious (but it is probably because both King and Arguelles were influenced by J. J. Hurtak [18]). However, in the Jon King interview [19] he makes it clear that he was given the dates of the Timegates during his contact experiences, which pre-dated the publication of Arguelles' book. This is *The Mayan Factor* version:

"*The final five-year period, AD 2007-2012, will be singularly directed to the emplacement of galactic synchronisation crews at all the planetary light-body grid-nodes.*" [20]

Unfortunately, there were some errors and inconsistencies made in *The Mayan Factor* concerning the Maya calendars, which, due to the book's popularity, have caused subsequent errors and confusion in the theories of other people who used it as their main source on Maya calendrics. [21] (See also page 46.)

This is how Arguelles visualizes the final moments as the 13-baktun cycle reaches a close:

"*Then, as if a switch were being thrown, a great voltage will race through this finally synchronized and integrated circuit called humanity. The Earth itself will be illumined. A current charging both poles will race across the skies, connecting the polar auroras in a single brilliant flash. Like an iridescent rainbow, this circumpolar energy uniting the planetary antipodes will be instantaneously understood as the external projection of the unification of the collective mind of humanity. In that moment of understanding, we shall be collectively projected into an evolutionary domain that is presently inconceivable.*" [22]

## Photon Belt

The *Photon Belt*, or *Photon Band*, is a persistent myth that is always being associated with 2012. By tracing it back to its origins and seeing how it has developed, we should be able to understand how much of this story is based in fact, and how much is pure fiction.

In the February/March 1991 issue of *Nexus Magazine*, there was a reprint of "*an obscure but popular 1981 article*", [23] which said that in 1961 "*satellite-borne instruments*" had discovered a "*photon band*" around the Pleiades star cluster. The article claimed that someone called José Comas Sola (a Catalan astronomer who is more famous for his observations of Saturn's largest moon, Titan, circa 1908) discovered that our solar system is part of the Pleiades constellation and that Paul Otto Hesse was the discoverer of the Photon Belt:

"*Paul Otto Hesse also made a special study of this system, of which our Sun is a part, and discovered, at absolute right angles to the movements of the suns, a PHOTON BELT or MANASIC RING, a phenomena [sic] which scientists have not yet been able to reproduce with laboratory experiments.*" [24]

One revolution of our solar system around the Pleiades is described as taking 24,000 years, which is made up of a 10,000-year period of darkness, followed by a 2,000-year period of light (passing through the band), followed by another 10,000-year period of

Fig.19.2: *The Photon Band/Belt concept displayed on the astronomical zodiac (signs arranged anticlockwise), showing current 13-baktun cycle and the positions of the previous four. Adapted from Clow [1995] and other sources.*

darkness and a second 2,000-year period of light. The article continues:

*"WE ARE NOW POSED* [sic] *TO ENTER THIS PHOTON BELT.   It is inevitable... between now and the end of this century - but it is inevitable!   We have completed the full circle and are back at the beginning.  It is described in detail in your Bible, by all books on mythology, by Nostradamus, and by modern day scientists."* [25]

The article predicts what will appear to be falling stars, as solar radiation interacts with the Photon Belt, and the sky will appear to be on fire. This may be preceded by 110 hours of darkness if the Sun enters first. People will experience something akin to putting their fingers into an electric socket, and then be converted from *"Corporeal"* people to *"Atmospherean"* people, but not all will survive the shift. There is also the following total mis-quote of the Nostradamus Quatrain 10:72:

*"Nostradamus, in his quatrain about the end of the world as we know it in 1999* [says] *'and it will rain no more, but in 40 years, all will be normal'"* [26]

The modern form of mediumship called channelling lent support to the theory, and as time went on, channelled information was published supporting the Photon Belt story, enlarging on it, but changing some of the details to match up with other prophecies. In 1991, a book by Peter O. Erbe was published in Australia [27] (home of *Nexus Magazine* and the original *Flying Saucer Research Magazine*, where the first article appeared), in which 'The Great White Brotherhood' channelled through a message saying that Earth completes its orbit around the Pleiades not every 24,000 years, but every 25,860 years:

*"... This particular cycle is nestled within a number of greater cycles, of which it is but a part - including the overall cycle of 206 million years - in one single point of convergence. This is also called the Harmonic Convergence."* [28]

206 million years equates approximately to 8,000 of the 25,860-year cycles, which are each close to the accepted current length of precession. We are further informed that we would enter the Photon Belt in 2011, which would trigger an ascension to *"fourth-level density"*. The book also notes that St. Germain (the famous immortal, who is one of the Great White Brotherhood, as related by the Theosophists) *"stipulates the month of December 2012 as the approximate date of the actual transition"*. [29] The alien race known as the Greys (usually thought to be from Zeta Reticuli) [30] were said to be in league with governments trying to abort the process. In some New Age circles, the Greys are seen as being the *"opposition"*, who made a deal with the American government after the Roswell UFO crash in 1947 or the Philadelphia Experiment in 1943, trading alien technology for permission to abduct humans for genetic experiments. According to Erbe, they feed on human fear and do not want to lose their food source.

In *Earth's Birth Changes*, [31] published around the same time, someone called *Azena* channels St. Germain, who says we will enter the Belt in December 2012, attaining a "*parallel universe*". This will represent "*the culmination - The Harmonic Convergence - of a 200 million-year evolutionary cycle*".

Sheldon Nidle channelled "*The Sirians*" and in 1994 published the results in *You Are Becoming a Galactic Human*. [32] The Sirian version was that we were scheduled to enter the Photon Belt by the end of 1996. [33] After five or six days in the "*Null Zone*" on the edge of the belt, while the geomagnetic field would be collapsed, the atoms of our bodies should have been modified, changing our physical bodies to semi-etheric bodies, at which point there would have been a mass landing of the Galactic Federation. In 2012-2013, our whole solar system was scheduled to travel down a wormhole in the direction of the Sirius system. The Photon Belt will alter DNA and give us six extra chakras for a total of thirteen, allowing us to use our inter-dimensional soul body for existence in a timeless higher dimension - the Fifth.

Barbara Hand Clow, whose grandfather was a Cherokee Indian, is an astrologer and the editor of Bear and Company (which publishes a wide selection of alternative books). In her 1996 book *The Pleiadian Agenda*, she channels *Satya*; a Pleiadian goddess who gives a version of the forthcoming shift that seems to unify all the other conflicting versions. Nibiru was originally a planet from the Sirius star system, [34] and travels from there to here and back every 3,600 years. It was last here 2,000 years ago and appeared as the Star of Bethlehem. In 1987 (Harmonic Convergence), the Galactic Synchronization Beam (Arguelles' Resonant Frequency Synchronisation Beam) reacted with the Photon Belt as we entered it. At Winter Solstice 2012, Earth's entire orbital path will be engulfed in the Belt; this will be the ascension or "*galactic orgasm*". We must prepare by meditating at sacred sites, to modify our DNA and emotional bodies. In 2013, "*the third dimension will dissipate on Earth.*"

Now it's time to burst the bubble with a few quick words from Cecil Adams, who claims to be the "*World's Smartest Human Being*" (he is joking), and runs a website (www.straightdope.com) that aims to clear up misconceptions:

*(1) No Photon Belt or other such region of increased energy has been discovered. Photons in any case are merely particles of electromagnetic energy, which we commonly experience as light. Upon exposure to excess photons, the most common transformation of your being is sunburn.*

*(2) There's no 'anomaly' near the Pleiades star cluster. The Pleiades are surrounded by a nebula, or gas cloud. This cloud is composed not of photons, but of dust and hydrogen gas.*

*(3) The Earth isn't heading toward the Pleiades, but away from them. In the 1850s it was conjectured that the Earth orbited the Pleiades, but this has long since been discredited.*

*(4) Paul Otto Hesse is a German author of a book on Judgement Day and is unknown to astronomers.* [35]

In 1973, Jim Hurtak wrote a book called *The Keys of Enoch*. This is a book that purports to have been projected into its author's third eye while he was *"before the throne"* - not channelled, therefore, but revealed like the *Book of Enoch* and St. John's *Book of Revelation*. On page 78, [36] he says:

*"Thus, this precession of the equinoxes is the length of time required for our solar system to make one complete revolution around the Pleiades, our greater parent sun, which calculates to a period of 25,827.5 years."* [37]

So this would seem to be the earliest provable reference to the solar system revolving round the Pleiades. The book also refers to an *"electromagnetic Null Zone"*, [38] which will propel the solar system into another dimension where fifth-dimensional bodies are needed.

The appeal of the Photon Belt concept could perhaps be explained by its simplicity and similarity to the scientifically feasible theories of galactic superwaves and magnetised plasma bands, and its common points with the popular Synchronisation Beam of Arguelles. As a modern myth encoding a cyclical encounter between Earth and some kind of radiation connected with Galactic Centre that is governed by, or coincidental with, precession, which may cause an evolutionary jump in mankind along with changes in the atmosphere and crust, then it retains some validity. However, considering its misleading association with photons, and its association with Hurtak's *"Null Zone"*, the Pleiades and failed prophecies, it is, on the whole, best forgotten.

## Realm Border Wave

The *Cassiopaea* website [39] holds a colossal repository of channelled messages from *"The Cassiopaeans"*, who claim to be *"sixth density beings"*, and in the section of the site called *The Wave*, it is explained how there is a cluster of comets on a 3,600-year orbit, which appears as a single body. Every time the comets come, the Annunaki arrive just beforehand, to feed on the soul energy created by fear. The Annunaki are from Zeta Reticuli (which effectively makes them the 'Greys' to some, as they allegedly originate from the same star system). Right behind the comet cluster is a *"Realm Border Wave"*, which returns every 309,000 years (twelve precessional cycles) and will merge this *Third Density* with the next one up - the *Fourth Density*. This is a *Realm Border Crossing*. Riding on this Wave is a colossal fleet of spaceships. Three immense ships are also coming from the direction of Orion, each carrying twelve million *Nephilim!* The Nephilim (literally, *"those who fell down"* in Hebrew), are mentioned in *Genesis* chapter six, and are usually thought to be the offspring of the union between the *"sons of God"* (or *Annunaki* - see Nibiru section in Chapter 7) and the *"daughters of men"*. However, a close reading of *Genesis* 6.1-4 reveals three non-human species, since the Nephilim were there before the sons of God arrived, and the offspring were the *"mighty men of old"*, who were giants according to the *Book of Enoch*.

The Cassiopaeans and Pleiadians are helping us to prepare for this shift, according to

Laura Knight Jadczyk, who is the channel. Those who successfully make the transition will merge with all other densities of their being for a short moment, which may seem to last forever. This sounds very similar to Ken Carey's scenario. Those who fail to make the transition will have to repeat the whole 309,000-year third Earth cycle. There will be physical side effects of the Wave, such as a shift of the "*magnetic axis*", and ozone depletion, which is already occurring. The Wave will arrive between now and 2012 (although in some quotations they say it could be as late as 2018); timing depends on whether it is speeded up by scientific projects currently underway, which sound similar to the Philadelphia Experiment.

Most of the Cassiopaean information was obtained using a *planchette* (a small board with wheels and a pencil that is supposedly caused to write spirit messages when a person's fingers rest lightly on it), or by using a Ouija board. It is said in spiritualist circles that only "*lower astral shells*" can be contacted through this method, and that "*higher spirit guides*" never make contact by it. Whether you agree with that statement or not, there is now a mass of information available that the Cassiopaean information is unreliable to say the least, but unfortunately, anybody who points this out is liable to be labelled as "*a psychopath*". [40]

## The Calleman 'Solution'

Swedish researcher Carl Johan Calleman noticed that since the tzolkin can be used as a map of the 13-baktun cycle, it could theoretically also be applied to the larger cycles that have been found on a few *stelae* (a stela or stele is an upright slab or pillar with an inscription or sculpture; the plural form is stelae) such as stela 1 at Coba - a ruined Maya city in the forest 60 miles east of Chichen Itza in the Yucatan. Then he noticed that if this is continued upwards, a cycle is discovered that is close to the scientifically accepted age of the universe. To explain this further, we must first look at the extended version of the Long Count calendar:

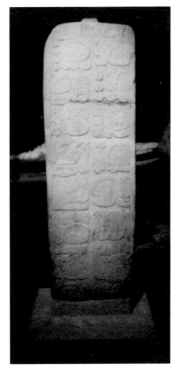

20 *kin* or days is one *uinal*. 20 days
18 *uinals* is one *tun*. 360 days
20 *tuns* is one *katun*. 7,200 days (about 20 years)
20 *katuns* is one *baktun*. 144,000 days (about 400 years)
20 *baktuns* is one *pictun*. 2,880,000 days (about 8,000 years)

*Fig.19.3: A stela at Tonina, showing 4 Ahau/8 Cumku at the top - the origin point of the 13-baktun cycle*

20 *pictuns* is one *kalabtun*. 57,600,000 days (about 160,000 years)
20 *kalabtuns* is one *kinchiltun*. 1,152,000,000 days (about 3.154 million years)
20 *kinchiltuns* is one *alautun* (about 63.08 million years)
20 *alautuns* is one *hablatun* (about 1.26 billion years)
20 *hablatuns* is about 25.2 billion years

What Calleman realized is that thirteen hablatuns would be equal to about 16.4 billion years, which is close to the usual estimate given for the age of the universe; about 15 billion years. If the pattern of the 13 x 20 Sacred Calendar or tzolkin encodes larger sacred cycles, such as the 13-baktun cycle, he reasoned that a whole cosmology of 13-unit cycles, rather than 20-unit ones, could be represented in a nine-step pyramid form, such as the Pyramid of the Jaguar at Tikal, Guatemala, the Pyramid of Kukulcan at Chichen Itza, Mexico, or the Temple of Inscriptions at Palenque, Mexico (the one that conceals the tomb of the ancient Maya ruler, Pacal). In this way, the top or ninth level would represent a 13-uinal period, while the bottom, or first level, would represent a 13-hablatun period.

So, the topmost layer represented the 260-day tzolkin of thirteen uinals. The next level down would be a 260-uinal cycle of thirteen tuns. The next level down would be a 260-tun cycle of thirteen katuns (this is a cycle normally known as the *Short Count*). Under this would be a 260-katun cycle of thirteen baktuns (this is the familiar 13-baktun cycle). Below this would be a 260-baktun cycle of thirteen pictuns, and so on. In this way, we would have a nine-level pyramid, where each layer is structured like the tzolkin, but twenty times larger than the layer above.

*Fig.19.4: The Pyramid of Kukulcan, Chichen Itza, Mexico. Nine-step pyramids are thought by Carl Johan Calleman to represent nine evolving states of consciousness. Photo: Lee Anderson.*

This is a very intriguing idea, showing how the development and evolution of the universe could be encoded into the structure of the Maya calendrical systems, from the creation of the universe until its final consummation at the end-point of 13.0.0.0.0. At the junctions of each level of the layered pyramid, humanity apparently gains another "*frame of consciousness*", and although Calleman says that speculation on the consciousness that will be accessed at the "*summit of the pyramid*" would seem to be "*almost pointless*", he does indulge the reader a little. It will be an end of time, in which no more calendars are needed:

"... *the attainment of a time-less cosmic consciousness, and an experience of unity with All-That-Is in its fullest sense, a disappearance of the line dividing life from death. Although many that live today have had temporary experiences of such a cosmic consciousness, these have only been temporary, due to our limiting frame of consciousness. At the end of Creation this may no longer be so and the eternal life may in fact manifest as a time-less cosmic consciousness.*" [41]

If this sounds quite similar to other interpretations we have covered, maybe that is because it is based on "*several ancient scriptures*" that turn out to be mainly the *Book of Genesis* and the *Book of Revelation*.

Anyway, you might wonder what it would imply for the Long Count notation, if there were cycles larger than the 13-baktun cycle. The Maya usually just used the last five positions; in fact, stela 1 at Coba implies that all the larger cycles have already reached thirteen, so you might think the 13.0.0.0.0 date should actually be written as 13.13.13.13.13.13.0.0.0.0 in Calleman's system. However, when you look closer, the logic breaks down a little. In fact, stela 1 at Coba shows cycles that are longer than the thirteen hablatuns since the start of the universe at the time of the theoretical Big Bang. The full Long Count date on the stela is written as:

13.13.13.13.13.13.13.13.13.13.13.13.13.13.13.13.13.13.13.0.0.0.0

Calleman says [42] this stela implies a hierarchy of creations, i.e. his multi-layered pyramid, but this Long Count date actually signifies a time span equivalent to about $6.5 \times 10^{22}$ years. This is trillions of years longer than the age of the universe; or in other words, the current universe is about the four billion-billionth universe of 16.4 billion years each! Calleman's pyramid would need 23 levels to show this. These larger cycles could, however, be a mythic representation of four previous eras (at a push).

Although the "*Creation*" date in 3114 BC is theoretically written as "*0.0.0.0.0*", wherever it is referred to on a stela it is written as "*13.0.0.0.0*" [43] and most Mayanists have thus concluded that every time we get to the end of the thirteenth baktun (which is baktun number twelve, since the first one was baktun zero), we reach a new Creation date and the count of baktuns, katuns, tuns, uinals and kin go back to zero. A record on a temple stairway at Yaxchilan [44] is said to show eight levels above baktun, and they are all still at '13' - 13.13.13.13.13.13.13.13.9.15.13.6.9. This means that when the baktuns, katuns, tuns, uinals and kin go back to zero at Creation, the larger levels all stay fixed where they were. If they were part of a functioning Long Count, then they would either all have gone back to zero, or the pictun level would have gone up to '14'. This Coba stela must then be simply depicting mythic time and underlining the importance of the creation dates.

Calleman supports the True Count, as opposed to the Lounsbury correlation, but he realised that his theory would be much neater if only the Long Count had ended on day 13 Ahau in the tzolkin, instead of 4 Ahau. Incredibly, he decided that the Maya got it wrong, and said that although he still agreed with the True Count of the tzolkin, the correlation between the Long Count and the tzolkin was wrong. This is something nobody had questioned before, since there has never been any doubt of the tzolkin-to-Long Count correlation; it was set by the Maya and wherever a stela shows the Long Count, it shows the relevant tzolkin date. Previous arguments had concerned how the calendars relate to the Gregorian calendar, not how they relate to each other. Calleman criticized Arguelles for creating his own New Age *Dreamspell* count, [45] yet has not seen the parallels to his own creation. In fact, he says in reference to later "*invented*" tzolkin correlations, "*Such disregard of the calendrical knowledge of the Classical Maya is not likely to lead to truth*" [46], but this applies equally to his own invented Long Count correlation. The result of the change in correlation means that Calleman sees the 13-baktun cycle as starting on June 17th 3115 BC and ending on 28th October 2011. [47]

There is a problem, however, because dividing by twenty works fine until we get to the level beneath the summit of the pyramid, when we find that thirteen tuns is 4,680 days, and a twentieth of this is 234 days, not 260 days. Calleman admits this, where he refers to "*The short universal cycle of 2011, probably totalling only 13 x 18 = 234 days, but possibly 260 days...*" [48] Two diagrams on p.77 of Calleman's book differ on the length of this last cycle -

Fig.19.5: Calleman's nine-level pyramid model of the nine evolving states of consciousness illustrates that if we retain the 20-fold pattern up to the top, we lose the pattern of 260 components, but if we retain the 260 components, we lose the 20-fold pattern.

one says 13 x 20 days (260) and the other says 13 x 18 days (234). If the tzolkin level (the *Universal Underworld*) is shortened to 234 days, so that the pattern (of each level being a twentieth the size of the one above) is retained, then the tzolkin as the key 260-unit *"filtration pattern of divine light"* is unable to form the top level of the pyramid. Alternatively, if the 260-unit tzolkin is retained as the top level of the pyramid, so that each level consists of 260 sub-units, then the top level will be only an eighteenth the size of the level below, whereas all other levels are a twentieth the size of the level below. Since both solutions lose the symmetry of the pyramid, Calleman is clearly undecided as to which is correct. This brings the validity of the whole pyramid construct into question.

If Calleman had stuck with the Maya Long Count correlation, the idea would have remained an interesting concept, but the idea that the tzolkin *"ends"* on the day 13 Ahau and *"begins"* on the day 1 Imix is, in fact, *"based upon a misconception of the tzolkin calendar"* [49] due to modern conventions in representing it, according to John Major Jenkins. Therefore the alteration to the Long Count was not necessary, and Calleman could have presented the idea without resorting to inventing his own correlation. Calleman now has quite a following, and supporters are presenting his theory as *"The Mayan Calendar"* or stating, *"The Maya say..."* when they should state, *"Carl Calleman says..."* His book is titled *The Maya Calendar: Solving the Greatest Mystery of Our Time*, but his solution is being taken as the genuine Maya Calendar, when it is an attempted explanation that got out of hand and ended up 'improving' the facts to fit the explanation. Amazingly, José Arguelles has written the introduction to Calleman's sequel book, just as several websites are attempting to combine the theories of Arguelles and Calleman... and even Jenkins. It seems that people are so wary of throwing out the baby with the bathwater, that they have poured all the water into one bath, inadvertently drowning the baby.

For further analysis of Calleman's theory, see the Jenkins-Calleman debate on the *Diagnosis 2012* website, in which each author simultaneously submitted a series of three articles to the debate. [50]

## Scallion Rap

Modern prophet or *"futurist"* Gordon Michael Scallion publishes his *Earth Changes Report* nine times per year. It is an eight-page newsletter focusing on his most recent visions. In his 1997 book *Notes From The Cosmos*, [51] he records an impressive list of uncannily accurate predictions that he made for the years 1991-1997 (that were published in *ECR*), plus the facts of what actually occurred. He is most famous for his prediction of the epicentre of the 1994 Northridge earthquake in California, which he made in 1993.

Scallion predicts that solar flares and sunspots will precede a reversal of the Sun's magnetic field, ready for a new age. This is the time of the Tribulation and, like the Native Americans, Scallion says that human consciousness is triggering the Earth changes. The Blue Star Kachina of the Hopi Indians will appear from behind the Sun, travelling towards Arcturus (a star in the Bootes constellation, near Virgo). This Blue Star is a *"companion to*

*Sirius B*", and will cause Earth's frequency to double to over fifteen cycles per second or 15 Hz (this is the Schumann Resonance, comprised of electromagnetic waves in the cavity between the Earth's crust and the ionosphere that Gregg Braden in Chapter 9 predicted would be at 13 Hz by 2012). Our subtle bodies will change, and we may experience palpitations, electrical sensations in the limbs and spinal column, migraines, flu-symptoms and intense dreams, as we adjust.

Between 1998 and 2002, the Earth's magnetic field was predicted by Scallion to begin to shift two or three times, by six or seven degrees each time. This would be the result of the interaction of an 11,600-year "*critical-axis-tilt-point*" cycle and a 3,750-year "*solar-magnetic reversal cycle*". The "*magnetic polar shift cycle*" is caused by "*the interaction between Earth, the Sun and other planets*", possibly implicating the 1999 total solar eclipse and the May 2000 planetary alignment. However, the Earth's magnetic field has *not* shifted by 12-21° between 1998 and 2002, so this is a failed prediction.

Scallion says that in a vision he saw the planet Mars wobble on its axis, causing its smallest moon, Phobos, to move in a "*snake-like motion*", pushed out of its orbit by the approach of the Blue Star, now like a second sun. Phobos spirals towards Earth's orbit and ricochets off our atmosphere, causing hurricanes and tidal waves, then earthquakes and volcanoes, then a melting of the ice-caps and global flooding. He seems to have covered it all here! (See also pages 189-190 for other Phobos predictions.)

While in Wiltshire, UK, looking at crop formations in 1993, Scallion received a "*direct communication*" from "*The Etherians*", who told him that the culmination point of these Earth changes was to be 2012, but that the cycle has been affected by humanity:

*"Solar-magnetic cycles - pole shifts - occur at the 11,600-year interval, with lesser cycles occurring at harmonic sub-junctures in the greater cycle. A full magnetic reversal would regularly occur on the Sun in the year 2012. However, due to the expansion of thought-forms and nuclear activity in your world, the cycle has been modified, and now occurs earlier, before preparations are completed. But knowing these cycles can enable shifts to occur in your world, so that the cycle can be corrected. In doing so, preparation will be facilitated in our combined worlds. The effect of such a solar reversal brings great changes to our combined worlds, making for new seasons, and, indeed, new species."* [52]

On the other hand, if you can find early copies of *Earth Changes Report*, some researchers [53] claim that Scallion made many dire predictions pre-1988, that have failed to happen, such as Mount Rainier exploding, huge fractures causing the west coast of America to split into islands, Japan sinking into the sea, and finally a "*shift in the Earth's poles*" that was predicted to follow all these events by the year 2001 at the latest! Shifting this on to 2002 didn't work either, so it seems he shifted it on another decade to 2012.

## Crystal Skulls

In 1924, British explorer Frederick Mitchell-Hedges was excavating a Maya city called Labaantun in the jungle of what is now Belize. His seventeen-year old daughter Anna climbed to the top of the tallest pyramid to admire the view and noticed something reflecting the sunlight between the stones of the pyramid apex. When the top stones were removed, she was lowered on a rope through the hole, and came out clutching a life-size replica of a human skull, carved out of a solid piece of quartz. Three months later, the lower jaw of the crystal skull was found in the main chamber of the pyramid. Mitchell-Hedges was told by a Maya priest that the skull had magical powers, and it remained in the possession of Anna Mitchell-Hedges throughout her life, but various psychics who spent time with it were said to have gone into trances, and channelled masses of bizarre information. Over the years, more of the skulls have come to light, including one in the British Museum in London, which was bought by them in 1898,

*Fig.19.6: Kathleen Murray's crystal skull, Mahasamatman.*

originally sourced from Mexico.  However, recent tests on this particular skull suggest the visible grinding techniques are more in keeping with it being less than 200 years old, and it has been dismissed by some as a 'fake'.

In *The Mystery of the Crystal Skulls,* [54] Chris Morton and Ceri Louise Thomas interview North and South American Indians, who claim that there were originally 52 crystal skulls, of which the Maya had thirteen. They say they were brought to Earth in the distant past by extra-terrestrials, having been encoded with information from twelve different planetary civilisations.

*"... The whole layout of Teotihuacan was like a huge clock-face, centred around the Pyramid of the Sun. The Avenue of the Dead, like one hand of a clock, pointed at where the Pleiades would have set on the southern horizon on 12th August 3114 BC, whilst the skull beneath the Pyramid of the Sun, like the other hand of the clock, pointed at the place on the horizon where the Pleiades set today".* [55]

Morton and Thomas also found that the three pyramids of Teotihuacan were a reflection of Orion's belt, in the same way that Robert Bauval claimed this to be the case for the Giza pyramids (there is disagreement on this from Egyptologists, but Dr Jan Harding announced in 2003 that Thornborough Henge in Yorkshire, UK, which pre-dates the Giza pyramids, also

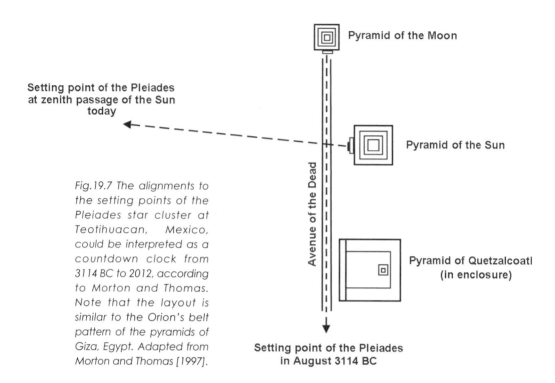

Pyramid of the Moon

Setting point of the Pleiades
at zenith passage of the Sun
today

Pyramid of the Sun

Avenue of the Dead

*Fig.19.7 The alignments to the setting points of the Pleiades star cluster at Teotihuacan, Mexico, could be interpreted as a countdown clock from 3114 BC to 2012, according to Morton and Thomas. Note that the layout is similar to the Orion's belt pattern of the pyramids of Giza, Egypt. Adapted from Morton and Thomas [1997].*

Pyramid of Quetzalcoatl
(in enclosure)

Setting point of the Pleiades
in August 3114 BC

symbolized the stars of Orion's belt - see *Ecstatic Fusebox* in Chapter 21). They were told by elders of the Hopi Indian people that the extraterrestrials that brought the crystal skulls were from Sirius, Orion and the Pleiades (where all that channelling comes from!). The information is held in the molecular crystal lattice, as in the silicon chips we use today, but can be accessed by consciousness. The Mitchell-Hedges skull was tested by Hewlett-Packard (experts in crystallography, since they use them in their computers and have a specially-equipped laboratory for testing crystals), but they could find no tooling marks on it, and they concluded that it would have taken 300 man-years to make it. Harley Swiftdeer, a *"Cherokee medicine man"* and *"war-chief of the Twisted Hairs Society's council of elders"* told the authors that, originally, the Olmecs had brought the skulls:

*"The skulls were kept inside a pyramid in a formation of tremendous power, known as the Ark. The Ark was composed of the twelve skulls from each of the sacred planets kept in a circle, with a thirteenth skull, the largest, placed in the centre of this formation. This thirteenth skull represents the collective consciousness of all the worlds. It connects up the knowledge of all the sacred planets."* [56]

Don Alejandro Cirilio Pérez Oxlaj (the Maya elder mentioned in Part One) is the Head of the

National Council of Elders of Guatemala, and he was the source for most of the material in the penultimate chapter of Morton and Thomas' book. Don Alejandro said that now is the *"Time of the Warning"*, also called *Time of the Awakening*, or *Time of the Quickening*, which is the transitional period between the end of the Nine Hell cycles, which ended on 17th August 1987, and the time of the Thirteen Heavens, which begins *"after sunset on 21st December, in the year 2012"*. The crystal skulls were left here to help us in this time of transition - we must change before 2012, showing love and respect for each other, life, and the planet, or we shall be cleansed from it by cataclysms. The modern Maya have been arranging a series of meetings for elders from indigenous tribes of North and South America and other countries, to culminate in a reunion of all the crystal skulls, and this will happen at a pre-destined time known only to the Maya day-keepers.

On page 349 of *The Mystery of The Crystal Skulls*, Don Alejandro is quoted as saying:

*"But the prophets said the Nine Hells would end between Long Count kin 1863022 and 1863023, between the days you call 16 and 17 August 1987, that the Time of the Warning would come to pass and that now is the time to prepare for the Thirteen Heavens. The Thirteen Heavens will begin after sunset on 21 December in the year 2012. The next day after that is written in our Long Count calendar as 13.0.0.0.0."* [57]

An analysis of this statement is very revealing. The first thing we notice is that the end of the Nine Hells is said to be exactly on the days that Tony Shearer calculated, and which were also repeated by José Arguelles in *The Mayan Factor*. If you look at note number 21 for this chapter of the book you hold now (the *Galactic Synchronization* section), you will see that there was an error of 221 days in this calculation. [58] The next thing is the *kin* numbers (days since the beginning of the count), 1863022 and 1863023. Again, these are exactly the same as the kin numbers given in *The Mayan Factor* for the Harmonic Convergence days. The trouble is, Arguelles made an error of 281 days [59] in calculating these numbers, and Don Alejandro has the same numbers. Since there are 1,872,000 days in the 13-baktun cycle, if we calculated forward to find the end of the cycle, we would arrive at a day 281 days short of 21st December 2012 (i.e. 15th March 2012). Since Don Alejandro goes on to give the correct end-date, we can only presume that the *"prophet"* who supplied him with the information, is none other than José Arguelles (or *Valum Votan*, alias Lord Pacal, who Arguelles claims is inhabiting his body nowadays). [60]

## Aeon of Maat

Magick is defined as *"the art of causing change to occur in conformity with the will"* (the spelling with a 'k' is a modern convention amongst occultists to avoid confusion with sleight-of-hand entertainers). Thelemites are magic(k)ians who follow the teachings of Aleister Crowley's Law of Thelema (Greek for *"will"*), centred around the *"Do what thou wilt shall be the whole of the law"* doctrine. *Maat Magick* is an extension of Thelemite ideas

*Fig.19.8: The magick practices and beliefs of Aleister Crowley have entered popular culture in more ways than one - here is Crowley's face appearing on a boot!*

and consists of techniques for accessing the power of the future age of Maat, the Egyptian Goddess of Truth and Justice, which is the sequel to the current Age of Horus. Maat Magick lists six aeons, which are the *Nameless Aeon* (pre-history, hunter-gatherers, shamanism), the *Aeon of Isis* (beginnings of agriculture, goddess worship, paganism), the *Aeon of Osiris* (cities, war, Abrahamic religions), the *Aeon of Horus* (atomic energy, radio, TV, atheism, existentialism, Thelema), the *Aeon of Maat* (quantum theory, genetic engineering, Internet, various Magicks), and the *Wordless Aeon* (when a new species emerges from Homo sapiens).

The Aeon of Horus, according to Thelemites, began in 1904 when Crowley received the *Book of the Law* (his wife Rose went into a trance in Cairo and channelled it). In 1974, when Andahadna received *Liber Pennae Praenumbra* (see below), the Aeon of Maat began to run concurrently with the Aeon of Horus, and since Maat is "*the Daughter, twin to Horus*", the influences will work together to change humanity by "*the awakening of the Racial Unconscious to Racial Consciousness*". [61] When humanity is thus transformed into a "*doubly conscious species*", the Wordless Aeon will start, and this will be an aeon in which "*physical speech is unnecessary with a shared consciousness*".

An even more recent development, *Chaos Magick*, is an unstructured approach to magick using any practices that get results, but without adopting the associated belief systems. Even here, there is an accepted aeon structure according to Peter Carroll's book *Liber Kaos*. [62] In this system, there are four aeons, the *Shamanic Aeon*, *Religious Aeon*, *Rationalist Aeon* and *Pandemon Aeon*, which is equivalent to the Wordless Aeon of the Maat Magick system. [63]

On the *Mutation Parlour* [64] website, Orryelle Bascule connects Chaos Magick and Maat Magick to the work of Jenkins, McKenna, and Arguelles, plus the Hopi Indian prophecy of the "*13th Tribe*", or *Rainbow Warriors*, to conclude that the Return of Quetzalcoatl will be the activation and rising of Kundalini, and awakening of collective consciousness for humanity. This will also be an activation of Gaia's Kundalini, the serpentine energy lines that connect Earth's sacred sites, the chakras of our planet. This is explained in his *Zuvuya* essay. [65] Orryelle has formed a microcosmic "*13th tribe*" of Rainbow Warriors from a variety of nationalities to perform a series of rites - "*the 13th Tribe Weaving*", involving "*chakra-piercing*", which is explained in his *Liber XIII*. [66] Magickal works are traditionally titled in Latin, hence *Liber XIII* means "*Book 13*", since the concept of twelve tribes is not just concerned with Jewish ancestry, but, says Bascule, also exists in Australian Aboriginal mythology, as well as that of the Hopi Native Americans, and represents twelve races and a thirteenth that unites them. Thirteen is also a most significant number for the Maya. The Anahata, or heart chakras, of the twelve initiates are woven together "*both etherically and with physical threads through piercings ritually executed in the Anahata chakra of each, by a Thirteenth*". These rites were to be performed at "*Gaia's seven chakra points*" in the years approaching 2012:

"*Activating group Kundalini at each of Gaia's chakras via these weavings, progressively towards 2012, will help to resonate humanity's awakening Groupmind with the intense awakening of these Great Serpents, the Ida and Pingala of Gaia's Kundalini.*" 67

Bascule thinks that in 2012, the Aeon of Horus will fuse with the Aeon of Maat. In light of the Aeon information above, this could also be interpreted as the arrival of the Wordless Aeon, or at least a possible access point to it, and the start of a new species of telepathic human.

## High Priestess of Maat

There are currently several organisations calling themselves the *Ordo Templi Orientis*, or the *Order of the Temple of the East*, but the branch run by Kenneth Grant, who is one of Crowley's executors, is called the *Typhonian O.T.O.* (Typhon was a Greek Goddess, according to Grant, though in standard Greek mythology Typhon was the son of Gaia and a snake-legged monster who attacked the Gods) to distinguish it from the other "*spurious organisations*". It is also called the Temple of the Rising Star, Sirius. Soror Andahadna, Priestess of Maat in the Typhonian O.T.O., who is now known as *Nema*, published the *Liber Pennae Praenumbra* 68 in 1976. The information was received while out-of-body during magickal workings, and concerns the Aeon of Maat, or the *Aeon of Truth and Justice*, which most occultists would not expect for another 2,000 years. 69 However, since the Manhattan Project in World War II, when nuclear explosions caused rips in space-time, a "*seal*" was dissolved on a gateway to another universe. This is where some very nasty beings live, known as "*the Elder Gods*", and if you have ever read any H. P. Lovecraft, that may sound familiar. For this reason, our evolutionary progression must be speeded up so the gateway can be re-sealed before the Elder Gods, who are "*Alien beyond human imagining*", enter and devour us. 70

The magickians have, since 1975, been working with *Maatians* (our future selves) to try and earth an evolving "*Cosmic Net*":

"*Once established, the Net will radiate a field akin to magnetism that will induce mass mutation in the genes of the Race of Man. By subtle atomic and molecular adjustments, it will unlock the [as] yet unused potential of the human brain, stimulate the human quality called 'genius', and vastly enlarge the capacity of Man on all planes...*" 71

# PART 4:
## Diagnosis

*T*he rise in levels of beta-carbolines seen in pineal glands as one ascends primate phylogeny - with the highest levels occurring in Homo sapiens - lends credence to the idea that the adaptation called consciousness may involve mutation of the metabolic pathways associated with serotonin, other trypamines, and harmine. The shift of emphasis from serotonin pathways to beta-carboline and methylated tryptamine pathways is, we speculate, the molecular evolutionary event that is responsible for the intimations of transfiguration that have recently characterized mass consciousness.

**Terence and Dennis McKenna, *The Invisible Landscape*** [1]

# Chapter 20:
# Analysis

## Three Questions

In Part One, we saw that as well as the 13-baktun cycle of the Maya, other calendars such as the Tibetan, Vedic and Jewish calendars all indicate 2012 as the end of a long-term cycle. We also saw how many indigenous people from North, Meso and South America, and even Africa and New Zealand have recently been saying that now is the time to reveal their ancient prophecies, and that they invariably mention dates that correspond to the western year 2012 as the time of either catastrophic Earth changes and/or a spiritual leap for Mankind. These prophecies seem to validate the conclusions from studying the calendars, but how reliable are the prophecies?

In Part Two, we looked at theories in which researchers have tried to find a possible cause for the prophesied changes. A lot of the interest shown in the year 2012 has originated from two best-selling books. These are *The Mayan Factor* by José Arguelles, and *The Mayan Prophecies* by Cotterell and Gilbert. As we have seen, despite some good points, both the books contain errors that have resulted in confusion about the Maya calendars, and this confusion has infected the theories of several researchers who have been influenced by the books. A third bestseller, Graham Hancock's *Fingerprints of the Gods,* has further confused matters by quoting a defunct 2011 end-date for the 13-baktun cycle. [1] The problem here is to sift out the infected parts of the theories, plus other errors - we don't always have to throw the whole theory out, but how much is left at the end of this process?

In Part Three we looked at modern sources of confirmation about 2012, including sacred plants, near-death and out-of-body experiences, UFO contact experiences, remote viewing, prophets, visionaries and magic(k)ians. The question here is: how many of these sources have also been infected, whether consciously or subconsciously, by existing prophecies and theories?

## Are The Prophecies Reliable?

In New Age circles, if a tribal elder or shaman gives a talk, he is usually surrounded by an aura of wonder. The presumption is that he or she is a holder of knowledge that has been carefully preserved by word of mouth, and that the elders have met and agreed that now is the time to release the wisdom and prophecies for the benefit of the world. In 2003 I spent a day with *Tlakaelel*, a Nahuatl "*man of knowledge*" from Mexico. Speaking through an interpreter, he explained that he did not want to be worshipped. A short while later, someone arrived who had spent time with Tlakaelel at his educational centre near Teotihuacan, and greeted him by kneeling on the floor and kissing his hand. I cringed. Tlakaelel said that he "*holds 48,000 years of history*" in his memory. He said this relates to four 12,000-year periods between the

Earth's crossings of a Photon Band that goes round Alcyone, the central star of the Pleiades. My heart sank at word of the very dubious Photon Band/Belt concept (see Chapter 19). He said that this is a time of purification and cataclysms, and that the last time we crossed the Band, the year changed from 360 days to 365 days, and that this time it will change back again. This provides a convenient explanation for the lack of a Long Count calendar among the Aztecs - in fact, Tlakaelel said that the 360-day tun-based Long Count calendar was "*superseded*" by the 365-day haab calendar, whereas Mayanists tell us that the haab and tzolkin both preceded the Long Count. [2]

He said that Tenochtitlan - the Aztec capital that once stood where Mexico City now stands - was founded on July 26th 1325, and finally fell to the Spanish on August 13th 1521, and that it lasted for a period of four Suns of 52 years each. Unfortunately, the period is *not* in actual fact 4 x 52 (208) years, but around 196 years. The year of 1325 as the founding of Tenochtitlan agrees with what the historians say. July 26th is the date of the zenith passage of the Sun at Teotihuacan and it is familiar as the "*Synchronization date*" or New Year's Day adopted by José Arguelles for his *Dreamspell* count, after the fashion of the post-conquest calendar reform of the Yucatec (from the Yucatan peninsula) Maya. The date of the fall was correct at 13th August 1521.

*Fig.20.1: An Aztec priest apparently adjusting a ratchet on a calendrical device. Museum of Anthropology, Mexico City.*

This was as much as Tlakaelel would say about the calendar. In fact, when I showed Bert Gunn, his interpreter, my booklet on the Aztec Sunstone (which accompanies the Aztec Sunstone animation I put together - see Chapter 16's *Aztec Pizza* entry), he asked me if *I* could give *them* any information about 52-year and 12,000-year astronomical cycles! In other words, it seems that these prophecies are already tainted by New Age sources, but are still incomplete.

An Internet search provided some additional information from an Aztec "*Carrier of the Word*" called Ehekateoti Kuauhtlinxan, [3] who says that from the date of the fall of Tenochtitlan on 13th August 1521, there were nine periods of 52 years that add to 468 years (together making up a period of darkness), until 13th August 1989. He then explained that due to the fact that the 1521 date was recorded in the Julian calendar, the equivalent date today would be 28th August 1989, and that this was the day on which the Aztec people started to "*come out*" to claim recognition as an ethnic group.

The period described by Ehekateoti is the same as the Nine Hells that we have already talked about, except that these Aztecs are measuring them from the fall of Tenochtitlan, rather than the landing of the Spanish, which means that their equivalent of Harmonic Convergence was on 28th August 1989. However, the first thing we notice is that there was a thirteen-day discrepancy between Julian and Gregorian dates by 1989, not a fifteen-day one. The next thing is that the calculation would be based on 365-day years - the Aztec *xiuhpohualli* (which the Maya called *haabs*), rather than solar years. When we then calculate 9 x 52 365-day years from 13th August 1521 (Julian Date), we arrive at 1st May 1989 (Gregorian Date). [4] John Mini, in *Day of Destiny*, [5] also made an error with this calculation, somehow coming up with August 13th 1999 - over ten years in error - but then he never did explain how he calculated it. [6]

So, having found that the New Age concept of the Photon Band had tainted the 'knowledge' of the "*Man of Knowledge*", and that the "*Carrier of the Word*" had tripped up on his numbers, I realized that Britt and Lee were not the only 'Elders' who had shot themselves in the foot (Britt and Lee Elders were the makers of the Mexican UFO wave videos discussed in Chapter 15, which incorrectly state 1991 as the Sixth Sun). In the *Crystal Skulls* section of Chapter 19, we have seen how Don Alejandro was quoting from *The Mayan Factor* and implying that this was ancient prophecy. It looks as if some of the elders have been looking to non-native researchers to pep up their knowledge base, while some of those same researchers have been changing their names to Maya names, Native American names, ancient Egyptian names, or even ancient Hebrew priest names (see note 5, Chapter 9) to give their theories and prophecies some authority. Another of Morton and Thomas's main sources of crystal skull information was "*Cherokee medicine man*" Harley Swiftdeer, but several Native Americans are now saying that he is not recognised by the Cherokee nation, and that his practices are not Cherokee practices. [7]

There are now websites with information on what they are calling "*plastic medicine men*", although some of this material is over the top in my opinion, even listing Michael Harner as an offender, for no particular reason except he has published a study on shamanic practices that is used as source material for workshops by self-taught techno-shamans. All I am saying is that we should proceed with caution concerning indigenous prophecies, and crosscheck them, rather than giving our power away.

Having said that, if we look back through the prophecies quoted, we notice that some of them say there will be a catastrophe of huge proportions, with just a handful of survivors, while other prophecies play down this element, just emphasising the changes to Mankind. Many versions include the concept of a period of purification or purging prior to 2012, but the starting dates vary as follows: 1985 (Patricio Dominguez - see note 3); 1987 (Senecas, Cherokees and Carlos Barrios); 1989 (modern Aztecs such as Ehekateoti Kuauhtlinxan, mentioned above); 1990-1993 (Q'ero); 1991 (Quetza-Sha); 1991-2001 (Gerardo Barrios); 1998-2000 (the Pueblo); 2000 (Q'ero, interviewed by Alberto Villoldo [8]). Others have said that the last katun of the 13-baktun cycle is the "*time of purification*", but have then given 1992 as the year in question, repeating an error in *The Mayan Factor*. [9] A katun is twenty tuns of 360 days, totalling 7,200 days, or approximately 19.72 years. The final katun started on 12.19.0.0.0, which was April 5th 1993. So the prophecies agree that there will be a period of purification lasting anything from 27 years to eleven years before the end of the final katun in December 2012.

If we filter out the prophecies that are infected with New Age dogma, we are still left with some impressive predictions. The Seneca medicine man Moses Shongo, for example, made his prediction around 80 years ago of a 25-year period of purification before 2012. I recently had an e-mail from my friend Len Stevens, who has been living at a meditation retreat at a temple in Thailand, in which he told me of the predictions of his teacher, who lives in Northern Thailand. He has three times received detailed information, while meditating, concerning forthcoming acts of war:

"[These events culminate] *in a pole reversal in 2012 - the destruction of everyone who isn't at least partially enlightened or in the presence of an enlightened one. I really don't think these people are aware of the other prophecies regarding 2012.*" [10]

The Maori prophecy (see page 38) is instructive here, showing how a misinterpretation can arise. The *"fall of the curtain"* was interpreted as the end of the world following the final scene of the play, but on further investigation it actually means the 'dissolving of the veil'. In fact many people are worried that in 2012 the world will end. They are right! The world *will* end; it will be the end of the Fourth World of the Hopi and Maya, and the start of the Fifth World. It is a World Transition, or the end of a World Era, and perhaps the end of the world *as we know it*. This is the same as the end of the Fifth Sun of the Aztecs, and the start of the Sixth Sun. The Earth changes have begun and there is a general agreement in the prophecies that the purification period will be a time in which mankind will have the opportunity to evolve, and that we can consciously help the process by visiting sacred sites to *"strengthen our energy bodies"* or to do exercises to *"engage our energy bodies"*. Some say that the progress we make on ourselves and on lessening our ecological impact on the planet could lessen the Earth changes. Phrases like *"destruction of unenlightened ones"* may be due to the insidious percolation of the Christian concept of the Judgement Day, but they may also be a warning to clean out our cerebral closets

Fig.20.2: Mural of the Four Suns *at Palenque. The tassles around the neck of the central god are Suns, or gods, or eras. The central god may be the equivalent of the central controlling deity on the Aztec Sunstone, who controls the fifth and final era in the set of five.*

before the locks are broken open and we are confronted with our own suppressed complexes. Judging by the effects of various self-help therapies in exorcising personal demons, this could be like all hell breaking loose in the mind before equilibrium is achieved.

## Theory Filtration

We have seen how Cotterell and Gilbert's interpretation of the 'Birth and Death of Venus' is faulted, and their supposed proof of Maya knowledge of sunspot cycles is a mess of graphs and calculations that lead nowhere. These misconceptions have infected all

Fig.20.3: *There were originally four solar deity heads in the* Mural of the Four Suns *at Tonina (page 72). Note the similar style to the 'tassles' in the previous picture. Notice the skull-like central controller at the top, perhaps governing the fifth and final period of the precessional era (26,000 tuns).*

Cotterell's later books - the whole series is based on *The Mayan Prophecies*; also infected were later books by Gilbert, including *Signs in the Sky*; Geryl and Ratinckx's *The Orion Prophecy*; Michael Poynder's *Pi in the Sky*; Morton and Thomas's *Mystery of the Crystal Skulls*; Nigel Appleby's *Hall of the Gods*; Elliot Rudishill's *E.Din Land of Righteousness*; William Gaspar's *The Celestial Clock* and even *The Unity Keys of Ananda*; and David Wilcock's *Shift of the Ages*. However, Cotterell and Gilbert were right about the increase in solar activity, and also in general about a solar megacycle, as we have seen. Also relevant is their mention of the effects of fluctuations of the geomagnetic field on the human endocrine system. They mention this as part of an attempt to prove that changes in the solar wind that appear on their graph in the year 627 AD were responsible for a drop in the fertility of the Maya, causing them to abandon their cities. Jenkins points out [11] that this actually corresponds to "*the Classic Period florescence of Mayan culture*" rather than the decline, which started around 800 AD. Cotterell indulges in some dubious graph work to make this point, [12] involving a 40° swivel to a graphed line of the solar cycle to align it with another line showing the production of follicle-stimulating hormone (FSH).

The errors in *The Mayan Factor* (in this case, the "*3113 BC*" start date not being clarified as an *astronomical* rather than a *historical* date, but other errors are fully listed in note 21 for Chapter 19) have caused a problem for Sergey Smelyakov and his Auric Time Scale theory, as we have seen. They also caused a problem on page 173 of Weidner and Bridges' *A Monument to the End of Time*, where the Arguelles date for the final katun was used - 1992 instead of 1993 (and unfortunately this has been repeated on page 335 of the latest expanded edition). [13] However, Arguelles' simple discovery that the tzolkin is a microcosmic version of the 13-baktun cycle (of 260 kins and 260 katuns respectively) is invaluable. His speculations concerning the I Ching and Franklin magic square (first aired in Earth Ascending) were prophetic, and his application of De Chardin's Noosphere concept is inspirational.

Even the dreadful book *Giza-Genesis* by Wilkie and Middleton-Jones managed to get something right - Rush Allen, the astro-mythologist who runs the *SiLoaM.net* website mentioned in Chapter 8, agrees that the theory was misinformation, but concedes that somehow James Wilkie and Howard Middleton-Jones came to the same conclusion as he did - that the Hall of Records will be opened on 21st December 2012 at 10:18:13 local Cairo time, though his interpretation of the event is a mass illumination of mankind.

## Cosmic Dust Increase

Paul LaViolette's galactic core explosion theory is a science-based concept that sounds feasible, and connects several ideas we have discussed, although only peripherally in some cases. A long-term solar cycle, geomagnetic reversals, legends of the Sun going dark and other Egyptian mythology, Mayan and Aztec mythology, the precession of the equinoxes; all these are explained by LaViolette's theory. He even points out [14] that José Arguelles' Galactic Synchronisation Beam, emitted from galactic centre, has certain common points with the galactic core explosion theory. He also has an essay on his website [15] in which he makes a case that the Photon Belt is a metaphor for a galactic superwave. LaViolette's theory also fits precisely into the predictions of the alchemist Fulcanelli, and the Hendaye Cross, as recounted by Weidner and Bridges. However, despite the fact that LaViolette tentatively links the theory to the 13-baktun cycle of the Maya, he told me that he disagrees with Kev Peacock's theory because: *"Mag[netic] pole flips are induced by major coronal mass ejections unlike anything that occurs at present. The Sun has to first become transformed as a result of a cosmic dust incursion."* [16] This implies that he doesn't really expect a major galactic superwave in the immediate future, but a minor one that would not bring a major change to the Earth's geomagnetic field or climate, but would carry an electromagnetic pulse or EMP that would cause high voltage surges in power lines and telephone lines. In his online essay quoted earlier, he points out that the minor superwave events have *"... EMP effects comparable to those of major superwaves,"* [17] but for a geomagnetic inversion to occur, cosmic dust would have to cause a major increase in solar activity, that would in turn affect the Earth's magnetic polarity.

LaViolette's comment to me (above) was made in the year 2000, before the solar maximum and subsequent unusual solar behaviour. On 4th November 2003, there was the largest solar flare ever recorded. The previous record was on 2nd April 2001, when we had an X-22-level flare (classified then as an X-20 because at that point the gauge only went up that far; increasing-size events have since led to larger scales being developed, including the tentative use of a 'Y' system). This time, estimates varied between X-28 and X-35 or more. [18] In fact, in March 2004, physicists from the University of Otago in New Zealand released the results of their *Ionospheric Impact Assessment*, [19] in which they concluded that the November 2003 flare had been an X-45, which is more than twice as big as any previous flare. Fortunately, it wasn't pointing towards Earth, since the X-ray flare of March 6th 1989 that was pointing towards Earth and shorted out the Canadian power grid, leaving six million people with no electricity (and also burned out a New Jersey nuclear power transformer) was somewhat less than an X-20! The 2003 flare came after a record-breaking nine major solar eruptions in the space of twelve days. All this happened after solar maximum, in a period when the Sun should have quietened down. Even before this event, on 2nd November 2003, *www.NewScientist.com* declared that Ilya Usoskin, a geophysicist, and colleagues from the University of Oulu in Finland working with scientists from the Max Planck Institute for Aeronomy in Germany, had just revealed that the Sun is now more active than it has been for over 1,000 years. [20] An even more recent announcement in July 2004, by Swiss scientists at the Institute for Astronomy in Zurich, confirms the increased activity of the Sun via a study of Greenland ice cores. Significantly, in April 2006, NASA predicted that an immense solar storm was likely to occur in 2012. [21]

On 11th August 2003 it was announced on *www.SpaceDaily.com* [22] that the *Ulysses* satellite had detected a three-fold increase in "*stardust*" flowing through the solar system since the last solar maximum, when the Sun's magnetic field weakened due to "*increased solar activity*". The stardust, which is usually kept out by the Sun's magnetic field, was predicted to "*create more cosmic dust by collisions with asteroids and comets.*" However, a few days later, on 20th August 2003, another article appeared, revising the reason that the dust was increasing:

"*Instead of reversing completely, flipping north to south, the Sun's magnetic poles have only rotated at halfway and are now more or less lying sideways along the Sun's equator. This weaker configuration of the magnetic shield is letting in two to three times more stardust than at the end of the 1990s. Moreover, this influx could increase by as much as ten times until the end of the current solar cycle in 2012.*" [23]

## Alcyone Examined

The concept of the Photon Band won't go away, no matter how many times its faults are pointed out - hackles rise on Internet discussion groups as the subject comes up, and then just when you think it is all settled, a new member starts the whole thing going again. It is as persistent as an archetype from the collective unconscious mind. Barbara Hand Clow describes the problem in *The Pleiadian Agenda*, [24] and says she wouldn't have given the matter much attention, except that her Cherokee grandfather, Grandfather Wise Hand, had told her many years ago that Alcyone - central star of the Pleiades - was her home. Then she noticed, in a book by Hunbatz Men, [25] in which he describes seventeen Maya calendars, that one of them is a 26,000-year cycle of the Sun's orbit around Alcyone. When she asked Hunbatz Men if the end of the Pleiadian cycle would coincide with the end of the 13-baktun cycle in 2012, he confirmed that it would.

As we have seen, the myth liberally mixes up fact and fiction, since these are the facts:

1) The precession of the equinoxes takes between 25,600-26,000 years.

2) The solar system moves around a *"central sun"* - Galactic Centre - but it takes 230-250 million years to complete one orbit around it.

3) The Maya had a 13-baktun cycle that ends in 2012, when the Solstice Sun is close to Galactic Centre and aligned to the centre of a *"belt of light"* called the Milky Way.

4) The Maya used the movement of the Pleiades constellation to measure precession, and thus, with the Pyramid of Kukulkan, set up a Pleiades alarm clock set for 2012.

In the Photon Belt myth, these facts are mixed up so that the solar system moves around a central sun in the Pleiades, and takes 26,000 years to do it, with the cycle ending in 2012. [26] The cycle used by Hunbatz Men encodes the important concepts that are connected; that the Pleiades are used to check precessional movement towards galactic alignment in 2012. The fact that the mythologised version of Earth revolving around the Pleiades is astronomically incorrect does not alter the fact that the important concepts have been preserved in that myth.

Alexey Dmitriev's magnetised plasma band seems to be much closer to the Photon Band concept than LaViolette's theory, and applies just as effectively to long-term solar cycles, geomagnetic reversals and precession. It might also be encoded in ancient mythology if anybody cared to spend enough time looking for it. However, the magnetised plasma band has some other fascinating implications.

## Plasmatic Communication from the Noosphere?

William C. Levengood is a biophysicist based in Michigan, USA, who specializes in agriculture and seeds. Since 1991 he has been studying samples taken from crop formations across the world, and has been publishing the results in peer-reviewed journals such as *Physiologia Plantarum*. Working with Nancy Talbott and John Burke, Levengood helped found BLT Research (BLT - Burke, Levengood & Talbott), and has been coordinating international efforts to establish scientific protocols for crop sample collecting. Samples are taken at pre-defined spacings and cross-sections of formations, and control samples (from measured distances away) are also collected and labelled, and sent off to Michigan for analysis. John Burke has also written up articles based on the results of the investigations. They have found several anomalies and phenomena that cannot be explained, most of which had never been seen in Levengood's 40-year career, before he started looking at crop formations.

Four of the main anomalies are as follows: [27]

1) The stalks are softened so they can bend without breaking.

2) Stalks sometimes have *expulsion cavities* (also known as *blown nodes*), holes at the stem nodes where the stalk has been rapidly heated from the inside, turning the moisture to steam so fast that a hole is blown and the sap comes out. This effect has been replicated in an industrial microwave oven (enlarged cell-wall pits are also due to internal heating).

3) An electrical charge has been found on the stalks, the amount of charge proportional to the amount of bending.

4) Bract tissue around the seed has been found to have an increased electrical conductivity.

Other effects include elongated plant stem nodes, stunted or malformed seed heads and unusual seed germination, but the four anomalies listed above are the ones relevant to the point I am making here. John Burke says [28] that the team looked for an agent that could be responsible for these effects and they realised that plasma (an electrically-charged gas, or gas with the electrons

Fig.20.4: Anomalies in stems from the crop formation at East Kennett, Wiltshire, 2 July 2000 (see colour pages). Above are stems bent and stretched at the nodal joint - a physical impossibility when laying crop manually. Below are shown 'expulsion cavities', holes blown in the nodes where some kind of heat appears to have exploded the plant moisture outwards. Photos: Melissa White of The White Studio, www.thewhitestudio.co.uk

stripped off) fits the bill nicely. Not only would it also move in a spiral when passing through the geomagnetic field, but it would also emit microwaves, heating the plants from the inside and causing the electrical changes. Meteorologist Terence Meaden had already suggested *plasma vortices* as the causative factor of crop circles, but the theory was abandoned because it was weather-dependent and the crop formations were found to be forming in a variety of weather conditions (and they were becoming more complex and thus less explicable as a natural phenomenon).

Looking around for an alternative source of plasma, the BLT team thought of lightning, which is a high-energy form of plasma, but that would cause charring of the crop. However, up in the ionosphere there are low-energy plasmas that glow when they become energized, in the form of the northern lights (*aurora borealis*) and the southern lights (*aurora australis*). The reflective layers of the ionosphere weaken at night, especially just before dawn (when the plasma is more likely to break through), the time many crop circles seem to appear.  Also, the number of free electrons in the atmosphere increase one hundred-fold at sunspot maximum, coinciding from 1988 to 1989 with record numbers of crop formations up to that time.  These observations led the team to take a closer look at the ionosphere. It turns out that there are forms of plasma now known as *sprites* that have recently been observed coming down from the ionosphere as far as cloud level, and BLT deduced that a similar phenomenon might be responsible for crop formations, since this would also explain two other oddities about the crop designs.

There have been instances (in two-thirds of the 32 crop formations where BLT had been able, by 1998, to obtain soil samples, according to John Burke) [29] when high concentrations (twenty to 100 times higher than the control samples) of micron-sized spheres of magnetite have been found in soil samples from crop circles. Despite claims of iron filing misdemeanours by one hoaxer, this effect - found in 21 formations around the world - is said by BLT to be meteoritic dust that has been heated and melted into microscopic spheres; and most meteoritic dust can be found up in the ionosphere! A spiralling plasma tube would bring that down and concentrate it in the resulting crop formation, but BLT wondered why the plasma tubes would mostly discharge in a small area of England. When

*Fig.20.5: The most important crop of the ancient Maya was maize; here is Yum Kaax, Maya maize god, based on a drawing in the Dresden Codex.*

they looked at a geological map of the area, the answer was obvious - Wiltshire is mostly chalk, and chalk is an aquifer, a sponge-like rock that holds a lot of water, trickling through and causing a negative electric charge. This would attract the plasma like a lightning conductor. In fact, Glenn Broughton and Steve Page had independently come to this same conclusion after checking geological maps of the UK and cross-referencing information from crop circle databases. About 90% of crop formations were found to lie on aquifers (which include limestone and greensand), and BLT checked a field that regularly gets formations using a *fluxgate magnetometer*, and found that the magnetic field that accompanied the charge vanished straight after a formation appeared.

The only thing left unexplained was how the complex and apparently meaningful patterns could result from a natural process. This is where it gets complicated, involving magnetohydrodynamics, chaos theory and waveguides, and the team are still developing that part of their theory. However, if we look at photographs of sprites, we find that above a sprite is an expanding disc called an *elf*, both their namesakes (sprites and elves) being types of fairy folk - sometimes blamed for creating the first recorded crop circles. In *Passport to Magonia*, [30] ufologist Jacques Vallee pointed out many parallels between fairies and today's extraterrestrials, such that he sees them as the same phenomenon. In fact, Alexey Dmitriev says of the *vacuum domains*, a category in which he includes elves and sprites, that he and his colleagues propose "*a new non-meteorological approach to the study of these violent processes, now growing stronger*". [31]

According to this theory, the crop formations seem to be caused by plasma from the ionosphere, and that is where the plasma has been collecting, bleeding through from the magnetised plasma band that Dmitriev says the solar system is travelling into. If Teilhard de Chardin's Noosphere, the evolving mind layer that surrounds the Earth, is located in the ionosphere, then perhaps the fact of the increasing numbers and complexity of crop formations is linked to the plasma build-up, and the Noosphere is attempting to communicate with us. If humanity is the evolving global neocortex - human neurons about to link into a unified component organ of the planet - then perhaps the 'fairy folk' and some of the 'extraterrestrials' are a lifeform that collectively represent another and older part of the global brain.

## Thermal Plasmas at Hessdalen

In the Hessdalen valley, in northeast Norway, unexplained lights have been under investigation since the early 1980s by a team led by Norwegian engineer Prof. Erling Strand. Since August 2000, Italian astrophysicist Dr Massimo Teodorani and his team have joined the research effort, using radio spectrum analysers, spectroscopes and other equipment. [32] In 2001, Teodorani published some results of the study, in which he found that the lights were 95% thermal plasmas (the other 5% were solid objects). The lights appear when there is a measured perturbation in the geomagnetic field, and the plasma is trapped in a magnetic cage that keeps it concentrated. They can shift out of visibility and become invisible (Teodorani says that at this point they shift from high-energy plasmas to low-energy plasmas), but are still evident on the radar. [33] Linda Moulton Howe [34] has seen the very same thing in the crop fields of Wiltshire, using an infrared scope, and I was myself present on one of these occasions. [35] These plasmas are not ball lightning (that only lasts for a few minutes at most, whereas these plasmas lasted as long as two hours), and the physics behind them is not currently understood.

There are continual eyewitness accounts of balls of light (BOLs) in the Wiltshire area, and of these, many have been seen in association with crop formations. Bert Janssen's video documentary *Contact* [36] presents a fascinating compilation of sequences of these balls of light filmed over crop formations. In 2001, Nancy Talbott herself witnessed a crop formation being created by tubes of light in The Netherlands. The following night, Talbott returned to the formation and took flash photographs. Every film (four to five rolls) showed numerous light orbs, some were quite large ("*four-five times larger than a soccer ball*") and almost transparent, while others were grapefruit-sized and more dense, but at the time the photos were taken none were visible to the naked eye. The photos and account can be seen at *www.rense.com*. [37]

In September 2003, it was announced at *NewScientist.com* [38] that Mircea Sanduloviciu and his colleagues at Cuza University in Romania had just succeeded in creating plasma balls in the laboratory, which were able to "*grow, replicate and communicate - fulfilling most of the traditional requirements for biological cells.*" Although the traditional view is that life can only be present if there is inherited genetic material, the Romanian team think that they may have found the explanation for how life on Earth began, since the plasma spheres were created in microseconds when they replicated early conditions on Earth by passing an electric arc through an argon plasma. Even more compelling is Sanduloviciu's conclusion:

*"The cell-like spheres we describe could be at the origin of other forms of life we have not yet considered."* [39]

An article at *www.guardian.co.uk* [40] specifically links this research to the separate studies of Paul Devereux and Andrew York in the UK, and Michael Persinger and Gyslaine Lafreniére in the USA, in which they correlated UFO sightings in Leicestershire and the USA, respectively, to geological fault lines (where layers of rock grind against each other). Persinger and Lafreniére suggested that the air above the fault would be ionised, in a piezo-electrical effect such as could be caused when crystals are compressed, resulting in a plasma light orb. So here we have some scientific evidence that the balls of light could actually be lifeforms in themselves. The coverage of the Romanian announcement on *The Encyclopaedia of Astrobiology, Astronomy and Spaceflight* website [41] suggests that the research implies the possibility that plasma life could be found in stars, planetary magnetospheres, areas of ionised hydrogen such as the Orion Nebula, and in ball lightning.

## Vacuum Domains

Alexey Dmitriev, the Russian geophysicist whose article on the magnetised plasma band we have already reviewed, has also done some research into tornadoes, [42] and has reported on the existence of balls of light within them. The tornado lights are only one of a group of phenomena that he calls "*vacuum domains*", which he says have the following properties: they rotate, emit light, and stop electronic devices due to a strong magnetic field. Dmitriev claims that vacuum domains, [43] which are only explicable in terms of the Zero-Point energy theory, are generally on the increase. Zero-Point is a vibrational energy retained by molecules even at the temperature of absolute zero, and which also exists in a vacuum - there is enough in one cup of coffee to evaporate all the world's oceans, according to physicists Richard Feynman and John Wheeler. Vacuum Domains also include ball lightning, earthquake lights, poltergeist lights, natural self-luminous objects (or plasmoids) and sprites.

Of these, plasmoids, earthquake lights and ball lightning are more frequently seen at the peak of solar activity, and all the vacuum domains have the ability to penetrate through solid matter. Several types are associated with electrical or magnetic fields, and in 1995 Paul Devereux measured a huge jump in the local geomagnetic field (800-fold), coincident with the appearance of an anomalous light (known locally as a *min-min* light) in the Australian outback. The light was about six miles away! [44]

Dmitriev notes that the strange electromagnetic fields in a tornado can have apparently impossible effects. [45] Reports of tornado effects include a maple leaf that was pressed into hard stucco (a kind of plaster/cement wall covering), the porous tip of a charred plank staying undamaged after puncturing a wall, and a pine stick that didn't break while puncturing an iron sheet. Wilcock cites cases where pebbles have gone through glass without breaking it, and straw has been embedded into window panes. [46]

## The Hutchison Effect

The kind of phenomena noted above are known collectively as *The Hutchison Effect*, after the Vancouver "*wild scientist*" John Hutchison, [47] who was studying the longitudinal waves discovered by Nikola Tesla. Hutchison, who did not receive a conventional scientific education, but had a lifelong fascination with machines and electricity, had a collection of equipment in his lab, including Tesla coils, Van de Graaff generators, radio-frequency generators, RF transmitters and many other devices. One day in 1979, [48] he turned on all the machines at once, "*to study possible field interactions*" and was amazed when a steel bar levitated into the air. Continued experiments caused very similar effects to those caused in tornadoes, such as the embedding of wood into metal without charring it or displacing any metal (cold-melting), continuing levitations (including hovering fires, lights appearing and vanishing), melted steel and aluminium, and coins embedded into metal. Video footage and photos of these impossibilities are available on the Internet at *www.hutchisoneffect.org.* [49] The effects were sporadic at first, but by 1990 he had refined his approach so that he could produce the effects about five times per hour. His lab was raided twice, and some of the machinery was confiscated - regular scientists could not explain it and it was thought to be "*a risk to national security*". He eventually sold what was left of the equipment to avoid further hassle, but is now looking for sponsorship to continue his experiments. [50]

You may recall that Terence McKenna was told by the self-transforming machine elves that the "*laws of physics will be transformed around 2012*". [51] Dmitriev seems to echo this when he says that all the hundreds of thousands of self-luminous formations, or plasmoids, are having an ever-increasing influence on the Earth's geophysical fields and biosphere:

"*The presence of these formations is the mainstream precedent to the transformation of Earth; an Earth which becomes more and more subject to the transitional physical processes which exist within the borderland between the physical vacuum and our material world.*" [52]

## Biochemistry of Galactic Alignment

It was over 45 years ago that Russian biochemist Simon Shnoll was working on muscle protein and noticed an irregularity in biochemical reaction rates [53] (an example of this kind of reaction rate would be to measure the time that it takes for acetylcholine to build up and dissipate from muscles). The results contradicted the theory, and when he asked his teacher, he was told that if he made less experiments, the anomaly would disappear! Over the ensuing years, he investigated "*anomalous statistical regularities in a wide range of physical, chemical and biological processes, from radioactive decay to the rates of biochemical reactions*". [54] In 1998, in the Russian physics journal *Uspekhi Fisicheskikh Nauk*, [55] Professor Shnoll published the results of over 30 years of experiments, in which he had made repeated histograms, or bar charts, showing rates of radioactive decay in which the decay never reached the ideal bell-curve that it should do, with increased trials. He found that the more readings he took, the more certain peaks were accentuated on the histogram. However, when he repeated the same experiment at the same time - in other words, had two or more identical experiments running at the same time - the histograms were almost identical. He then used a computer to compare the closeness of all the histograms, and a pattern finally emerged. There were clear peaks at intervals of just under 24 hours, 27.28 days and "*at three time intervals close to a year: 364.4, 365.2 and 366.6 days.*" [56] The first period corresponds "*quite precisely*" to a sidereal day (i.e. in relation to the stars), not a solar day. The second period is exactly one rotation of the sunspots - a *Carrington Rotation*. [57] Of the last three, one could either be a solar year of 365.2425 days or a sidereal year of 365.256363 days. The others are unknown. [58]

So, biological processes, chemical reactions and radioactive decay are all affected by astronomical cycles, including solar activity and sidereal cycles. This means that the orientation of the Earth to the Milky Way has biological, chemical and radioactive effects. This is exactly what the 13-baktun cycle is tracking: our orientation towards the equatorial plane of the Milky Way. As it now seems that the interaction of the geomagnetic field with the solar field and the galactic field can affect our biochemistry, this could be another factor in any forthcoming consciousness changes. We have seen convincing evidence that the geomagnetic inversion has already started, and this is what Dmitriev says on the matter:

"*... The currently observed polar travel acceleration is not just a shift or digression from the norm, but is in fact an inversion of the magnetic poles; in full process.*" [59]

The results of a separate scientific study support Shnoll's findings. In 1997, James Spotiswoode published a paper called *Apparent Association Between Effect Size in Free Response Anomalous Cognition Experiments and Local Sidereal Time*, in which 2,500 trials were performed using remote viewing and *Ganzfeld experiments*. This is where a mild sensory isolation is induced by special goggles or half ping-pong balls combined with the wearing of headphones that emit *white noise* (combined frequencies), or *pink noise* (white noise without high frequencies). Anomalous cognition is another term for ESP or extra-sensory perception, and the idea of the experiment was to increase understanding of how ESP works, by finding "*a physical parameter which clearly modulated AC performance*". The results showed not only that the time of the sidereal day (about four minutes shorter than a solar day) had a significant effect on the results, but, specifically, that at a Local Sidereal Time (LST) of about 13.5 hours plus or minus an hour or so, which corresponds to the rising time of Galactic Centre on the horizon, there is a massive increase in human "*intuition*" or psychic ability. The implication is that the galactic alignment process could significantly boost human psychic abilities. See *www.diagnosis2012.co.uk/new7.htm#intuit*

## Implosion Point

John Major Jenkins has laid down a solid base with his comprehensive analysis of Maya archaeology and calendrics, showing that the galactic alignment process lies at the heart of the 2012 phenomenon. David Wilcock is constantly building around this base, synthesising obscure findings as he goes. His approach of looking for scientific confirmation for the Ra material has produced some interesting finds, including Dmitriev, Shnoll and Smelyakov. Wilcock believes that as we travel further into the magnetised plasma band, we pass through "*ripples*" that are spaced out by the phi ratio, either side of the band. [60] These are Smelyakov's *bifurcation points*. The plasma bands he sees as spaced out in a galactic-sized version of the Parker Spiral (the Catherine-wheel spiral in which plasma bands curve out from the Sun, as explained in Chapter 12), about 25,920 years apart. This is how he combines Dmitriev's magnetised plasma band and Smelyakov's Auric Time Scale.

As we have seen, Smelyakov's Auric Time Scale did not re-appear until October 2004, following the start-date problem. When it did re-appear, only the start-date, end-date and bifurcation points had been amended, but there were no amendments regarding the second point I made about the fact that the series does not end in 2012 as implied by David Wilcock, but continues until 2037. When I told Wilcock about the 2037 implosion point, [61] his reply insinuated that he thought I had misunderstood the Auric Time Scale [62], and said, "*I do not view this actually as a spiral formation in hyperspace*". [63] However, he had already implied that the series terminated in 2012, in his essay *The Ultimate Secret of The Mayan Calendar*, in which he said "*... the entire cycle decreases to a certain final moment at the end of the cycle*". [64] More specifically, in an interview with Wynn Free, Wilcock said "*... Dr Smelyakov was simply to take the beginning and ending point of the said Mayan calendar cycle and to separate this cycle into partitions such that they are divided by phi with a spiral imploding toward 2012*". [65]

When I also informed Sergey Smelyakov at the same time, he said I had raised some valid points that had not occurred to him at the time (see Chapter 12). During the two-year and four month period waiting for the modified version of the Auric Time Scale to appear, rather than waiting around any longer, I spent an afternoon working out a phi-based series

| BIFURCATION POINT (B.P.) | B.P. INTERVAL | |
|---|---|---|
| 11,407 B.C. | 5125.366126 YEARS | a |
| 16 DEC 6282 B.C. | 3167.65 YEARS | b |
| 11 AUG 3114 B.C. | 1957.72 YEARS | c |
| 28 APR 1156 B.C. | 1209.93 YEARS | d |
| 4 APR 55 A.D. | 747.78 YEARS | e |
| 14 JAN 803 A.D. | 462.15 YEARS | f |
| 10 MAR 1265 A.D. | 285.63 YEARS | g |
| 26 OCT 1550 A.D. | 176.53 YEARS | |
| 6 MAY 1727 A.D. | 109.10 YEARS | |
| 11 JUN 1836 A.D. | 67.43 YEARS | |
| 15 NOV 1903 A.D. | 41.67 YEARS | |
| 18 JUL 1945 | 25.75 YEARS | |
| 20 APR 1971 | 15.92 YEARS | |
| 20 MAR 1987 | 9.84 YEARS | |
| 20 JAN 1997 | 6.08 YEARS | |
| 18 FEB 2003 | 3.76 YEARS | |
| 22 NOV 2006 | 2.32 YEARS | |
| 19 MAR 2009 | 1.43 YEARS | |
| 25 AUG 2010 | 10.68 MONTHS | |
| 15 JUL 2011 | 6.60 MONTHS | |
| 31 JAN 2012 | 4.08 MONTHS | |
| 3 JUNE 2012 | 2.52 MONTHS | |
| 19 AUG 2012 | 1.44 MONTHS | |
| 5 OCT 2012 | 29.21 DAYS | |
| 3 NOV 2012 | 18.05 DAYS | |
| 21 NOV 2012 | 11.15 DAYS | |
| 2 DEC 2012 | 6.89 DAYS | |
| 9 DEC 2012 | 4.26 DAYS | |
| 13 DEC 2012 | 2.63 DAYS | |
| 16 DEC 2012 | 1.63 DAYS | |
| 18 DEC 2012 | 1.01 DAYS | |
| 19 DEC 2012 | 14.92 HOURS | |
| 19 DEC 2012 | 9.22 HOURS | |
| 20 DEC 2012 | 5.70 HOURS | |
| 20 DEC 2012 | 3.52 HOURS | |
| 20 DEC 2012 | 2.18 HOURS | |
| 20 DEC 2012 | 1.35 HOURS | |
| 20 DEC 2012 | 49.90 MINUTES | |
| 20 DEC 2012 | 30.84 MINUTES | |
| 20 DEC 2012 | 19.06 MINUTES | |
| 20 DEC 2012 | 11.78 MINUTES | |
| 21 DEC 2012 | 7.28 MINUTES | |
| 21 DEC 2012 | 4.50 MINUTES | |
| 21 DEC 2012 | 2.78 MINUTES | |

"Vertical" Intervals:  $a=c(1+\phi)$

or  $c=\dfrac{a}{1+\phi}$

"Horizontal" Intervals: $b=\dfrac{a}{\phi}$   $d=\dfrac{c}{\phi}$   etc.

*OPPOSITE: Fig.20.6: The projected Mach 2 version of Karpenko and Smelyakov's Auric Time Scale, with amended start point and re-calculated with an improved fit to the 13-baktun cycle, reaching the centre of the whorl on December 21st 2012 - Peter Russell's "white hole in time". The same phi series as the original was used (see Fig.12.8), except that here, bifurcation points are all on the left, and intervals are all on the right. Phi was taken as 1.6180339 and, starting with the length of the 13-baktun cycle to six decimal places, the calculation was done with nine decimal places carried through, but with each interval rounded off on the diagram.*

with the same criteria as The Auric Time Scale that terminates on 21st December 2012. I present the result in Fig.20.6, and you can see that I have conceived it as a spiral, like the spiral of Peter Russell, that converges on a white hole in time, or implosion point, in December 2012. If you prefer to see it as a series of ripples approaching the band of plasma, imagine viewing it looking into the spiral, centred on the part of the band that we shall meet on Winter Solstice 2012. As we cross the lines of the spiral, we meet the bifurcation points of the Smelyakov theory. When I compared the new dates of the bifurcation points to the events listed by Smelyakov, they compared well, with some even closer to the events listed. Most impressive of all, though, was the fact that there is a new bifurcation point on July 18th 1945, which is only two days after the Trinity Test. This was the first time (as far as we know) that a nuclear explosion ever occurred on planet Earth, and being within two days, makes it more significant than all the original bifurcation points. It thus comes into a fairly close relationship with Timewave Zero, since that was based around the Hiroshima bomb - the first nuclear detonation over a populated area.

# Chapter 21:
# Synthesis

## Contaminated Trance?

It seems that everyone has a piece of the puzzle, whether small or large, so let's look at question three - how much contamination is there between the many sources of information in Part Three: *Beyond the Veil* and the already existing information and misinformation on 2012?

Terence and Dennis McKennas' book *The Invisible Landscape* was first published in 1975, when there was hardly anything in print about 2012. Frank Waters' book *Mexico Mystique* was also published in 1975, but put the end of the 13-baktun cycle at 2011. Terence modified the end of the Timewave by 34 days in the second edition, since he had heard by then about the 13-baktun cycle. If Terence had heard of the Maya calendar ending in December 2012, he would have fixed the end-point there in the first edition, rather than November 2012, so *The Invisible Landscape* is obviously an independent source on 2012, and it was revealed through the alteration of consciousness via DMT (close relatives of DMT; psilocybin and psilocin, to be exact) and harmine.

Since Terence McKenna later became a kind of evangelist for the use of sacred plants, many of the people who got 2012 information via sacred plants would have already been familiar with the 2012 scenario, it seems. Yet the Syrian Rue user previously quoted in Chapter 13 was surprised at his revelation, having given no credence to McKenna beforehand. Dannion Brinkley had his near-death experience in September 1975, so it is just possible he could have seen *The Invisible Landscape*. Ken Kalb, on the other hand, had a near-death experience in Mexico in 1969, which led to the writing of his book *The Grand Catharsis*, about the history of consciousness between 1987 and 2012, a period in which he sees the entire planet having a near-death experience, but he wrote it in 1995, so was probably influenced by *The Mayan Factor*. However, I have personally spoken to Jon King and he told me that he knew nothing about the Maya, 2012 or McKenna when he had his contact experience. I have also spoken to Robert Gilson, who assures me that he knew nothing about 2012 when he had his vision of a *"Period of Justification"*.

In my opinion, there is enough independent corroboration here to show that this 2012 information is bubbling up from some deep communal level of mind and emerging from various human transmitters in order to give us a spiritual kick up the Aristotle! [1] We have seen how the Timewave Zero concept sprang from a vision provided by the same mushroom that the Maya took. We have also seen how pure DMT allowed the *"machine-elves"* to tell Terence McKenna of a forthcoming change in the laws of physics around 2012. Dr Rick Strassman's research provides convincing evidence that DMT is involved in birth, death and near-death experiences, as well as mystical experiences and close encounter experiences. When you also take into account the UFO wave that has been happening in Mexico since 1991, and consider that Mexico is the land of the Aztecs and the earlier Maya who originated the calendar cycle that terminates in 2012, the pieces of the puzzle start to fall into place. We have also mentioned Dr Callaway of the University of Kuopio, Finland, whose research demonstrated that the near-death experience, out-of-body experience and death itself are based on internal secretion of pinoline, DMT, and 5-meo-DMT.

In other words, since many of the prophecies of Earth and consciousness changes in 2012 originate from shamans or medicine men using exogenous (outside the body) DMT and pinoline, while other 2012 prophecies originate from mystical experience, contact experiences, near-death and out-of-body experiences, which are linked with endogenous (inside the body) DMT and pinoline release, we therefore have a massive connection between pineal hormones and a major event due in, or close to, 2012. Rick Strassman considered the possibility that a solar flare or some other astronomical event could trigger a mass-turning on of the N-methylating enzyme responsible for DMT production. Serena Roney-Dougal pointed out that the pineal responds to lunar and sunspot cycles via the changing geomagnetic field, and that sudden changes in the field correspond to poltergeist and ghost activity. A drop in the field, if you remember, increases the incidence of clairvoyance and telepathy, corresponding to secretion of a member of the telepathine family, pinoline.

## Enter the Shepherdess...

We have seen that several people claim that Salvia divinorum has given them access to 2012 information, and also that this plant has a connection to pre-conquest Mexico. Some users refer to the deva or consciousness of the plant as the *Shepherdess*, or the *Green Goddess*. Salvia divinorum was not known to bind to any receptor sites - in other words, it was not understood how it produced a hallucinatory effect - until August 2002, when a paper was published [2] showing that Salvinorin A (now known to be one of two psychoactive constituents of Salvia divinorum) binds to the kappa-opioid receptors. Most other visionary drugs work on the serotonin (specifically the 5-HT-2a receptor) system, including the DMT family, so this enables us to cancel DMT out of the 2012-visionary equation for a moment and look from another angle.

After reading dozens of accounts of experiences people have had using DMT and Salvia, [3] I realized that one thing that is often described by users of both entheogens [4] is an out-of-body experience, or OOBE, and that there are also well-known similarities between OOBEs and NDEs (near-death experiences). There are equally well-known similarities between alien abduction experiences and OOBEs. So if we refocus on the OOBE, rather than the external or internal means of achieving it, we can see that the source of information about 2012 seems to be the place that consciousness travels to when it vacates the body - what those in the esoteric world call the *astral realm* or *astral plane*. Remote viewers, or psychic spies, who can remote view in time as well as space, work via the astral plane, and we have already heard about the block reported by some remote viewers around 2012.

I mentioned that the most interesting thing in Cotterell and Gilbert's *The Mayan Prophecies* was a reference to the effects of fluctuations of the geomagnetic field on the human endocrine system. They quoted a passage from a 1987 paper by Dr Ross Adey of Linda Hospital, California:

*"About 20% of pineal cells in pigeons, guinea-pigs and rats respond to changes in both direction and intensity of the Earth's magnetic field (Semm, 1983). Experimental inversion of the horizontal component of the Earth's magnetic field significantly decreases synthesis and secretion of the peptide hormone melatonin, which powerfully influences circadian rhythms, and also reduces activity in its synthesizing enzymes (Walker et al., 1983)."* [5]

So there is evidence that the secretion of pineal hormones can be affected by a change in the geomagnetic field, and we have already seen how not only Gregg Braden, but also mainstream scientists, are saying that a geomagnetic reversal is imminent, and that the magnetic field is approaching a 100,000-year peak that corresponds to a 100,000-year solar cycle. This 100,000-year cycle is about the same length as four cycles of the precession of the equinoxes, and has been linked to the

Maya calendar by William Gaspar. Braden linked the forthcoming magnetic field change with the need for an extra-dimensional body. So is there any evidence linking out-of-body experiences with changing magnetic fields? Recall that in Chapter 9 we reported the phenomenon of body polarity reversal during OOBEs discovered by the Monroe Institute, [6] and its implication of a possible mass-OOBE induced by geomagnetic reversal or fluctuation circa 2012.

## TLE

Temporal lobe epilepsy (TLE) is caused by *"unusual electrical activity in the brain's temporal lobes"* [7] and people suffering from TLE often report spiritual or religious feelings. In Clifford Pickover's essay, *Transcendent Experience and Temporal Lobe Epilepsy*, he includes the testimony of one un-named female sufferer who says:

*"With TLE, I see things slightly different than before. I have visions and images that normal people don't have. Some of my seizures are like entering another dimension, the closest to religious or spiritual feelings I've ever had. Epilepsy has given me a rare vision and insight into myself, and sometimes beyond myself, and it has played to my creative side. Without TLE, I would not have begun to sculpt."* [8]

The symptoms of an epileptic seizure have several points in common with feelings reported by alien abductees, according to TLE researcher Eve LaPlante. [9] These include heat on one side of the face, a ringing in the ears, seeing flashes of light prior to abduction, an unnatural silence, a feeling of anxiety, a sensation of bugs crawling on the skin, and yet more symptoms. LaPlante says that religious prophets such as Mohammed, Moses and St. Paul are all thought to have suffered from TLE, since the descriptions of their experiences all show several signs of it. The Russian writer Dostoevsky, who was himself a sufferer, recognised these signs in the stories of Mohammed. Other famous sufferers include the poet Tennyson and the artist Van Gogh, showing that the condition can have positive, creative effects. It is interesting to note here that the bifurcation points on Sergey Smelyakov's Auric Time Scale showed a correspondence to the coming of great religious teachers and philosophers, including St. Paul.

Very small fluctuations in the geomagnetic field have been found to affect people suffering from epilepsy (as mentioned in Chapter 13), and the (disputably) psychedelic tryptamine bufotenine has been found in the urine of people suffering from epilepsy, [10] but tryptamines including bufotenine have been found in smaller quantities in the urine of those not prone to epilepsy. [11] Steve Scott (a.k.a. Ian Hard) has Temporal Lobe Epilepsy, and he brought my attention to the fact that since childhood he has sensed the importance of 2012. [12] A BBC TV *Horizon* programme called *God on the Brain* (17th April 2003) dealt with the connection between TLE and religious experiences. It covered the work of Dr Michael Persinger of Laurentian University in Canada, whose research indicates that people with TLE may be especially sensitive to magnetic fields. He has a specially designed helmet that directs controlled magnetic fields to the temporal lobes, and he has been able to trigger several types of religious experiences, including out-of-body sensations, physical feelings (such as being grabbed by the shoulders or leg for example), and even visions of alien abduction in some cases. [13]

Earth mysteries researcher Paul Devereux was director of the *Dragon Project*, which started in 1977 and was an attempt to monitor energy anomalies at sacred sites. [14] Many sites have been found to have magnetic anomalies, such as Carn Ingli, the "*Peak of Angels*" in Wales, which has areas of reversed magnetic field. Devereux says: "*Persinger and colleagues have produced some exciting statistical evidence that suggests that there is a link between some forms of psi activity in humans and the activity of the geomagnetic field*". [15] Devereux, who has tried Persinger's magnetic helmet, notes that a stone, shaped like a seat, in the Gors Fawr stone circle in Wales, not only affects compass needles, but is also one of a pair of outliers that align to sunrise on the Summer Solstice:

"*The sitter's head leans back against exactly that part of the stone that most disturbs the compass: the cerebral cortex is in close proximity to the natural magnetic effect. The stone is also involved in a midsummer-sunrise alignment. Would the effect be somehow enhanced then? Or does that clue tell us when the ritual was carried out at the magnetic 'spirit' stone? Alas, we have much yet to learn in our fledgling study of geopsychedelics.*" [16]

Are magnetic effects at sacred sites enhanced at the solstices? Will the Winter Solstice in 2012 trigger an even more far-reaching effect? Should we be at such a sacred site for the galactic alignment event (which is actually every Winter Solstice from 1980 up to 2016 - see page 247), or will the changes in the background geomagnetic field affect the weak magnetic field that surrounds all our heads? Perhaps being present at a sacred site might protect us from changes in the background geomagnetic status. There is an Argentinean webpage (in Spanish language on the www.argemto.com.ar site) that explains how Russian

*Fig.21.1: Stone seat at Cairn T, Loughcrew Mountains, Ireland. The passage of the cairn is aligned to the equinox sunrise.*

cosmonauts exposed to a magnetic field of 0 gauss (the gauss is the unit of magnetic induction equal to one ten-thousandth of a Tesla, so 0 gauss therefore means no measurable magnetic field) experienced *"confusion, aggression and madness"*, and postulates that Earth's magnetic field will drop to 0 gauss by 2012. [17]

## Acute Schizophrenic Break Syndrome

At the moment of the Summer Solstice sunrise in 1972, Michael O'Callaghan was standing inside a Neolithic passage-cairn called Tibradden on the hills above Dublin in Ireland. He underwent an experience in which he saw the city below as a huge organism eating into the hillside, slowly poisoning itself with its own excretions. As the Sun rose over the horizon, shining directly up the ancient passageway onto him, Michael's vision metamorphosed into a classic mystical experience:

*"In this ecstatic condition, I had the delicious feeling of being utterly at one with nature, no longer a separate 'skin-encapsulated ego', but a living extension of the biosphere in human form that could simultaneously look back upon - and identify with - the larger portion of its global Self, 'outside looking in,' as it were."* [18]

He saw Humankind emerging from the womb of history like a newborn baby, the flower at the end of a 4.6 billion-year germination process, with a huge potential - if only we could reach out and grab it. The Sun was the answer to the energy problem, he saw, with its free solar power, and if we could stop our rampant consumerism in time, we could find ourselves at the beginning of the Solar Age.

O'Callaghan came to realize that an acute schizophrenic break syndrome was like an extended version of his solstice experience, and the *world itself* is on the brink of a schizophrenic break. He clears up one thing from the start:

*"Contrary to popular misunderstanding, the term 'schizophrenia' does not refer to the multiple personality syndrome; the Greek etymology of the word actually means 'broken soul' or 'broken heart.'"* [19]

Cases of schizophrenia (often classed as *"mental breakdown"* by the mainstream psychiatric community) were seen by the psychologist Carl Jung as the start of a healing experience, if approached correctly. The experience, if handled carefully by support and not repression or use of sedatives, usually lasts about 40 days (and 40 nights...). Very often it will include a death and re-birth, experience, or 'inner apocalypse'. This is often projected outwards and interpreted as the end of the world and an end of time.  In fact, O'Callaghan points out that the word *apocalypse* means 'a revealing', and this is a process of the unconscious mind revealing itself by archetypal imagery. Dr R. D. Laing, who helps schizophrenic people through the healing process, says that the *Book of Revelation* is obviously about an internal process of the destruction and re-integration of the ego. [20] St. John the Divine is said to have written it while he was *imprisoned in a cave* on the Greek Island of Patmos (a dark-room retreat).

Jung said that schizophrenia can be defined as "*when the dream becomes real*", [21] and this is the title of the brilliant four-chapter essay that Michael O'Callaghan has written on the subject. [22] Jung saw dreams as messages from our unconscious minds; when the dreams break into waking consciousness, we can no longer ignore them.

Schizophrenia is currently affecting approximately 2% of the population of the world, and we are not dealing with it properly. The current 'treatment' is that people are just drugged to stop the whole process, while what they actually need is to be in a supportive environment for the 40 days, by which time they will start to re-integrate - a process in which the three months following the 40-day schizophrenic break is spent at the facility, then another three months in a half-way house, then back to the outside world. This approach was tried in the 1970s by Dr John Weir Perry at the *Diabasis* facility in San Francisco, and it was 100% successful, with no relapses. In indigenous societies, anyone showing signs of an approaching 'break' is taken and shown that the experience is a gift, and it is integrated into their subsequent training for a career as a shaman. The apprentice can then learn to navigate the otherworld, and re-invoke the experience at will by using trance techniques that often include sacred plants. [23]

As Ken Kalb saw it, *the Earth itself* is having a near-death experience. It is poised on the edge of an abyss where we must choose to cross on the bridge of ecological sustainability or jump using our "*Yama-zaki*" supercharged rocket plane with only half a pint of fuel left in the tank. Have you ever wondered why the (much flouted) Kyoto Protocol, an international agreement to cut pollution to target levels, has a deadline in the year 2012? We have already seen the link between shamanism and the 2012 phenomenon, and that the re-integration following the break can lead to a feeling of oneness with nature, so these messages seem to be sourced from the collective unconscious, which is another concept that started with Jung. The same message is bubbling up through diverse terminals or human neurons in the developing global brain. The source could also be seen as the Gaian mind, or some would even say, the Galactic Federation, or the "*wee folk*". It is being broadcast through the astral plane, or the fourth and fifth Dimensions, or the next density level, or even via 'voices in the head'. Choose your favourite terminology, but we are being told in myriad ways that the Earth is about to enter a transition phase around the Gregorian year 2012, and that there will be geomagnetic effects that may open our pineal eyes. The "*first flowerings*" are the schizophrenics and psychics, those with TLE, channels, shamans and visionaries, who are more sensitive to the first and smaller magnetic changes. As the Earth's field gets nearer to reversal, it seems likely that there will be more pineal-openings, and those of us who have not confronted our inner selves and our accumulated emotional blockages may find this experience to be more hellish. The fact that "*tryptamines other than serotonin*" (and different from those found in control subjects) and, later, DMT itself, were found in the urine of schizophrenic people [24] demonstrates the

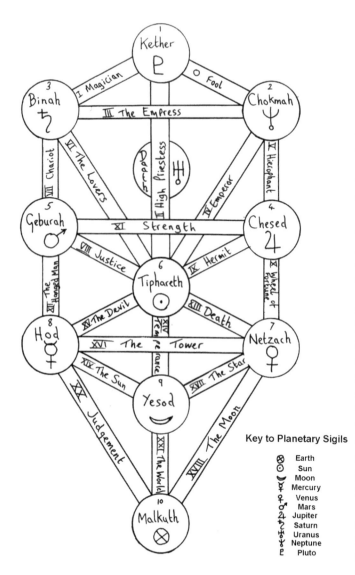

Fig.21.2: The kabbalistic Tree of Life showing the eleven Sephiroth, or spheres, with their planetary attributions, and the 22 paths with their Tarot attributions. This is the standard interpretation (the Crowleyan interpretation used by groups such as the AA and the OTO reverses the position of The Emperor and The Star).

Key to Planetary Sigils

⊗ Earth
☉ Sun
☽ Moon
☿ Mercury
♀ Venus
♂ Mars
♃ Jupiter
♄ Saturn
♅ Uranus
♆ Neptune
♇ Pluto

likelihood that the condition is connected with an altered pineal output - the first blurred opening of the pineal eye.

## Gnostic Soulcraft

In Graham Hancock's book *Heaven's Mirror: Quest for the Lost Civilization*, [25] he concludes that the survivors of the Ice Age civilization that ended around 10,500 BC passed on not only a knowledge of astronomy and precession, related to the cyclic catastrophe that ended the Ice Age, but also a *"science of immortality"*. This was a technology of the soul, in which techniques acquired over millennia of study and experimentation could be used in ways to preserve consciousness beyond the veil of death. Hancock says the knowledge was passed down through secret societies, and traces can be found in the Gnostic writings found at Nag Hammadi.

In Gnostic versions of the *Genesis* myth, the forbidden fruit gives knowledge of light and darkness. The Tree of Knowledge can easily be seen as some sort of hallucinogenic plant that made those who had eaten it aware of other planes of existence and, via out-of-body experiences, they would have seen that consciousness can exist without the physical body. The *"Tree of Life"* thus became perceptible; the kabbalistic tree of life is a map of the paths of the netherworld, and the middle pillar relates directly to the chakras in our subtle body, situated along our own middle pillar - the spine. By certain exercises involving the chakras or power zones, and the snakelike Kundalini energy, it seems that the astral body can be perfected or transformed into a vehicle with a much longer lifespan.

So, Hancock's study traced this science of Soulcraft from a pre-diluvian race, through ancient civilizations in Mexico, Egypt and other places, suggesting that it is linked to the precession cycle.

Some of the information can still be found in the Bible. In Matthew 22, the *"kingdom of heaven"* is compared to a marriage, at which those who are not wearing the *"wedding garment"* will not get to witness the wedding. In Luke and Matthew, we are informed about the pineal eye:

*"Your eye is the lamp of your body; when your eye is sound, your whole body is full of light; but when it is not sound, your body is full of darkness. Therefore be careful lest the light in you be darkness. If then your whole body is full of light, having no part dark, it will be wholly bright, as when a lamp with its rays gives you light."* [26]

This theme is expanded in Matthew 25: 1-13, in which we are told to have our lamps fully fuelled up and burning, ready for the arrival of the bridegroom for his marriage feast. As to exactly what this means, John Major Jenkins, in *Galactic Alignment*, has provided us with a clue from a book called *The Celestial Ship of the North*, by Valentia Straiton, in which someone called Edgar Conrow is quoted:

*"The pineal gland is the 'North Gate'. This, in man, is the central spiritual creative centre. Above in the heavens, it is found in the beginning of the sign Sagittarius, and is the point from which spiritual gifts are given. It is called 'Vision of God,' and is the Light within, a gift to the pure in heart, who verily may 'see God,' but to the impure, or those who abuse this great gift, the consequences are terrible.*

*This North Gate, the creative centre in man, the most interior centre in the body, has become atrophied, and redemption or regeneration means its restoration to creative ability, by having the electrical, or positive, and the magnetic, or negative, forces restored in equal balance in man or woman."* [27]

The alignment of the solstice Sun with the Galactic Equator, close to Galactic Centre at the start of Sagittarius, is thus a time when the Galactic Pineal Eye will radiate its light and restore our individual pineal eyes to their full potential of transmundane vision. However, not everyone will qualify. Luke's gospel implies that only the unmarried will qualify, [28] but it seems that he means male sexual energy should not be 'wasted' in ejaculation, but used instead for the higher purpose of modifying our subtle body into its fully flowered form.

## Egyptian Shamanism

You can find an expanded essay on this subject, called *Soulcraft*, at *www.diagnosis2012.co.uk/soul.htm*, in which all the traces of the knowledge are exhumed and compared, but, briefly, we can trace it back to Egyptian sources to get quite an early version. The Egyptians had a shamanic religion, in which the Pharaoh would induce an astral flight by means of techniques including hallucinogens, light and sound [29] (see Appendix 2), meditations timed by lunar phases, and possibly a darkroom retreat, to become Osiris (who was cut into pieces and then re-assembled) in a death-rebirth experience. Isis reassembled the fourteen pieces of Osiris, having collected them in the Land of the Phoenix (Phoenicia - now Lebanon), during the fourteen days of the waning Moon (except for the phallus, which was lost), then bound him up like the pupa of a butterfly. She then used a wooden phallus to conceive Horus, and Osiris ascended to Heaven (possibly encoding the higher use of sexual energy). The phoenix was retained as the symbol of an immortal bird, but is also connected with the recurrence of a long cycle of time.

The Egyptian winged disk, according to Charles Muses, [30] represents the "*non-molecular body*" that is developed as the vehicle for these flights. The timing of the whole 70-day mummification process was synchronised with the 70-day disappearance of Sirius into the Duat (the period when Sirius is not visible). Muses points out the parallels between mummification and the process of metamorphosis from caterpillar, via cocoon and pupa (chrysalis) into butterfly. The wrapping of the body in bandages represents the silk-enswathed larva (caterpillar), and the folded wings embossed on the sarcophagus lids represented the visible wing shapes that are visible on the pupa or chrysalis case. The Mes-khent, or "*birth tent of skin,*" that was placed around the mummy represented the outer cocoon, while the ancient Egyptian word for the funeral chamber is literally "*the birth chamber*". [31] Humanity is seen as a larval stage in preparation for the final metamorphosis. [32] The 70-day embalming period was a later metaphor for a metamorphic transformation - one that was commenced while the physical body was still alive, leading to the birth of the "*winged form*", or immortal body.

## Non-Molecular Body

The Egyptian soul-science ("*psyche-ology*") is quite complex, with several non-physical bodies being involved, but Jeremy Naydler has reconstructed the scheme in quite a convincing way in *Temple of the Cosmos*. [33] The *khat* is the physical body (symbolized by a fish hieroglyph), and the *ka* (symbolized by upturned arms), or *double*, can be seen as "*vital force*" - an energy body that seems to be equivalent to an etheric body. The *ba* (symbolized by a bird with a human head), although often translated as "*soul*", is better understood as a seed-soul consciousness, since it is "*but a preliminary to a yet more exalted state of consciousness*". [34] It is consciousness externalised, and seems to be the equivalent of the astral body. "*As a ba, a person had the experience of looking at his or her body as if from an outsider's standpoint. This experience was central to the Osirian initiation."* [35] The *khaibit*, or *shadow* (symbolized by a dark human silhouette), represents *"all the untransformed earthly appetites and obsessions that fetter the ba to the physical realm and prevent it from moving on"* [36] (the astral body is also known as the emotional body). The *akh*, also called *akhu* or *khu* (represented by a bird - the Crested Ibis), means *"shining one"*, or *"illuminated one"*. It is also called *"the imperishable one"* that returns to its source beyond the Duat.

Naydler says *"The akh may be understood as the ba divinised"*, [37] but in order for the akh to be released from the body, a new spiritual body had to be germinated from the physical body as a vehicle for the akh. This spiritual body is the *sahu*. This sounds like the immortal man in Taoist Yoga, who is gestated in the abdomen and expelled through a psychic opening in the top of the head to appear as a person sitting on a lotus within a golden sphere, as we shall see shortly. The lotus was also a symbol of rebirth in Egypt. Naydler says the re-membering following the dismemberment was an essential part of the Osirian initiation, which is a germination process in which the sahu is formed and the akh is attained, allowing access to the stellar realms beyond the Duat.

Naydler's interpretation implies that the conscious mind resides in the khaibit (shadow) and the unconscious mind in the ba (astral body). If the shadow can be conquered, then it can unite with the ba to form the akh (khu). At the same time, the sahu can be germinated

*TOP (L-R): Fig.21.3: The Egyptian hieroglyph for the* khat, *or physical body.*
*Fig.21.4: The Egyptian hieroglyph for the* ka, *or etheric body.*
*Fig.21.5: The early Egyptian hieroglyph for the* ba *or astral body.*

*MIDDLE (L-R): Fig.21.6: A later Egyptian hieroglyph for the* ba.
*Fig.21.7: The depiction of the* ba *in the Egyptian Book of the Dead, or, literally, the Book of Coming Forth by Day - in this case, the Papyrus of Ani.*
*Fig.21.8: The Egyptian hieroglyph for the* khaibit, *or shadow.*

*LOWER (L-R). Fig.21.9: A crested Ibis -the Egyptian hieroglyph for the* akh, *or khu.*
*Fig.21.10: An alternative hieroglyph for the* akh *or khu.*
*Fig.21.11: The Egyptian hieroglyph for the* sah *or sahu.*

from the ka, which now has access to more vital energy - the sexual energy, that is no longer being diverted into emotional blockages since the cleaning up of the shadow. This interpretation provides a scheme of the unification of male and female (conscious and unconscious), while retaining the evolution of the higher bodies.

This all seems to support the contention of Charles Muses that there were three post-mortem paths that could be followed by the newly-deceased Egyptian: *The Hippo Path*, in which the soul's vehicle disintegrated and the soul reincarnated; *The Cow Path*, in which the soul experienced a dream-like existence in the Duat, or Underworld, from where it could either reincarnate or ascend; and *The Lion Path*, where a higher body allowed access to a higher dimension.

In the epilogue of Naydler's *Temple of the Cosmos*, he recognises the connection between Napoleon's invasion of Egypt and "*his desire to discover the sources of Masonic Lore - which he believed lay in ancient Egypt...*" [38] He also recalls the Masonic Great Seal of America, with its implication that the "*New Order of the Ages*" was coming up and represented a "*general spiritual awakening*" linked to a re-emergence of Egyptian knowledge (symbolized by the return of the capstone to the Great Pyramid). We have already seen how the Great Seal encodes the year 2012 on the top of the pyramid.

### The Spiritual Wedding

Just as Feng-Shui, the Chinese system of geomancy, has an *Earth Ch'i* and a *Heaven Ch'i*, Mary Scott has found evidence that the fire-serpent, or Kundalini, which is said by the Hindus to lie coiled and sleeping at the base of the spine, is actually an Earth-force. This Kundalini is "*the Shakti or divine cosmic energy with particular dominion over the physical world*". [39] The evidence suggests that "*some energies may enter the chakra at the base of the spine, from below, a point not stressed in Tantric texts*" [40] (part of the evidence was from meditators who had a condition called physio-kundalini, the symptoms of which are concentrated in the pelvic area, but which start with sensations in the feet and legs). The Kundalini is "*coiled three and a half times around the Linga, the Shiva line of force which enters the body from above*". [41] Shakti, including Kundalini, is the feminine aspect of the divine in manifestation, while Shiva is the male aspect.

Kundalini Yoga is a collection of techniques to raise the Kundalini up the spine, cleansing the chakras on the way until finally the two aspects of the Divine, the male Shiva force and the female Shakti (Kundalini), reunite in the *Sahasrara* chakra at the crown of the head. This results in the ego-annihilating *Samadhi*, or *trance of ecstasy*. It is quite a dangerous practice, and needs to be learnt from a Yogi. The Kundalini energy is not *prana* (vital energy contained in the air we breathe), but works in close association with prana. Mary Scott says that "*Kundalini is called the* Logos *in bodies, and this has to be taken to cover galaxies as embodiments of Brahman, as well as bodies in the usual sense of the word.*" [42] The prana and Kundalini blend in the *Muladhara*, or *Root chakra* at the base of the spine. In a similar way, Scott tells us, there must be a blending of forces in the Earth - terrestrial centres and channels through which cosmic energies pass, and in which they blend.

## Earth Ch'i Meets Heaven Ch'i

This concept of a force from above meeting a force from below, and the meeting of the two taking place in the human body, was suggested over 50 years ago. In the Theosophical booklet *Kundalini - An Occult Experience*, [43] published in 1947, G. S. Arundale suggests that there is an *Earth-Kundalini* and a *Sun-Kundalini*, which may be seen as two poles - negative and positive respectively (similar to the Chinese Earth Ch'i and Heaven Ch'i). The booklet does not mention prana, but says that Earth-Kundalini flows up through the feet and limbs to the Root or Muladhara chakra at the base of the spine, where it is concentrated together with the Sun-Kundalini so that, in the rare cases when the system works at its full evolutionary potential, the human acts as a rod connecting the two terminals and experiences a higher consciousness of union with the Divine, together with clairvoyance and other paranormal side-effects. These higher states Arundale calls *Buddhic* and *Nirvanic*, which may perhaps be equivalent to Global Consciousness and Solar Consciousness.

Arundale also suggests that there are inter-planetary and inter-solar streams of Kundalini, and that not only does Earth have chakras, but the Earth and the Sun may themselves be chakras in larger systems. He also suggests that Kundalini concentrates in hills and mountains, and places of repeated ceremonial gatherings such as churches, temples, and mosques, which he says are "*magnetised areas*". He says that this Kundalini "*waxes and wanes*" or "*ebbs and flows*", which suggests a lunar influence (though *he* doesn't actually say so). He hints at the connection between sexuality and Kundalini in that "*such remnants of sexual nature as there may have been*

*Fig.21.12: The snake heads at the base of the stairway on the pyramid of Kukulcan, Chichen Itza, Mexico. The Maya Daykeeper Hunbatz Men has demonstrated that the Maya had a spiritual technology utilising the chakra and serpent/Kundalini energy, in which one aspired to become Kukulcan (Quetzalcotal), the feathered serpent. He sees the pyramid as a reminder of the process (Men, 1990, p.109-145). Photo: Lee Anderson*

seem to be transmuted and transformed into their true purpose... Godliness." [44] Since "*Kundalini Fire is the essence of the Love of God*", [45] perhaps some kind of 'love' in our sexual centre is being converted to Love, or the Holy Spirit: Eros converting to Agape.

Mary Scott does not mention Arundale, but has independently investigated the findings of dowser Guy Underwood, and found many connections to Kundalini lore. Underwood detected deep underground streams, and called these "*water lines*", which he saw as lines of force which cause discontinuities in a background force-field coming from the Earth. He also detected two other types of lines, that he called "*track lines*" and "*aquastats*". All these convoluted lines were found to have an intimate relationship with prehistoric sacred sites, and in the course of his investigations Underwood excavated to check his results, and found he had actually discovered several prehistoric circles, barrows, mazes and stone-paved tracks, which have since been declared genuine sites. Blind springs are coils where lines converge, and which occur on all three types of line. Water lines and aquastats, which often interweave with each other, converge on blind springs with seven coils, or with multiples of seven (49 was the maximum number found by Underwood). Track lines converge on spirals of three and a half, or multiples of three and a half, just as Kundalini is said to be resting in a coil of three and a half turns.

Scott says the lines correlate to the water veins and Yin and Yang dragon currents of the Chinese system, while the straight alignments known as *ley lines* correspond to the Chinese spirit paths. The snake/dragon theme is preserved in the names of many hills in Britain, and many of the churches built over sacred sites have been named after Saint Michael - the one who slew the Dragon (Michael was the biblical prototype for St. George, England's patron saint). Scott points out that Underwood found each blind spring had an associated "*geospiral*" and a pair of "*halos*" surrounding it, both of which altered according to the phases of the Moon. Since Feng-Shui (the Chinese art of geomancy) places importance on planetary influences, and some earthworks trace planetary movements, she concludes that the ley lines are indeed spirit paths, with influences from the Sun and major planets, while the aquastats and tracklines are the Yang and Yin dragon paths of Feng-Shui, which are associated with energies of the Earth and Moon system. At sacred sites, the two types of path meet in blind springs:

"*If this is so, the phases of the Moon and the lunar year would play an important role in the circulation of the intrinsic energies, while solar cycles and planetary movements would determine phases of activity and quiescence along ley lines. The priests and priestesses of the old pre-Christian religion in Britain must have been conversant with all the relevant astronomy, as we can gather from Sir Norman Lockyer's research into the subject.*" [46]

As I mentioned in Chapter 1, in John Major Jenkins' *Galactic Alignment* [47] he reasons that that the process of galactic alignment will allow the Kundalini/Shakti to flow through us, resulting in the shift to a more exalted state of consciousness. He sees the peak of the process occurring now, during the 36-year "*window of opportunity*" that coincides with the period it takes for the Winter Solstice Sun to cross the Galactic Equator (approximately 1980 to 2016, centred on 1998, but flagged by the Maya at 2012). According to Joan Parisi Wilcox's book about the Incas, *Keepers of the Ancient Knowledge*, [48] we are in a window of opportunity between 1993 and 2012, during which we can contribute to the coming transition by forming *saiwas*, or "*columns of energy*," that connect the upper world to the underworld, via our bodies. This, again, sounds like Earth Ch'i meeting Heaven Ch'i.

Brian Stross of the University of Texas has written an essay called *The Sacrum Bone: Doorway to the Otherworld*, [49] in which he shows that the Maya conceived of the *sacrum* (the fused vertebrae that lie in the centre of the pelvis) as a kind of skull. The skull and the sacrum were seen as portals to the underworld, and it is a fact that our own language acknowledges this with the skull's 'temples' and the word sacrum, which means "*holy bone*". Joining them together, we have the 33 vertebrae of the spine that are related to the 33 degrees of Freemasonry. Stross says the Maya saw the spine as a microcosm of the World Tree or axis (as did the Egyptians - the *djed* columns represented the spine of Osiris-Orion and the Earth's axis). However, the Maya associated the "*portals*" at each end of the spine with the celestial gates, where the ecliptic crosses the Galactic Equator. The galactic sacrum was the *Place of Creation* in Orion, where the solar god *One Hunahpu* burst out of a turtle shell. The galactic temples were at the Dark Rift, where galactic alignment will occur through 2012, when the World Tree aligns with the Galactic Tree and One Hunahpu emerges from the mouth of the jaguar-toad. Here we have a strong suggestion that galactic alignment will inaugurate a merging of Heaven and Earth (or the merging of the upper world, lower world and physical world, as in the Peruvian prophecy), or the coming together of Rangi and Papa of the Maoris - Geb and Nuit of the Egyptians - in an ego-annihilating meeting of Shiva and Shakti.

## Hendaye Revisited

Jay Weidner and Vincent Bridges have published an updated and extended version of their book *A Monument to the End of Time*, [50] called *The Mysteries of the Great Cross of Hendaye: Alchemy and the End of Time*. [51] The book shows in even more detail how the knowledge of a cyclic event connected with the cycle of precession was encoded into alchemy and Gnosticism, along with a science of transformation. A Hermetic text called *Isis the Prophetess* indicates that this is a threefold transmutation (which I repeat) of "*the cerebrospinal energies and fluids*", [52] the use of those energies to perform physical transmutations, and the transmutation of time, converting the Iron Age to the Golden Age. Isis was in charge of the process and it could not begin "*until the stars were in the proper place*". [53] Isis is connected with Venus, and we are reminded of the transits of Venus in 2004 and 2012, that Will Hart suggested would be some kind of trigger. However, Isis is also connected with Sirius, so this brings to mind Charles Muses' suggestion of Sirius as the trigger (the Maya version of the rebirth of *First Father*, which signifies the galactic alignment as the trigger, could be equated to the rebirth of Osiris, which was enabled by the wooden phallus episode of Isis). Again, the secret is traced by Weidner and Bridges (but in even more detail in the new edition) through Coptics, Gnostics, Hebrews, Islam, the Knights Templar, Cathars, Priory of Sion, Troubadours and grail romances to the building of the cathedrals, where it was encoded in stone just in time before the Church burned everyone at the stake.

As we saw in Chapter 8, the authors conclude that a galactic core superwave, as predicted by Paul LaViolette's theory, will bring a *"double catastrophe,"* but they also say that *"it could also be a window of opportunity for profound change, perhaps even the moment of ascension or the mass attainment of the* Diamond Body, *an immortal light body described in Tibetan Buddhism."* [54] We also saw in Chapter 8 how the authors decoded the anagram in the inscription of the Hendaye Cross as *"Inca cave, Cusco, Peru,"* and *"Hail to the Cross at Urcos."* Then, during a conversation with Dr Juan Nunez del Prado, a professor of Anthropology at Cuzco University who was doing a lecture tour of the USA, they found out that there *was* a cross at Urcos. They later visited it, and also found caves near Cuzco, but the original cross had been replaced and the caves didn't give any answers either. However, the Hendaye cross had predicted a catastrophe in the northern hemisphere, and intimated that Peru was a place of refuge. Cuzco and Urcos are just North of the Altiplano, which is a high plateau surrounded by even higher mountains, and would thus be well protected from tidal waves. It is also in the southern hemisphere. But perhaps the word *cave* should be taken in its Latin meaning of *beware,* or more aptly, 'be aware' - in other words, be aware of the Incas near Cuzco, Peru.

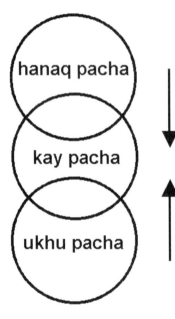

Fig.21.13: *According to Andean prophecy,* hanaq pacha, *the upper world, and* ukhu pacha, *the lower world, will converge on* kay pacha, *the everyday world, to form "one cohesive and paradisiacal world" around 2012. We can aid the process by performing* ayni - *digesting heavy energy - and by creating* saiwas *, columns of energy connecting the three worlds. See* Wilcox [1999].

In the new book, the authors mention another Peruvian link they have found, which could be significant. They have spoken to Alberto Villoldo, a psychologist and medical anthropologist who has been studying the Q'ero priests and Quechua shamans of Peru for twenty years. Villoldo says that the word *pachakuti* that Joan Parisi Wilcox referred to (see Chapter 2) as a cosmic transmutation, or overtuning of space-time can be further analysed. *Pacha* means both *Earth* and *time,* while *kuti* means, 'to turn upside down' or 'to set right'. [55] Therefore the meaning is both a turning upside down of Earth, and a turning upside down of time, but also setting them right - in other words, turning them the right way up again, according to

Villoldo. It is interesting that some people translate *pachakuti* as "*earthquake*", since this is the meaning of Ollin - the central symbol on the Aztec Sunstone that rules this era and its transition. The prophecies of the Q'ero speak of "*a tear in the fabric of time itself*", and "*the end of time*," [56] according to Villoldo. However, both Joan Parisi Wilcox and Elizabeth Jenkins say that the pachakuti ended on 1st August 1993, while Villoldo uses the term to cover what they (Wilcox/Jenkins) call the first phase of the *Taripay Pacha* from 1993 to 2012 (the "*full-blown form*" is not expected until 2012, when the sixth-level priests emerge). *Taripay Pacha* means "*The Age of Meeting Ourselves Again*", which sounds just like the spiritual wedding.

**The Peruvian Solution**
Joan Parisi Wilcox spoke of the "*engaging of the energy body*" as a technique that will aid the spiritual evolution of mankind during the first initial phase of Taripay Pacha, from 1993 to 2012, following a pachakuti from 1990 to 1993. Villoldo has a slightly different version, in that he puts the pachakuti between the year 2000 and 2012, [57] but Wilcox and Elizabeth Jenkins (see below) have split the initial nineteen-year phase of the Taripay Pacha into two sub-phases; the first is a seven-year period from 1993 to 2000, and the second is a twelve-year period from 2000 to 2012. Chaski puts the start of the pachakuti in 1992, [58] which is also the start of the twenty-year period leading to 2012 signified by the Hendaye Cross, though Weidner and Bridges say the pachakuti is between 2002 and 2012 (the cross flags 2002 as the halfway-mark in the twenty-year period). We shall shortly go 'straight to the horse's mouth' for the origin of these various versions, but we can say that whether we see the pachakuti as a three-year phase preceding a nineteen-year phase, or simply as a twenty-year phase, the window of opportunity is happening now!

Jay Weidner has recently made a film with Alberto Villoldo, *Healing the Luminous Body: The Way of the Shaman*, [59] and spoke about it in a radio interview on *Network X* in January 2004, but here, he seems to imply that the pachakuti *starts* in 2012:

"... *Villoldo tells us that the Incan shamans believe that 2012 heralds what they call a pachakuti, or period of upheaval and renewal that occurs at the end of time, in which the world will be turned right side up again. He tells us, 'There will be a tear in the fabric of time itself, a window into the future through which a new human species will emerge. They call this new species, Homo Luminous'. I don't know if this is what is really happening, but if the pursuit of alchemy is to turn lead into gold, so perhaps the real goal of time and history is to turn the lead of the human body into the gold of Homo Luminous. Perhaps, like the ancient Egyptians believed, we will become stars in the heavens being born in the Bardo dreams of Orion. To be honest though, I don't really know.*" [60]

On Villoldo's website, he says that the prophecy of the *Return of the Inka* or *Return of Pachakuteq* will herald the end of time. [61] The Inka (I use this spelling to differentiate between the people - Incas - and the god-men) Pachakuteq was the ninth man-god and was the one who built Machu Picchu, and after him there were four more, if you count the one-year reign of Atahualpa, but he was very cruel and so does not seem to qualify. Atahualpa succeeded his brother Huaskar, but both are said to have failed in their duties as Inkas, and are said to currently be in the Underworld, helping the beings there to prepare for the forthcoming merging of the three planes. The twelfth true Inka will emerge between 2000 and 2012:

*"The Star Rites are held at the Snow Star, at Mt. Ausangate. They are believed to summon the return of the Inka. Before Spanish rule, the Inka were the political and spiritual leaders of a mighty empire that spanned a large part of South America. But the shamans are not speaking about the return of a ruler that will re-establish the now-forgotten glory of the empire. They speak of the possibility of Luminous Ones emerging among us."* [62]

This statement contradicts what Juan Nunez del Prado says, but before commenting, lets look at another extract from Villoldo's *www.thefourwinds.com* website:

*"The processes the Inca shamans have been the keepers of are known as Karpay, the great rites of passage. The Karpay connect the person to an ancient lineage of knowledge and power that cannot be accessed individually - it can only be summoned as a village. This power can ultimately provide the fuel for an individual to leap into the body of an Inka, a luminous one, someone who is directly connected to the source that fuels stars. A person who completes the cycle of ceremony of the Karpay is able to emerge into the Fifth Sun, similar to the Hopi prophecies of emerging into the Fifth World. They can become the Luminous One, also known as 'Man (or Woman) who walks in Peace.'"* [63]

### The Horse's Mouth

I recently had the opportunity to talk to Juan Nunez del Prado and to ask about the prophecies. [64] He confirmed the versions written in Joan Parisi Wilcox and Elizabeth Jenkins' books. The return of the Inka means the process by which the first twelve fifth-level priests emerge, with the first one emerging from the Mount Ausangate (*Qoyllur Riti* or *Snow Star*) festival, and eventually a group of twelve doing a ceremony in which two sixth-level priests emerge. These are the *"shining ones"* who will lead Peru and the world into a new era of peace; so, presumably, the fifth level of consciousness will have to become established before the Luminous Ones of the sixth level begin to increase. I shall enlarge on this below.

In Villoldo's second paragraph above, he says that the Karpay process cannot be accessed by individuals, whereas del Prado provides a Hatun Karpay fourth-level initiation for individuals all over the world. The reason for this disagreement seems to be that Villoldo has not found any Andean priests who know about the Hatun Karpay initiation process. However, del Prado's teachers were Don Andreas Espinosa and Don Benito Qoriwaman, who were the last of the great paqos, and who died in 1981 and 1988 respectively. Juan Nunez del Prado initiated Alberto Villoldo in 1993.

It was Don Benito Qoriwaman who gave del Prado the formula for the pachakuti (this information was passed on sometime before 1987). He said that the pachakuti would last three years, followed by a seven-year period of preparation, followed by a twelve-year period of manifestation. Then the Taripay Pacha would begin. On 1st January 1990, two masters came to del Prado's house to tell him that at a meeting of paqos they had all agreed that the pachakuti would start on 1st August 1990. Then, del Prado applied the date to Don Benito's formula and ascertained that in August 1993 [65] the pachakuti

*Fig.21.14: Juan Nunez del Prado prepares a despacho to Pachamama - the Mother Earth. The despacho is an offering consisting of several items such as flowers, leaves and sweets, infused with sami, or refined energy, then folded into a bundle.*

would end and the seven-year period of preparation would start. The seven-year period would then end and the twelve-year period of manifestation would therefore start on 1st August 2000. The end of the whole transitional process would end on the first day of the Taripay Pacha: 1st August 2012 (1st August is the Q'ero New Years day).

Juan Nunez del Prado confirmed that at the time he got the second part of the prophecy in 1990, he had heard nothing about the Maya calendar; nor had he even travelled outside Cuzco.

## The Urcos Connection

There is another connection between the cross at Hendaye and Peru. Weidner and Bridges decoded *"Urcos"* from the inscription on the cross, but since the original cross at Urcos had been replaced, they remained mystified about its connection to the enigma. The answer lies in the book by Elizabeth Jenkins, *Initiation: a Woman's Spiritual Adventure in the Heart of the Andes*. [66] It was published in 1997, two years earlier than Joan Parisi Wilcox's book, and is a similar story of a woman who undertook the fourth-level initiation under the guidance of Juan Nunez del Prado, who explains that *"attaining the fourth level has to do with developing the astral body"*. [67] Wilcox tells a story about the emergence of twelve fifth-level paqos (priests). In Elizabeth Jenkins' version, she goes into a little more detail. She had just taken her Hatun Karpay, or initiation into the fourth level, when she was told the prophecy of the twelve fifth-level paqos. The fifth level is a level of consciousness that allows miraculous healing abilities. There will be six males and six females - the priests are called *Inka mallku* and the priestesses are called *nust'a*. The first Inka mallku will emerge at the aforementioned festival of *Qoyllur Riti* - an annual festival at a very high altitude, at the base of a glacier. At this festival, 30-70,000 people (sources vary) produce a huge bubble of living psychic energy, visible to those initiates who have developed their clairvoyance:

"[The first Inka mallku will] *follow a specific travel route to the village of Urcos, and there, at the door of the church, he must meet and recognise another Inka mallku who has risen simultaneously here, near the Temple of Wiraqocha. These two must then travel together to Cuzco, where they will meet and recognize the third Inka mallku, who will rise at the public ritual of Corpus Christi on the main square in front of the central cathedral of Cuzco, the ancient Temple of Wiraqocha in Cuzco.*" [68]

Elizabeth Jenkins was told this by Juan Nunez del Prado when she was at the Temple of Wiraqocha at Raqchi (not the one in Cuzco). The story continues that the three Inka mallku travel on to Lima, where they meet the fourth and the first nust'a. The five continue on, gathering the rest of the twelve at specific times and places, and they all return to the Temple of Wiraqocha to perform a *"coronation ritual"*. This will cause the emergence of the new *sapa Inka* and *qoya* - the supreme Inka ruler and his sister-wife - the first initiates of sixth-level consciousness. The sixth level beings will have a visible shining aura. Then the mythical hidden city of Paytiti will materialise, just like the prophecies of the New Jerusalem and Shambhala, and the Golden Age will begin. After this, the seventh and highest level of consciousness is possible. This level is called *titantis ramji*, or *deity incarnate*. These seven levels seem to correlate exactly to the seven man types of Boris Mouravieff (see the online essay *Soulcraft* for more details on this) [69] and the seven Worlds of the Hopi.

So, the church at Urcos - where there must surely be another cross of some form - will play a key part in the coming shift, when the first two fifth-level priests meet there to begin the process leading up to the emergence of the sixth level. The emergence of the sixth-level priests is expected to be *"around 2012 or so,"* [70] according to Elizabeth Jenkins:

*"This time period, from 1993 to 2012, represents a 'critical period' in the development of human collective consciousness. These nineteen years mark the time when a significant percentage of humanity can and must pass from the third to the fourth level. We must be able to leave fear behind and learn to share our cultural gifts and achievements. If we can truly learn to live* ayni *- sacred reciprocity - and to share all of our accumulated knowledge without fear of each other, then we can discover our wholeness, like putting together pieces of a puzzle that make up our human family, our* ayllu. *It is up to the people of the Earth, us, to maximize this critical period in order to bring in the Taripay Pacha. We must not waste this opportunity!"* [71]

The first step to prepare people for the coming change is one of *"cleansing"*. In the Karpay ceremonies, the paqos use their medicine bundles to *"extract any huchas, or heavy energies associated with our past - the pain, grief and discontent that we all carry from our personal histories, as well as the violence we carry within us."* [72] Alternatively, fourth-level paqos can perform *Hucha Mikhuy*, in which they digest the hucha, or heavy energy of other people, absorbing it through the *qosqo* (see below). The fourth-level initiation, as Elizabeth Jenkins described it, also involves the use of several caves, some of which are close to Cuzco, to connect with *Pachamama* (Mother Earth or Gaia) in order to cleanse the energy-bubble (subtle body) of heavy energy and absorb finer energies (*sami*). Could this be the reason that the Hendaye Cross points to the caves around Cuzco? The caves are places of living energy that have been in continuous ceremonial use for centuries, and are thus potent tools for developing the subtle body.

As we have seen, emotional blockages divert the vital energy from its true purpose of feeding our energy bodies, and thus from being ready to *"meet ourselves again"*. There are plenty of people who specialise in this very technique of helping people to release all attachments, fears, complexes and other baggage, so a trip to Peru should not be necessary for this. The process can be continued by practising the exercises in the back of Wilcox's book. Elizabeth Jenkins' Wiracocha Foundation (*www.inka-online.com*) also runs courses and expeditions to initiate students to the fourth level - Hatun Karpay. Laurence Lucas, author of *The 21st Century Book of the Dead*, [73] provides another route, that combines the knowledge of the Maya, Egyptians, Tibetans, Chinese *Qi Gong*, yoga and astrology, to form a *"liquid lightbody"* or *"holographic energy field"* specifically to prepare for 2012 (see *www.stardrum.com/21stc_bod.htm*). Also with 2012 in mind, Ananda Bosman does a *Vortexijah* or *Diamond Body* training, based around the *"secret Tibetan Buddhist teachings of the Vajra Chakra: the Diamond Body"*, cross-referenced to findings from superconductive physics (see *http://phoenix.akasha.de/~aton/DIAMOND1.html*). Although his site says he wouldn't be doing any more after 2001, he did run another course in Switzerland in May 2004 and there is a video available.

### The Coricancha and the Golden Sun Disc

The Incas had a similar concept to that of the Hindu chakras, but they are seen as energy belts with a focal point, four of which can perceive as kinds of eye, so that the pineal eye is called the *"seventh eye"*, rather than the third eye. The energy belt at the navel or solar plexus position is the one through which most of the energy exchange is performed, and is called the *qosqo*. This correlates to the place where many people report that their astral body connects to their physical body via a silver cord. The city of Cuzco thus means *navel*, and is seen by some as the navel (chakra) of the world. The centre, or navel, of the city was the Sun temple, or *Coricancha*, which stood where the cathedral now stands, and in the cathedral grounds the original egg-shaped omphalos stone still survives. The Coricancha was the centre-point of a system of 41 *ceques*, or alignments, of sacred places (or *huacas*),

Fig.21.15: A replica of the golden Sun Disc of Coricancha, seen here on display in the Museum of Anthropology, Lima, Peru.

which have been totalled to 328. The system was a giant lunar calendar of twelve months of an average 27.3 days each (a sidereal month of 27.3 days is the passage of time for the Moon to return to the position of a given star), according to Dr Tom Zuidema of the University of Illinois [74] This is also very close to the 27.28-day 'Carrington Rotation' of the sunspots, found by Simon Shnoll to affect biochemical reaction rates. Knowing that the Incas had a Soulcraft technology, and that Charles Muses has found a direct link between Soulcraft and the lunar calendar, perhaps one use of the ceque system was for the timing of those operations. According to Paul Devereux, the ceques were essentially "*the physical correlates of the routes of shamanic flight in the spirit landscape; lines either marking the designated ways over the landscape for the disembodied mind of the shaman, or recording where the shaman's spirit had travelled, or both.*" [75] Juan Nunez del Prado has been working with Q'ero paqos to reconnect the sacred sites of South America by laying down "*energy filaments*". At the same time, they cleanse and reactivate the *chunpis*, or energy belts of Pachamama (Earth Mother).

In the Coricancha, which still has intact solstice alignments, there once stood a massive golden Sun Disc that is at the centre of several myths. [76] It was said to have reflected the morning sunlight onto the mummies of the Inka rulers. Other myths connect it with the pachakuti (but many Internet sources say that the pachakuti is a 500-year period, and two patchakutis make one *Inti*, or Sun) and say it also represented the central Sun of the galaxy. [77] According to www.spiritjourneys.com, "*It has been prophesied that during the time of the tenth pachakuti, which began in 1992, the Solar Disc would be reactivated... 2002 was the opening and activation of the Temple of Illumination on the Ethereal Plane. With this opening, the energy frequency of the Solar Disc will finally be restored to its original power.*" [78] Note that the 1992 and 2002 dates also connect to the Hendaye Cross. However, the location of the disc is not yet known, since it was removed by the Incas to stop the Spanish from getting hold of it and is said to be either in Lake Titicaca, or in the hidden city of Paytiti. The cover of this book shows a full-size reconstruction of the Solar Disc, which is displayed in a museum in Lima, Peru (there is also a miniature version of five and a half inches in diameter in the Museum of the American Indian in New York), and it shows a central deity with protruding tongue, like the Aztec Sunstone. It represents the fulfilment of the prophecy, when Joan Parisi Wilcox says that the three realms - the Upper Realm, Earth Realm and Underworld (*hanaq pacha, kay pacha* and *ukhu pacha*) will merge or coalesce into "*one paradisiacal world here on Earth*". [79] This is very similar to the "*dissolving of the veil*" predicted by the Maoris for 2012, in which the sky and Earth will meet.

# Chapter 22:
# Prognosis

## Taoist Yoga

There is an important point to consider, if we are to find ourselves navigating the "*invisible landscape*" of the astral realms, and this knowledge has arisen from a study of Neolithic sacred sites, combined with certain clues from Taoist yoga, so we shall follow the clues in the next few paragraphs.

In Taoist yoga, [1] breathing and visualisation exercises are practised in which the generative force is diverted from its normal route (ejaculation) and is circulated around a system of power-zones that closely resemble the Hindu chakras. In a leaflet from the occult bookshop *The Sorcerer's Apprentice*, [2] the system is claimed to be similar to Kundalini yoga, but safer. During a long process of internal alchemy, the original spirit cavity is located and transformed into the "*precious cauldron*" (which is equivalent to the activation of the pineal gland), and an "*immortal foetus*" starts to develop.

Eventually, the spirit body separates from the physical body, then a golden light emerges from the physical body (up from the precious cauldron, through the top of the head, or "*heavenly gate*") and combines with the spirit body. In the version given by Lu K'uan Yu, the *immortal man* or spirit body sits upright within "*a mass of golden light, the size of a large wheel*": [3]

"*When spirit manifests for the first time, it should only be allowed to leave the physical body in fine weather and it should be well looked after, like a baby just born. Its egress should on no account take place when there is thick fog, heavy rain, gale, thunder and lightning.*" [4]

The spirit body is "*very sensitive to fear and awe, which should be*

*Fig.22.1: The Taoist system conceives of three channels, and on the central channel we have A: cardinal point North - the mortal gate; N: the solar plexus; M: the heart; P: the centre of the brain, and G: cardinal point South - the heavenly gate. After Luk [1970, 1996].*

圖 胎 道

圖 胎 出

*Fig.22.2: The developing* immortal foetus *(left), from which the* immortal man *emerges in a mass of golden light (right). After Luk [1970, 1996].*

*avoided at all costs."* [5] This immortal man within a golden wheel is reminiscent of the original merkabah [6] (Hebrew for *chariot*) that was seen by Ezekiel, enlarged on by Hurtak, developed further by Drunvalo Melchizedek and connected by Gregg Braden with the zero-point in 2012. Braden said that when the component tetrahedrons were counter-rotating, [7] the whole Mer-Ka-Ba (he spells it like this to emphasise that the concept includes the Egyptian *Ka*, or etheric body, and *Ba*, or astral body) would look like a flying disk. Lu K'uan Yu also describes the spirit body as a *"golden ball of light"*.

## Kilner

In 1911, Dr Walter J. Kilner of St. Thomas's Hospital in London published the results of experiments prompted by Baron Karl Von Reichenbach's earlier conclusions about the existence of an aura around the body that could theoretically be used as an aid to medical diagnosis.

After his eyes were *"sensitised"* by looking at daylight through a dark screen, Kilner looked at human subjects against a black background, through a lighter screen made from dicyanin dyes sandwiched between sheets of glass. [8] What he saw was an envelope of energy composed of three layers, the innermost of which he called *"the etheric double"*. The other two he named the *"inner aura"* and the *"outer aura"*, which together extend at least a foot from the body:

*"The entire aura was sensitive to magnets, and when subjected to the negative current from a Wilmshurst machine - a device for producing an electric charge - it vanished completely, then reappeared with an increased intensity."* [9]

In 1970, biophysicists and biochemists from Kirov State University of Kazakhstan in Russia published the results of a study in which they had been studying the human *"energy body"* by means of an electron microscope, following up on the discoveries of Seymon Kirlian, a Russian electronics engineer who, in 1939, discovered that a photographic plate placed between human skin and the electrode of a high-frequency electrotherapy machine recorded a luminescent shape surrounding the body. The Kirov State university team called this the *"biological plasma body"*, because they found it to be *"some sort of elementary plasma-like constellation made of ionised, excited electrons, protons and possibly other particles... It is not a chaotic system. It's a whole unified organism in itself."* [10] The Russian scientists also showed that the plasma body is charged up by the oxygen we breathe - particularly by ionised air, and that it is affected by the eleven-year-plus sunspot cycle, the Moon, thunderstorms, strong winds, illnesses, emotions, the thoughts of others, and changes in the planets! A plasma is a gas that can be created in electric storms or thermonuclear reactions, causing all the electrons to be stripped from the nuclei of the atoms. In *Supernature*, biologist Lyall Watson points out that not much is known about plasmas, or how they could be created at body temperature, but it is known that *"the only thing that will contain its energy effectively is a magnetic field - and we know that the body has one of these."* [11] But maybe it is possible that the plasma is created outside the body, and invades it in the manner Philip K. Dick's *plasmate*.

## Plasmatic Invader

Philip K. Dick was a science-fiction writer, now famous as the author whose stories have been made into films like *Bladerunner*, *Total Recall* and *Minority Report*. His writings were thought-provoking mixes of psychology, philosophy and weirdness, and he already had 40 books in print when in February 1974 he had a mystical experience that changed his life.

Dick was under a lot of stress at the time, and in pain with an impacted wisdom tooth, waiting for a delivery of prescribed painkillers. The girl who delivered the medication was wearing a necklace with a golden fish pendant, like the fish symbol worn by the early Christians. Dick was hypnotised by the pendant initially; then it reportedly fired a beam of pink light at his head, causing *"anamnesis"*, which is a Greek word meaning *"loss of forgetfulness"*, in which an existence as a second-century secret Christian superimposed itself onto his contemporary existence. Dick interpreted this as an invasion of his mind by a *"transcendentally rational mind"*, which he called *Valis* (Vast Active Living Intelligence System). It *"was equipped with tremendous technical knowledge. It had memories dating back over 2,000 years, it spoke Greek, Hebrew, Sanskrit; there wasn't anything that it didn't seem to know."* [12] Like Jung, Dick found that his visions had much in common with the philosophy of the Gnostics, fragments of whose scriptures were unearthed in 1945, when 49 *codices*, or Gnostic books, were found near the ancient town of Chenoboskion in Egypt. They are known as the 'Library of Nag Hammadi', as that is the name of the nearest modern town.

Dick played with various interpretations of the experience in his remaining books, but in *Valis*, in an appendix, he presents his most enduring take on it. He saw the experience as an invasion by the *"immortal one"*, which he called a *"plasmate"*, since it is a form of energy. In *Valis*, the plasmate had been slumbering in the form of the buried Gnostic scrolls, until it awoke when they were unearthed and read:

"*As living information, the plasmate travels up the optic nerve to the pineal body. It uses the human brain as a female host in which to replicate itself to its active form. This is an interspecies symbiosis.*" 13

The Gnostics have a notion that the soul of each of us is a Divine Spark - a fragment of the Godhead scattered throughout creation - and that every fragment will eventually be re-connected into the Godhead. This will occur at the end of time.

## Neolithic Earth-Net

The Taoist warning against thunderstorms may have wider relevance. Lightning invariably strikes at the crossing points of water lines (underground streams), according to dowsers, and sacred sites have been found by dowsers to invariably be positioned at these points, on what dowsers call *blind springs*. However, in his book *Earth Lights* 14 Paul Devereux makes the observation that nearly all the stone circles in the UK are in areas of low thunderstorm activity. These facts seem at first to contradict each other, until you hear the old wives' tale about a thunderstorm happening if a barrow is desecrated. This is not just a reference to the wrath of the gods, as we shall see, but it certainly must have crossed the minds of a certain research group, as reported by dowser Tom Graves. 15 The group were surveying a stone circle, and when they hammered a stake into the ground, triggered an immediate two-minute rainstorm.

In his book *Needles of Stone*, 16 Tom Graves presented evidence that the Neolithic network of alignments that join up sacred sites was designed - at least partially - as a weather-control system. Standing stones next to barrows acted like lightning conductors, or to be more accurate, like Wilhelm Reich's 'cloudbuster'. Reich was a psychologist who claimed to have discovered evidence that Sigmund Freud's hypothetical *libido* - the life energy that he said was essentially sexual energy - was real and could be captured and stored in a specially designed box. Reich called the energy "*orgone*", since it powers the orgasm, and the box was called an "*orgone accumulator*" and was composed of alternate layers of organic and inorganic materials. He designed a machine that looked like an anti-aircraft gun, a collection of various lengths of metal tubes on a swivelling base, connected by a steel cable to a body of water. This was the cloudbuster. When pointed at clouds, it dispersed them, and when pointed at empty sky, it could create clouds, and even storms on some occasions. It is only in recent years that Reich's ideas have been taken seriously and researchers have successfully repeated his experiments.

In the case of a barrow and standing stone, Graves explained that a negative charge from an underground stream was passed up the stone and into a positively-charged cloud, thus neutralizing it and causing rain; or the positive charge from the cloud was passed down via the stone, along the underground stream and into the barrow, which stored it (a barrow is made up from alternate layers of organic and inorganic layers, like an orgone accumulator, says Graves). This also neutralized the cloud and avoided lightning. The charge then slowly leaked back into the sky via stream and stone, or was neutralized by the negative charge from the underground stream (see diagram on page 261). The two polarities involved would be orgone and DOR (Deadly Orgone Radiation, the stagnant, negative version of orgone life energy), which are *ch'i* and *sha* in the Chinese system. The system is still actually working after all these years, since Graves points out that the Isle of Jura has a lot of megalithic sites, and thunderstorms are very rare there.

Why would the Neolithic people have wanted to avoid lightning at all costs? This is a question that has gone unanswered until now. Two facts mentioned by Graves have a bearing on this. Firstly, several of Graves' correspondents had told him that the telepathic transmission of complete mental images was easier between sacred sites than elsewhere, and we have already seen that telepathy works better when geomagnetic activity is quiet. It so happens that in *Places of Power*, Paul Devereux reports that stone circles are areas where the geomagnetic field is *lower* than the background level. [17] This implies that the sacred sites were used for telepathic message relaying, but that is only part of the story.

The second fact from Graves is that his magician friends told him that they had found both forms of astral travelling - "*projection of the imagination, and projection of the entire personality*" - to be much easier "*by hitching a ride on the energy that passes along ley lines or overgrounds.*" [18] However, the interpretation of leys as energy lines is no longer very viable following Paul Devereux's work (though this does depend on one's definition of the word "*energy*"), and it might be better to follow Mary Scott's lead and describe convoluted lines as *dragon currents* and straight lines ("*overgrounds*") as *spirit paths*. Devereux, as editor of the *Ley Hunter* magazine for sixteen years, and one of the founders of the *Dragon Project* - an ongoing investigation into sacred sites and their effects - makes a strong case that the ley line network is the remnant of a system of shamanic flight alignments, where ancient barrows, standing stones, stone circles and even pre-reformation churches (built on sacred sites) were aligned in straight lines. The surviving beliefs of the Kogi tribe of Columbia back up the theory. Their shamans or seers are called *Mamas*, and they are trained from birth and kept in the dark for their first nine years, so they can tune in to the *aluna*, or *Spirit Earth* (here we have some evidence that Ananda's dark-room retreats are a genuine ancient technique of shamanism). Interestingly, as reported in Alan Ereira's 1990 BBC TV documentary on the Kogi, and quoted by Devereux, they also refer to the *aluna* as the life force and the Mother:

"[The Mama walks spirit paths] *in a world visible only to the mind's eye, the world of aluna... they were lines of thought, not lines on the ground. But there were points where the two worlds used to meet. ... The Mamas used to travel in aluna and meet other people from other places there. But as the years passed, there were fewer and fewer people who reached the spirit world to talk with them. Now there is no one. It is deserted.*" [19, 20]

Devereux also traces the use of hallucinogens back through medieval times when our modern stereotype of the witch had its origin. Wise old women, who had accumulated knowledge of medicinal plants over a longer-than average life, brewed up tropane-containing plants like henbane, mandrake, datura (thornapple) and belladonna in their cauldrons. Tropanes are known for causing sensations of flight, and also for their ability to be absorbed through semi-permeable membranes. The wise old ladies lived alone at the edge of town as outcasts among people who mostly died around 30 years of age (the classic witch appearance is simply an exaggerated old person, whose teeth have fallen out and the nose appears to touch the chin, with long white hair, wrinkles and hairy growths). The flying ointment was stirred up in the cauldron with a broomstick, and the broomstick was then "*ridden*" (rubbed between the labia). [21] Devereux shows that the tradition of out-of body flight is rooted back in pre-history, [22] and it seems that the Neolithic shamans would use the low-magnetic environment of stone circles as a sacred space in which to shamanise, or achieve trance.  Remember that Earth's magnetic field strength is dropping as we approach 2012...

## Ecstatic Fusebox

Finally, we can perhaps answer the question of why the Neolithic people needed weather control. First, remember what was said about the immortal body in Taoist Yoga - there was a warning to the student never to come out of the body during thunder or lightning. Then recall Kilner's dycyanin aura filter. The aura was visibly affected by a magnet and the electric current from the Wilmshurst machine caused it to completely disappear. Could this be the reason that the megalithic priesthood feared lightning? If they were out of their body on an astral flight, a sudden bolt of lightning would at best send their astral form back to their body in a state of shock, and at worst cause death, and possibly even the loss of their astral body. Since lightning is naturally attracted to the nodal points of their system, the priesthood would have needed a lightning-prevention system, like a kind of integral fusebox. This is exactly what Graves described as the function of a barrow and standing stone (see Fig. 22.3).

The two functions we have associated with the ancient grid are the very same two abilities enhanced by our natural pineal hallucinogens; the beta-carbolines (like pinoline) triggering telepathy, and the tryptamines (like DMT) triggering out-of-body experiences (literally ecstasy, from the Greek, *ekstasis*, "*standing outside oneself*"). What this all means is that the changing geomagnetic environment is probably going to cause the place the Kogi call aluna to become populated again, as more people find they are "*standing outside themselves*" in a normally invisible landscape.

Like the witchcraft mythology of hags, broomsticks and cauldrons, the pointed hats that are still used in our caricatures of witches and wizards conceal another secret. In 2003, the National Museum in Nuremberg held an exhibition in which, for the first time, four golden hats from the Bronze Age were displayed together. The most recent find, which was bought by the Berlin Museum of Archaeology in 1996, has been subject to a detailed study by Professor Wilfried Menghin, director of the Berlin Museum. It is about 3,000 years old, 30 inches high, and was found in Switzerland in 1995. It is covered with a total of 1,739 Sun and Moon symbols, and when compared with the other hats, it was found that the embossed symbols on it represented a quarter of a Metonic cycle, which is a nineteen-year cycle discovered by Greek astronomer Meton in the fifth century BC. Meton

Fig.22.3: *Two modes of ancient thunderstorm control, with the stone-and-barrow system (after Tom Graves).*

found that 235 lunar months are equal to nineteen solar years, after which the lunar phases repeat on the same solar calendar date. The Ezelsdorfer hat which was found in Germany, has 1,737 symbols, and the hats together show that the 1,735 days in 57 lunations (a quarter of the 235 lunations of the Metonic cycle) had been recorded as a logarithmic table, which, according to Professor Menghin, "*enables the movements of the Sun and Moon to be calculated in advance*" and "*they suggest that Bronze Age man would have been able to make long-term empirical astrological observations.*" [23]

A third golden cone-hat found near Schifferstadt in Germany in 1835 still had a chin-strap attached, and is dated the earliest of the four, at 1300 BC. The fourth surviving hat was found in France, but there are reports of five similar cone-hats found by peat-diggers in Ireland in the seventeenth and eighteenth centuries that have now disappeared, according to the research of Professor Sabine Gerloff of Ehrlangen University, Germany. Gerloff has also suggested that the Gold Cape of Mold (a kind of low-slung solid gold embossed collar designed to attach to a cloak), found in Wales in 1831, was another part of the ceremonial dress of the priest-kings. [24]

So, our Halloween fancy-dress outfits of Merlin, with his Sun, Moon and star-covered cape and hat, are actually based on the calendrically encoded ceremonial dress of

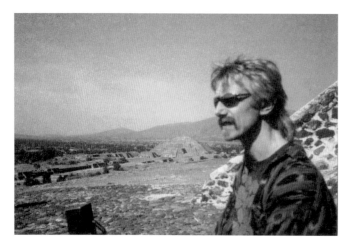

*Fig.22.4: The Pyramid of the Moon at Teotihuacan, Mexico, as seen from the Pyramid of the Sun, with the author in the foreground. Like a number of other ancient monuments, the layout of the complex appears to represent the belt of the constellation Orion.*

Bronze Age *"king-priests"* who would have been revered as Lords of Time. (See the colour pages for a demonstration of the wearing of these hats and collars.)

Since 1994, Dr Jan Harding from the University of Newcastle has been studying Thornborough Henge, a line of three massive henges in Yorkshire, [25] and has concluded that the complex included alignments to the Summer Solstice, lunar standstills, and the rising of the constellation of Orion. In 2003, [26] he announced that the whole complex was a reflection of the belt of Orion, and the aerial shots seem to confirm this, with the three henges in a row, one slightly offset. The third henge is not immediately visible, since there is a copse of trees now growing on it, but it has been well preserved within the trees. The site was inhabited from 3500 BC to 2500 BC, so it looks as though this Orion groundplan preceded the one at Giza (according to the officially accepted chronology, in which the Great Pyramid was built around 2500 BC). The pyramid layout at Teotihuacan in Mexico also appears to be a representation of Orion's belt. We have seen evidence that both Ancient Egypt [27] and Neolithic England had shamanic priesthoods who travelled out-of-body and were thus able to get an aerial view of the terrestrial belts of Orion that they had constructed.

In *Shamanism and the Mystery Lines,* [28] Paul Devereux reveals that, according to tribal people all over the world and to modern investigators of out-of-body travel, the astral body can sometimes appear as a light-ball. Although he said in *Earth Lights* that there is no evidence to associate ley lines with UFOs, he does admit the following about a random sample of leys selected for his book *The Ley Hunters Companion*:

*"... 37.5% of the leys we were selecting showed some evidence of UFO events occurring on them or in their immediate vicinity. It was impossible to determine whether this UFO incidence was associated with the alignments as such, or with the sites forming the alignments."* [29]

It could be that the electromagnetic conditions are only conducive to the physical manifestation of the light-balls at the nodes - the sacred sites with their unusual energy fields (they are also commonly witnessed at crop formations). Balls of light recorded at Hessdalen could still be tracked on radar after passing out of the visible spectrum.

## Enoch's Glorious Device

*The Book of Enoch* (1 Enoch or the *Ethiopic Enoch*, as opposed to the later book, *The Secrets of Enoch*, also called Enoch 2, or the *Slavonic Enoch*) [30] has been dated to the years between 200 BC and 100 BC (between the Old Testament and New Testament). Specialists in Jewish religious texts have agreed that much of the New Testament used Enoch as source material. It is an apocalypse (revealing) similar in some ways to St. John's *Book of Revelation*. [31] Its attribution to Enoch as the author is thought to be a calendrical reference, since Enoch is stated in *Genesis* [32] to have been seventh in line from Adam, and to have lived to the age of 365 years. There is a lot of calendrical information in the book, and when Robin Heath (author of several books on megalithic sites) analysed it using a simple computer program, [33] he found that the observations were taken from somewhere far to the North of Israel - in fact, from the latitude of Stonehenge! In *Sun, Moon and Stonehenge,* [34] Heath further showed that the descriptions of the Sun and Moon-rises within six portals in the east, and the settings within six portals in the west, refer specifically to observations made from a location known as The Grave (at the 'entrance' to the trilithon-horseshoe), through the "*portals*" between the sarsen stones at Stonehenge. This fits perfectly with Enoch chapter 34, where he is taken by the angel Uriel "*towards the north to the ends of the earth, and there I saw a great and glorious device...*" [35] Christopher Knight and Robert Lomas (see below) point out that Enoch also seems to have visited Newgrange in Ireland (a passage tomb built around 3000 BC that is covered in brilliant white quartzite), when he visited a "*wall built of crystals*". [36]

Robin Heath remarks that in the Celtic book *The Tales of Taliesin*, the author states, "*I was instructor to Eli and Enoch*". He is also mentioned in *The Mabinogion*, another Celtic book, dating to circa 1300; there is even a hill called Carn Enoch, near Preselli, in Wales, where the bluestones of Stonehenge originated. [37] I have also discovered that the original ancient name of the county which borders the Boyne valley in Ireland, where Newgrange is situated, was *Uriel*. [38]

Enoch was the great-grandfather of Noah, and in the *Book of Enoch*, not only is Enoch given calendrical information, but he is also told about the forthcoming flood and passes the information down to Noah. Robin Heath points out that before 3000 BC, astronomical alignments were mostly stellar. He suggests that just prior to 3000 BC, Earth had a close encounter with an asteroid, which is the origin of the worldwide flood myth. He suggests an approximate date of 3300 BC. Knight and Lomas suggest 3150 BC, and also suggest that the Grooved Ware people of Neolithic Britain actually predicted this, after making observations following the previous impact with a comet that they put at 7640 BC. We have already seen that other researchers put the flood at 3114 BC, along with the start of the 13-baktun cycle.

Knight and Lomas, who are Masons, have researched ancient Lodge documents in an attempt to trace the roots of masonic tradition. They started looking at Enoch, since he is mentioned in several masonic degrees. They have traced back masonic ceremonies to the Knights Templar (so convincingly that many previously incredulous Masons now concur); the original nine knights were direct descendants of Jewish Temple priests. The Templars excavated under the Temple of Jerusalem and found the huge stash of treasure described in the Copper Scroll from Qumran, plus accompanying secret texts - contemporary writings to the Dead Sea Scrolls. These were then buried under Rosslyn Chapel in Scotland, which is a copy of Solomon's Temple, complete with nine vaults. The information in the scrolls was encoded into Cathedrals sponsored by the Templars - this is when the masonic guilds started, who laid out the stonework.

The Grooved Ware people were trading in the Mediterranean area (e.g. tin for bronze production), and their beliefs were passed onto the Caananites and Phoenicians, who bequeathed them to the Israelites when they arrived from Egypt.

Knight and Lomas pointed out (after Martin Brennan) that if a lens tracks the midday Sun for 366 days and the dots are joined, the resulting figure is two spirals around the solstices, with flattened curves at the equinoxes. [39] Presumably, if the shadow from a post or *gnomon* is marked at midday every day for 366 days, the same result would be achieved. Thus, a spiral represents a quarter of the year. There are many spirals at Newgrange, which is aligned so that the Winter Solstice sunrise illuminates the chamber each year. There is a conspicuous triple spiral in the inner chamber at Newgrange. According to the Knight and Lomas theory, a triple spiral would represent three seasons: nine months, or the gestation period of humans. This is the period around which the Maya tzolkin of 260 days is based, and, as we know, the 13-baktun cycle that ends in 2012 is structured like a giant tzolkin of 260 katuns, possibly representing a planetary gestation that precedes the birth of the next Sun (rebirth of One Hunahpu) on the Winter Solstice of 2012.

Fig.22.5: *The triple-spiral engraved in the central chamber at Newgrange, Ireland.*

Enoch compares all the righteous and elect at the time of Judgement to *"fiery lights"*; [40] they shall have been *"clothed with the garments of glory"*. [41] He says, *"ye shall shine as the lights of heaven and the portals of heaven shall be opened to you"* [42] and they *"shall go where the days and seasons are prescribed for them"*. [43] Is this a description of the golden light-ball bodies in the timeless astral dimension? Despite the fact that the flood myth borrows heavily from the Sumerian myth of *Utnapishtim*, perhaps the whole apocalyptic genre of Judaism and Christianity has its roots in Britain, and the megalithic attempt to predict the next catastrophe. But perhaps it is in essence a prediction of the next geomagnetic fluctuation that will cause the mass opening of the pineal eye, and *exosomatic* (literally, *outside the body*) transition. A clue here is the *"forty days and forty nights"* that the rain fell upon the Earth while Noah was in the Ark. [44] We have already seen that this is the period of the Acute Schizophrenic Break Syndrome, with its altered pineal output. Other biblical instances of it are Moses' forty days and forty nights on Mount Horeb in the Sinai desert, talking to God, [45] Elijah's escape to the desert, where he sees an angel and continues for forty days and forty nights to Mount Horeb and hears God speaking to him, [46] and Jesus' forty days and forty nights in the desert, being tempted by the Devil, then visited by angels. [47]

Having seen the connection between the *Book of Enoch* and Stonehenge and Newgrange, we might notice that Newgrange was designed to identify the Winter Solstice sunrise, and that the orthodox position (after Professor John North's 1996 book *Stonehenge - Neolithic Man and the Cosmos* [48]) now is that the primary alignment at Stonehenge is

*Fig.22.6: The passage and lightbox at Newgrange, Ireland, showing a close-up of the quartz blocks that form most of the perimeter wall.*

towards the Midwinter (Winter Solstice) sunset. The Summer Solstice sunrise, attended by thousands at Stonehenge each year, in which the first gleam of the Sun appears just next to the Heel Stone, and when fully risen sits exactly on it, is an alignment that did not exist when the monument was constructed. The change in the obliquity of the ecliptic has caused the Sun to move between one and a half and two Sun-widths towards the Heel Stone. This changing obliquity cycle of 41,000 years is exactly divisible by the 13-baktun cycle, as William Gaspar pointed out. The Earth's axis takes 20,500 years to go from minimum to maximum tilt, and another 20,500 years to go back. This means it takes exactly four 13-baktun cycles for a half-cycle, and we are just at the end of the Fourth World, or Sun, of the Hopi and Maya that ends on a Winter Solstice. At Newgrange, the changing obliquity has moved the light beam back, so it no longer fully illuminates the triple-spiral of gestation, [49] but falls in the centre of the chamber where it would (if the basin was still in its original position) hit the central stone reflecting basin, lighting up the whole chamber and signifying an emergence of humanity from its techno-chrysalis into fully-metamorphosed [50] *imago* forms.

Crop formations, as we have seen, are attracted to aquiferous geology, and these are the same areas where most sacred sites are preserved. The Avebury area of Wiltshire is the central focus of the activity, and also is the location of the world's largest stone circle, which encircles the whole village of Avebury, subsequently built within it. The crop circle phenomenon is undoubtedly interacting with sacred sites, and this was especially noticeable in 2003. On 5th July of that year, a line of Bronze Age barrows at North Down, Wiltshire, UK, had a formation appear as an extra 'barrow' in the sequence, but with the appearance of a Bronze Age shield (see pictures). Three sacred site formations also appeared in Yorkshire in 2003; the first of these three appeared next to Thornborough Henge on 21st June (see *Ecstatic Fusebox*, above), alerting many people to the existence of this little-known earthwork and attracting attention to the fact that it is under threat from quarrying, thus prompting a campaign to save the site. It has since been featured in a BBC TV documentary about the Orion connection discovered by Dr Jan Harding. Another crop formation, which appeared on 9th July, was visible from the Rudston Monolith, the highest standing stone in the country (26 feet), and yet another arrived on 3rd August at Boroughbridge in the same field as the Devil's Arrows standing stones.

Not only are the crop formations helping to focus our attention on sacred sites, but they may also be having effects on our endocrine system. Circle researcher Lucy Pringle conducted an experiment in which hormone levels were ascertained using an ESR (Electrical Skin Resistance) meter on a woman aged 72 and a man aged 54, before and after entering a crop formation. After visiting the circle, their melatonin levels had *"increased considerably"*. [51] Melatonin is made in the pineal gland and is the raw material

for producing internal hallucinogens. There are also several women who have reported either post-menopausal bleeding, or unexpected menstruation, during visits to crop formations (two of these are friends of mine; others have been reported by Lucy Pringle). [52] This could also implicate the pineal as well as other endocrine glands, since it is involved in the feedback loops of human sexual hormone production. Both effects may be connected to magnetic fields, since

*Fig.22.7: A crop formation resembling a Celtic shield joins a line of burial mounds at North Down, near Avebury, Wiltshire, 6 July 2003. Photo: Nick Nicholson*

Jerry Decker of the website *www.keelynet.com* (a site about free energy, gravity control and alternative health) says "*a steady state magnetic north pole field will stimulate the production of melatonin and eliminate PMS, as long as field strength in the vicinity of the pineal is in the 400mg. range.*" [53] PMS is premenstrual syndrome.

Tom Graves compared the sacred sites to a system of acupuncture points, since these show a measurable

*Fig.22.8: Closer view of the Celtic shield crop formation. Photo: Nick Nicholson*

difference in skin resistance from surrounding areas, which has been measured with a device called a *Tobiscope* [54] and photographed using Kirlian photography. The points are exactly where the Chinese always said they were. In a similar way, the Earth acupuncture points (sacred sites) show a measurable difference in geomagnetic field from surrounding areas, and would seem to be nodal points in a network of meridians on the planetary body, where we can access higher dimensions of mind. We are being shown the relevance of the Neolithic mindset - this is what Terence McKenna called "*the archaic revival*".

## Third Eye Magnetised

Jerry Decker reports on *Keeleynet* [55] that in a telephone conversation with Walter Rawls (co-author with Albert Roy Davis of four books on magnetism), [56] Rawls told him about an experiment in which a mask [57] was made to hold a long cylindrical magnet over the pineal gland, worn for between ten and 30 minutes per day for three to four weeks [58] (this must be done with a long bar magnet, to separate the poles, and it must be the north pole, since the effects of a south pole could be dangerous to the health):

"*Within the first week, he was sitting at his desk reading documents when he noticed something move, out of the corner of his eye. As he looked up, the ghostly figure of a man had walked through one wall, moved across the room and disappeared through another wall. The figure was totally unaware of Walter. Further exposures to this north pole field took place over a second and third week. The second week, the same ghostly figure moved through the room and glanced toward Walter as he passed through. This time, the figure appeared to have slightly more detail, not quite so ghostly. The third week, busy working on documents, Walter noticed a change in the room. When he looked up, the wall had dissolved away and he was looking at a small hill where a man and woman sat beneath a tree. It was the same ghostly male figure who he'd seen on the other occasions. He sat quite still, watching this pastoral scene for several minutes. The man looked over toward Walter and appeared startled. It was as if he clearly SAW Walter this time and possibly recognized Walter as the ghost HE had seen the previous week! The image faded away and the wall restored to its normal condition. From that moment on, Walter never used the pineal stimulator again.*

*In conversations about this, with Walter and other interested people, it was mentioned that there is a theory that we have multiple energy bodies, much like the Ka and the Ba of ancient Egypt. Each energy body lives in another reality, yet communicates with our consciousness here in this reality. Another comment was that consciousness simply creates an energy body in whatever reality it VISITS. Prolonged presence in a given reality increases the density of the energy body, moving from a phantom, ghostly form that is at first not easily perceptible to the inhabitants of the other reality until the intruding energy body has become sufficiently dense to trigger their senses. That could explain why repeated exposures would add density to Walter's other reality body, allowing its denizens to perceive him, thus the startled reaction from the male figure."* [59]

The American Centre for Psychical Research has commented that ghost sightings and paranormal activity are more frequent during times of high solar emissions; [60] there were also increased sightings of the 'American Yeti', Bigfoot, at the time of the last solar maximum, and there have also been reports of increased admissions to mental hospitals during these periods. This illustrates that as the Sun gets nearer to its megacycle peak, more people's magnetic cerebral switches are activated.

We all have *"significant deposits"* of magnetite (a naturally-occurring magnetic oxide of iron) in the pineal gland, and also layers of magnetite in the sphenoid and ethnoid bones of our sinuses, with which we detect magnetic fields, according to the findings of Manchester zoologists Baker, Mather and Kennaugh. [61] Anaemic people have an absence of these deposits. There are two types of people who are even more sensitive to these fields, according to the work of Albert Budden. [62] What is known as *electromagnetic hypersensitivity* (EMH) occurs when the magnetism of the pineal (and sphenoid/ethnoid) magnetite is increased by environmental factors. In EMH Type A, this happens by *"prolonged irradiation at a hot spot, often where the fields involved emanate from a natural geological source, i.e. tectonic activity at faults"*. [63] Stone circles, as Devereux found, lie mostly on or near geological faults (UFO sightings are also common in these areas). [64]

Electromagnetic hypersensitivity is acquired in Type B by exposure to a major electrical event or MEE. These include being close to a lightning strike, major electrocution, proximity to ball lightning or earthlights, ECT (electroconvulsive therapy) and defibrillation (resuscitation following heart attacks, etc.). People with Type A hypersensitivity tend to see angels, guides and friendly apparitions, while those with Type B hypersensitivity tend to have 'alien' abduction experiences, says Budden, whose wife is a Type B. Whitley Streiber, who has written several books about his abduction encounters, was not only exposed to "*multiple MEEs*" in his earlier life, but he also experienced nosebleeds and the feeling of "*knots*" in his sinuses. [65] Streiber recognises that electromagnetic hypersensitivity plays a part in his experiences, [66] but still sees his experiences as real. It could be that sudden magnetisation of the internal magnetite tunes us in to a different part of the astral plane - what is known in the esoteric world as the *lower astral*, whereas a slow, steady magnetisation gives access to the *higher astral*.

Carn Ingli is a peak on the Preselli hills overlooking Newport on the coast of Wales, and it would be an example of the kind of environment that would slowly increase pineal magnetic sensitivity. The name Carn Ingli means "*The Peak of Angels*", and is named after the experiences of St. Brynach, who lived the life of a hermit on the peak, where he communicated with angels. In *Places of Power*, Paul Devereux reports that the hill has some unusual magnetic anomalies, including a few places where the field is fully reversed by 180°, which can be checked with a compass. In 1987, a woman felt she was "*being subjected to waves of some kind of force*" [67] coming from the peak, and the closer she got, the stronger the feelings became. This is how the reversed field came to the notice of *Dragon Project* investigators.

## Telepathic Interplay

We have seen that many catastrophe theories associated with 2012 are seriously faulted; yet Earth changes are increasing by the month. Either the field-effect energy reversal suggested by John Major Jenkins, or our entry into the magnetised plasma band may be the mechanism anticipated by ancient cultures that will trigger not only increased solar activity and weather extremes, but also a geomagnetic reversal, during which time itself may seem to slow down (I know exactly what this is like from a motorcycle accident in 1976, in which I wrote off a Fiat with my elbow - it was like a slow-motion film). This also happens in dreams, where you can have a whole dream of falling for thousands of feet, based on a physical fall from the bed to the floor. This is Ken Carey's "*moment of quantum awakening*"; an out-of body experience into a timeless realm caused by a magnetically-induced pineal eye opening. Some have even suggested that our memories will be wiped by the magnetic reversal. If this interpretation is correct, then it is certainly an interesting time to be alive, to be part of an evolutionary quantum leap which may be seen as the boundary between Homo sapiens and our descendent, *Homo spiritus*.

Preparation for an event such as this would involve confronting our shadows, a clearing out of the subconscious or unconscious mind of all repressed feelings, forgiveness of all those who have caused us problems in the past; a letting-go of all bitterness, resentment, negative emotions, self-doubt and ego problems, a dissolving of learned fear and anger responses; getting ready to treat others as ourselves, as in the Maya greeting "*In lake'ch*" - "*I am another yourself*". [68] This process is *metanoia* - a Greek word meaning *mind-change*, but which generations of biblical scholars have mis-translated as *"repentance"*. These are exactly the issues that are sorted out by years of meditation (contemplation, or real prayer), but since we need to get a move on, there are all kinds of workshops available to help with this, as well as practising techniques of out-of-body travel and familiarising ourselves with the geography of the Otherworld. We might even try taking iron pills, as recommended by dowsers, to improve our magnetic sensitivity (or drink iron-rich spring water, such as that from Chalice Well in Glastonbury), and spend more time at sacred sites, to gently increase pineal and sinusoidal magnetic sensitivity. Then perhaps we will be ready for what Alice Bailey called *"a telepathic interplay which will eventually annihilate time"*, in which we can co-operate as human neurons in a global brain.

Archaeologist Laurette Séjourné has interpreted the end of the Fifth Sun of the Aztecs in a similar way:

*"We know that the Fifth Sun appears after four others have come and gone, and that this Fifth Sun is itself destined to be superseded by another. We cannot believe that these myths of solar cataclysms were inspired only by the eternal cosmic renewal manifest in natural cycles. Apart from the fact that Nahuatl religious phenomena, which are so spiritual, could never be so simply explained - in terms that is, that have no inner meaning - there are various indications that the Fifth Sun is the creator of a great and indestructible work: that of freeing creation from duality... ... The essence of the Nahuatl religion is contained in the revelation of the secret which enables mortals to escape destruction and to resolve the contradiction inherent in their natures by becoming converted into luminous bodies"* [69]

Fig.22.9: *"Human emerging as butterfly". A shield design from the Tepatlaoztoc Codex. After Brotherston [1992].*

So we could look upon the Earth as a large hibernating creature like a bear that is re-cycling its body waste, but can only keep it up for a certain amount of time before it either has to wake up or poison itself. The unconscious mind of the bear knows when Spring is coming, the trigger that will arouse it from its slumber, just as the year 2012 is emerging from the collective unconscious as the end of time, or year of ascension, or the year of catastrophe, or the deadline for cleaning up the planet by the Kyoto Protocol. As we get nearer, there should be more outbreaks of telepathy and clairvoyance, like a pan of maize on a stove that starts with a few pops and speeds up until the whole pan goes crazy.

## Conclusion

In our quest to investigate the meaning behind 2012, we have seen that the tribal elders are divided in their expectations of Earth changes at the end of the 13-baktun cycle. We have looked at catastrophic theories of axis shift, crustal displacement, rogue asteroids and wandering planets, but most of these theories are unconvincing due to errors and inconsistencies. Paul LaViolette's galactic core explosion theory is quite convincing, but not firmly linked to 2012... until we consider Weidner and Bridges' study of the Hendaye Cross. The enciphered message on the cross seems not only to be warning of a cyclic catastrophe, but the alchemists behind the message have given clues that this event might also act as the trigger of an evolutionary leap to a new kind of human with a functional shamanic luminous body, or vehicle.

The magnetised plasma band theory of Dmitriev and Wilcock is also intriguing, explaining all the changes going on in the solar system, and also implying that there is a link to a forthcoming evolutionary leap and to the increase of "*self-luminous formations*" in the atmosphere, which some branches of science are on the verge of accepting as a new kind of lifeform. Both these theories, of Weidner and Bridges and of Dmitriev/Wilcock, would allow an explanation of the 100,000-year solar cycle that now seems to be emerging, since it is about four cycles of precession in length, and both these theories are linked to the precession cycle, which is, of course, what is being measured by the Long Count calendar of the Maya.

A third fascinating idea emerges from the findings of Professor Simon Shnoll, combined with John Major Jenkins' work, and implies that the galactic alignment process itself may cause biochemical or neurochemical changes in humanity, which may be part of a process of a mass awakening of Kundalini.

Gregg Braden's observation about the falling geomagnetic field strength being the sign of a forthcoming magnetic reversal is borne out by several scientists, while there is also a trend for greater bursts of geomagnetic activity at the time of the solar maximums (and during the progressively more frequent and more intense solar storms), as discovered by Kev Peacock. When we consider the findings of Michael Persinger and Serena Roney-Dougal, it seems that we can expect a general increase in telepathy, interspersed with more bouts of poltergeists, UFOs and other paranormal phenomena that may correspond to increased output of pinoline or DMT respectively. Rick Strassman's suggestion of a sudden switching-on of the N-methylating enzyme that controls DMT production is a similar scenario.

Persinger's findings regarding those suffering from TLE, combined with the story of Michael O' Callaghan, suggests that the geomagnetic fluctuations could prompt a mass schizophrenic break for humanity, the *Inner Apocalypse* or *Revealing*, in which our suppressed complexes will emerge in visible form. This may be a healing process and part of a near-death experience for the Earth itself, as its mega-mind is congealed from its constituent human particles. There is a similar kabbalistic doctrine of the *Heavenly Man*, which says that throughout the cycles of history, certain individuals manage to achieve perfection and become part of an evolving mega-being:

*"This process is repeated, so says the tradition, through seven great epochs of evolution, until at the end there is to be found one Heavenly Man, which consciously mirrors the mind and consciousness of the Eternal, that mind and consciousness which is immanent in all manifestation, and which in the Qabalah is known as Adam Kadmon."* [70]

In Persinger and Lafreniére's book *Space-Time Transients and Unusual Events*, they suggest the concept of a geopsyche:

*"Our concept of the geopsyche essentially involves the interaction between large numbers of biological systems and the geomagnetic environment within which they are immersed. It contends that at certain critical numbers of biological units (of a species), a matrix is formed with the capacity to be energized by the intense geophysical forces of nature. When energized, this matrix acquires the potential to display behaviours and patterns of its own."* [71]

They go on to explain how this transformation could be brought about, using the analogy of thin wires that are all in the same relatively small space, but together constitute a cable:

*"Now, suppose a moving magnetic field is applied to the entire population of the little wires. The result would be the induction of an electric current in each of those wires and the production of an electric field over the entire volume. Within limits, increasing the number of wires in the cable would amplify the intensity of the field. Although the electric field would in principle be produced by the individual wires, it would take on the properties of a matrix with properties of its own.*

*In the principle of the geopsyche, the elements are not thin wires, but the electronic units of human organisms - the brains of individual people, millions of people. They are not packaged into cables, but are clustered into areas of high population density. The geopsyche emerges when a changing magnetic field is applied to the population of individual electronic units."* [72]

In the geopsyche concept, presuming the "*energizer*" to be consistent with previous geomagnetic storms, or electrical disturbances, Persinger and Lafreniére say the duration of the phenomenon would be anything between a few seconds and a week. In other words, it is only transient. This is not really what Teilhard de Chardin was talking about when he predicted a "*planetized humanity*" that has "*a communication of mind and spirit that will make the phenomenon of telepathy, still sporadic and haphazard, both general and normal*", [73] but it gives us another way of looking at it.

    Although we have been unable to reach a definite conclusion at this point as to what we can expect around 2012, hopefully we have been able to sift out some of the misinformation and have increased our understanding so that we can pool our knowledge more effectively, and work together to manifest a 'Golden Age'. In the words of Terence McKenna:

*"We are the inheritors of a million years of striving for the unspeakable, and now with the engines of technology in our hands, we ought to be able to reach out and actually exteriorise the human soul at the end of time; invoke it into existence like a UFO and open the violet doorway into hyperspace and walk through it; out of profane history and into the world beyond the grave, beyond shamanism, beyond the end of history, into the Galactic Millennium that has beckoned to us for millions of years across space and time... This is the moment! A planet brings forth an opportunity like this only once in its lifetime and we are ready and we are poised and as a community we are ready to move into it, to claim it, to make it our own. It's there! Go for it! And thank you..."* [74]

Good luck, readers!

# APPENDICES
# & REFERENCES

# APPENDIX 1

# Two Accounts of Out-Of-Body Experiences

This account of an out-of-body experience by Robert Anton Wilson appeared in his introduction to a book called *Brainchild* [1] by David Jay Brown, and was induced in 1986 by a prototype *"brain machine"* made by retired NASA engineer, Mike Hercules. Hercules already had a machine on the market called *Pulstar*, but the new one was called *Pulstar-2* and unfortunately never went into production, since Mike died the following year. For the second trip, he also had Wilson hooked up to a *"second generation"* electroencephalograph (EEG) that shows separate readings for all four types of brainwave - beta (waking), alpha (relaxed, light meditation), theta (dreaming, deep meditation), and delta (deep sleep). The *Pulstar-2* had four electrodes that were attached to Wilson's head at the *"right and left, front and back"*, and Wilson started sending electromagnetic waves of 6.5 hertz into his brain. He went rapidly into a state of deep meditation, which he recognised as being normally very difficult to attain. Mike Hercules turned it down to 4.0 hertz and Wilson left his body and had *"an interesting tour"* of the Rocky Mountains. He later heard that 4.0 hertz is the frequency used by Robert Monroe's *Hemi-Sync* tapes, which are designed to produce OOBEs by *"binaural beat"* sounds. Mike asked if he'd like to repeat the experience, with the electroencephalograph attached to his skull as well. Wilson agreed, and this is his account:

*"Mike turned the frequency down to 4.0 hertz and then lower, and lower, and I went deep, deep into the quiet serene place of hypnosis and then away from the bodily sensation-and-emotion circuits and then up and out, over the Rockies, over the North Pole, down past Iceland to Ireland, to Dublin Bay, and I found the hill of Howth on the north rim of the bay and swooped gently down on the old street, curiously called* The Haggard, *where I was living at that time. I entered my house and found my wife reading in the living room and became very concerned with not doing anything to frighten her, and then I browsed a bit around Howth Hill and went back over the North Pole and found the Rockies and pursued the Continental Divide and found Boulder and Mike's house and went back into my body in his laboratory.*

*I was feeling as happy as a cat in a tuna factory. It had been a glorious trip, like* Lilacs in the Sky *with Delphiniums.*

*Then Mike showed me the EEG for the period of my Far Journey. The lines were flat. My brain showed no beta, no alpha, no theta, no delta. Nothing. Void. Clinically, it looked like the graph of a dead brain. Whatever was going on during my flight over the pole, I was not using my imagination, which would have produced high delta and some beta, at least."* [2]

Notice that, to get to Ireland from Boulder, Colorado, and to return again, Wilson went via the

North Pole, suggesting an interaction between the astral body and the geomagnetic field. The second account is from Terence McKenna in *True Hallucinations*, [3] in which, while in Katmandu, Nepal in 1969, he produced a similar effect to Wilson's experience, but via exoegenous DMT, following an earlier dose of LSD, combined with a sexual encounter (this was not an uncommon kind of activity in Katmandu in the 1960s). After finding himself amongst the *"machine-elves"* (the morphing multi-coloured beings mentioned in Chapter 13, that told McKenna the laws of physics would change in 2012), at the moment when the whole vision would normally have faded, the scene changed:

*"I suddenly found myself flying hundreds of miles above the Earth and in the company of silver disks. I could not tell how many. I was fixated on the spectacle of the Earth below and realized that I was moving south, apparently in polar orbit, over Siberia. Ahead of me I could see the Great Plain of Shang and the mass of the Himalayas rising up in front of the red yellow waste of India. The Sun would rise in about two hours. In a series of telescoping leaps, I went from orbit to a point where I could specifically pick out the circular depression that is the Kathmandu Valley. Then, in the next leap, the valley filled my field of vision. I seemed to be approaching it at great speed. I could see the Hindu temple and the houses of Kathmandu, the Temple of Svayambhunath to the west of the city and the Stupa at Boudanath, gleaming white and a few miles to the east. Then Boudanath was a mandala of houses and circular streets filling my vision. Among the several hundred roof tops I found my own. In the next moment I slammed into my body and was refocused on the roof top and the woman in front of me."* [4]

Again, the astral traveller was moving in polar orbit, showing the relationship between the geomagnetic field and the astral body, and he was flying in the company of *silver disks*, giving the impression that not only do astral bodies have the appearance of UFOs, but as astral forms they are also subject to the geomagnetic field. This is all very relevant to the essay that follows, *The Astral Transition*.

# APPENDIX 2

# The Astral Transition:
# Clues From Egypt and Siberia Suggest a Shamanic Experience in 2012

## Ecdysone and the Non-Molecular Body

As mentioned in Chapter 21, Dr Charles Muses, alias *Musaios*, suggested in his 1985 book

*The Lion Path* [1] that the Egyptians had developed a technology in which tones, lights and a then-unidentified plant (later identified as *khat*) were used to *"open a rusty valve"*, or trigger the production of hormones similar to the ecdysone (ecdydsterone) produced by larval forms of insects, which allows the adult form to emerge. In this way, they would encourage the gestation of a non-molecular body that would allow the survival of consciousness beyond physical death. As already mentioned, every external mummy case has folded wings on it, in imitation of the embossed wings found on a chrysalis. The process was started well before death, and completed during the 70-day embalming period, connected to the 70-day disappearance of Sirius.

Muses, a mathematician, philosopher and computer scientist, was convinced that the synchronous *perihelion* (closest point of planetary orbit to the Sun) of Pluto, with the *periastron* (closest approach of two stars to each other) of Sirius B and Sirius A, which both occurred in 1994 and only happen together every 90,000 years, allowed a flow of resonant energies, and the possibility of an evolutionary jump for those prepared to follow the clues left by the Egyptians. He produced a series of audio cassettes of sounds consisting of special frequency combinations, designed to be used at astrologically pre-determined times while meditating, in order to produce *"the higher human analogue of the lepidopteran metamorphic hormone, ecdysterone"*. This would then *"activate certain genes whose functions would otherwise remain inaccessible"*. The transformative energies would start slowing in January 1999, and stop by May 2000, and Muses says that those unable to complete their development before then would have to *"reincarnate on the life-bearing planets of other solar systems that are on a later (and non-Plutonic) Meta-Cycle"*. He expected a culmination of the whole process on November 12th 2004, when he said that Earth changes would start. [2]

## The Pyramid Texts
In Wm. R. Fix's 1979 book *Star Maps*, [3] the author shows the correspondence between shamanic flight and the initiation rituals of Egypt. In the 4,300-year old *Pyramid Texts*, on the walls of the Pyramid of Unas, it is stated repeatedly that, *"He is not dead, this Unas is not dead"*. In fact, Fix makes it plain that the reason why no bodies have ever been found in any pyramids - even those which were sealed - is because the pyramids were designed for initiation, to facilitate an OOBE (out-of-body-experience), in which the Pharaoh would be gone for about three days, first orbiting the planet, and then going to the circumpolar stars, to become a purified spirit (hence the term *astral projection*). Upon his return, Unas was told, *"Put on thy body"*.

Shamans too, traditionally fly to the polar stars. The *Axis Mundi*, or *World Tree*, which represents the Earth axis (and connects with the underworld below, and heaven above), is shown on some of their drums as the route taken to the polar stars. Shamans usually employ drumming, fasting and powerful plants to access the other planes, and typically experience dismemberment, where they are torn to pieces, then put back together again, as a kind of rebirth. This is exactly what happened to Osiris when his brother Set (plus 72 conspirators) tricked Osiris into getting into a coffin and then threw it into the Nile. The coffin became embedded in a tamarisk tree and was eventually used as a pillar in a palace. Isis found the coffin and hid it, but Set discovered it and cut Osiris into fourteen pieces. With the help of Thoth, Isis found all the pieces except one - the phallus - and re-assembled Osiris. With Thoth's magic, and a wooden phallus, Isis conceived Horus. Then Osiris ascended.

## Mystery Religions

These shamanic themes formed the Osiris cult, then found their way into other 'mystery religions', such as the Greek mysteries of Dionysus at Eleusis, Attis in Asia Minor, Bacchus in Italy, and Mithras in Persia. The life stories of all these god-men involved a voluntary death, a flight from the body, a descent into the underworld, an ascent to heaven, then a resurrection. They also had a sacrament, which in later versions was wine, but in the Mysteries of Mithras, "*developed from older rites which used consecrated bread and water mixed with the intoxicating juice of a psychedelic plant called* Haoma". [4] The various cultures all adapted one of their gods to take on the role of the resurrecting god-man, but, when a Jewish sect wanted their own mystery religion, it was a bit more difficult, since they only had one god, so they based the mysteries around the figure of the Jewish Messiah, resulting in Christianity. Timothy Freke and Peter Gandy, in their book *The Jesus Mysteries*, [5] have pointed out 30 correspondences between the Dionysus/Osiris Mysteries and Christianity. I have also found Mithraism/Christianity correspondences in *Pears Cyclopedia*, and these can be seen in the chart opposite.

## Precession Encoded

Giorgio Santillana and Hertha von Dechend, in their 1969 book *Hamlet's Mill*, [6] have shown that there has been knowledge of the precession of the equinoxes for millennia, and that it has been encoded into mythology all over the world. This concerns the slow movement of the Earth's axis in a circle, which takes about 26,000 years to complete. Plato called this the *Great Year* of 25,920 years. The Vernal (spring) Equinox slowly moves through all twelve zodiac constellations over the 25,920 years, until it comes back to its starting point. Actually, it is the background stars that are moving - the equinox stays in roughly the same place. Each constellation takes 2,160 years to cross the equinoctial point, and it takes 72 years for each of the 360° of the sky to rotate. The constellations also oscillate up and down over the precession. Robert Bauval and his co-authors [7] have shown that the Egyptians were measuring this movement from the First Time of Osiris (*Zep Tepi*), which they put at 10,500 BC, when Orion was at its lowest point, to the Last Time of Osiris, which is coming up soon (half a precessional cycle later), when Orion reaches its highest position.

These precessional numbers, 72, 360, 2,160, 4,320 (2 x 2,160) and 25,920, have been found encoded into Egyptian myths, such as the one where Ra, upon discovering his wife's

## Dionysus/Osiris Mysteries

| | Mystery of Mithras (Mithraism) | Mystery of Jesus (Christianity) |
|---|---|---|
| 1. Virgin birth of "Son of God" | Miraculous/Virgin birth of sun-god | Virgin birth of Son of God |
| 2. Born in cave on 25th December | Born on 25th December - originally the Winter Solstice | Born in "stable" (original = "cave") on 25th December |
| 3. Crucifixion (or stuck to/in a tree) to atone for sins of humanity | Mithras sacrificed a bull to save humanity from sin | Crucifixion to atone for sins of humanity |
| 4. Birth prophesied by star | | Birth prophesied by star |
| 5. Three shepherds visited the birth | "Magi" are astrologer-priests of Mithras | "Magi" (Matt) or 3 shepherds (Luke) visited birth |
| 6. Baptism of initiates | Baptism of initiates | Baptism of Jesus and initiates |
| 7. Water into wine | | Water into wine |
| 8. Miracles | | Miracles |
| 9. Transfiguration | | Transfiguration |
| 10. Twelve disciples | Mithras surrounded by 12 signs of the zodiac | Twelve disciples |
| 11. Eating of bread and wine (= flesh and blood) to commune with the god | Initiates took "Holy Communion" of watered-down wine with bread and wafers embossed with the cross | Jesus & disciples shared wine and bread; initiates take Holy Communion of wine and bread or wafers embossed with the cross |
| 12. Death of saviour redeems sins of the world | Death of bull redeems sins of the world | Death of saviour redeems sins of the world |
| 13. Descends into Hell and resurrects after three days | Mithras (Sun) "dies" at Winter Solstice and is "reborn" after a 3-day standstill | Descends into Hell and resurrects after three days |
| 14. Ascends to Heaven to appear as judge at the end of time | Mithras waits in heaven for the End of Time when he will return to Earth to awaken the dead and pass judgement | Jesus ascends to heaven for the End of Time when he will return to Earth to awaken the dead and pass judgement |
| 15. 3 women followers visit empty tomb | | 3 women followers visit empty tomb |
| 16. | Sunday is the holy day | Sunday is the holy day |
| 17. | Use of bell, holy water and candles | Use of bell, holy water and candles |

*The striking similarities between the stories of Dionysus, Mithras and Jesus, and the methods of worship adhered to by followers of the religions which sprang up around them.*

infidelity, said she was not to bear children on any of the 360 days of the year. Thoth intervened and played a game of draughts (*senet*) with the Moon, and won one 72nd part of the Moon's light, creating the extra five *epagomenal* days, on which were born Isis, Osiris, Set, Nephthys and Horus the elder (360/72=5). Encoded here is 72 x 360 = 25,920. Remember also the 72 conspirators of Set, who caused Osiris to become part of the tree!

Every year, the Egyptians held a festival for *Raising the Djed*. The *Djed* was a pillar with four rings on it, which represented the backbone of Osiris, the tree he was entombed in, and the axis of the Earth. In her book *Catastrophobia*, [8] Barbara Hand Clow has pointed out that the relief showing the Raising of the Djed in the Temple at Abydos, shows the Djed at an initial angle of "*20 to 25° off vertical*" - the same as the angle of tilt on Earth's axis. When measuring the image with a protractor, it is actually within a degree of the 23.5° tilt angle. Clow says that around 9,500 BC, at the end of the Ice Age, the catastrophe pinpointed by Allan and Delair in *When the Earth Nearly Died*, [9] when supernova debris passed close to Earth, caused the start of the precession cycle by knocking the axis away from vertical.

## Djed = Axis Mundi = Tree of Life = Tree of Knowledge

Some Egyptian papyri show the World Tree administering spiritual nourishment, thereby combining the concepts of the World Tree, Tree of Life and Tree of Knowledge. This connection is also emphasised on Stela 25 from Izapa, Mexico (see Fig.1.6, page 25), which shows "*Hunahpu with Seven Macaw in his polar perch*". The polar axis is shown looking very similar to a Djed pillar, with Seven Macaw representing the Big Dipper (Plough/Great Bear) constellation. In his book *Maya Cosmogenesis 2012*, John Major Jenkins has shown [10] that the Maya were tracking precession, and that this is what is behind the Long Count calendar. The Crocodile Tree on the stela represents the Milky Way, and Hunahpu is shaking Seven Macaw off his perch, representing the precessional movement of the Big Dipper away from the celestial pole (and also signifying the change in preferred shamanic destination to Galactic Centre, via the Crocodile/Caiman Tree). Notice that there is a snake wrapped around the two trees!

In Plaincourault, France, there is a mural showing the Tree of Knowledge with the snake wrapped around it, and Eve talking to the snake. The Tree is a Fly Agaric mushroom! The Fly Agaric is, of course, a hallucinogenic, and John Allegro, who translated the Dead Sea Scrolls, went as far as to suggest that the early Christians used it as a sacrament. Bishop Jim Pike (a friend of sci-fi author Philip K. Dick) found the argument so convincing that he went to the desert near Qumran on the Dead Sea in search of Fly Agarics, but unfortunately died of dehydration while there. Gordon Wasson's book *Soma, Divine Mushroom of Immortality* identifies the Fly Agaric with Soma, the sacrament of the Hindus (meaning "*body*", which gives us the word *somatic*), but Ananda thinks that Soma was like an alternative Ayahuasca, made from Syrian Rue and Acacia.

## Taking the Pee?

Every year at Christmas, we re-enact our own mystery play, which has somehow survived to remind us of all this. December 25th used to be Winter Solstice. It is the birthday of the god-man Osiris/Dionysus/Mithras/Jesus, who, as Osiris, represents the polar axis (Djed) and its 72 x 360-year precession cycle. We now pretend that a wise old man called Santa Claus flies through the sky, pulled by reindeer (having frozen time, so he can visit everyone), and enters via the chimney. He is depicted as wearing a red and white outfit (though this is a more contemporary depiction, after St Nicholas, Bishop of Myra, who wore those colours - originally he was shown as wearing green or other variations, though the gifts were always traditionally wrapped in red and white), leaving presents under a pine tree that we have brought indoors, or in socks hanging over the fireplace. Then he flies off to the North Pole!

In Siberia, since time immemorial, around Winter Solstice, shamans have gathered the red and white Fly Agaric mushrooms from under the very same pine trees we put in our living rooms, and distributed them from a sack. In Siberia, the entrances to homes are in the roof, and double as a smoke outlet, so they *really are* entering via the chimney! The mushrooms are left to dry out by hanging them over the hearth. The mushrooms have to be gathered quickly, because the reindeer love them. However, it is a fact that the psychoactive ingredient can be recycled several times, and unpleasant side effects such as vomiting are thus avoided. It is also a fact that the reindeer love eating yellow snow! If a reindeer herder wants to gather his herd, he only has to urinate, and they all come running.

That is why the reindeer all fly along in frozen time. Even the reindeer names reinforce the encoding (see www.solsticestudios.net [11] for more information). The Christmas tree also represents the Axis Mundi, with the candles or lights and baubles representing stars, and the star on the top representing the Pole Star. It is usually a five-pointed star, and therefore encodes 72, since a pentacle is formed by 5 x 72° angles. Santa lives at the North Pole, which encodes the OOBE destination, and Santa's helpers, the elves, are either the fourth-dimensional astral beings encountered, or even our higher-dimensional selves - also represented by the angel/fairy on the tree.

What crazy kind of world is this? Is Jack's trip up the beanstalk to get the golden eggs another version? Is Humpty Dumpty an exploded planet?

## What Does it all Mean?

As we have seen, Jenkins has shown that the Maya were tracking precession with the Long Count calendar, but rather than the Vernal Equinox, they were tracking the movement of stars (the Milky Way) against the Winter Solstice. He also showed that the Maya 13-baktun cycle (5,125 years) ends on Winter Solstice 2012. What is more, the Maya used to take hallucinogens, including toad venom and psilocybin mushrooms. Jenkins has also found some evidence that they may have taken *Amanita Muscaria* (Fly Agaric), [12] but they mainly used the psilocybin mushroom. This contains a close relative of DMT, which is also produced in the pineal gland, or third eye, and which is shaped like a pine cone. It was after ingesting these mushrooms that the McKenna brothers were inspired to investigate the I Ching-encoded Timewave that ends in 2012.

Some have suggested that the Egyptians also took psilocybin mushrooms. They did take the blue water lily, which, says Paul Devereux in *The Long Trip: A Prehistory of Psychedelia*, *"was the form in which Isis restored the murdered Osiris, and was thus a symbol for him"*. [13] The lily has hypnotic effects. Devereux says the Egyptians also had access to opium (which gave Errol Flynn an out-of-body experience) and khat, which produces a dream-like state. Also, in the Americas, a different species of tobacco was taken, and in huge doses. A near-lethal dose can give an OOBE. We have heard recently of the *"cocaine mummies"* found in Egypt (examination of mummified tissues showed traces of cocaine, which must have come from the Coca plant that grows only in South America). Well, they also contained large amounts of nicotine, another plant that should not have been in Egypt - very upsetting for Egyptologists!

Devereux has shown that most of these power plants can cause OOBEs when taken in large enough doses, or in combination (though they can be very dangerous or unpleasant in some cases), and that they have been used for just such purposes for thousands of years. In another book, *Shamanism and the Mystery Lines*, [14] Devereux makes a very strong case that these magical shamanic flights were associated with the alignments we know as *ley lines*, where ancient barrows, standing stones, stone circles, and even pre-reformation churches (built on sacred sites), are aligned in straight lines.

Will the *"Galactic Winter Solstice"* in 2012 allow a mass out-of-body experience? Will celestial and terrestrial grids align? Will a passing celestial body re-align the Axis Mundi to its pre-fall state? Or maybe the falling geomagnetic field will lead to a magnetic reversal and switch our polarity (OOBE researcher Robert Monroe found that the body's polarity reverses while the consciousness is out of body). Maybe the solar mega-cycle or galactic alignment will trigger it... or perhaps it will be stimulated by the magnetised band of plasma through which the solar system is passing.  Better get practising those OOBEs!

*First posted on* Diagnosis 2012 *website, August 2001*

# APPENDIX 3

# Cropgnosis:
# Crop Circle Research from a Gnostic Perspective

In the *Plasmatic Communication from the Noosphere* section of Chapter 20, we found that there may be a connection between Alexey Dmitriev's theory of our entry into a magnetized band of plasma, and the mechanism behind crop formations as proposed by John Burke of BLT Research. It is a logical step from this position to wonder whether the effects observed in crop formations could be a foretaste of the physical effects that we will experience as the solar system becomes further embedded in the plasma band. So, does this mean our kneecaps will explode, like the crop-stem nodes? Let's hope that on a global, less concentrated level, the more severe effects will not be triggered - after all, the Earth has passed through the plasma bands many times before without wiping out all life-forms (once every 25,920-year cycle of precession, according to Wilcock's theory, but there are arguments for other lengths of interval, such as four cycles of precession, around 100,000 years).

## Plant Effects as Precursor and Metaphor of Human Effects

It was while reading through the *Stunted, Malformed Seeds and Germination Effects* section of the *Plant Abnormalities* page [1] on the BLT website that the possibility of similar plasma effects on humans jumped out at me. BLT has discovered four levels of effects on seeds and germination, according to the stage of crop maturity at the time of exposure:

*a) Immature crop (before flowering): the plant develops normally, but is totally devoid of any seeds.*

*b) Young crop where seed is forming: seeds will be smaller, with reduced germination.*

*c) More mature plants with fully formed embryo: seeds small, with no growth variability. All germinating seeds exhibit synchronised growth.*

*d) Mature plants with fully formed seeds: massive increase in growth rate and vigour. Seedlings can tolerate extreme stress without harm.*

So, if humanity is to be affected in a similar way in the near future, what exactly could this mean? There are several possible interpretations. Here is the first one that occurred to me:

## If "seed" represents spiritual preparation:

*a) Those totally unprepared: will be unable to make a dimensional transition.*

*b) Those who have started preparation: will make a partial transition.*

*c) Those who have almost completed preparation: will make a low-level transition to the same state.*

*d) Those who have completed their spiritual development: will make a complete transition to a comparatively god-like state.*

## The second interpretation. If "seed" represents fertility:

*a) Those totally unprepared: will be totally sterilised.*

*b) Those who have started preparation: will be partially sterilised. Reproduction may produce a race of mutants or dwarves.*

*c) Those who have almost completed preparation: reproduction may produce a race of clones.*

*d) Those who have completed their spiritual development: the next generation will be a race of gods.*

As a possibly corroborative factor to what may seem like crazy speculation above, the BLT *Other Facts* page 2 tells us that after visiting the 1996 'Julia Set' fractal formation at Stonehenge, "*more than a dozen women reported menstrual abnormalities, the most unusual of which was the re-occurrence in several post-menopausal women of their previous normal menstrual cycles.*" As already mentioned, according to Lucy Pringle's experiments, 3 this is probably connected with an increased secretion of melatonin from the pineal gland that sometimes occurs in the crop circle environment. So perhaps plasma can have effects on human reproduction. This pineal activation could also be involved in the god-like developments, with the rising of Kundalini and the Spiritual Wedding that we covered in Part Four of the book.

## The Sower

I hesitate to continue to the next part, since I am not an advocate of modern Christianity. However, it is now accepted by some researchers that there were inner teachings used by the early followers of "*The Way*", and that these early followers were actually Gnostics. Anyway, I remembered at this point the parable in the Bible called *The Sower*, so I located it in three versions: Matthew 13, Mark 4 and Luke 8. Incredibly, it is a parable of four kinds of seed germination:

*a) Seeds that fell on the path: eaten by birds.*

*b) Seeds that fell on rocky ground: brief germination, then withering.*

*c) Seeds that fell among thorns: seedlings grew a little, but became choked.*

*d) Seeds that fell on good soil: grew to full size and produced a huge amount of grain - "some a hundredfold, some sixty, some thirty".*

Even more incredibly, the parable is explained (for the benefit of the disciples, or inner Gnostic brotherhood), as representing four types of spiritual development:

*a) Those who misunderstand "the word".*

*b) Those who accept the word for short time (until stressed).*

*c) Those who accept the word for a longer time (until distracted).*

*d) Those who accept the word and understand it: they bear fruit and yield 100, 60 or 30-fold.*

Matthew 13 continues with another wheat parable, about weeds choking the crop, and then gets very sinister, talking about harvest time, when the grain is collected into the barn and the weeds are burned. The harvest is *"at the close of the age"* and the reapers are angels. The theme is then expanded on in *Revelation* 14, the *"Harvest of the World"*, which is very nasty. However, some bible scholars think that the author added these parts to an original text (called *proto-Matthew*, or *the Q-gospel*).

The "word", of course, is *Logos* in Greek, and is a Gnostic term that has been universally misunderstood, so perhaps a good place to start would be a website called *The Outlawed Logos Teachings of Jesus* at www.gnosticchristianity.com, [4] and in particular the page *Details of the Five Stages of Consciousness.* [5] This finds many models from psychology, mythology, palaeontology, and several religions, that all agree on five stages of development in human society and in individuals, as an evolution of consciousness, or *"intellectual metamorphosis"*. The mass of humanity is stuck in stages two and three - stage five is, in Teilhard de Chardin's model, *"'the convergence' or 'mega-synthesis' of hyper-personal consciousness, oriented toward God, the Omega Point"*. Also, the parable of the sower is seen from the same Gnostic perspective as the very same five-stage model, where the fifth stage is a result of the *"100-fold yield"*

In summary, here are the five stages of Gnostic consciousness:

*Stage I refers to non-rational beings.*

*Stage II refers to rational beings without a conscience.*

*Stage III refers to rational beings with a conscience.*

*Stage IV refers to the expanded consciousness (enlightenment) achieved by using both judgmental and non-judgmental laws of logic.*

*Stage V refers to an amplified form of consciousness in which the whole is more than the sum of the parts.*

So, concealed in the results of scientific research, we find a clue that the side effects in humans of forthcoming plasmatic exposure (as the solar system becomes more embedded in a magnetised beam of plasma) may depend upon the evolved state of each individual at the time of maximum immersion. Those who are *"ripe"* will become fully functioning neurons in the planetary brain, as Gaia completes her gestation. This will allow all functioning human neurons to communicate telepathically, so *"ripeness"* would signify a readiness to have every thought telepathically broadcast. The timing of maximum immersion seems likely to be co-incident with the end-point of the Maya 13-baktun cycle, which is a 260-katun macroscopic version of the 260-day tzolkin. While the tzolkin governs individual gestation, the 13-baktun cycle seems to govern planetary gestation, and the due date is Winter Solstice 2012 AD.

*First posted at www.swirlednews.com, October 2002*

# NOTES & REFERENCES

If you find that a web page referenced here is no longer online, try looking in the Internet Archive at *www.archive.org or http://web.archive.org*

## Introduction

1. Thanks to the work of John Major Jenkins - see Jenkins [1998].
2. Arguelles [1987]
3. McKenna [1975]
4. Arguelles [1984]
5. *www.diagnosis2012.co.uk* - also known as *2012: Dire Gnosis*, where *Dire* means serious or urgent, as well as dreadful, and thus sums up the ambiguous nature of the 2012 phenomenon. *Dire Gnosis* therefore means, primarily, 'important knowledge' as well as inferring a diagnostic approach.

## Part 1: Ancient Calendars and Prophecies

1. Dick [1991]

## Chapter 1: The Maya Calendar

1. Jenkins [1994] p.110
2. Aveni [1997] p.42
3. Jenkins [1994] p.110 & p.113
4. Ibid. p.111. Barbara and Dennis Tedlock were apprenticed to a daykeeper who confirms this.
5. Scofield [1991] p.5
6. Ibid.

7. Arguelles [1987]
8. The time it takes for the equinoxes to precess back through all twelve signs of the zodiac.
9. Jenkins [1998]
10. Ibid. p.328
11. Jenkins [1998] p.330
12. Ibid.
13. This is because the rate of precession is slowing down from the classic rate of 25,920 years (the "*Platonic Year*", which was correct around the time of Plato) by around eleven years per century. Precession is caused by the approximate 23° tilt of the Earth's axis, and the variation in the rate of precession is caused by a variation in the tilt over 41,000 years - a cycle known as "*the variation in the obliquity of the ecliptic.*"
14. Jenkins [1998] p.212
15. Ibid.
16. Brotherston [1992] p.299. As well as the Aztecs and Toltecs, the Zuni, Navaho and some Incas say that we are in the *Fifth Sun* or *World*, while the Maya, Hopi and some other Incas say we are in the *Fourth Sun* or *World*. Encoded into these two versions, we have the precession of the equinoxes, where five cycles of 5,200 tuns (or 5,125 years) add to 26,000 tuns (25,627 years), and a half-cycle of the change in the obliquity of the ecliptic or axis tilt cycle, where four cycles of 5,200 tuns (5,125 years) add to 20,800 tuns (20,500 years) - half of the 41,000-year cycle. *www.diagnosis2012.co.uk/new4.htm#ages*
17. Quoted in Gilbert and Cotterell [1995] p.70, "... *an anonymous manuscript from 1558 entitled Leyenda de Los Soles, seemingly derived from one or other of two earlier documents, the Chimalpopoca Codex and the Cuauhtitlan Annals...*"
18. Séjourné [1957, 1978] 1978 edn. p.138
19. Shearer [1975]
20. e.g. José Arguelles' *The Transformative Vision* (1975) p.14 "... *for this fifth age, Ollin, means 'Earth-Shaking,' change or movement. It spans at the most a little more than a millennium, consisting of thirteen 52-year Heaven cycles, from 843 to 1519, and nine 52-year Hell cycles, from 1519 to 1987.*" The Cherokee, Dan Troxell, agrees.
21. However, there was a substantial error made in calculating Harmonic Convergence, and it should have been on 7th January 1987. This is an error of 221 days and is explained fully in note 21 of Chapter 19.
22. Jenkins [1994] pp. 288-289

## Chapter 2: Tribal Prophecies

1. Men [1990]
2. *http://web.archive.org/web/20030218184249/http://www.greatmystery.org/mayaspring2002.html http://web.archive.org/web/20030404171024/http://www.greatmystery.org/mayaspring2002initiation.html*
3. *www.galacticmaya.com/English/Interview.htm*
4. In *Valis*, Philip K. Dick defined plasmate as follows: "*I term the immortal one a plasmate, because it is a form of energy; it is living information. It replicates itself - not through information or in information - but as information.*" PKD continued with: "*The plasmate can crossbond with a human, creating what I call a homoplasmate. This annexes the mortal human permanently to the plasmate. We know this as 'birth from above' or 'birth from the Spirit'.*"

5. www.latinola.com/archives-com_13.html

6. www.chiron-communications.com/communique7-10.html

7. See Note 22 of Chapter 1. Barrios uses August 1987, taken from Shearer/Arguelles, but this is an error.

8. (1998) www.kachina.net/~alunajoy/timekeeper.html

9. Skinner [1994] p.157. See also www.kachina.net/~alunajoy/awake.html

10. Wilcox [1999]

11. Waters [1969]

12. Ibid. p.30

13. Ibid. p.178

14. Ibid. p.11

15. Ibid. p.33

16. Ibid. p.408

17. Quoted all over the Internet - here is an example: http://seventhmoon3.tripod.com/hopi.htm

18. Timms [1994] p.157

19. Waters [1969] p.408

20. www.dreamscape.com/morgana/pan.htm

21. McFadden [1991]

22. http://users.pandora.be/gohiyuhi/frauds/frd0019.htm
http://nativenet.uthscsa.edu/archive/nl/9201/0113.html

23. Waters [1969] pp. 143-144

24. Waters [1975]

25. Ibid. pp.272-273

26. See Coe [1966, 1971] 1966 edn. p.149 and 1971 Penguin paperback p.174.

27. Hope [1990] p.191

28. Scallion [1997]

29. Temple [1976, 1998]

30. Ibid. 1998 hardback edn. pp.324-325

31. Ibid. p.298

32. www.lightnews.org/December98/fifth_world_of_peace_and_l.htm

33. Hail [2000]

34. http://www.amazon.com/exec/obidos/tg/detail/-/0892818042/qid=1080309050/sr=1-1/ref=sr_1_1/102-5288386-9508124?v=glance&s=books

35. http://trox11.tripod.com/snake/snake.htm

36. www.2012.com.au/hitler.html

37. Grandmother Twylah Nitsch is author of several books: *Creature Teachers; Entering Into the Silence; The Seneca Way*; also co-author of *Other Council Fires Were Here Before Ours: A Native American Creation Story as Retold by a Seneca Elder and Her Granddaughter*.

38. www.alternativeapproaches.com/magick/amerind/amerind3.htm

39. www.livinglakes.org/stlucia/credomutwa.htm

40. www.wam.umd.edu/~tlaloc/archastro/ae32.html

41. http://forums.abovetopsecret.com/viewthread.php?tid=558


## Chapter 3: Oriental/Asian Calendars

1. Jenkins [2002]

2. Godwin [1981]

3. Ibid. quoted in Hope [1991] pp.108-109

4. Santillana de [1969, 1977] pp.242; 290; 409

5. Jenkins [2002] pp.244-245

6. Ibid. p.268

7. Note that the Mesoamerican calendars also incorporate animals into their systems, but as day-signs rather than year signs. Seven of them are the same as the Tibetan animals; *snake* follows *dragon* in both systems, and 2012 is the year of the Dragon in Chinese and Tibetan calendars. Tibet uses the Chinese calendar system of five elements combined with twelve animals, to give a 60-year cycle, the *Rab-byung*, and in both Chinese and Tibetan systems 1986 was the year of the *Fire Tiger*. Most sources agree that the year *Fire Tiger* started on 9th February 1986 and ended on 28th January 1987 in China. In the Chinese version, the 60-year cycle begins with a *Wood Rat* year, but the Tibetan calendar started in 1027, when the Kalachakra teachings were introduced to Tibet, and this was the fourth year of the Chinese 60-year cycle; the year *Fire Rabbit* (or *Fire Hare*). So the Tibetan 60-year cycle starts three years after the Chinese 60-year cycle. "*Chinese and Tibetan new years, however, do not always coincide. This is because each of these calendar systems has its own mathematical formulas* [formulae] *for adding leap-months and for determining the start and length of each month.*" (*The Berzin Archives: www.berzinarchives.com/astro_sc.html*). In 1986, the year *Fire Tiger* started on 9th February in Tibetan and Chinese systems, but the following year, *Fire Rabbit* began on 28th January 1987 in China and 28th February 1987 in Tibet.

   While the previous 60-year Chinese cycle ended on February 1st 1984, and the current 27th (some say 78th) Chinese cycle began on 2nd February 1984, in the Tibetan version, the 60-year cycle that ended in 1986/87 was the sixteenth 60-year cycle since the Tibetan calendar started in 1027, with the introduction of the Kalachakra teachings.

8. Jenkins [2002] pp.74-85

9. Jenkins has 18.51 years on pp.77 and 273-274, but this incorrect. *www.alignment2012.com/Table%20of%20Contents-2.htm*

10. Jenkins [2002] pp.84-85

11. Bernbaum [1980, 2001]. Edwin Bernbaum's book *The Way to Shambhala*, originally published in 1980 (republished in 2001), was my source for the Kalachakra information, which clarifies and completes various versions circulating on the Internet and in books that have only part of the story.

12. Arguelles [1975]

13. Ibid. p.302

14. Shearer [1971]

15. Shearer [1975]

16. Bernbaum [1980, 2001]

17. Ibid. p.83

18. I used Cybersky for this, which can be downloaded as a free demo here: *http://cybersky.com/csky322s.exe*

19. *www.acusd.edu/~lnelson/risa/d-kalki.html*. This page is not currently online, though the main site still exists, so find it archived here: *http://web.archive.org/web/20030724223249/www.montclair.edu/risa/d-kalki.html*

20. *www.skyboom.com/ddasa/index12.html*. This page is not currently online, so find it archived here: *http://web.archive.org/web/20010418000605/http://www.skyboom.com/ddasa/index12.html*

21. *www.livinginjoy.com/gc/booklet_e.html*

22. Grasse [2002] p.17

## Chapter 4: Ancient Chinese Lunar Calendar

1. McKenna, Terence and Dennis [1975, 1993]
2. 18th November if you take the non-US time of 6th August 1945 as the date of the bomb.
3. *www.levity.com/eschaton/sheliak/seg_8.html*
4. McKenna, Terence and Dennis [1975, 1993] 1975 edn. p.189; 1993 edn. p.196
5. Ibid.
6. Ibid.
7. *http://groups.yahoo.com/group/timewavezero2012/*
8. 23rd December 2012 is the second most popular end-point for the 13-baktun cycle, and is known as the *Lounsbury correlation*, the *584285 correlation*, or the *GMT3*.
9. Emperor Huang Ti was a book-burner and there is no record of him having developed an I Ching sequence. It seems likely that Peter Meyer produced this sequence as a test for Timewave theory, and just arbitrarily named it after any old emperor.
10. This is less so for the Kelley and Watkins waves, and further less so in the case of the Huang Ti wave.
11. Michell [1969] pp.110-111
12. To see an animation of the ways that the Franklin Magic Square adds to 260, see:
*www-personal.une.edu.au/~lgrunwa2/une/KLAs/maths/Benfranklin_magicsquare.html*
13. Peter Meyer is only interested in the Timewave as a mathematical form of entertainment nowadays.
14. The 384 quantification values did not begin or end with a zero, so that the resulting graph did not descend to the point of maximum novelty. Therefore the wave has no beginning or end point. For the Timewave calculations, see *Time Wave Zero 2012* discussion group message thread from message 1722: *http://groups.yahoo.com/group/timewavezero2012/message/1722*

## Chapter 5: Abrahamic Religions

1. Cain [2002]
2. www.magicmusicmyth.com
3. Whiteside [2002]
4. www.godsweb.com
5. www.geocities.com/bob_hunter/jesusreturn.html
6. www.jvim.com/catalog/leftbehind.html
7. www.siscom.net/~direct/revelation/ - The *Book of Revelation Website*, now available as a book, *The Final Days of Mankind* - see Howard [2002]
8. Dan 9: 24
9. See also Psalm 90: 4 and Ezekiel 4: 6
10. www.be-ready.org/when.html
11. Matt 24: 32-35; Mk 13: 28-31; Lk 21: 29-33
12. Lk 21: 29-33
13. Psalm 90: 10
14. Rev 11:2; Rev 13: 5
15. Rev 12: 14
16. Dan 7: 25; Dan 12: 7

17. Rev 12: 6 and Rev 11: 3. The trampling in *Daniel* is 2,300 "days", which would seem to be affected by the day=year rule, but in *Revelation* it is 1,260 days, whereas the 1,260-day figure in Daniel seems to refer to actual days - three and a half years - so we can presume that the five instances of 1,260 days in *Revelation* also refer to actual days, two of these periods adding to the seven-year period usually called the *Tribulation*.

18. www.authorsden.com/visit/msgboard.asp?AuthorID=10788

19. www.christiantrumpetsounding.com/7_yr_come_again.htm

20. Keene [2002]

21. Crockett [2001]

22. http://aplus-software.com/thglory/7000year.htm

23. http://victorian.fortunecity.com/byzantium/56/y6k.html

24. http://aplus-software.com/thglory/7000year.htm. This website is no longer online, but you can find it on the Internet archive:
http://web.archive.org/web/20030405022140/http://aplus-software.com/thglory/7000year.htm
The fourth part of the article is not linked to it, but can be found here:
http://web.archive.org/web/20021230192522/aplus-software.com/thglory/rapture5.htm

25. www.teshuvah.com/#T

26. www.sichosinenglish.org/books/timeless-patterns/06.htm

27. www.austinchronicle.com/issues/vol18/issue28/xtra.y2ksmarty.html

28. www.islaam.com/books/13_when_shall_it_be.htm

29. Keter Publishing house Ltd. Israel 1973; now available as a CD ROM.

30. Alford [1996] p.237. Alford refers to a papyrus in Cairo Museum, ref. 30646, that was found in a tomb in Thebes and mentions a "*Game of 52*" that Thoth challenged mortals to play, and which they usually lost. Alford sourced this information from Zecharia Sitchen's *Lost Realms* (Sitchen [1990b] pp.82-83.

31. Drosnin [1997]

32. Noah [2002]

33. Gordon Michael Scallion said in his book *Notes From the Cosmos* (1997) that he had seen Phobos loosened from its orbit (see Chapter 19, *Scallion Rap* section), and Glen Deen actually predicted its arrival on 18th September 2012, which is *Rosh Hashanah*, or *Judgement Day* in the Hebrew calendar. However, Deen predicted this by working from a presumed "*loosening*" date of 5th June 2000 - not 2010... He has since said it was loosened in 2001, rather than 2000. Glen Deen now says Planet X could impact Mercury circa March 2nd 2012, and Mercury could impact Venus circa June 6th 2012, resulting in a rendezvous of Venus/Mercury with Earth on 11th December 2012.

34. Elliot Rudisill, in his book *E.Din: Land of Righteousness*, sees the seven heads as one celestial body - Leviathan - and the ten heads as another - Behemoth - see Chapter 7, *Behemoth and Leviathan* section.

35. Note that Cassandra Musgrave also saw Japan slip into the sea in 2012, in her NDE revelation - see Chapter 14, *Near-Death Experiences* section.

36. Drosnin [2002]

37. http://exodus2006.com

## Part 2: 2012 Theories

1. www.gnosis.org/naghamm/asclep.htm

## Chapter 6: Sunspot Cycles

1. Gilbert and Cotterell [1995]
2. *www.alignment2012.com/mproph.htm*
3. Cotterell [1988]
4. Cotterell [1997]
5. Cotterell [1999]
6. Cotterell [2001]
7. In fact, I have found varying timings given for the differential rotation of the Sun, and none of these agree with Cotterell's figures of 26 days at the solar equator and 37 days at the solar poles; most quote 25 days and 35 days respectively. These figures would alter all the findings of Cotterell - for example, if we substitute the rotational periods of 25.38 and 35 for the 26 and 37 of Cotterell, then his 87.454545-day bits come out at 92.3385 days. This means that all his larger cycles that multiply up from this are wrong.
8. *www.alignment2012.com/mproph.htm*
9. *www.gsfc.nasa.gov/gsfc/spacesci/sunearth/solarmax.htm*
10. The e-Book *Something Is Wrong With Our Sun* is now available at Kev Peacock's new updated website *www.spin.net.au/aeitower/CDBook*. The original solar magnetic fields theory page was at *http://people.mail2me.com.au/~vk4vkd/Geomagnetic.htm* and you can access it at the web archive: *http://web.archive.org*
11. Jazz Rasool's website: *www.bodymind.co.uk*
12. Poynder [1992]
13. Telephone conversation 1/2/2004
14. Poynder [1992] p.131
15. See note 7 above.
16. Jenkins [1998] p.366 and *www.alignment2012.com/mproph.htm*
17. Brennan [1994] p.7
18. *Kindred Spirit* magazine Vol.2, No.1 (1990) p.24

## Chapter 7: Astronomical Claims

1. Mardyks and Alana-Leah's [1999] website - now offline. *Galactic Astrology:* *www.geocities.com/Area51/Nebula/9172/gac.html*
2. Mardyks and Alana-Leah [1999] p.106-107
3. *www.fieldwerks.com/galactic_alignment.htm*
4. *www.geocities.com/Area51/Nebula/9172/play.html*. This site is no longer online.
5. *http://edj.net/mc2012/truezone.htm*
6. It takes 243 years for Venus to return to the exact point where it started in relation to the stars, which is 152 of the 584-day cycles (the true average is around 583.92). This is equal to 30.4 pentagrams, or 30 pentagrams plus two extra 584-day cycles (or two points of a pentagram), bringing it into alignment with the original five points. NB. This is not a complete revolution of the pentagram, but a 72° revolution. It takes more than a multiple of the eight-year pentagram because the constellations have also precessed over 240 years, by about 3.3°. One complete revolution of the pentagram takes 1,199 years. I have checked all these movements on astronomical software - thus, the pattern which starts with a

standstill on 14th May 2012 AD is a repeat of the pattern which started 243 years previously on 12th May 1769 AD, and these are both repeats of the pattern which occurred 1,199 years previous to 2012, on 26th April 813 AD. For more information on the retrograde loops of Venus, see the Review of *The Orion Prophecy* at: *www.diagnosis2012.co.uk/orp.htm*

7. *http://hem.passagen.se/alkemi/gaia2012.htm*

8. *http://sunearth.gsfc.nasa.gov/eclipse/eclipse.html*

9. Hart [2003]

10. *www.diagnosis2012.co.uk/5thsun.htm*

11. Russell [1982]

12. Download software from here: *http://cybersky.com*

13. Velikovsky [1950, 1972]

14. Ibid., and Brasseur, *Histoire des Nations Civilsées du Mexique*, I, 311 and I, 120, paraphrased in Velikovsky pp.158-159

15. Bauval and Gilbert [1994, 1995]

16. Jenkins' full unabridged review of *The Mayan Prophecies* can be seen at:
 *www.alignment2012.com/mproph.htm*

17. Download shareware online at *www.angelfire.com/zine/meso/meso/skyglo36.zip*

18. Excellent free Maya calendar software can be downloaded from *http://members.shaw.ca/mjfinley/Maya.htm*. It is not obvious from most astronomical software screen shots when exactly Venus becomes visible/invisible due to solar glare - this is when you need the *Burden of Time* software - but don't forget to set the start-date to 11th August every time you use it.

19. On the *SkyGlobe* software, the astronomical configurations are correct for the given dates, but it is not that simple. The 584-day Venus cycle is split up into an eight-day period of invisibility (when it nears and passes in front of the Sun at inferior conjunction), then the *heliacal rise* happens (the first visible rising, close to the Sun). This is followed by a 263-day period of visibility, followed by *heliacal set*, then a 50-day period of invisibility (when it nears and goes behind the Sun at superior conjunction), and then another 263-day period of visibility. If we check on the *Burden of Time* Maya calendar software, which gives Venus phases, we find that, as John Major Jenkins pointed out, Venus' last appearance as "*morning star*" was on 1st August 3114 BC. Venus was actually in the phase when it was approaching the end of a 263-day period of visibility, and was nearing the Sun again, for heliacal set, which was due on 17-18th August 3114 BC.

20. Phillips [1998]

21. Appleby [1998]

22. Sitchin [1976, 1978]

23. Appleby [1998] p.211

24. Ibid. p.60. Appleby is quoting *The Washington Post* 30/12/83. You can see a photocopy of the newspaper cutting at *www.enterprisemission.com/images/pulsar-Wash-post1.gif*. See Appleby [1998] p.61 for *Newsweek* 13/7/87 quote.

25. Appleby [1998] p.58

26. Hope [1990] p.221

27. Temple [1976, 1998] 1998 edn. p.239

28. Santillana de and Dechend, von [1969, 1977] pp.430-437

29. *http://nibiruancouncil.com/html/nibirureturnarticle.html*

30. Clow [1995] p.30

31. *www.yowusa.com/authors/jvdworp/0300/phobos/phobos1.html*

32. *www.yowusa.com/authors/jvdworp/0300/phobos/phobos2.html*

33. *http://groups.yahoo.com/group/astro-revelation/message/1265*

34. Rudisill [2001, 2002]

35. Ibid. p.210

36. Ibid. pp.282-286

37. Ibid. p.344

38. Ibid. p.267

39. Ibid. p.268

40. Ibid. p.329. Something the author overlooked is the possible connection to the 49-year *Sigui* period of the Dogon (based around the orbit of Sirius B), who Robert Temple traced to Egypt, and who also based their calendar around Sirius, where the heliacal rise (with the Sun) of Sirius coincided with the annual Nile Flood.

41. Ibid. p.328

42. Ibid. p.329

43. Ibid. p.344

44. Ibid. p.333

45. *www.edinnet.com/CommentsonDiagnosis2012.htm*

46. Ibid. p.285

47. Ibid. p.329

48. Following my critique, this essay has been removed from the site.

49. *www.2near.com/edge/maya/hunter-2.html*

50. The numbers are not harmonics of each other. Even if we ignore the error between the calculated obliquity figure for 2012, 1406.263785 minutes and the ideal number it should be (1406.25 minutes), this is still not a harmonic of the 1.0040625 figure for oblateness.

51. E-mail: 20/09/03

52. Ibid.

53. LaViolette [1997]

54. Ibid. p.301

55. Ibid. p.314

56. Ibid. p.107

57. Ibid. p.187

58. *Galactic Tsunami* by David L. Souers at: *http://members.tripod.com/galactictsunami/chapbychap.html*

59. *http://therealmidori.tripod.com/disaster.html*

## Chapter 8: Alternative Archaeology

1. Schwaller de Lubicz [1961, 1988]

2. Hancock [1995]

3. Collins [1998]

4. Ibid. p.209

5. Ibid. p.200

6. Bauval and Gilbert [1994, 1995]

7. Michael Mandeville's book *The Return of the Phoenix* was self-published in 1997, but can be found in updated form online at *www.michaelmandeville.com/phoenix/phoenix.htm*

8. Appleby [1998] p.360

9. *www.michaelmandeville.com/phoenix/phoenix.htm*

10. Appleby's source for the date of the last magnetic reversal (10,500 BC) was probably Alan Alford (*Gods of the New Millennium*, p.225 and 625), who says the Swedes reported in *New Scientist* 6/1/1972, p.7, that "*a reversal of the Earth's magnetic field had occurred 12,400 years ago*," which equates to 10,428 BC. This event is known as the *Gothenburg Magnetic Flip*, and occurred 12,700 years ago (10,700 BC) according to Dr Paul LaViolette; other sources say 12,500 years ago and 12,600 years ago. There seems to be some disagreement as to whether this event was a magnetic reversal or just a local fluctuation. LaViolette calls it a "*substantial geomagnetic disturbance*". Gregg Braden quotes a later Swedish paper, which indicates that it was a 180° shift, due to new evidence from the southern hemisphere, and that it occurred 13,200 years ago. However, Alford has since written a book theorising that the Phoenix myth is about exploded planets (*The Phoenix Solution*).

11. West [1993]

12. In *Hall of the Gods*, Appleby gets the dates right on p.362, but on pp.363-364, says 12,500 BC, when he meant 12,500 BP - before present.

13. Appleby [1998] p.296

14. Bauval and Hancock [1996]

15. Ibid. p.283

16. Ibid. p.70

17. Bauval and Hancock calculated these dates with *SkyGlobe* software, but when I checked them with the same software, I found that from the 1960s on to 2800 AD, the altitude of the Orion star Al Nitak remains at 58.0° (from Cairo looking due south). This means that we are in the *Last Time of Osiris/Orion* now.

18. Appleby [1998] p.317. This is when he says the causeway of Khafre pyramid was pointing to cross-quarter sunrise.

19. Ibid. p.359

20. Jenkins [1998] p.76

21. Ibid. p.81-87

22. Collins [2000]

23. Ibid. p.354

24. Ibid. p.355

25. Ibid. p.355

26. Ibid. p.354

27. Dick [1981, 1991]. *Valis* means "*Vast Active Living Intelligence System*." See Appendix (p.229 in the Vintage Books edn.).

28. Raymond Mardyks' website, *Galactic Astrology Centre* is no longer online. It was at this address: *www.geocities.com/Area51/Nebula/9172/gac.html*

29. *www.rense.com/ufo5/undergiza.htm*. This page on *Rense.com* is the first version, as far as I know. No references are given for this statement, but I have traced it to a book called *Tracing Our White Ancestors* by Frederick Haberman, pages 22-23, which in turn sources the statement from a book called *History of Phoenicia* by George Rawlinson. The Haberman paragraph is quoted online here (but I have corrected the title of Rawlinson's book): "*Let us now analyse the word 'Phoenician' and 'Phoenicia.' Professor George Rawlinson, in* History of Phoenicia, *tells us that Phoenicia derived its name from the forests of date or Phoenix palms which grew there in great luxuriance. So far so good; but whence did the Phoenix palm derive its name? Horapollo says: 'A palm branch was the symbol of the Phoenix.' Yes, but what or who was the Phoenix? Sanchoniathon, the Phoenician writer, states that 'Phoenix was the first Phoenician.' Phoenix, then, was a man. Now, the word Phoenix is the Greek form*

of the Egyptian term 'Pa-Hanok', the house of Enoch. In Hebrew, Enoch also is Hanok. Thus the mystery of that ancient race is solved: they were the sons and descendants of Enoch and of Noah and his three sons, who after the Flood started their westward march."
www.childrenofyahweh.com/Teaching%20Letters/letter_27.htm

30. Hurtak [1977 - 1996] p.xiii. Hurtak confirms that he saw the next "*great cycle*" starting in the year 2004. Hurtak [1977 - 1996] p.549

31. Appleby [1998] p.360

32. The article was originally here: http://cob250.dn.net/members/panspermia/quickening.htm and has since gone, but can be found on the Internet archive at www.archive.org

33. Sitchin [1990, 1995] p.328. "*It can be simply illustrated that when the planet's perihelion was in Cancer, its first appearance had to be from the direction of Sagittarius.*"

34. www.ambilac.com

35. *http://cob250.dn.net/members/panspermia/quickening.htm* No longer online - see www.archive.org

36. Middleton-Jones and Wilkie [2001]

37. See the article *Crystal Clear* (if only it was!) at *http://howardmj.freeyellow.com/page5.html*

38. Lehner [1997]

39. Ibid. p.108

40. *www.siloam.net/jenkins/ambilac.html*

41. *www.siloam.net/jenkins/ambilac.html*

42. Fulcanelli [1926, 1957]

43. Rayner Johnson [1980]

44. Weidner and Bridges [1999]

45. Ibid. p.177

46. *www.earthportals.com/earthportals/Portal_Market/timms.html*

47. Weidner and Bridges [1999] p.164

48. José Arguelles gives 1992 as the start of the final katun in the last baktun of the 13-baktun cycle, and this date is also mistakenly quoted by Weidner and Bridges... see Chapter 19, note 13.

49. Weidner and Bridges [1999] p.196

50. Ibid. p. 231

51. In *Stalking the Wild Pendulum* p.33-36 and 54-56, Bentov explains that in meditative states the breathing is so gentle that it no longer interferes with the feedback of the aorta, allowing the system to become resonant so that the whole body resonates at the same frequency as the Earth - 7.8 Hz. How this is affected by the increasing rate of Schumann Resonance remains to be researched.

52. For more on this, see the essay by Vincent Bridges, *Star Birth Bardo in the Body of Orion*: www.sangraal.com/bardorion.htm

53. Weidner and Bridges [1999] p.234

54. *http://vincentbridges.com/RaisingtheDjed.htm*

55. *www.vincentbridges.com/millennium/update.html*

56. 12,000 stadia - Rev. 21: 16

57. Weidner and Bridges [1999] See appendix G; pp.274-279 and:
www.sangraal.com/library/gnomon.htm

58. *www.vincentbridges.com/millennium/update.html*

59. Ibid.

60. *www.vincentbridges.com/update.html*

61. E-mail: 26th September 2002. Ian Crane said he was positioned approximately 100m due east of

the paws of the Sphinx at dawn on 22nd, 23rd and 24th September from 5.30 AM and saw nobody on the causeway up to the Great Pyramid, or in front of the Sphinx, so presumes that the Nicky Scully group were positioned on the plateau. He said, "*To be on the plateau at that hour of the morning would have either required a permit from the Egyptian Antiquities Department (Zahi Hawass and co.), or necessitated a large amount of baksheesh to have changed hands!*"

62. Gilbert [2000]

63. Ibid. p.262

64. June 21-22nd 2000 and also on June 29th 2000

65. Gilbert [2000] p.265. Or 2500 AD - the date of its highest altitude as stated in *The Orion Mystery*. Both these dates were calculated with *SkyGlobe* software. To see why they are wrong and why the *Last Time* is now, see note 17 of this chapter.

66. In *The Orion Mystery* by Gilbert and Bauval, the *First Time of Osiris* was called *Zep Tepi*, and Bauval and Hancock both call it *Zep Tepi* in later works, as do several other authors. However, Gilbert mistakenly reverses the phrase to *Tep Zepi* throughout this book.

67. Gilbert [2000] p.232. See Matt. 22 for the wedding garment parable, and also Rev. 19: 7-9 for the Wedding of the Lamb.

68. Jenkins [1998] p.389. Astronomers vary between 1998 and 1999 in their calculations of the exact time of the galactic alignment, so the end of the process varies between 2016 and 2017, with 2018 being the first definite year when the process is over.

69. Gilbert [2000] pp. 269-270

70. Geryl and Ratinckx [2001]

71. *www.diagnosis2012.co.uk/orp.htm*

72. The loop starts on 12th February 9389 BC.

73. The possibility of a correspondence between other stars in Orion (in addition to just those in Orion's belt) to pyramids on the ground is something that Bauval and Gilbert suggested in *The Orion Mystery*, (p.296-300 paperback edn.), but Bauval later admitted that only the correlation of the Giza pyramids to Orion's belt is convincing.

74. *http://ourworld.compuserve.com/homepages/dp5/pole1.htm*


## Chapter 9: The Geomagnetic Field

1. Braden [1993-1997] p.19

2. Various scientific websites confirm these claims of a declining magnetic field, though they differ in details - e.g. *Brittanica.com:*
*www.britannica.com/bcom/eb/article/6/0,5716,108976+16+106190,00.html*
This website says the average time between reversals is 300,000 to a million years, and takes 5,000 years to reverse, but it does shrink to zero during reversal, allowing entrance to cosmic rays that would cause mutations. *The Answer Man* (*www-spof.gsfc.nasa.gov/Education/FAQ.html*) says the average is every 500,000 years, and the last one was 700,000 years ago, and that the field strength has dropped 8% in the last 150 years. *Ask the Space Scientist* (*http://image.gsfc.nasa.gov/poetry/ask/amag.html*) says it reverses every 250,000 years, is decreasing at 0.07% per year and will be at zero in 4,000 years; the reversal can take less than 100 years, and the last one was 250,000 years ago; *American Scientist* (*www.sigmaxi.org/amsci/articles/96articles/Fuller.html*) says it was 780,000 years ago; *Science Frontiers* (*www.science-frontiers.com/sf041/sf041p13.htm* and *www.science-frontiers.com/sf101/sf101g11.htm*) says the Steens mountain volcanic record indicates that a 180° reversal took 4,500 years, but included

three periods of very rapid change; In *Earth Under Fire*, Dr Paul LaViolette says that the Steens mountain information shows that a reversal would take only two months; Andrew P. Roberts (*http://earth.agu.org/revgeophys/robera01/robera01.html*) suggests that confusion arises because people fail to differentiate between *"polarity transitions and excursions of the geomagnetic field"*; More recently, sources have been agreeing that the last reversal was 780,000 years ago, that the average time between reversals is 250,000 years, and that at the current rate it will be 1-2,000 years before a reversal, though some sources now admit that certain researchers say it could happen in a few weeks. The latter would be preferable, since that means we would not be without our protection from the solar wind for long.

3. The situation regarding Schumann Resonance is harder to answer. Scientists in USA and Western Europe are mostly saying it hasn't changed (Braden got his information from Russia and Norway), yet the climatology department of Arizona State University is using changing Schumann Resonance values as an accurate measure of global temperatures, so the jury is still out on this one.

4. There is disagreement as to whether this *"Gothenburg flip"* was just a local field change, or a full reversal; see note 10 of Chapter 8 above.

5. Braden [1993-1997] p.51. The Merkabah was the divine vehicle of light described by the Hebrew prophet Ezekiel as having the appearance of *"wheels within wheels,"* and made its first appearance in New Age literature in 1973 in J. J. Hurtak's *Keys of Enoch*, as combinations of interlocking pyramids: bi-pyramids or tri-pyramids, for example. Hurtak describes an *Order of Melchizedek*, who administer to Man through the Merkabah in order to prepare mankind for the *"fear-inspiring day of Jehovah, when the Sons of Light will appear"*(p.590). Merkabah meditation has now become a widespread practice, but in April 2000 Hurtak said in an interview that *"Sacred teaching like the Merkabah... is not given to those who wish 'instant nirvana' nor experiences based on multi-level marketing. In order to work universally through Merkabah, it requires the rigours of inner development, for some, over a whole lifetime, or many lifetimes, and is NOT in the realm of simple meditation and dream time experiences, which operate on a global as opposed to universal level."* (*www.lightnet.co.uk/informer/interviews/hurtak0004.htm*).

Hurtak's *The Keys of Enoch* describes five bodies that must be fully developed before the *Christ body* or *Overself body* can be worn. Only then can a Merkabah take his *"physical body and consciousness body"* off the planet for the next phase. See Hurtak [1977-1996] p.446. Bernard Perona, who changed his name to Drunvalo Melchizedek, claims to be the current authority on the *"Merkaba"*, as he spells it, and it is his version to which Braden is referring, but Melchizedek sent out a *"sequel to an open letter"* in January 2003, which said, *"The Melchizedek tradition does not teach, nor has it ever, that we spin the top tetrahedron one-way and the bottom one the other way. Anyone who has studied this work carefully knows this is not true. This is wrong, and I clearly say so."*

6. Braden [1993-1997] p.32

7. There is some evidence that the pyramid interacts with the geomagnetic field, since there is a patent registered in 1949 (*www.amasci.com/freenrg/tors/drbl.html*) with the Patent Office in Prague, Czechoslovakia for a cardboard replica of the Great Pyramid that will sharpen razor blades if they are put inside with the sharp edge facing East-West, while the pyramid is aligned North-South. However, this suggests an enhanced magnetic field rather than a reduced one. There are rumours that magnetometer readings in the King's chamber show a higher than background level (*www.sacredsites.com/2nd56/378.html*), but I have been unable to trace the source of this information as yet. There is, however, a very high radiation measurement in the King's chamber, since the granite walls under the weight of all the limestone exude radon gas, giving it a similar saturation to some stone chambers of Cornwall (Devereux [1990, 1999] pp. 194-197). Dr Paul Brunton experienced a stunning

spontaneous projection of the astral body when he spent the night in the King's Chamber (see Brunton [1935-1969] pp.57-78). Paul Devereux, who co-ordinated the *Dragon Project* - a study of energies at sacred sites - confirms that at the Rollright stone circle in Oxfordshire, there was "*some evidence growing of a fluctuating field within the circle relative to outside, changing over a period of hours*". Devereux [1990, 1999] p.91

8. Hutchison [1994]

9. *http://ebeltz.net/classes/histgeo3.html*

10. *www.telegraph.co.uk/connected/main.jhtml?xml=/connected/2002/04/17/ecfhead.xml*

11. Simulations performed by Dr Gary Glatzmaier of the University of California, Santa Cruz, and Dr Paul Roberts of UC, Los Angeles.

12. *http://observer.guardian.co.uk/international/story/0,6903,837058,00.html*

13. Ibid.

14. *http://news.bbc.co.uk/1/hi/sci/tech/2889127.stm*

15. LaViolette [1997] p.92

16. J.R.Petit, J. Jouzel et al. *Climate and atmospheric history of the past 420,000 years from the Vostok ice core in Antarctica, Nature* 399 (3 June, pp.429-436, 1999);

*www.nature.com/cgitaf/DynaPage.taf?file=/nature/journal/v399/n6735/full/399429a0_r.html&filetype*

17. *www.aist.go.jp/aist_e/new_research/20020329/20020329.html*

18. Published in the June 10 issue of *Earth and Planetary Science Letters* (Elsevier, volume 199, issues 3-4)

19. *www.eurekalert.org/pub_releases/2002-06/dc-1c060602.php*


## Chapter 10: Ice Cycles

1. Gaspar [1999]

2. Ibid. p.80

3. Ibid.

4. Allan and Delair [1995]

5. This differs by about 1,200 years from the estimate of astrophysicist Dr Paul LaViolette at 12,700 years ago with his Galactic Superwave theory in *Earth Under Fire*, and by 1,700 years from geologist Gregg Braden's Magnetic Reversal theory in *Awakening to Zero Point*. However, Allan and Delair concluded that the flood was caused by the close fly-by of a large planetoid. Unlike Sitchin, however, they don't suppose it to be on its way around an elliptical orbit, but instead consider it to have continued onwards to collide with the Sun. *Uriel's Machine*, by Knight and Lomas, concludes that the Earth was hit 9,640 years ago (7640 BC) by seven comet fragments, causing massive tidal waves, and that this was the date of Noah's flood. Andrew Collins has criticized Knight and Lomas (claiming that they failed to reference him as one of their sources), but Collins' own conclusion in his book *Gateway to Atlantis* is that the comet impact occurred 10,600-10,500 years ago (8600 - 8500 BC). Hapgood's model, according to Graham Hancock, puts the flood (caused by crustal displacement) at 14,500 BC to 12,500 BC, whereas Hancock himself goes for 10,500 BC (though since ice cores have now shown Antarctica to have been fully glaciated for much longer, Hancock no longer suggests Antarctica as the former Atlantis, and in *The Mars Mystery* he suggests that crustal displacement/the flood was triggered by comet or asteroid impact.

6. *www.homepage.montana.edu/~geol445/hyperglac/time1/milankov.htm*

7. Ibid.

8. *www.ngdc.noaa.gov/paleo/milankovitch.html*

9. *http://aa.usno.navy.mil/faq/docs/seasons_orbit.html*

10. Ibid.

11. There is a good explanation of the Milankovitch cycles at: *www.d.umn.edu/~hmooers/geology/Glacial_Geology/Notes2.pdf*

12. *www.atmos.washington.edu/1998Q4/211/project2/moana.htm*

13. It is on Adobe Acrobat software, and every time I try to download it I get half, then my computer crashes, so beware, but it is at: *http://allusions.wcp.muohio.edu/ClimateChangePrediction/ImminentClimateChg2000.pdf*

## Chapter 11: 0.0.0.0.0

1. Published in *The Express* on 13/3/99. *www.nunki.net/PerDud/TheWorks/Express/MountainArk.html*

2. Ibid.

3. Brotherston [1992] p.115

4. Furlong [1997]

5. Furlong's article (posted on his website) *What on Earth was Happening in 3100 BC?* sums up the cogent points: *www.kch42.dial.pipex.com/3100bc.htm*

6. *http://personal.eunet.fi/pp/tilmari/*

7. Baillie [1999]

8. Ibid. p.178

9. Ibid. p.179

10. *http://abob.libs.uga.edu/bobk/ccc/ce102103.html*

11. *http://abob.libs.uga.edu/bobk/ccc/cc111003.html*.  The quoted report about the work of Dr Lonnie Thompson of Ohio State University can be found at: *http://researchnews.osu.edu/archive/quelcoro.htm*

12. Hope [1990] p.221

13. Ibid. p.21

14. The ratio between solar and lunar years (1.0307) is where a sidereal year of 365.256 days is divided by a lunar year of 354.3672 days, made up of twelve synodic lunar months of 29.5306 days each.

15. Keene [2002]

16. Joel has three articles about these coincidences; *Cosmic Coincidences* (*www.diagnosis2012.co.uk/jjk.htm*), *Celestially Challenged* (*http://www.diagnosis2012.co.uk/jjk2.htm*) and *Continually Coordinating Circumstances* (*www.authorsden.com/visit/viewshortstory.asp?id=11420&AuthorID=10788*).

## Chapter 12: Fringe Science

1. *www.mirrorsedge.com/attop.htm*

2. *www.ascension2000.com/Shift-of-the-Ages/index.htm*

3. E-mail: 11th June 2001

4. *www.ascension2000.com/ConvergenceIII*

5. E-mail: 11th June 2001

6. *www.ascension2000.com or http://ascension2000.com*

7. *www.ascension2000.com/DivineCosmos*

8. Ibid.

9. 1997; updated in 1998. *www.tmgnow.com/repository/global/planetophysical.html*

10. *http://news.bbc.co.uk/2/hi/science/nature/3052467.stm*

11. *www.ascension2000.com/DivineCosmos/08.htm*

12. *www.ascension2000.com/09.28.03.htm*

13. *www.tmgnow.com/repository/global/planetophysical1.html*

14. *Some Lines of Investigations on Properties of Self-Luminous Formations Using a Model of Non-Homogenous Physical Domains* (*www.tmgnow.com/repository/solar/Dmitriev.html*) See also: *Electrogravidynamic Concept of Tornadoes* (*www.tmgnow.com/repository/planetary/tornado.html*) and *Planetophysical Function of Vacuum Domains*
(*www.tmgnow.com/repository/planetary/pfvd.html*)

15. *www.tmgnow.com/repository/global/planetophysical4.html*

16. Professor James McCanney and his Plasma Discharge Comet model, which predicts the arrival of Planet X "*sometime in the next ten years*"; in other words, 2002-2013. *www.jmccanneyscience.com*

17. Professor Sergey Smelyakov: *www.diagnosis2012.co.uk/sme3.htm*

18. *www.goldennumber.net*

19. E-mail: 28th May 2002

20. *www.timeofglobalshift.com/Science/Ulti_Secr.html*

21. *www.timeofglobalshift.com/Science/AMCC.pdf*

22. E-mail: 16th May 2002

23. E-mail: 19th May 2002

24. The Julian calendar preceded the Gregorian calendar and, as an alternative to back-calculating Gregorian dates, archaeologists often use Julian day numbers, avoiding the dreaded 'year zero' error, since the Julian calendar's zero point is in 4714 BC (Gregorian equivalent). The Julian day numbers correspond to a Julian date, which is different from the Gregorian. For example, the start-date for the 13-baktun cycle 0.0.0.0.0 is 11th August 3114 BC (in "*True Count*" correlation), back-calculated in the Gregorian calendar, but in the Julian calendar it was 6th September, on Julian day number 584283. To find the end-date from this Julian day number, just add 1,872,000 (the number of days in the 13-baktun cycle) to 584283 and you arrive at JD number 2456283. Then use the online converters or a table to find the Gregorian equivalent (21st December 2012). See *www.diagnosis2012.co.uk/mlink.htm* for online Julian Date and Julian Day calculators.

25. E-mail: 22nd May 2002

26. E-mail: 23rd May 2002

27. E-mail: 1st June 2002. I am not trying to boast that I out-thought a maths professor, just pointing out that he agreed that I had a good point, for reasons that become clear further on in the chapter. I have more recently re-read Karpenko and Smelyakov's paper and found that on pages 31-32 they remark that in their projection of Chinese population levels, which they use to cross-reference the Auric Time Scale, the levels theoretically spiral to infinity between 2036 and 2037. They point out that their calculation of the exact date of this - April 7th 2036 - has no real meaning, since their calculation was just an approximation.

28. *www.timeofglobalshift.com/Science/Ulti_Secr.html*

29. Russell [1982]

30. Russell [1992]

31. Ibid. p.200

32. Ibid. pp.202-203 & note
33. Russell [1992] p.205
34. Wilson R.A. [1982]
35. Ibid. p.29-32
36. Wilson R.A. [1990]
37. Ibid. p.17
38. Ibid. p.17
39. Wilson R.A. [1983] p.240
40. Wilson R.A. [1990] p.18
41. Atwater [1999]
42. Atwater [1999] p.215
43. Carey [1991] p.125
44. Ibid. p.125
45. Carey [1985] p.67
46. Carey [1991] p.128
47. Carey [1985] p.62
48. Ibid. p.54
49. Carey [1982] p.22
50. Carey [1982] p.22 and Carey [1991] p.47
51. It seems that Frank Waters, in *Mexico Mystique*, quoted the December 24th 2011 date from Michael Coe's book *The Maya* (1966), but in later works Coe used the *Lounsbury correlation* that fixes the 13-baktun end-point (13.0.0.0.0) as 23rd December 2012.
52. Carey [1982] p.22; Carey [1986] p.28; p.67; Carey [1991] p.47; p.159
53. Carey [1991] p.127

## Part 3: Beyond the Veil

1. Weidner and Bridges [1999] p.234

## Chapter 13: Shamanism

1. This is found today in the Sonoran desert of Mexico and should not to be confused with the Colorado cane toad, Bufo marines, or Bufo americanus, the venom from which only contains Bufotenine. Mexico *"represents without a doubt the world's richest area in diversity and use of hallucinogens in aboriginal societies."* Devereux [1997] p.105
2. While Bufotenine is also a tryptamine (5-hydroxy-DMT), its hallucinogenic effectiveness is disputed (see www.erowid.org)
3. Also called *Stropharia cubensis*
4. McKenna [1991]
5. *http://users.skynet.be/lightworkers-tempel/engvision.html*
6. E-mail: 3rd June 2004
7. Called adrenoglomerulotropine. McKenna [1975, 1993] 1993 edn. p.65
8. 6-methoxytetrahydroharman Naranjo [1967], quoted in McKenna [1975, 1993] 1993 edn. p.65

9. These are: tetrahydro-beta-carboline and 6-Methoxy-tetrahydro-beta-carboline (McKenna [1975, 1993] 1993 edn. p.97) and a possible third one, which has been synthesized from melatonin in vitro (in a test-tube): 6-methoxyharmalan: Naranjo [1967], quoted in McKenna [1975, 1993] 1993 edn. p. 65, which has also been said to be formed from Serotonin: Roney-Dougal [1997, 2002] p.101 quoting McIsaac, Khairallah and Page [1961]

10. Roney-Dougal [1997, 2002] 2002 edn. p.101. Pinoline is the second compound in note 8 above: 6-MeOTHBC for short.

11. Guichhait RB [1976]: pp.187-190, quoted by Ananda at *www.akasha.de/~aton/NeoDMT.html* and see also *www.inclusivescience.org/pinealproject.htm*

12. *www.diagnosis2012.co.uk/dmt.htm*

13. Strassman [2001]

14. Caroline Taylor's review of *DMT: The Spirit Molecule: www.diagnosis2012.co.uk/dmt.htm*

15. *www.diagnosis2012.co.uk/dmt.htm*

16. Roney-Dougal [1997, 2002]

17. Ibid. p.100

18. Ibid. p.139

19. Ibid.

20. Ibid.

21. Devereux [1990, 1999] pp.129-130

22. Ibid. p.63

23. Roney-Dougal [1997, 2002] pp.140-141

24. Ibid. pp.140-142

25. *www.akasha.de/~aton/NeoDMT.html*

26. *http://phoenix.akasha.de/~aton/Unidance.html*

27. *http://phoenix.akasha.de/~aton/CV.html*

28. *www.akasha.de/~aton/NeoDMT.html*

29. Ibid.

30. A special attention to diet is necessary because beta-carbolines inhibit a substance called MAO: monoamino-oxidase, which protects us from the effects of tyramine, which is in many foods and normally rendered harmless by MAO. This is why shamans usually go on a fast before taking ayahuasca. *www.erowid.org/chemicals/maois/maois_info2.shtml*

31. Callaway [1988]

32. Airaksinen M. M. *et al* [1991] and [1993]

33. Callaway [1988]

34. These will include *The Soma Conspiracy*, about inner and outer alchemy, *The Rig Veda*, in which Ananda has just discovered a 2012 connection, and a PDF online version of *Unity Keys of Emmanuel*. See *2012 Books* webpage for updated information: *www.diagnosis2012.co.uk/books.htm*

35. From *Ananda's Grailzine Newsletter*, September 2003

36. Original web address: *www.psychonaut.org* may be archived at the Internet Archive: *http://web.archive.org* or go to *www.diagnosis2012.co.uk/new5.htm#rue* for more information

37. Original web address: *www.psychonaut.org/psilo/mushroom3.htm*. See note 35

38. Original web address: *www.psychonaut.org/psilo/mushroom4.htm*. See note 35

39. Original web address: *www.psychonaut.org/psilo/mushroom5.htm*. See note 35

40. E-mail: 15th February 2002

41. Ibid.

42. E-mail: 12th May 2002

43. Canul replied to my article in *Salvia Divinorum Magazine - Salvia Divinorum: Key to the Paradigm Shift in 2012*. The reply thread follows the article. *www.salvia.us/magazine/viewtopic.php?p=9#9*
44. *www.diagnosis2012.co.uk/new5.htm#salvia*
45. E-mail: 7th July 2003


## Chapter 14: Other Altered States

1. *http://members.aol.com/yesloveisgod/says/prophecy3.html*
2. Ibid.
3. Ibid.
4. Kalb [1998]
5. The NDE of Mellen-Thomas Benedict lasted for at least an hour and a half, verified as an hour and a half from the time the body was discovered by Benedict's hospital caretaker, using a stethoscope, blood-pressure readings and heart-rate monitor. Whether this counts as *"clinically-documented"* or not is unknown. See *www.near-death.com/experiences/reincarnation04.html*
6. Brinkley [1994, 1995]
7. *www.mikepettigrew.com/afterlife/html/dannion.html*
8. Ibid.
9. *www.inlightimes.com/archives/2-Dannion-Brinkley.htm*
10. *www.inlightimes.com/1999/12-99/dannion.htm*
11. *www.gracemillennium.com/spring01/pmh.htm*
12. The concept of seven root races, which relate to the development of the seven chakras, was brought to the west via Madam Blavatsky, and also used by Rudolph Steiner and Edgar Cayce. The base chakra was developed in the first root race, the Polarians; then came the Hyperboreans, then the Lemurians, then the Atlanteans and then the Aryans (nothing to do with Nazi beliefs). Since each chakra relates to a colour, the current outbreak of psychic children, known as 'Indigo children' due to the colour of their aura, is taken by many to be a sign of a coming transition to the sixth root race. Indigo relates to the colour of the sixth chakra, the Ajna or Pineal Eye. Atwater originally put the start of the fifth root race around the time of Christ, whereas other sources put it much further back - her more recent work now concurs with this. Each root race has seven sub-races, and we are said to be in the fifth sub-race. The implication is that we may simply be at the juncture of the fifth and sixth sub-races. The next sub-race is called *"Nova men"*. See *www.kheper.net/topics/Theosophy/root_races.html* for more information. For information on psychic/Indigo children, see *www.psychicchildren.co.uk*
13. *www.geocities.com/nulliusinverba/AR3.htm*
14. *www.happycampnews.com/coast2coast/2001_12_02_archives.html*
15. *www.soundwellness.com/ofrank/of/of2doc/ParApocalyp.html*
16. *www.religionen.at/irsilverb01.htm#top*
17. LaBerge [1998] p.61
18. *www.lucidity.com/LucidDreamingFAQ2.html#OBE*
19. Harary & Weintraub [1990] pp.89-90
20. See discussion at *www.robertpeterson.org/obe-vs-lucid.html*
21. *www.dreamofpeace.net*
22. *http://pub53.ezboard.com/fsorceryfrm26.showMessage?topicID=158.topic*. This webpage is no longer online - nor is it available at the web archive, but there is a slightly differently-worded version of the same dream here: *www.tortuga.com/cgi-bin/ikonboard.pl?s=406be92d029cffff;act=ST;f=1;t=458*

23. *www.dreamofpeace.net/sealife/viewtopic.php?t=1175*   Find all relevant links at: *www.diagnosis2012.co.uk/7.htm/dream*

24. Dream dates to 28th November 1998. *http://sstoth0.tripod.com/dreamimages/id26.html*

25. *www.cropcircleresearch.com/thoth/dream_pv0001.html*

26. *www.greatdreams.com*

27. *www.womenandwisdom.org/article1.shtml*

28. Karpinski [2001]

29. Karpinski [2001] p.31

30. Weldon [2003]

31. Clow [2001]

32. Allan and Delair [1995]

33. *www.hindustantimes.com/news/181_72097,001100010001.htm*

34. Ibid.

## Chapter 15: UFOs and ETs

1. Video footage: *Messengers of Destiny* - 1991-1992 footage (50 + clips); *Masters of the Stars* - 1992-1993 footage (55 + clips); and *Voyagers of the Sixth Sun* - 1993-1996 footage (90 + clips), by Genesis 111.

2. *www.diagnosis2012.co.uk/new4.htm#dresden*

3. Mike Finley's website is called *The Real Maya Prophecies: Astronomy in the Inscriptions and Codices* and can be found at: *http://members.shaw.ca/mjfinley/mainmaya.html*

4. *www.diagnosis2012.co.uk/new4.htm#dresden*

5. E-mail: 15th October 2002

6. *UFO Reality* Issue 7, April/May 1997

7. Ibid.

8. Ibid.

9. Ibid.

10. *UFO Reality* Issue 4, October/November 1996

11. Hurtak [1977-1996]. This book is also listed in Arguelles' bibliography, so that is possibly why some of the *TUMI* column sounds familiar, although by the time the magazine was published, Jon King (living in Glastonbury) would have been familiar with Arguelles' *The Mayan Factor*.

12. *UFO Reality* Issue 1, April/May 1996

13. Ibid.

14. Ibid.

15. William and Birnes [2000] pp.234-235. See also this quote of an article by Bill Hamilton, Pam's husband, though it says the prediction was for 2011: *www.noveltynet.org/content/paranormal/www.brotherblue.org/libers/pamsrep.htm*

16. *UFO Reality* Issue 4, October/November 1996

17. Conversation with the author, August 2003

18. *UFO Reality* Issue 4, October/November 1996

19. Ibid.

20. *UFO Reality* Issue 5, December/January 1997

21. Ibid.

22. *http://www.karinya.com/watchers.htm*

23. Ibid.

## Chapter 16: Crop Circles

1. Thomas [1998, 2002]
2. Davis [1992] p.53
3. Wilson [1990] p.17 and *www.rawilson.com/trigger2.shtml*
4. *Chambers's 20th Century Dictionary*
5. e.g. 'The Maltese Cross', Morestead, Hampshire, 1997
6. Séjourné [1957, 1978] and Waters [1975, 1989]
7. Wilson T. [1998]
8. Waters [1975, 1989] p.180
9. Look out for the forthcoming animation with accompanying booklet - *Secrets of the Sunstone* (see *www.diagnosis2012.co.uk*)
10. Men [1990] p.34
11. Lucy Pringle's website: *http://home.clara.net/lucypringle*
12. Thomas (Ed) [1999]
13. Thomas [1998, 2002]
14. Thomas [1998, 2002] 2002 edn. p.80
15. *www.kachina.net/~alunajoy/*
16. *www.kachina.net/~alunajoy/98july.html*
17. *www.swirlednews.com/article.asp?artID=110*
18. Boerman [2000]
19. Michel [1969]
20. Alford [1996] p.588
21. Ibid.
22. Alford calculated a date for the Great Flood, using Babylonian and Sumerian mythology, as 10,983 BC. He says that this is the date that precession started - in other words, the Earth's angle of tilt was perpendicular to its orbit around the Sun until 10,983 BC, when a close pass of Nibiru caused an axis shift and the subsequent flood. After this, Alford says that the *Sars*, or ages of Sumeria (each ruled by a different god), changed from 3,600 years to 2,160 years, which is one zodiac age, or a twelfth of the classic precessional cycle of 25,920 years. He also points out the strange fact that 2,160 - the length of a zodiacal age - is 3-6-0-0 when written in the sexagesimal Sumerian system, yet implies that Nibiru is still on a 3,600-year orbit, although he admits that it might have been forced "*into a slightly different orbit*" (Alford [1996] p.569). This means that, working forward, the next pass of Nibiru is due in 3,418 AD (adding a year to compensate for the missing year zero). However, if Nibiru's orbit changed to 2,160 years, as could be implied by all Alford's information, then when would the next pass be? 1978 AD is the answer (adding a year to compensate for the missing year zero), and since it didn't come then, that can't be right. But Alford calculated that the next precessional age starts in 2012 (Alford [1996] pp.586-588) using the current value of precession (25,776 years, as suggested by Egyptologist Jane Sellers). So, how did he work that out? One current zodiac age is a twelfth of 25,776 years, and works out as 2,148 years. But before calculating, we have to take into account the 108-year delay or *destiny determining time* (Alford [1996] p.333; pp.355-356; p.359; p.360; p.366; p.368). This phrase comes from the Sumerian *Lugal-e* text quoted by Sitchin (*The Wars of Gods and Men*, p.165) and tells that Nergal was sent to tell Marduk that he had returned to Babylon too early, since his destiny determining time was not yet due. Alford says the discrepancy alluded to here is 108 years, because 108 years is 1.5° of precessional movement (72 + 36), which he feels is the minimum time needed to detect the precession cycle (pp. 358-359). If we start at Alford's date for the flood at 10,983 BC and subtract the 108 years, we

get 10,875 BC. So, six Sars of 2,148 years each (12,888 years) after this corrected date for Marduk's destiny determining time brings us to 2013, except we have to add another year to compensate for the missing year zero, as in all calculations across the BC-AD divide (due to the fact that the year after Jesus' hypothetical birth was 1 AD and the year before was 1 BC - your calculator allows for a zero that isn't there, so it must be added on somewhere). In other words, using Alford's figures, we get 2014, not 2012. Oh dear, it's two years out! So how did Alan Alford get 2012? The calculation is given on page 662, note 58: "*10983 BC - 107 = 10,876 BC*". He mistakenly used the number 107, when he had already stated three times that it should be 108 (Alford [1996] p.359; p.366; p.368). Alford's second error was that he forgot about the missing year zero, so we have to add yet another year to the calculation (Alford [1996]). On p.457 and p.458, he says the 13-baktun cycle began in 3113 BC, which he may have used to back-calculate his original flood date. If he did use 3113 BC to back-calculate, then all his BC dates will be Gregorian astronomical dates, so no compensation for the missing year zero is necessary, and his calculation will only be a year out.

23. The variation of the obliquity of the ecliptic, or axis tilt cycle, causes the length of the precession of the equinoxes to vary over time. 2,160 + 2,158 + 2,156 + 2,154 + 2,152 + 2,150 represents the cumulative years of six zodiacal ages, while precession is changing from 2,160 years per zodiac age to 2148.


## Chapter 17: Secret Government

1. Berlitz and Moore [1979]
2. Ibid. pp.115-116 & pp.165-166
3. Ibid. p.15 & p.176
4. *http://home.inreach.com/dov/ttstrnge.htm* is no longer online, but can be found at the web archive here: *web.archive.org/web/20020202055415/http://home.inreach.com/dov/ttstrnge.htm*. Gibbs now has his own website at *www.hdrenterprises.net*, but a much better display of his products is here; *www.futurehorizons.net/time.htm*. For more on do-it-yourself time machines, see this incredible page: *www.keelynet.com/energy/dimshift.htm*
5. *www.futurehorizons.net/time.htm*
6. *www.allthingsspooky.com/letter.html* (this is an alternative to the archived address at note 4)
7. Frissell [1994]
8. *www.freezone.de/english/mc/e_conv04.htm*
9. Ibid.
10. *www.2013.com*
11. *www.2013.com/faq*
12. Ibid.
13. Interview with Art Bell on January 30th 1997
14. *http://mindcontrolforums.com/hambone/dame0197.html*
15. Ibid.

## Chapter 18: Nostradamus

1. Cheetham [1973-1976]
2. Ibid. p.417

3. *http://members.nbci.com/centuries/future.html*. Now offline and unfortunately not on the Internet Archive.

4. Ibid.

5. Hogue [1997]

6. Rev 6: 13; Rev 8: 7; Rev 11: 19; Rev 12: 4; Rev 15: 21

7. Rev 8: 5; Rev 8: 8; Rev 8: 10-11; Rev 9: 1

8. Rev 6: 12; Rev 8: 5; Rev 11: 13; Rev 16: 18

9. Quatrains 1:69; 2:15; 2:41; 2:43; 2:46; 2:62; 4:67; 5:32; 6:6

10. Quatrains 2:18; 2:81; 2:92; 2:96; 4:100; 5:98; 6:97; 8:2; 8:10; 8:77

11. Quatrains 1:87; 6.66; 9:31; 9:83; 10:67

12. www.geocities.com/Athens/Atrium/3933/2003-2012page.htm

13. www.escape666.com/nostindex.htm

14. www.home.mastersites.com/kingofterror

15. Dimde [2001]

16. www.tmgnow.com/repository/cometary/76P_phobos1.html

17. Ibid.

18. Ibid.

19. *http://petragrail.tripod.com/codes.html*

20. www.angelfire.com/wizard/magick2/2.html and www.angelfire.com/rebellion/newworld_1/666.html

21. Ibid.

22. Cheetham [1973-1976] p.417

23. *http://howardmj.freeyellow.com/page5.html*

24. www3.telus.net/themist/myrddin.htm

25. Rev 6: 12

26. Rev 6: 12

27. Rev 6: 13

28. *http://sunearth.gsfc.nasa.gov/eclipse/SEcat/SEdecade2011.html* and www.eclipse.co.uk/solarspirit/solar_sequence3.htm

29. The American format for dates is month, day, year, while the British format is day, month, year. In this way, a quick glance at the end-date of 12/21/12 can be confused with 21/12/12, especially if you also confuse the start-date, when day number one (the day after 0.0.0.0.0) was 12th August 3114 BC.

30. www.nostradamus-repository.org/shipton.html

31. www.wilders.force9.co.uk/BeyondEarth/comets.htm and www.mkzdk.org/hammer/hammer.html

## Chapter 19: New Age

1. *http://www.aquarian-age.net*

2. The statement is as follows: *"While acknowledging the zero point of the zodiac to be defined as the point where the true galactic equator crosses the ecliptic between Taurus and Gemini, and recognizing the J2000 galactic equator defined by the galactic north pole of 12h 51.4m, 27° 8' to be representative of the B1950 definition of the galactic coordinate system, by virtue of Sagittarius A\* being recognized as the dynamical centre of the galaxy with the true galactic equator passing through Sagittarius A\*, and by virtue of the Sun being at 90° 00' 32" past the point of the crossing of the J2000 galactic equator and the ecliptic at the Spring Equinox of 20 March 2000, 0735 GMT, we declare*

*the Age of Aquarius to have unequivocally arrived. Pax Aetatis Aquarii vobiscum!"*

3. http://www.aquarian-age.net

4. From *Testimony Magazine* - www.testimony-magazine.org/back/jun2001/piperov.pdf

5. http://ancientegypt.hypermart.net

6. E-mail: 24th July 2001

7. Clow [2001]

8. Clow and Fletcher's calculations forget about the lack of a year zero in our calendar, so they are both a year out.

9. E-mail from Vincent Bridges 12th May 2001

10. See especially Stanley Messenger's articles, *Lucifer and Ahriman under the Bed* www.isleofavalon.co.uk/GlastonburyArchive/messenger/sm-lucifer.html and *Crop Circles as a Path From Space into Time* (2), www.isleofavalon.co.uk/GlastonburyArchive/messenger/sm-ccircles2.html

11. Watson [1979, 1980] pp.174-177. 'Hundredth monkey' is a term that caught on after Lyall Watson described some behaviour changes of monkeys on a Japanese island. One female discovered that washing the sweet potatoes in the sea, to clean them and add a salty flavour, made them much more palatable. Over several months, other monkeys slowly began to copy her, until one day, a critical number was reached (the 'hundredth' monkey), and by the end of that day, *all* the monkeys on *all* the islands - without any physical communication having taken place between them - changed their behaviour permanently to the washing of potatoes before eating them.

12. E-mail: 1st June 2001

13. José Arguelles gives "1992" as the start of the final katun in the last baktun of the 13-baktun cycle, and this date is quoted by Weidner and Bridges in their book *A Monument to the End of Time* on page 173 - but they have confirmed to me that this page is flawed, since they agree that the last katun started in April 1993 (e-mail from Vincent Bridges, 12th May 2001). Unfortunately, the error is also repeated on p.335 of the new revised and expanded edition, *The Mysteries of the Great Cross of Hendaye*. However, in the Long Count correlation invented by Carl Calleman - the *Calleman correlation* - the final katun begins on February 10th 1992. In Calleman's system, the 13-baktun cycle ends on October 28th 2011, not December 21st 2012. There is more on this later in the chapter.

14. www.nvisible.com

15. http://aa.usno.navy.mil/data/docs/EarthSeasons.html

16. Arguelles [1987] p.154

17. Ibid. p.158

18. But it might just be that they have both been influenced by Hurtak's *The Keys of Enoch* - cited by Arguelles in his bibliography - see note 11 of Chapter 15.

19. *UFO Reality* Issue 7, April/May 1997 and Issue 8, June/July 1997.

20. Arguelles [1987] p.194

21. For example: *1)* (p.45; p.110) *The Mayan Factor* says that the zero day of the Long Count was in 3113 BC instead of 3114 BC. 3113 BC is only correct if viewed as an astronomical date, implying that an extra year has been substituted for the missing year zero, to ease calculation across the BC/AD divide. Since the references at the back of *The Mayan Factor* include several books by J. Eric. S. Thompson, one of these was probably the source. Thompson wrote these books in the 1950s and 1960s, and since then the convention for indicating astronomical dates has been updated to using a negative determinant, such that *3113 BC astronomical* is now written as *year -3113*. This is equivalent to *3114 BC historical*, but many readers would simply have misunderstood the start-date as *3113 BC historical*. This was most certainly the cause of the one-year error in Sergey Smelyakov's *The Auric Time Scale*, as Smelyakov uses Arguelles' *The Mayan Factor* as the main source of information on Maya calendrics.

**Error = +368 days**. *2)* On p.29, *The Mayan Factor* says that Good Friday in 1519 was the day 1 Reed in the Aztec calendar (1 Ben in the Maya); this is an **error of +12 days**, since 1 Reed was on 4th May Julian (JD) or 14th May in the Gregorian calendar (GD), and Good Friday occurred on 22nd April (JD) or 2nd May (GD). Good Friday actually occurred on the day 2 Imix (Alligator) according to the True Count. *3)* On p.131, *The Mayan Factor* says that 20th June 1986 was the tzolkin day 10 Ben, whereas it was actually the day 8 Kawak in the True Count. This is an **error of +54 days**. *4)* On p.131, *The Mayan Factor* says that 20th June 1986 was the haab day 9 Kayeb, whereas it was actually 12 Zotz. This is an **error of -108 days**. *5)* On p.131, *The Mayan Factor* also says that 20th June 1986 was the Long Count date 12.18.14.18.9, whereas it was actually 12.18.13.1.19. This is an **error of +690 days**. *6)* On p.131, *The Mayan Factor* says that 20th June 1986 was 1,862,599 days after zero-day, whereas it was actually 1,862,319 days after zero-day. This is an **error of +280 days**. *7)* On p.148, and p.169, *The Mayan Factor* says that the first day of Harmonic Convergence, 16th August 1987, was day number 1,863,022, after the zero-day, whereas it was actually day number 1,862,741 after zero-day. This is an **error of +281 days**. Anyone using the Long Count figures or the Day numbers above to calculate forward to the end of the Long Count, would calculate the end-point (day 13.0.0.0.0. or 1,872,000 days after zero day) to be 16th March 2012, 15th March 2012, or 31st January 2011. *8)* On p.196, *The Mayan Factor* says that 8th October 1986 was the tzolkin day 1 Imix, whereas in the True Count, this was the tzolkin day 12 Manik. This is an **error of +52 days**. *9)* On p.196, *The Mayan Factor* says that 8th October 1986 was the day 12 Zotz in the haab calendar, whereas it was actually 0 Yax. This is an **error of -110 days**. *10)* Final Katun: On p.161, 179 and 200, *The Mayan Factor* says that the final (260th) katun of the 13-baktun cycle will start in 1992. In *Dreamspell*, he later refines this to July 26th 1992. It actually started on April 5th 1993. A katun is 7,200 days - approximately 19.72 years, not twenty years! This is an **error of -254 days**. *11)* Harmonic Convergence: Tony Shearer first calculated Harmonic Convergence as being nine 52-year *Hell cycles* after the arrival of Cortés (interpreted as the return of Quetzalcoatl by the Aztecs), which he took as 21st April 1519 (JD), the day before Good Friday. He calculated that 9 x 365.25 x 52 days (or 170,937 days) after Cortés's arrival would be August 16th 1987. However, the answer should have been 21st April 1987 JD, which is 4th May 1987 in the Gregorian calendar. But this is just the first error, since Hell cycles are Calendar Rounds, which are each 52 haabs in length, and a haab is a 365-day year, not the 365.25-day Julian year. This means there was an **error of +117 days** (there are 117 leap days in 52 x 9, or 468 years), and the end of the nine Hell cycles should have been 117 days earlier, which is 25th December 1986 (JD) or 7th January 1987 (GD). Shearer should have used 9 x 52 x 365 days, or 170,820 days. Instead of adjusting 117 days back, the date was adjusted 117 days forward from 21st April 1987 (JD) to 16th August 1987, but this was taken as a Gregorian date, rather than a Julian date. This seemed to be a meaningful date, because in the correlation Shearer was using (*corr#584284*, or one day away from the True Count), August 16th 1987 was the day 13 Ahau, which is the *"last day"* in the tzolkin. The 17th August 1987 was thus (in the 584284 correlation) the day 1 Imix, or the *"first day"* of the tzolkin. So, Harmonic Convergence should have been on 25th December 1986 (JD) or 7th January 1987 (GD). **Total error = +221 days** or (2 x 117) - 13 (where 13 is the accumulated difference between Julian and Gregorian dates).

Some people who have tried to understand how Harmonic Convergence was calculated have concluded that it must have been calculated from the day that Cortés met the Aztec emperor Moctezuma, since, coincidentally, this happened 117 days after 21st April (when he landed), on August 16th 1519 (JD). Exactly 468 Julian years later (9 x 52 Julian years, or 170,937 days) would be August 16th 1987. This calculation incorporates both errors of 117 days and the Gregorian/Julian error.

Arguelles used Shearer's calculation for Harmonic Convergence, but subsequently developed an Aztec/Maya-based calendar system called *Dreamspell*, that used the same 54-day error tzolkin count featured in *The Mayan Factor*, p.131 (see above). This system ignores the leap-year day of February 29th every four years, and the result is that the 54-day error is reducing by one day every four years. In March 2004, the error was down to 49 days. In the *Dreamspell* count, Harmonic Convergence 16/17th August 1987 happened on the days 3 Men and 4 Cib, which means that all the meaning involved in calculation of Harmonic Convergence as 13 Ahau and 1 Imix - as the start/end of the tzolkin - is lost.

In his *Response to the Count Controversy*, Arguelles says, "*The Harmonic Convergence*, The Mayan Factor, and the Dreamspell *are all based on the July 26 synchronization date. It was by following the calendar based on this synchronization date that I was able to verify the Harmonic Convergence as a test of Mayan time science.*" We can only presume that he is referring to the next 26th July after Harmonic Convergence - 26th July 1988 - which was 13 Reed (Ben) in the Dreamspell Count. However, this was a meaningful day to the Aztecs - not the Maya. (*www.resonateview.org/places/writings/mayan/joseres.htm*) See also *Investigating the Origins of Dreamspell*: *www.diagnosis2012.co.uk/dspell.htm*

22. Arguelles [1987] p.194
23. *www.beyond-the-illusion.com/files/Orvotron/Newsletters/92marapr.txt*. Halfway down the page, repeated from a 1981 article in the Australian *Flying Saucer Research Magazine*.
24. Ibid.
25. Ibid.
26. Ibid.
27. Erbe [1991]
28. Ibid. p.225
29. Ibid.
30. Since the Betty and Barney Hill case - the first ever recorded alien abduction with subsequent hypnotic regression - happened in September 1961.
31. Azena [1991]
32. Essene and Nidle [1994]
33. Ibid. p.53
34. See Roberto Solarion for more on this - he thinks the Sirian Nibiru will return in 2012: *www.apollonius.net/sirius.html*
35. *www.straightdope.com/classics/a4_042.html*
36. This is the hardback version; for other versions, we are talking about Key 1-0-8; 32
37. Hurtak [1977-1996] p.78
38. Ibid. p.79
39. *www.cassiopaea.org*
40. *www.vincentbridges.com/cassiopaea.html* and *www.cassiopaea.net*
41. Calleman [2001] p.207
42. Ibid. p.75
43. From the accompanying Calendar Round date of 4 Ahau 8 Kumku, Mayanists know this refers to the start of the current 13-baktun cycle in 3114 BC
44. *www.wilsonsalmanac.com/converg.html* or *www.alley29.com/Sphinx%20Group/calendar.html*
45. *http://edj.net/mc2012/calleman.htm*
46. Calleman [2001] p.157
47. Calleman's reason for correlating the start-point to June 17th 3115 BC was that the creation story of Palenque said that the solar god *First Father* had his seventh birthday the previous day. Ibid. p.236
48. Ibid. p.206. Table 6 and Fig. 27, both on p.77 of Calleman's book *The Mayan Calendar*, each indicate a different length for the *Universal Underworld* (the highest level of the pyramid). Table 6 says it is 13 x 20 kin (260 days) and Fig. 27 says it is 13 x 18 kin (234 days).

49. *www.diagnosis2012.co.uk/jmj.htm*

50. The debate is accessible from the index page of *www.diagnosis2012.co.uk* and see the readers' responses at John Major Jenkins' site *Alignment 2012.com* (*www.alignment2012.com/fiasco.html*)

51. Scallion [1997]

52. Ibid. p.226

53. *www.citilink.com/~mjfitz/gmscallion.htm* and *End-Time Visions - the Road to Armageddon* by Richard Abanes p.53-56

54. Morton and Thomas [1997]

55. Ibid. p.143

56. Ibid. pp.322-323

57. Ibid. p.349

58. 52 haabs of 365 days makes a Calendar Round, and nine of these add to 170,820 days. If we count that number of days forward from the day that Cortés landed, we come to 7th January 1987 in the Gregorian calendar - an error of 221 days.   See note 21 for more.

59. See note 21 of this chapter.

60. *www.earthportals.com/Portal_Messenger/josevotan.html*

61. *www.dplanet.ch/users/prkoenig/staley/nema10.htm*

62. *http://homepage.sunrise.ch/homepage/prkoenig/nema13.htm*

63. Carroll [1992]

64. *www.crossroads.wild.net.au/index.html*

65. *www.crossroads.wild.net.au/zuv.htm*

66. *www.crossroads.wild.net.au/lib13.htm*

67. Ibid.

68. Andahadna [1976], quoted in Grant [1980]. She is also known as Maggie Cassady and Margarete Ingalls. See *www.hermetic.com/wisdom/pennae_praenumbra.html*

69. According to most Thelemites, we have been in the *Aeon of Horus* since 1904, when Crowley received *The Book of the Law*. See her book *Maat Magick: Nema* [1995]

70. Grant [1980] p.242

71. Ibid. p.185, quoting Andahadna in an unpublished paper on the Mysteries of Maat.

72. Ibid.

## Part 4: Diagnosis

1. McKenna [1975, 1993] p.106

## Chapter 20: Analysis

1. The 2011 end-date was inherited from Frank Waters' 1975 book *Mexico Mystique*, which in turn got the start date from *The Maya* by Michael Coe (1966). The start date of 3113 BC should have said *year -3113*, or should have clarified that it referred to *3113 BC astronomical*, as opposed to *3113 BC historical*. To get an end-date of 2011, you would think the calculation must have been made from a 3115 BC start point, which is equivalent to year -3114 (*3114 BC astronomical*), but it is probably just a case of error due to the missing year zero: 3113 + 2011 + a missing year = 5,125 years, whereas the

correct calculation is either the historical one (3114 + 2012 = 5,126 minus year zero = 5,125) or the astronomical one (3113 + 2012 = 5,125).

2. *http://members.shaw.ca/mjfinley/calnote.htm*

3. *www.traditionalstudies.org/journal/s_america/aztec.html*

4. I used the free *Geditcom* date calculator for this calculation. Download it at: *www.geditcom.com/DateCalc.html* Another version of this Nine Hells cycle was revealed by Patricio Dominguez at the Confederation of Indigenous Elders of America, in which he said that the Nine Hells started in 1517 when the Spanish landed in the land of the Maya, and ended in 1985. See *www.diagnosis2012.co.uk/books2.htm*

5. Mini [1998]

6. John Mini hints (Mini [1998]) that the day 13 Reed represents the end of the Fifth Sun, and that it was on August 13th 1999 (hence its position among the snake rattles, which are a warning). He probably arrived at this date by counting the twelve years from 87 to 99 (if 87 = 1 Reed, 88 = 2 Knife, 89 = 3 House, 90 = 4 Rabbit, 91 = 5 Reed... 99 = 13 Reed), then subtracting three days from August 16th, to compensate for the three intervening leap days. Day 13 Reed in Year 13 Reed does work out as 1999, but either 17th January 1999 or 4th October 1999, not August 13th. Mini also said on p.173 that there are only eight dots on each of the fire-snake segments surrounding the Aztec Sunstone, and included a fold-out diagram at the back of the book showing only eight dots per segment. It is plain, even by looking at a photo of the *real* Sunstone, that there are 10 dots per segment.

7. See these sources: *http://users.pandora.be/gohiyuhi/frauds/index.htm* and *www.iktome.freewebsites.com*

8. *www.thefourwinds.com/AProphecy.html*

9. Arguelles [1987] pp.161, 179, 200

10. E-mail: 15th June 2003

11. *www.alignment2012.com/mproph.htm*

12. Gilbert and Cotterell [1995] pp.249-250

13. Now re-named as *The Mystery of The Great Cross of Hendaye: Alchemy and the End of Time* in a new updated and expanded edition. Weidner and Bridges [2003].

14. LaViolette [1997] p.104

15. Now online again at *www.etheric.com/LaViolette/Disinformation.html*

16. E-mail: 1st September 2000

17. *http://therealmidori.tripod.com/disaster.html*

18. *www.earthchangestv.com/mitch/november_2003/05flare.htm*

19. *http://news.bbc.co.uk/1/hi/sci/tech/3515788.stm*

20. *www.newscientist.com/news/news.jsp?id=ns99994321*

21. *http://news.bbc.co.uk/2/hi/science/nature/3869753.stm* and *http://reports.discoverychannel.ca/servlet/an/discovery/1/20060503/discovery_solar_storm_060505/20060504?hub=DiscoveryReport*

22. *www.spacedaily.com/news/milkyway-03a.html* See also *http://spaceflightnow.com/news/n0308/10ulysses/*

23. *www.spacedaily.com/news/milkyway-03b.html*

24. Clow [1995] p.47

25. Men [1983]

26. See *Exploding the Myth of the Photon Belt*: *www.worldlightfellowship.org/classes/photon_belt.htm* *www.diagnosis2012.co.uk/blt1.htm*

27. *The Physics of Crop Formations*: *www.diagnosis2012.co.uk/blt2.htm*, best read after Nancy Talbott's *Crop Circle Analysis Shows That Most are not Hoaxes* at: *www.diagnosis2012.co.uk/blt1.htm*

28. *www.diagnosis2012.co.uk/blt2.htm*

29. Ibid. The highest concentration of meteoritic dust - about 100 times normal soil concentration - was found at a crop formation known as the *"H-Glaze formation"* at Yatesbury, Wiltshire in 1993, and studies on samples from this contributed to BLT's conclusions. However, a more recent scientific study by R. Ashby (Jan 2005) at *www.xstreamscience.org* concludes that the formation was hoaxed by paranormal debunker Rob Irving. Irving supplied a sample of the powdered iron consisting of microscopic spheres that he claimed to have used, and this was used on crop and chalk samples that were subjected to similar conditions that existed when the pattern appeared. This produced results that were very similar to those found in the formation. However, Burke says that about twenty other formations yielded similar *"meteoric dust"* of at least twenty times normal soil concentration, and these were distributed over thirteen states of the USA and five countries, and were clearly nothing to do with Irving.

30. Vallee [1970]

31. *www.tmgnow.com/repository/planetary/pfvd.html*

32. *http://hessdalen.hiof.no/reports/*

33. When radar was first invented, these invisible blobs were known as *"radar angels"*, and some radar equipment was modified to filter them out.

34. *http://dwij.org/pathfinders/linda_moulton_howe/linda_mh9.htm*

35. *www.earthfiles.com/news/news.cfm?ID=164&category=Real+X-Files*

36. Bert Janssen and Janet Ossebaard. 2001. *www.bertjanssen.nl*

37. *www.rense.com/general17/talbot.htm*

38. *www.newscientist.com/news/news.jsp?id=ns99994174*

39. Ibid.

40. *www.guardian.co.uk/life/farout/story/0,13028,1048649,00.html*

41. *www.daviddarling.info/encyclopedia/H/HII.html*

42. *www.tmgnow.com/repository/repository.html*

43. *www.tmgnow.com/repository/planetary/pfvd.html*

44. *www.acemake.com/PaulDevereux/earthlights.html*

45. *www.tmgnow.com/repository/planetary/tornado.html*

46. *www.timeofglobalshift.com/Science/scieblue.html*

47. *www.geocities.com/ResearchTriangle/Thinktank/8863/main.html*

48. *www.winstonbrill.com/bril001/html/article_index/articles/151-200/article158_body.html*

49. *www.hutchisoneffect.org*

50. Ibid.

51. Lecture by Terence McKenna at the University of London Student Union (ULU) on 25th September 1991: *World Youth Culture, Shamanism, Gaia, Chaos and Plant Hallucinogens*

52. *www.tmgnow.com/repository/global/planetophysical4.html*

53. *http://noosphere.princeton.edu/shnoll2.html*

54. *http://21stcenturysciencetech.com/articles/time.html*

55. See S. E. Shnoll, V. A. Kolombet, E. V. Pozharskii, T. A. Zenchenko, I. M. Zvereva, and A. A. Konradov, 1998, *Realization of discrete states during fluctuations in macroscopic processes*, in *Uspekhi Fisicheskikh Nauk*, Vol. 41, No. 10, pp.1025-1035. A new paper is currently in preparation. Shnoll's group is based at Moscow State University. From *http://21stcenturysciencetech.com/articles/time.html*

56. *http://21stcenturysciencetech.com/articles/time.html*

57. *www.museum.vic.gov.au/planetarium/solarsystem/sun.html* and *http://umtof.umd.edu/pm/crn/carrtime.html*

58. Thanks to David Wilcock again for uncovering this Shnoll material:
*http://ascension2000.com/ConvergenceIII/c303.htm*
*www.tmgnow.com/repository/global/planetophysical2.html*
59. E-mail: Wilcock to Stray: 28th May 2002
60. E-mail; Stray to Wilcock: 28th May 2002
61. E-mail; Wilcock to Stray: 28th May 2002
62. Ibid.
63. *www.timeofglobalshift.com/Science/ultisecr.html*
64. This was actually Ra through Wilcock: *www.fieldwerks.com/2003davidwilcock.htm* and *http://ascension2000.com/12.05.02.htm* (see also comments and quotes in Chapter 12).

## Chapter 21: Synthesis

1. This is an example of a 'secondary' cockney rhyming slang; Aristotle - bottle; bottle and glass - arse; as in the famous expression - *"move yer aris!"* The full 'tertiary' slang would be *"move yer April!"*, where April in Paris = Aris. This is the approximate location (the muladhara or root chakra), in which the Kundalini serpent is coiled up, asleep, according to Indian philosophy.
2. *www.erowid.org/plants/salvia/salvia_info5.shtml*
3. *http://www.erowid.org*
4. An entheogen is a psychoactive sacrament; a plant or chemical substance taken to occasion spiritual or mystical experience: theo = god, spirit; gen = creation.
5. Dr Ross Adey of Loma Linda Hospital, California: *Cell membranes, Electromagnetic fields and Intercellular Communication,* 1987 (no further refs. given). Gilbert and Cotterell [1995] p.24. Adey is quoting Walker et al., 1983, who is also quoted by Serena Roney-Dougal here: *http://paranormal.se/psi/tallkottskoerteln.html*
6. Hutchison [1994]
7. *www.meta-religion.com/Psychiatry/The_Paranormal/trascendent_experiences.htm*
8. Ibid.
9. LaPlante [1993]
10. On this page (*www.akasha.de/~aton/NeoDMT.html*), Ananda gives the following reference: Kärkkäinen J, Räisänen M, Naukarinen H, Spoov J and Rimon R (1988), *Urinary excretion of free bufotenin by psychiatric patients; Biological Psychiatry* 24:441-446. However, it seems that the patients with epilepsy whose urine showed traces of bufotenin (or alternative spelling *bufotenine*) were also autistic. *www.erowid.org/chemicals/bufotenin/bufotenin_journal2.shtml*
11. Bumpus and Page, and also Evarts, referenced in Rinkel [1960] pp.58; 214
12. E-mail: 10th July 2003. See also *www.ianhard.2ya.com*
13. Budden [1998] p.113 and Devereux [1990, 1999] 1999 edn. p.7. Persinger has also demonstrated a relationship between the intensity of geomagnetic disturbance the day after birth, and later visions and auditory hallucinations. Hodge K. A. and Persinger M. A. [1991] pp.205-8. *www.lycaeum.org/drugs/abstracts/L4.cgi?mode=keys&kwand=epilepsy*    No longer available - see archive:
*http://web.archive.org/web/20030708015243/http://www.lycaeum.org/drugs/abstracts/L4.cgi?mode =keys&kwand=epilepsy*
14. Devereux [1990, 1999]
15. Ibid. p.207 (in both editions) See also Devereux [1989] pp.203-225

16. Ibid. p.208 (in both editions)

17. *www.argemto.com.ar/mayas.htm*  Google translation: *www.google.com/intl/en_ALL/help/faq_translation.html*

18. *www.global-vision.org/dream/dreamch4.html*

19. *www.global-vision.org/dream/dreamint.html*

20. *www.global-vision.org/dream/dreamch1.html*

21. Paraphrased

22. *www.global-vision.org/dream/index.html*

23. *www.madness.crowcity.com*

24. Rinkel [1960] p.219 and Rodnight [1976], pp. 649-657: "[This research project] *studied the excretion of dimethyltryptamine (DMT) in 122 recently admitted psychiatric patients and twenty normal Ss* [subjects]. *DMT was detected in the urine of 47% of those diagnosed by their psychiatrists as schizophrenic, 38% of those with other non-affective psychoses, 13% of those with affective psychoses, 19% of those with neurotic and personality disorders, and 5% of the normal Ss. 99 of the patients were interviewed in a semi-standardized fashion, and also categorized according to a variety of operational definitions of the psychoses. The operational definitions failed to reveal any group significantly more correlated with urinary DMT than did the hospital diagnosis of schizophrenia, but a discriminate function analysis of symptomatology could be used to define a group of 21 patients of whom 15 (71%) excreted detectable DMT. There was a general relationship between psychotic symptoms and urinary DMT, but specifically schizophrenic symptoms did not appear to be major determinants of DMT excretion.*" From *http://deoxy.org/annex/daytripr.htm#6*

25. Hancock [1998 (b)]

26. Lk 11: 34 -36 and Matt 6: 22

27. Straiton [1927] quoted in Jenkins [2002] p.140

28. Lk 20: 35

29. A copper bell, according to Charles Muses/Musaios [1985-1990]

30. Charles Muses wrote several books, but he wrote *The Lion Path* under the pseudonym of Musaios. Musaios [1985-1990]

31. Musaios [1985-1990] p.33-35

32. See Appendix 2: *The Astral Transition*

33. Naydler [1996]

34. Ibid. p.201

35. Ibid. p.209

36. Ibid. p.205

37. Ibid. p.208

38. Ibid. p.285

39. Scott [1989] p.77

40. Ibid. p.96

41. Ibid.

42. Ibid. p.77

43. Arundale [1947]

44. Ibid. p.64

45. Ibid.

46. Scott [1989] p.116

47. Jenkins [2002]

48. Wilcox [1999]

49. *www.utexas.edu/courses/stross/papers/sacrum.htm*
50. Weidner and Bridges [1999]
51. Weidner and Bridges [2003]
52. Ibid. p.61
53. Ibid.
54. Ibid. p.398
55. *www.thefourwinds.com/Articles/AProphecy.html*
56. *www.thefourwinds.com/prayers_ceremony.htm*
57. *www.thefourwinds.com/Articles/AProphecy.html*
58. Merejildo, James Arévalo (Chaski). *The Awakening of the Puma Initiation Path: Evidences of Archeo Astronomy in the Andes.* English translation by Alain Goormaghtigh (Cuzco, Peru: Chaski), 1997, quoted at *http://tonebytone.com/hatunkarpay/14.shtml*
59. *www.sacredmysteries.com/allVideos.htm#healingbody*
60. *www.sacredmysteries.com/netx1.htm*
61. *www.thefourwinds.com/Articles/AProphecy.html*
62. Ibid.
63. Ibid.
64. While attending Juan Nunez del Prado's two-day workshop in Richmond, London, on May 25-26th 2004.
65. Joan Parisi Wilcox and Elizabeth Jenkins both have August 1st 1993 for the end of the pachakuti, but Juan Nunez del Prado said August 3rd 1993 when I spoke to him. However, although I double-checked this with him, in light of the fact that August 1st is the New Year ceremony for the Q'ero, and the other four dates in the sequence are all August 1st, it may be that this should also be August 1st.
66. Jenkins, Elizabeth B. [1997]
67. Ibid. p.113
68. Ibid. p.237
69. *www.diagnosis2012.co.uk/soul.htm*
70. Jenkins, Elizabeth B. [1997] p.230
71. Ibid.
721. *www.thefourwinds.com/Articles/AProphecy.html*
73. Lucas [2002]
74. See Devereux [1992] pp.78-83 and Aveni [1997] pp.147-176
75. Devereux [1992] p.191
76. However, many of these myths have their source in a 1961 book called *Secret of the Andes* by Brother Philip, who was actually a ufologist-theosophist called George Hunt Williamson.
77. *www.misionrahma.com/ingles/disc_solar.htm*
78. *www.spiritjourneys.com/everyone/calendar/peruthomsondtl.html*
79. Wilcox [1999] p.22

## Chapter 22: Prognosis

1. Luk [1970, 1996]. The method described is only applicable to males.
2. *The Sorcerer's Apprentice* is a Leeds-based (UK) supplier of books and paraphernalia for occultists. *www.sorcerers-apprentice.co.uk*
3. Luk [1970, 1996] p.185

4. Ibid. p.186

5. Ibid.

6. The kabbalistically correct spelling according to Hurtak.

7. But Drunvalo Melchizedek sent out a statement in January 2003 saying that the tetrahedrons should not spin in opposite directions. J. J. Hurtak, on the other hand, has implied that Drunvalo has got the whole merkabah concept totally wrong. See Chapter 9, note 5.

8. These "*aura goggles*" can still be obtained from the Society of Metaphysicians. *www.metaphysicians.org.uk*

9. Wilson C. [1986] p.387

10. Ostrander and Schroeder [1973] p.224. See also pp.225-242 and Watson [1973-1980] pp.146-147 (Coronet paperback edn.)

11. Watson [1973-1980] p.147 (Coronet paperback edn.)

12. *Gnosis* magazine, Vol.1, Winter 1985, p.7 - article by Jay Kinney: *The Mysterious Revelations of Philip K. Dick*

13. Dick [1981]. Appendix, paragraph no. 25

14. Devereux [1982]

15. Graves [1978]

16. Graves [1978]

17. Devereux [1990, 1999] pp.87-88 (in both editions)

18. Graves [1978] p.167 (Granada edn.)

19. Devereux [1992] p.199. Devereux is quoting from From *Heart of the World*, a BBC TV documentary, 4th December 1990.

20. Ereira [1990] in Devereux [1992] p.201

21. Devereux [1992] p.p150, 179 and Devereux [1997] pp.100-104

22. Devereux [1997]

23. *http://portal.telegraph.co.uk/news/main.jhtml?xml=/news/2002/03/17/wwiz17.xml&sSheet=/news /2002/03/17/ixworld.html*

24. *www.geocities.com/loddfaf/hexarch.html*

25. *www.friendsofthornborough.org/about.htm*

26. BBC 2 TV programme - *Time Flyers*, 4th November 2003

27. See Appendix 2 - *The Astral Transition*

28. Devereux [1992]

39. Devereux [1982] p.228-229

30. Charles [1917, 1997]

31. In *The Apocalypse of Weeks* (Enoch chapter 93 and part of 91, replaced to original order, as in the SPCK edition) the whole creation is predicted, from Adam to Judgement. There is a series of weeks, starting with the week from Adam to Enoch, in which Enoch is the seventh-born. This is not the same as the Seven Days of Creation that we covered in Part 1. There are ten of these periods called *weeks*, and the first five are easily identified from the Jewish Patriarch mentioned in it (by description, not by name). I have looked at the Genesis genealogies and there does not seem to be a regular period encoded, but the weeks seem to be between 600 and 1,000 years long. The Partriarchs of the first five weeks are Enoch, Noah, Abraham, Moses, and Solomon. The next week is the one in which the *Book of Enoch* was officially written down, and it predicts that in it, "*a man shall ascend*" and at its close, "*the house of dominion shall be burnt with fire*". These could well refer to the crucifixion in 33 AD and the destruction of the temple in 68 AD (70 AD according to some sources). This is a pretty amazing

prediction, considering that this part is the oldest part of the *Book of Enoch*, at around 200 BC, regardless of whether you take the ascension story literally. The seventh week describes the rise of an "*apostate generation*", which could refer to the Arab take-over of Jerusalem and building of the Al Aqsa Mosque on the site of the Temple in Jerusalem in 691 AD. At its close was to be elected "*the elect righteous of the eternal plant of righteousness,*" possibly the nine original knights of the Knights Templar in 1118. In the eighth week "*a righteous judgement would be executed on the oppressors ...*" and at its close, the oppressed would be re-housed. This seems to be the Jewish reclamation of Israel in 1947-1948. This means we are now in the 'ninth week', during which the Judgement will be revealed to the world, and the works of the godless will vanish and the world will be "*written up for destruction*". The Last Judgement of the fallen angels and the New Heaven and New Earth is not to be expected until the end of the next week, which will be between 1,500 and 2,000 years in the future (St. John interprets it as 1,000 years).

32. Gen 5: 23. Also mentioned in the New Testament: Heb 11: 5
33. Heath [1998] p.147
34. Heath [1998]
35. 1 Enoch 1: 55 (R.H.Charles edn. p. 93)
36. Knight and Lomas [1999] pp.263-264.  Enoch 14: 9, 71: 5 (pp.41, 93 SPCK edn.)
37. Heath [1998] p.149
38. www.mythicalireland.com/ancientsites/gaelicmap.gif
39. Knight and Lomas [1999] p.227; Knight and Lomas [2003] p.197. Knight and Lomas say this double spiral is based on an experiment by artist Charles Ross, and Martin Brennan shows the same diagram in his book *The Stones of Time*; Brennan [1994] p.190
40. Enoch 39: 7
41. Enoch 62: 16
42. Enoch 104: 2
43. Enoch 108: 15
44. Gen. 7: 12
45. Ex. 34: 28
46. 1 Kings 19: 8
47. Matt 4: 2
48. North [1996]
49. O'Brien [1992] pp.34-39
50. *Meta-morphe* is Greek for *change of form*.
51. http://home.clara.net/lucypringle/articles/points.html
52. Ibid.
53. www.keelynet.com/interact/Arc_7_98-12_98/00001143.htm (PMS is pre-menstrual syndrome).
54. Ostrander and Shroeder [1973] pp.236-238
55. www.keelynet.com/energy/dimshift.htm
56. Walter Rawls' website: www.magnetlabs.com
57. The mask was made out of a modified pair of glasses. www.keelynet.com/interact/Arc_1_98-7_98/00001120.htm
58. www.keelynet.com/biology/biomag2.htm
59. www.keelynet.com/energy/dimshift.htm
60. http://ascension2000.com/ConvergenceIII/c310.htm
61. Baker, Mather and Kennaugh [1983], referenced in Budden [1998] p.80
62. Budden [1998]

63. Budden [1998] p.82
64. Devereux [1982]
65. Budden [1998] p.89
66. Budden [1998] p.231
67. Devereux [1990, 1999] p.124 (in both editions)
68. See also *http://ascension2000.com/09.28.03.htm*
69. Séjourné [1957, 1978] p.157
70. Butler [1978] p.93
71. Persinger and Lafreniére [1977] pp.242-243
72. Persinger and Lafreniére [1977] pp.243-244
73. Teilhard de Chardin [1959] quoted in Devereux, Steele and Kubrin [1982, 1989] p.142
74. *Alien Dreamtime* - a live multi-media performance with *Space Time Continuum*. Recorded live on February 27th 1993 in San Francisco USA. Available on CD (Astralwerks/Caroline Records. inc) and DVD (Magic Carpet Media 2003)

## Notes to Appendix 1

1. Brown [1988]
2. Ibid. pp.1-2
3. McKenna T [1993]
4. Ibid. pp.60-61

## Notes to Appendix 2

1. Musaios [1985-1990]
2. *www.house-of-horus.de/lpfinal.html*
3. Fix [1979]
4. Freke and Gandy [1999] p.61
5. Ibid. p.61
6. Santillana de and Dechend, von [1969-1992]
7. Bauval and Gilbert [1995]; Bauval and Hancock [1996]
8. Clow [2001]
9. Allan and Delair [1995]
10. Jenkins [1998]
11. *www.solsticestudios.net/santawriting.htm*
12. Jenkins [1998] p.193
13. Devereux [1997] p.88
14. Devereux [1999]

## Notes to Appendix 3

1. *www.bltresearch.com/plantab.html*

2. www.bltresearch.com/otherfacts.html
3. www.nhne.com/specialreports/srcropcircles/int.pringle.html
4. www.gnosticchristianity.com
5. www.gnosticchristianity.com/ch9.htm

# BIBLIOGRAPHY

**Airaksinen M.M., Gunther J., Poso A., Callaway J.C. and Navajas C.**
1991. *Structural requirements for high binding affinity to the 5-HT uptake transporter for beta-carbolines.* In *British Journal of Pharmacology* 104: p.370

**Airaksinen M.M., Callaway J.C., Rägo L., Nykvist P., Kari E. and Gynther J.**
1993. *Binding sites for (3H) pinoline* (in *Melatonin and the Pineal Gland*. pp.83-86). Amsterdam, The Netherlands. *Excerpta Medica.* Elsevier Science Publishers B.V.

**Alford, Alan**
1996. *Gods of the New Millennium: The Shattering Truth of Human Origins.* London, UK. Hodder and Stoughton

**Allan, D.S. and Delair, J.B.**
1995. *When the Earth Nearly Died: Compelling Evidence of a Catastrophic World Change 9,500 BC.* Wellow, Bath, UK. Gateway Books. American edn: *Cataclysm! Evidence of a Cosmic Catastrophe in 9,500 BC.* Santa Fe, Bear and Co. 1997

**Andahadna, Soror**
1976. *Liber Pennae Praenumbra* (in the *Cincinnati Journal of Ceremonial Magick* Vol.1 No. 1). Cincinnati, Ohio, USA

**Appleby, Nigel**
1998. *Hall of the Gods: The Quest to Discover the Knowledge of the Ancients.* London, UK. William Heinemann

**Arundale, G.S.**
1947. *Kundalini: An Occult Experience.* Adyar, Madras, India. The Theosophical Publishing House

**Arguelles, José**
1975. *The Transformative Vision: Reflections on the Nature and History of Human Expression.* Berkeley, California, USA. Shambhala Publications
1984. *Earth Ascending: An Illustrated Treatise on the Laws Governing Whole Systems.* Boulder, Colorado, USA. Shambhala Publications Inc.
1987. *The Mayan Factor: Path Beyond Technology.* Santa Fe, New Mexico, USA. Bear and Co.

**Arthur, James**
2000. *Mushrooms and Mankind; The Impact of Mushrooms on Human Consciousness and Religion.* San Diego, California, USA. Book Tree

**Atwater, P.M.H.**
1999. *Future Memory.* Charlottesville, Virginia, USA. Hampton Roads Publishing Company Inc.

**Aveni, Anthony**
1997. *Stairways to the Stars: Skywatching in Three Great Ancient Cultures.* London, UK. Cassell

**Azena**
1991. *St. Germain: Earth's Birth Changes.* Perth, Australia. Triad Publishers PTY Ltd

**Baigent, Michael; Leigh, Richard and Lincoln, Henry**

1982-1990. *The Holy Blood and the Holy Grail*. London, UK. Corgi (Transworld Publishers) 1982 edn: Jonathan Cape

1991-1993. *The Dead Sea Scrolls Deception*. Ealing, London, UK. Corgi (originally Jonathan Cape 1991)

**Baillie, Mike**

1999. *Exodus to Arthur: Catastrophic Encounters with Comets*. London, UK. B.T. Batsford Ltd.

**Baker, Dr Douglas**

1977. *The Opening of the Third Eye*. Wellingborough, Northamptonshire, UK. The Aquarian Press

**Baker, R.R., Mather J., and Kennaugh, J.**

1983. *Magnetic Bones in Human Sinuses*, in *Nature* 301. 6th Jan 1983

**Bauval, Robert and Gilbert, Adrian**

1994 [1995]. *The Orion Mystery: Unlocking the Secrets of the Pyramids*. London, UK. William Heinemann Ltd. (1995 paperback; London, UK. Mandarin)

**Bauval, Robert and Hancock, Graham**

1996. *Keeper of Genesis: A Quest for the Hidden Legacy of Mankind*. London, UK. William Heinemann Ltd.

**Berlitz, Charles and Moore, William**

1979. *The Philadelphia Experiment: Project Invisibility*. UK edn: London, UK. Souvenir Press

**Bernbaum, Edwin**

1980, [2001]. *The Way to Shambhala: A Search for the Mythical Kingdom Beyond the Himalayas*. Boston, MA, USA, and London, UK. Shambhala Publications Inc.

**Boerman, Robert J.**

2000. *Crop Circles, Gods and Their Secrets*. Brummen, The Netherlands. The Ptah Foundation

**Braden, Gregg**

1993-1997. *Awakening to Zero Point: The Collective Initiation*. Bellevue, Washington, USA. Radio Bookstore Press

**Brennan, Martin**

1994. *The Stones of Time: Calendars, Sundials and Stone Chambers of Ireland*. Rochester, Vermont, USA. Inner Traditions (first published in 1983 as *The Stars and the Stones: Ancient Art and Astronomy in Ireland*. London, UK. Thames and Hudson)

**Brinkley, Dannion**

1994, 1995. *Saved by the Light: The True Story of a Man Who Died Twice and the Profound Revelations he Received*. New York, USA. Harper Mass Market Paperbacks (a division of Harper Collins)

**Brotherston, Gordon**

1992. *The Book of the Fourth World: Reading the Native Americas Through Their Literature*. Cambridge, UK. Cambridge University Press

**Brown, David Jay**

1988. *Brainchild*. Las Vegas, Nevada, USA. Falcon Press.

**Brunton, Dr Paul**

1935-1969. *A Search in Secret Egypt*. London, UK. Rider and Co.

**Budden, Alfred**

1998. *Electric UFOs*. London, UK. Blandford

**Budge, E.A. Wallis**

1999. *The Book of The Dead*. New York, USA. Gramercy Books

**Butler, W.E.**

1978. *Magic and the Qabalah*. Wellingborough, Northamptonshire, UK. The Aquarian Press

**Cain, Ivan and Dora**
2002. *The Year 2012*. Frederick, Maryland, USA. PublishAmerica Inc.
**Callaway, J.C.**
1988. *A proposed mechanism for the visions of dream sleep*, in *Medical Hypotheses* 26: 119-124
**Calleman, Carl Johan**
2001. *The Mayan Calendar: Solving the Greatest Mystery of Our Time*. Coral Springs, Florida, USA. (Also Basingstoke, Hampshire, UK). Garev Publishing International
**Carey, Ken**
1982. *The Starseed Transmissions: An Extra-Terrestrial Report*. Kansas, Missouri, USA. Uni-Sun
1985. *Vision*. Kansas, Missouri, USA. Uni-Sun
1991. *Starseed: the Third Millennium - Living in the Posthistoric World*. San Francisco, California, USA. Harper
**Carroll, Peter**
1992. *Liber Kaos*. Boston, Massachusetts, USA. Red Wheel/Weiser
**Charles, R.H. (translator)**
1917, 1997. *The Book of Enoch*. London, UK. SPCK
**Cheetham, Erika**
1973-1976. *The Prophecies of Nostradamus*. Ealing, London, UK. Corgi Books (Transworld Publishers Ltd.)
1973 edn. Spearman
**Clow, Barbara Hand**
1995. *The Pleiadian Agenda: A New Cosmology for the Age of Light*. Santa Fe, New Mexico, USA. Bear and Co.
2001. *Catastrophobia: The Truth Behind Earth Changes and the Coming Age of Light*. Rochester, Vermont, USA. Bear and Co.
**Coe, Michael D.**
1962, 1977, 1984. *Mexico*. London, UK. Thames and Hudson
1966, 1971. *The Maya*. London, UK. Thames and Hudson
**Collins, Andrew**
1998. *Gods of Eden: Egypt's Lost Legacy and the Genesis of Civilisation*. London, UK. Headline Book Publishing
2000. *Gateway to Atlantis: The Search for the Source of a Lost Civilisation*. London, UK. Headline Book Publishing
**Cotterell, Maurice M.**
1988. *Astrogenetics*. Saltash, Cornwall, UK. Brooks Hill Robinson and Co.
1997. *The Supergods*. London, UK. Thorsons
1999. *The Tutankamun Prophecies: The Sacred Secret of the Mayas, Egyptians and Freemasons*. London, UK. Headline Book Publishing
2001. *The Lost Tomb of Viracocha: Unlocking the Secrets of the Peruvian Pyramids*. London, UK. Headline Book Publishing
**Crockett, Stephen E.**
2001. *The Prophet Code: Precessional Encryption and the Apocalyptic Tradition*. Mount Gilead, North Carolina, USA. Aethyrea Books LLC
**Crowley, Aleister**
1986. *Magick*. London, UK. Guild Publishing
**Davis, Beth (ed.)**
1992. *Ciphers in The Crops: The Fractal and Geometric Circles of 1991*. Bath, UK. Gateway Books

**Devereux, Paul**

1982. *Earth Lights*. Wellingborough, UK. Turnstone Press

1989. *Earth Lights Revelation*. London, UK. Blandford Press

1990, 1999. *Places of Power: Measuring the Secret Energy of Ancient Sites*. London, UK. Blandford

1992. *Shamanism and the Mystery Lines: Ley Lines, Spirit Paths, Shape-Shifting and Out-of-Body Travel*. Slough, Berkshire, UK. Quantum

1997. *The Long Trip: A Prehistory of Psychedelia*. London, UK. Arkana (Penguin Group)

**Devereux, Paul, Steele, John and Kubrin, David**

1982, 1989. *Earthmind: Communicating with the Living World of Gaia*. Rochester, Vermont, USA. Destiny Books

**Dick, Philip K.**

1981, 1991. *Valis*. 1991 edn. New York, USA. Vintage Books (Random House)

1991. *In Pursuit of Valis: Selections from the Exegesis*. Lancaster, Pennsylvania, USA. Underwood-Miller

**Dimde, Manfred**

2001. *Nostradamus, Das Apokalyptische Jahrzehnt*. (*Nostradamus, the Apocalyptic Decade: the Crucial Years Until 2012*). Munich, Germany. Heyne Buchen

**Drosnin, Michael**

1997. *The Bible Code*. London, UK. Weidenfeld and Nicolson

2002. *The Bible Code 2: The Countdown*. London, UK. Weidenfeld and Nicolson

**Erbe, Peter O.**

1991. *God I Am - From Tragic to Magic*. Perth, Australia. Triad Publishers PTY Ltd.

**Ereira, Alan**

1990. *The Heart of the World*. London, UK. Jonathan Cape

**Essene, Virginia and Nidle, Sheldon**

1994. *You are Becoming a Galactic Human*. Santa Clara, California, USA. Spiritual Education Endeavors Publishing Company

**Fix, Wm. R.**

1979. *Star Maps*. London, UK. Octopus Books

**Freke, Timothy and Gandy, Peter**

1999. *The Jesus Mysteries*. London, UK. Thorsons

**Frissell, Bob**

1994. *Nothing in This Book is True, but it's Exactly How Things Are*. Berkeley, California, USA. Frog Ltd.

**Fulcanelli**

1926, 1957. *Le Mystere des Cathedrals*. Paris, France. J. Schmeit (1957 edn. Paris, France. Jean-Jacques Pauvert). 1971 edn. Jersey, Channel Islands, UK. Neville Spearman

**Furlong, David**

1997. *The Keys to the Temple*. London, UK. Piatkus Books

**Gaspar, Dr William A.**

1999. *The Celestial Clock*. New Mexico, USA. Adam and Eva Publishing

**Geryl, Patrick and Ratinckx, Gino**

2001. *The Orion Prophecy: Will the World be Destroyed in 2012?* Kempton, Illinois, USA. Adventures Unlimited Press

**Gilbert, Adrian and Cotterell, Maurice M.**

1995. *The Mayan Prophecies: Unlocking the Secrets of a Lost Civilization*. Shaftesbury, Dorset, UK. Element Books

**Gilbert, Adrian**

2000. *Signs in the Sky: Prophecies for the Birth of a New Age.* London, UK. Bantam (Transworld Publishers)

**Gillette, Douglas**

1997. *The Shaman's Secret: the Lost Resurrection Teachings of the Ancient Maya.* New York, USA. Bantam

**Godwin, Joscelyn**

1981. *Mystery Religions in the Ancient World.* London, UK. Thames and Hudson

**Grant, Kenneth**

1980. *Outside the Circles of Time.* London, UK. Frederick Muller Ltd.

**Grasse, Ray**

2002. *Signs of the Times: Unlocking the Symbolic Language of World Events.* Charlottesville, Virginia, USA. Hampton Roads Publishing Company Inc.

**Graves, Tom**

1978. *Needles of Stone.* St Albans, Herts, UK. Granada (original edn. by Turnstone)

**Guichhait R.B.**

1976. *Biogenesis of 5-methoxy-N,N-dimethyltryptamine in human pineal gland,* in the *Journal of Neurochemistry 26*

**Gurdjieff G.**

1950. *All and Everything (Beelzebub's Tales to his Grandson).* London, UK. Routledge & Kegan Paul Ltd.

**Hail, Raven**

2000. *The Cherokee Sacred Calendar - A Handbook of the Ancient Native American Tradition.* Rochester, Vermont, USA. Destiny Books

**Hancock, Graham**

1995. *Fingerprints of the Gods: A Quest for the Beginning and the End.* London, UK. William Heinemann Ltd.

1998. *The Mars Mystery: A Tale of the End of Two Worlds.* London, UK. Michael Joseph Ltd.

1998 (b): *Heaven's Mirror: Quest for the Lost Civilization.* London, UK. Michael Joseph Ltd.

**Harary, Keith and Weintraub, Pamela**

1990. *Lucid Dreams in 30 Days: The Creative Sleep Programme.* Wellingborough, Northamptonshire, UK. The Aquarian Press (Thorsons Publishing Group). [First published by St Martin's Press, New York, USA, 1989]

**Hart, Will**

2003. *The Genesis Race: Our Extraterrestrial DNA and the True Origin of the Species.* Rochester, Vermont, USA. Inner Traditions International Ltd.

**Heath, Robin**

1998. *Sun, Moon and Stonehenge: Proof of High Culture in Ancient Britain.* Cardigan, Wales. Bluestone Press

**Hodge K. A. and Persinger M. A .**

1991. *Quantitative increases in temporal lobe symptoms in human males are proportional to postnatal geomagnetic activity: verification by canonical correlation. Neuroscience Letters.* 1991. Apr 29. 125 (2)

**Hogue, John**

1997. *Nostradamus: The Complete Prophecies.* Shaftesbury, Dorset, UK. Element Books Ltd.

**Hope, Murry**

1990. *Ancient Egypt: The Sirius Connection.* Shaftesbury, Dorset, UK. Element Books

1991. *Time: The Ultimate Energy.* Shaftesbury, Dorset, UK. Element Books

**Howard, Kenneth W.**

2002. *The Final Days of Mankind*. Middletown, Ohio, USA. Direction Inc.

**Hurtak, J.J.**

1977-1996. *The Keys of Enoch*. Los Gatos, California, USA. The Academy for Future Science

**Hutchison, Michael**

1994. *Mega Brain Power: Transform Your Life with Mind Machines and Brain Nutrients*. New York, USA. Hyperion

**Jenkins, Elkizabeth B.**

1997. *Initiation: A Woman's Spiritual Adventure in the Heart of the Andes*. London, UK. Piatkus

**Jenkins, John Major**

1994. *Tzolkin: Visionary Perspectives and Calendar Studies*. Garberville, California, USA. Borderland Sciences Research Foundation

1998. *Maya Cosmogenesis 2012: The True Meaning of the Maya Calendar End-Date*. Santa Fe, New Mexico, USA. Bear and Co.

2002. *Galactic Alignment: The Transformation of Consciousness According to Mayan, Egyptian and Vedic Traditions*. Rochester, Vermont, USA. Bear and Co.

**Kalb, Ken**

1998. *The Grand Catharsis*. Lucky Star Press; ISBN: 0964292769

**Karpinski, Gloria**

2001. *Barefoot on Holy Ground: Twelve Lessons in Spiritual Craftsmanship*. Wellspring/Ballantine Albuquerque, New Mexico, USA

**Keene, J.J.**

2002. *Cosmic Locusts: The 2012 Convergence of Nostradamian Mayan & Biblical Prophecy*. Privately published: ISBN: 0-9724582-0-4

**Knight, Christopher and Lomas, Robert**

1999. *Uriel's Machine: The Prehistoric Technology that Survived the Flood*. London, UK. Century

2003. *The Book of Hiram: Freemasonry, Venus and the Secret Key to the Life of Jesus*. London, UK. Century

**LaBerge, Stephen**

1998. *Lucid Dreaming*, New York, USA. Ballantine Books

**LaPlante, Eve**

1993. *Seized*. New York, USA. Harper Collins

**LaViolette, Paul**

1997. *Earth Under Fire: Humanity's Survival of the Apocalypse*. New York, USA. Starlane Publications

**Lehner, Mark**

1997. *The Complete Pyramids*. London, UK. Thames and Hudson

**Lucas, Laurence**

2002. *The 21st Century Book of the Dead*. UK. StarDrum Books: www.stardrum.com

**Luk, Charles (Lu K'uan Yu)**

1970, 1996. *Taoist Yoga*. London, UK. Rider

**Mardyks, Raymond and Alana-Leah, Stacia**

1999. *Maya Calendar: Voice of the Galaxy*. Sedona, Arizona, USA. Star Heart Publications

**Masters, Robert**

1988. *The Goddess Sekhmet: the Way of the Five Bodies*. New York, USA. Amity House

**McFadden, Steven**

1991. *Profiles in Wisdom*. Santa Fe, New Mexico, USA. Bear and Co.

**McIsaac, W.M., Khairallah, P.A. and Page, I.H.**

1961. *10-methoxy harmalan, a potent serotonin antagonist which affects conditioned behaviour*. In *Science* 134. pp 674-5

**McKenna, Terence**

1993. *True Hallucinations*. San Francisco, USA. HarperSanFrancisco

1991. *World Youth Culture, Shamanism, Gaia, Chaos, and Plant Hallucinogens*. Lecture at ULU, London, UK. 25th September 1991

**McKenna, Terence and Dennis**

1975, 1993. *The Invisible Landscape: Mind, Hallucinogens and the I Ching*. New York, USA. Seabury Press [Revised and updated 1993 edition: New York, USA. Harper Collins]

**Men, Hunbatz**

1983. *Calendrios Mayas Y Hunab K'U*. Juarez, Mexico. Ediciones Horizonte

1990. *Secrets of Maya Science/Religion*. Santa Fe, New Mexico, USA. Bear & Co.

**Michell, John**

1969. *The View Over Atlantis*. London, UK. Sphere Books Ltd.

**Middleton-Jones, Howard and Wilkie, James Michael**

2001. *Giza-Genesis: The Best Kept Secrets Vol. 1*. Tempe, Arizona, USA. Dandelion Books

**Mini, John**

1998. *Day of Destiny: Where Will You be August 13, 1999?* Sausalito, California, USA. Trans-Hyperborean Institute of Science Publishing

**Monroe, Robert A.**

1994. *Ultimate Journey*. New York, London, Toronto, Sydney, Auckland. Doubleday

**Morton, Chris and Thomas, Ceri Louise**

1997. *The Mystery of the Crystal Skulls: Unlocking the Secrets of the Past, Present and Future*. London. UK. Thorsons

**Mouravieff, Boris**

1989. *Gnosis: Study and Commentaries on the Esoteric Tradition of Eastern Orthodoxy. Book One: Exoteric Cycle*. Robertsbridge, East Sussex, UK. Praxis Institute Press

1992. *Gnosis: Study and Commentaries on the Esoteric Tradition of Eastern Orthodoxy. Book Two: Mesoteric Cycle*. Robertsbridge, East Sussex, UK. Praxis Institute Press

1993. *Gnosis: Study and Commentaries on the Esoteric Tradition of Eastern Orthodoxy. Book Three: Esoteric Cycle*. Robertsbridge, East Sussex, UK. Praxis Institute Press

**Muldoon, Sylvan and Carrington, Hereward**

1929. *The Projection of the Astral Body*. London, UK. Rider & Co. Ltd.

**Musaios (Charles Muses)**

1985 - 2001. *The Lion Path - You Can Take it With You: A Manual of the Short Path to Regeneration for Our Times*. Sardis, Canada. House of Horus

**Muses, Charles and Young, A.M. (eds.)**

1972. *Consciousness and Reality*. New York, USA. Outerbridge and Lazard

**Naranjo, Claudio**

1967. *Psychotropic properties of the harmala alkaloids*, in *Ethnopharmacologic Search for Psychoactive Drugs*. Ed. Donald Efron, Bo Holmsted, and Nathan S. Kline. Washington DC, USA. Public Health Service Publication No. 1645

**Naydler, Jeremy**

1996. *Temple of the Cosmos: the Ancient Egyptian Experience of the Sacred*. Rochester, Vermont, USA. Inner Traditions

**Nema (Margarete Ingalls)**
1995. *Maat Magick: a Guide to Self-Initiation*. Boston, Massachusetts, USA.  Red Wheel/Weiser
**Noah, Joseph**
2002. *Future Prospects of the World According to the Bible Code*. Cameron Park, California, USA. New Paradigm Books
**North, John**
1996. *Stonehenge: Neolithic Man and the Cosmos*. London, UK. Harper Collins
**Novak, Peter**
1997. *The Division of Consciousness: The Secret Afterlife of the Human Psyche*. Charlottesville, Virginia, USA. Hampton Roads Publishing Company Inc.
**O'Brien, Christian**
1985. The Genius of the Few. London, UK. Turnstone Press
**O'Brien, Shane**
1998. *The Venus Legacy: When the Moon Turns to Blood*. Telford, UK. Cumorah Hill
**O'Brien, Tim**
1992. *Light Years Ago*. Dublin, Ireland. The Black Cat Press
**Ostrander, Sheila and Schroeder, Lynn**
1973. *Psychic Discoveries Behind the Iron Curtain*. London, UK. Sphere Books
**Persinger and Lafreniére**
1977. *Space-Time Transients and Unusual Events*. Chicago, USA. Nelson-Hall.
**Petit, J.R., Jouzel, J., et al.**
1999. *Climate and atmospheric history of the past 420,000 years from the Vostok ice core in Antarctica*, in *Nature* 399.  3rd June 1999
**Phillips, Graham**
1998. *Act of God: Tutankhamun, Moses and the Myth of Atlantis*. London, UK. Sidgwick and Jackson
**Poynder, Michael**
1992. *Pi in the Sky; A Revelation of the Ancient Wisdom Tradition*. London, UK. Rider
**Ratsch, Christian (ed.)**
1990. *Gateway to Inner Space: Sacred Plants, Mysticism and Psychotherapy*. Lindfield, New South Wales, Australia. Unity Press
**Rayner Johnson, Kenneth**
1980. *The Fulcanelli Phenomenon*. Jersey, Channel Islands, UK. Neville Spearman
**Reyner J.H.**
1989. *The Gurdjieff Inheritance*. London, UK. Turnstone Press
**Rinkel, Max M.D. (ed.)**
1960. *Chemical Concepts of Psychosis*. London, UK. Peter Owen Ltd.
**Rodnight, R., et al**
[1976]. *Urinary dimethyltryptamine and psychiatric symptomatology and classification*, in *Psychological Medicine*; 1976 Nov., Vol. 6 (4) 649-657
**Roney-Dougal, Serena**
1997, 2002. *Where Science and Magic Meet: Exploring our Psychic Birthright*. Frome, Somerset, UK. Vega (Chrysalis Books PLC.)
**Rudisill, Elliot ("El")**
2001, 2002. *E. Din: Land of Righteousness*. USA. 1st Books Library. *www.1stbooks.com*
**Russell, Peter**
1982. *The Awakening Earth: The Global Brain*. London, UK.  Ark Paperbacks

1992. *The White Hole in Time: Our Future Evolution and the Meaning of Now*. Chatham, Kent, UK. Aquarian Press

**Scallion, Gordon Michael**

1997. *Notes from the Cosmos: A Futurist's Insights into the World of Dream, Prophecy and Intuition*. W. Chesterfield, New Hampshire, USA. Matrix Institute Inc.

**Scofield, Bruce**

1991. *Day-Signs: Native American Astrology from Ancient Mexico*. Amherst, Massachusetts, USA. One Reed Publications

**Scott, Mary**

1989. *Kundalini in the Physical World*. London, UK. Arkana [Previously published: 1983 London, UK. Routledge & Kegan Paul]

**Séjourné, Laurette**

1957, 1978. *Burning Water: Thought and Religion in Ancient Mexico*. London, UK. Thames and Hudson

**Santillana de, Giorgio and Dechend, von, Hertha**

1969-1992. *Hamlet's Mill: An Essay on Myth and the Frame of Time*. 1977-1992 editions: Boston, Massachusetts, USA. David R. Godine Publisher Inc.

**Schwaller de Lubicz, R.A.**

1961, 1988. *Sacred Science: The King of Pharaonic Theocracy*. 1988 edn.: Rochester, Vermont, USA. Inner Traditions International Ltd.

**Shearer, Tony**

1971. *Lord of the Dawn*, Quetzalcoatl. Healdsburg, USA. Naturegraph Press

1975. *Beneath the Moon and Under the Sun; a Poetic Appraisal of the Sacred Calendar and the Prophecies of Ancient Mexico*. Albuquerque, USA. Sun Books

**Sitchin, Zecharia**

1976, 1978. *The Twelfth Planet*. New York, USA. Avon Books, Inc.

1990, 1995. *Genesis Revisited*. New York, USA. Avon Books, Inc.

1990 b. *The Lost Realms*. New York, USA. Avon Books, Inc.

**Skinner, Stephen**

1994. *Millennium Prophecies: Predictions for the Year 2000 and Beyond from the World's Greatest Seers and Mystics*. London, UK. Virgin Books/Carlton Books

**Strassman, Rick (MD).**

2001. *DMT: The Spirit Molecule - A Doctor's Revolutionary Research into the Biology of Near-Death and Mystical Experiences*. Rochester, Vermont, USA. Park Street Press

**Straiton, Valentia**

1927. *The Celestial Ship of the North*. New York, USA. Albert & Charles Boni

**Teilhard de Chardin, Pierre**

1959. *The Future of Man*. Fontana

**Temple, Robert**

1976, 1998. *The Sirius Mystery: New Scientific Evidence for Alien Contact 5,000 Years Ago*. London, UK. Century (revised edn.)

**Thomas, Andy**

1998, 2002. *Vital Signs: A Complete Guide to the Crop Circle Mystery and Why it is NOT a Hoax*. Seaford, East Sussex, UK. S.B. Publications [in USA - Frog Ltd; Spain - Ediciones Siruela]

1999. *SC: The Bimonthly Journal of Crop Circles and Beyond*. Issue 84. May/June 1999 (as ed.)

2003. *Swirled Harvest: Views from the Crop Circle Frontline*. Lewes, East Sussex, UK. Vital Signs Publishing

**Timms, Moira**
1994, 1996. *Prophecies to Take You Into the Twenty-First Century*. New York, USA. (1996 edn: Thorsons. London, UK)

**Vallee, Jacques**
1970, 1975. *Passport to Magonia: From Folklore to Flying Saucers*. London, UK. Tandem Publishing Ltd.

**Velikovsky, Immanuel**
1950, 1972. *Worlds in Collision*. 1972 edn. London, UK. (Abacus) Sphere Books

**Waters, Frank**
1963, 1969. *Book of the Hopi*. New York, USA. Ballantine Books (1963 edn., Viking Press Inc.)
1975, 1989. *Mexico Mystique: The Coming Sixth World of Consciousness*. USA. Swallow Press/Ohio. University Press Books

**Watson, Lyall**
1973-1980. *Supernature: A Natural History of the Supernatural*. Sevenoaks, Kent, UK. Hodder and Stoughton
1979, 1980. *Lifetide*. Sevenoaks, Kent, UK. Hodder and Stoughton (Coronet)

**Weidner, Jay and Bridges, Vincent**
1999. *A Monument to the End of Time: Alchemy, Fulcanelli and the Great Cross*. Mount Gilead, North Carolina, USA. Aethyrea Books LLC
2003. *The Mysteries of the Great Cross of Hendaye: Alchemy and the End of Time* (re-working of the 1999 *Monument* book, with much extra material). Mount Gilead, North Carolina, USA. Aethyrea Books LLC

**Weldon, Randolph**
2003. *Doomsday 2012: a Survival Manual*. Indianapolis, Indiana, USA. Cork Hill Press

**West, John Anthony**
1993. *Serpent in the Sky: the High Wisdom of Ancient Egypt*. Wheaton, Illinois, USA. Quest Books (the Theosophical Publishing House)

**Whiteside, Richard Henry**
2002. *God's New Millennium*. California, USA. God's Web Publishing Company

**Wilcox, Joan Parisi**
1999. *Keepers of the Ancient Knowledge - the Mystical World of the Q'ero Indians of Peru*. Shaftesbury, Dorset, UK. Element Books

**William, Harold and Birnes, Burt**
2000. *Unsolved Mysteries: The World's Most Compelling Cases of Alien Encounter*. New York, USA. Aspect (Time Warner Book Group)

**Wilson, Colin**
1986. *Mysteries*. London, UK. Grafton Books

**Wilson, Robert Anton**
1982. *Right Where You Are Sitting Now: Further Tales of the Illuminati*. California, USA. And/Or Press
1983. *Prometheus Rising*. Phoenix, Arizona, USA. Falcon Press
1990. *Trajectories Newsletter - The Journal of Futurism and Heresy*. Spring 1990 (Number 7). San Jose, California, USA. Permanent Press

**Wilson, Terry**
1998. *The Secret History of Crop Circles: The True, Untold Story of the World's Greatest Mystery*. Paignton, Devon, UK. The Centre for Crop Circle Studies

# INDEX

# THE AUTHOR

Geoff Stray has been studying the meaning of the year 2012 since 1982. Around 1996, he started to compile the information into a stapled booklet called *Beyond 2012*. In September 2000, he made it available on the internet via the website *Diagnosis 2012* (*www.diagnosis2012.co.uk*). Since then the website has become renowned as the most comprehensive database available on 2012, and has gathered input from every corner of the globe (except that globes have no corners). This book is the project's ultimate evolution.

Geoff has given presentations across England and in countries as far afield as Finland, the USA and Peru. He is also the author of *The Mayan and Other Ancient Calendars* and the mini-guide *2012 in Your Pocket*, and has contributed articles for *Caduceus*, *New Dawn*, *Hera* and other magazines. He has featured in TV programmes and documentaries around the world, as well as making several appearances on Sky Channel 200, *Controversial TV*.

In his spare time he makes handmade footwear, rides a dirt bike and plays the blues harmonica to passing sheep. He currently lives in Glastonbury, UK.

## PS. Pushing up the Crazies

"*A fortune-teller is so sure he is going to die in 2012, he has bought himself a grave and a cross, inscribed with the date. The healthy 70-year-old claims to have had visions which allowed him to calculate the year of his demise. In 1991, Alexandru Marin saw a 'big star' in an unusual position and, a year later, a 'strong light' shone in his house. 'In 2012 we will see if I am right,' he said. A priest said his purchase had shocked residents in the village of Branistea, Romania.*"

**London Metro, 3rd October 2001** (Thanks to Laurence Lucas & Neil Kilburn)